The Ethics Project in Legal Education

The contributions in this volume suggest that 'the ethics project in legal education' is increasingly an international one. Even though the strength of commitment by both the profession and the legal academy to 'ethics learning' within law schools varies, two fundamental questions confront all who work in this area. First, what is it that we want our students to learn (or, perhaps, in what manner do we want our students to develop) from the teaching of 'legal ethics'? Second, how can we create a learning environment that will encourage the nature and quality of learning we think is important?

All the contributors to this volume take a strong stand on the importance of ethical legal practice and the role of law schools in developing students' capacities in this area. They share a belief in the essential need to encourage law students to engage with the moral dimensions of legal practice. The questions that these scholars grapple with are therefore not of the 'should we be teaching this?' variety, but '*how* might we best to go about doing this, so that our efforts within law schools really make some difference?' Each of the chapters in this volume adds uniquely to our understanding of these matters.

Michael Robertson is Professor and Head of the School of Law at the University of Southern Queensland, Australia.

Lillian Corbin is Acting Head of Griffith Law School at Griffith University, Australia.

Kieran Tranter is a Senior Lecturer and Managing Editor of the Griffith Law Review at Griffith University, Australia.

Francesca Bartlett is a Lecturer at the T.C. Beirne School of Law, The University of Queensland, Australia.

Routledge Research in Legal Ethics

Titles in this series include:

Alternative Perspectives on Lawyers and Legal Ethics
Francesca Bartlett, Reid Mortensen and Kieran Tranter

Reaffirming Legal Ethics: Taking Stock and New Ideas
Kieran Tranter, Francesca Bartlett, Lillian Corbin, Reid Mortensen and Michael Robertson

The Ethics Project in Legal Education

Edited by Michael Robertson,
Lillian Corbin, Kieran Tranter
and Francesca Bartlett

LONDON AND NEW YORK

First published 2011
by Routledge
2 Park Square, Milton Park, Abingdon, Oxon, OX14 4RN

Simultaneously published in the USA and Canada
by Routledge
270 Madison Avenue, New York, NY 10016

Routledge is an imprint of the Taylor & Francis Group, an informa business

Typeset in Baskerville by
RefineCatch Limited, Bungay, Suffolk
Printed and bound in Great Britain by
MPG Books Group, UK

British Library Cataloguing in Publication Data
A catalogue record for this book is available
from the British Library

Library of Congress Cataloging-in-Publication Data
The ethics project in legal education / edited by Michael Robertson . . . [et al.].
p. cm.
Includes index.
ISBN 978-0-415-54651-5 (hardback)
1. Legal ethics—Study and teaching.   2. Legal ethics.   I. Robertson, Michael, 1954–
K103.L44E87 2011
174′.30711—dc22
2010016028

ISBN13: 978–0–415–54651–5 (hbk)
ISBN13: 978–0–203–84085–6 (ebk)

Contents

vi *Contents*

Preface

This is the third and final volume in the series of publications flowing from the Third International Legal Ethics Conference held in Australia in 2008. The organizers of that conference, most of whom are also the editors of this volume, were eager to place special emphasis on the pedagogical dimensions of lawyers' ethics in law school education. Learning and teaching about lawyers' ethical responsibility was therefore a major theme of the conference and attracted a substantial number of papers. Most of the chapters in this volume have grown out of those contributions.

The conference was hosted jointly by the Griffith Law School at Griffith University and the T.C. Beirne School of Law at the University of Queensland. This conference, building on the successes of the first two in the series – in Exeter, United Kingdom in 2004 and in Auckland, New Zealand in 2006 – was one of the largest specialist gatherings of legal ethicists in the new millennium.

For us, the privilege of working with the contributors in this book followed on from the success of the conference itself. It is fitting that our expressions of thanks extend to our colleagues from many countries who assisted in making the conference and this volume possible. We would first like to thank Kim Economides and Julian Webb for their foundational work in establishing the international legal ethics conference series, and for their encouragement in organizing the third conference. We would also acknowledge Tim Dare's role in organizing the second conference, which provided the platform for the third. We owe a particular debt to Brad Wendel, Christine Parker, Adrian Evans and Neil Watt for their help and enthusiasm over the two years of planning for the Gold Coast conference. Our thanks are also due to our respective Deans and others who contributed to the resources needed to run the conference: Charles Rickett and Ross Grantham from the TC Beirne School of Law, and Paula Baron and Richard Johnstone from the Griffith Law School; and to Teola Marsh from the University of Queensland and Linda Brauns from Griffith University. Substantial financial support for the conference was also given by the College of Law, for which we are especially grateful.

We extend our thanks to the contributors to this volume for their willingness to work with us and for their patience during the editing process. We would also like to thank Katie Carpenter and Khanam Virjee from Routledge for their support and encouragement. And a special mention must go to Griffith Law School student Stevie Martin, who not only worked tirelessly as the administrator for the conference, but also joyfully undertook the task of helping to edit the manuscripts in her final year at law school.

Finally, we wish to express our heartfelt thanks to colleagues, friends and most importantly to our families for their faith and support over these past few years.

Michael Robertson
Lillian Corbin,
Kieran Tranter and
Francesca Bartlett
March 2010

Contributors

Charlotte Alexander is the Deputy Director, National Institute for Teaching Ethics and Professionalism, Georgia State University, Atlanta, GA, USA. Her email address is calexander@gsu.edu

Francesca Bartlett is a Lecturer at the TC Beirne School of Law, University of Queensland, Brisbane, Australia.

David Chavkin is Professor of Law at the American University Washington College of Law, Washington, DC, USA.

Lillian Corbin is a Senior Lecturer and Acting Head of School at the Griffith Law School, Griffith University, Brisbane, Australia.

Lynda Crowley-Cyr is a Senior Lecturer at the James Cook University Law School, Townsville, Australia.

Clark Cunningham is the W. Lee Burge Professor of Law and Ethics, Georgia State University College of Law, Atlanta, GA, USA and Director of the National Institute for Teaching Ethics and Professionalism (NIFTEP). The NIFTEP home page is http://law.gsu.edu/niftep/. His email is cdcunningham@gsu.edu and his home page is http://law.gsu.edu/cunningham/

Linda Haller is a Senior Lecturer at the Melbourne Law School, University of Melbourne, Australia.

Helen Kruuse is a Lecturer in the Faculty of Law, Rhodes University, Grahamstown, South Africa.

David McQuoid-Mason is a Professor at the Howard College School of Law, University of KwaZulu-Natal, Durban, South Africa.

Donald Nicolson is the Director of Strathclyde Law Clinic and Professor of the University of Strathclyde, Glasgow, United Kingdom.

Michael Robertson is Professor and Head of the School of Law, University of Southern Queensland, Toowoomba, Australia.

Justine Rogers is a graduate of the Centre for Socio-Legal Studies, Law Faculty, Oxford University, United Kingdom.

Cassandra Sharp is a Senior Lecturer in the Faculty of Law, University of Wollongong, Australia.

Kieran Tranter is a Senior Lecturer in the Griffith Law School, Griffith University, Brisbane, Australia.

Julian Webb is Professor of Legal Education in the Law School at the University of Warwick, Coventry, United Kingdom.

1   Introduction

Michael Robertson, Lillian Corbin, Kieran
Tranter and Francesca Bartlett

A common starting point for all the chapters in this book – the third and final volume in the series of publications flowing from the Third International Legal Ethics Conference held in Australia in 2008 – is that law schools worldwide *do* have an important role to play in preparing law students for the ethical challenges of legal practice. This fundamental assumption has not always been widely shared, and some resistance to the proposition continues. In fact, law school ethics teachers in most, if not all, of the countries represented by the contributors to this volume continue to see themselves as a minority in law school education. Not only are legal ethics teachers still relatively few and far between, but many who have chosen – sometimes passionately – to work in this area and to develop a scholarship on the pedagogy of legal ethics continue to see their mission as one that needs to be advocated constantly within wider legal and academic communities.

This is because legal education as a whole, even in countries like the United States, the United Kingdom and Australia, has yet to accord legal ethics teaching the degree of importance that the contributors to this volume, among many others, have long taken for granted. However, the traditional ambiguity and sometimes indifference towards the legal ethics project in legal education has gradually been giving way to an acceptance of the importance of this area of learning. In comparison to ten or even five years ago, there is now a wider acceptance of the need to take seriously the challenge of teaching and learning ethical responsibility for legal professional practice. One recent and significant example of this growing recognition is contained within the core messages of the influential 2007 Carnegie Report in the United States. This report underlines in the strongest possible terms the future importance of legal ethics learning and teaching in American law schools – or what it refers to, *inter alia*, as 'ethical-social apprenticeship' – and this powerful message is likely to be influential in international legal education for many years to come. For example, the authors of the Carnegie Report make the following observation:

> Insofar as law schools choose not to place ethical-social values within the inner circle of their highest esteem and most central preoccupation, and insofar as they fail to make systematic efforts to educate towards a central

moral tradition of lawyering, legal education may inadvertently contribute to the demoralization of the legal profession and its loss of a moral compass, as many observers have charged.[1]

Taken together, the contributions in this volume suggest that what we refer to as 'the ethics project in legal education' is increasingly becoming an international one. Even though the strength of commitment of both the profession and the legal academy to 'ethics learning' within law schools inevitably differs across (and within) jurisdictions, it seems likely that two fundamental questions confront all those who work in this area. First, what is it that we want our students to learn (or, perhaps, in what manner do we want our students to develop) from the teaching of 'legal ethics'? Second, how can we create a learning environment that will encourage the nature and quality of learning we think is important? Of course, neither of these questions invites a straightforward or uncontroversial response, as many of the contributions in this volume demonstrate.

Generally speaking, the kinds of answers that the contributors – who come from different parts of the world – give to these two questions nevertheless reflects a common belief in the vitally important social roles that lawyers perform, no matter where lawyers practise. This is despite the international variations in resources and depth of commitment to the ethics project, together with variations in the character of the political and legal systems within which law schools are located. Hence, a common underlying concern is about the importance of graduating future lawyers who recognize that legal practice *sans* ethical practice is almost always antithetical to the needs of the kinds of societies we inhabit. In communities in which special emphasis is placed on the rule of law and the sometimes precarious rights of citizens, lawyers have an indispensable role to play in assisting individuals in numerous ways. This includes providing citizens with principled advice and access to core democratic institutions. Lawyers' work that is disrespectful of the moral imperatives of legal representation and assistance is, ultimately, costly and counter-productive. It is therefore hardly surprising that, notwithstanding differences in emphasis, all the contributors to this volume take a strong stand on the importance of ethical legal practice and the role of law schools in developing students' capacities in this area. Put simply, they share a belief in the essential need to encourage law students to engage with the moral dimensions of legal practice. The questions with which these scholars grapple are therefore not of the 'Should we be teaching this?' variety, but rather '*How* might we best to go about doing this, so that our efforts within law school really make some difference?'

Each of the chapters in this volume adds uniquely to our understanding of the ethics project in legal education. Inevitably, each dwells to a lesser or greater extent on some of the basic challenges surrounding legal ethics learning and teaching in law schools. As anyone who works in this area well knows, a familiar theme in much of the existing literature on legal ethics teaching in law schools is the inadequacy or impotency of traditional law curricula in encouraging the kind of learning that really seems worthwhile. It is therefore not surprising that the contributors to this volume share these concerns, and this seems like a convenient point to begin this overview of what each contributor brings to this volume.

Lynda Crowley-Cyr, in her arguments for a greater 'ethical literacy' and also 'reflexivity' among law students in an Australian context (Chapter 8), notes some of the failings commonly ascribed to traditional legal education. Likewise, David Chavkin, in his chapter on the importance of bringing experience and practice to the teaching of legal ethics (Chapter 4), begins by suggesting that the major 'deficiency' in legal education in the United States and elsewhere lies in the area of the teaching of professional responsibility. He highlights a grave concern shared by many contemporary critics of legal education, which is that law schools too often focus 'on the transmission and temporary retention of information'. Clark Cunningham and Charlotte Alexander also echo these concerns about the mainstream approach to legal ethics in American Law Schools in Chapter 5, drawing at some length on the Carnegie Report to highlight the shortcomings of a focus on avoidance of professional disciplinary action or civil liability rather than on 'mature professional identity'.

Julian Webb, in his discussion about the crucial need to take values more seriously in legal education (Chapter 2), notes that in England and Wales the professional ethics teaching that does take place tends 'to be of a highly instrumental rule-based character'. Helen Kruuse, in her examination of the practices and challenges facing an ethics education in South Africa (Chapter 6), also strikes a familiar chord in noting the unfortunate effects of a legal education that over-emphasizes 'rule craft' in many parts of the curriculum. One of the consequences of this preoccupation is the stultifying effect it has on moral reasoning in the 'ethics classroom'. Linda Haller makes a similar point in her argument about the need to be willing to encourage students to read traditional cases in a non-traditional way (Chapter 10). Serious concerns about the shortcomings of a rules-based learning agenda in Scotland are expressed by Donald Nicolson in his contribution about the unique contributions that clinics can offer in this area, including their potential to influence student moral development (Chapter 9). And Justine Rogers, in her chapter on the very significant challenges associated with assessment of legal ethics learning (Chapter 11), emphasizes the limited objectives of ethics teaching and learning through the way that common assessment practices often require and reward mere reproduction of knowledge, such as that contained within the ethical codes.

Most, if not all, contributors recognize, at least implicitly, the importance of placing emphasis on student *learning* rather than teacher *teaching* – and therefore the role of teachers in creating an effective learning environment for their students. This represents an important shift. Traditionally, the role of the teacher was to *teach* – that is, to transmit or impart knowledge to students. However, contemporary educational theory has altered the relationship between teacher and student by placing the student at the centre of the learning process. Much of this theory holds that students are themselves responsible for their learning, and therefore it is they who need to commit to and engage with the learning opportunities presented. Under this model, the role of teacher is recast from that of transmitter to one of facilitator. But this is not to suggest that the teacher's role has become any less important. In fact, it is probable that the responsibility of developing learning opportunities that encourage law students to reflect on their own views of what it means to act professionally and ethically is far more challenging for teachers than is implied by the 'transmitter' role.

Explicit statements evidencing this understanding of the changed teacher–student relationship are evident in Chapter 8 by Crowley-Cyr. In her view, an approach to teaching that holds up the teacher as someone who has superior knowledge, and who is therefore able to teach the students what they are required to learn, is flawed. Crowley-Cyr advocates an andragogical approach in which students are acknowledged as self-directed reflexive learners, with the teacher taking a facilitative role in the learning process. Similarly, Cassandra Sharp in Chapter 3 accepts that students are 'active viewers of legal popular culture . . . constantly interpreting, transforming and producing meaning in relation to the images and stories as presented in fiction'. In this, she implicitly recognizes that it is the students themselves who are driving their own learning, from which they construct who they believe they are – that is, their own identity.

In suggesting that students are capable of developing a sense of democratic intellect through a process of engaging in moral reflection, Webb too (in Chapter 2) implies that the teacher's role is not to be prescriptive, but rather is one that involves the use of debates, discussions and even the regular methods of lectures and tutorials to challenge students to develop their own ethical understandings and self-identity.

In saying that students are responsible for their learning, it is noticeable that many of the authors make reference to the idea that students are constructing their own knowledge. Although these contributors do not specially mention any particular educational theory, it appears that some are really reflecting aspects of constructivism.[2] Within constructivism, learners are seen to be 'actively constructing' knowledge through their own experiences. In this way, learners construct their own perspectives of meaning. Sharp, for instance, writes in Chapter 3 of the need for students to self-reflect around issues of morality and ultimately 'construct identity' – or, put in another way, 'reflexive law students could reflect on their own experiences . . . and actively construct identity in light of those reflections'. Similar ideas are evident in Chavkin's discussion in Chapter 4 about students 'creating' and 'developing' their knowledge, and also in Webb's references in Chapter 2 to 'self-work', which involves students developing 'confidence, interpersonal skills [and] the capacity for mature reflection', which in turn leads to their own self-identity.

Another noteworthy feature of many of the contributions is the commitment shown by the authors to reaching into other disciplines for guidance and additional resources. These efforts inevitably assist in enriching our understanding of the possibilities for developing our own and our students' learning in this area. For example, Rogers, Crowley-Cyr and David McQuoid-Mason all find special relevance for law students in engagement with bio-ethical principles, while Nicolson, Cunningham and Alexander rely to a great extent on contemporary moral psychology in offering better understandings of what may be important and possible for the ethics learning project.

At this point, it is convenient to return to the first fundamental question referred to above, which is about *what it is that we want our students to learn* or *in what manner we would like them to develop* from our teaching endeavours. Although the chapters in this volume provide a variety of responses to this question, it is possible to identify a number of common perspectives on what the authors advocate.

Taking each contribution in turn, and in no particular order, Nicolson is clearly interested in encouraging law students to develop 'an attitude of ethical professionalism'; however, he wants to take this further so that legal education might 'positively influence the development of students' moral character', which he sees as offering 'the best hope for influencing the future behaviour of lawyers'. Although Kruuse does not employ such phraseology, it is likely that she has similar learning outcomes in mind in wanting students to 'develop a sense of ethical judgment', the meaning of which she links to what is referred to as 'second-order reasoning'. Ultimately, she wants law students to 'develop in their own ethical practice'. Likewise, Cunningham and Alexander, drawing heavily on the insights and recommendations of the Carnegie Report, are strongly committed to the goal of developing law students' capacity for what they refer to as professional judgment. Haller, in her call for a careful rereading of seemingly 'benign' cases, sees opportunities for developing in students a valuable and critical reflection on lawyers' social and professional roles, which includes a greater sense of their moral responsibilities.

Like Nicolson, Sharp is interested in students' moral development, but her position suggests less certain learning outcomes. While she recognizes the 'vital importance . . . [of making] possible the enhancement of student capacity for self-determination', she is careful to add that this should not involve an agenda to 'mould' certain kinds of thinking. Ultimately, students should be provided with opportunities 'for effective and appropriate personal and professional decision-making, enabling them to develop and evaluate their values and attitudes in a self-reflective manner'.

Crowley-Cyr believes one of the goals of legal education must be to 'educate future professionals who have internalized an autonomous capacity to apply ethics in the practice of law'. In advocating an andragogical (adult learning) approach based on the bio-ethical principles of autonomy, beneficence, non-maleficence and justice, she shares some common ground with both McQuoid-Mason and Rogers. For McQuoid-Mason, these principles are a valuable resource for legal ethics teaching and learning, not least because they resonate strongly with the core values of legal practice. The principles provide 'a simple tool for busy practitioners and aspiring lawyers and resource-starved legal ethics instructors in developing Commonwealth countries, to navigate their way through their local professional rules of conduct'. Used carefully as a learning resource, these principles 'simplify rather than complicate ethical issues for legal practitioners and aspiring lawyers so that they do not feel overwhelmed and disempowered by them'. Rogers, in drawing on an assessment model from biomedical ethics that posits ascending levels of ethics learning from 'knowledge' through to 'habituation' and 'action', argues for a 'deeper, more reflective ethics education . . . cultivating responsibility, judgment and sensitivity rather than the "right" answer'.

An appreciation of the significance of 'values' in legal education is evident in a number of contributions, but Webb gives this topic the closest attention. In calling for far more emphasis on values, he states, for example, that 'one of the functions of legal education should be to provide an opportunity to develop that kind of critical evaluation of and reflection on one's values within a legal context'. The values he sees as calling for more attention in the development of students' abilities include 'the values of 'society' at large; the values of law as a social and political construct; the ethics and values of legal professionalism; and those 'of liberal higher education itself'. Chavkin's position on what students might learn in this area overlaps with those of others in a number of ways. For example, he too advocates the application of adult learning principles, and wants students to develop a sense of professional responsibility for their interactions with clients – through experiences that encourage self-reflection on the values that inevitably emerge within the practice of law.

Moving on from the question about the nature and quality of learning that is regarded as important, if not vital, it is now worth noting the kinds of approaches and strategies that might be used to create the conditions necessary to achieve these kinds of learning outcomes. Not surprisingly, some of these accounts are based upon the authors' own experiences as legal ethics teachers. It is also worth making the observation that, given the variation in these approaches, there is much to be said for recognizing the need for and value of diversity in creating the conditions necessary for this kind of learning. As the contributions collectively demonstrate, these opportunities arise through a variety of traditional and innovative strategies, be they in the classroom, through simulations, within the clinic, or even elsewhere – and they are all worth taking seriously in the quest for a more holistic approach to and understanding of legal ethics learning in law school education.

Cunningham and Alexander, Chavkin, and Nicolson all recognize the special opportunities offered by and through the legal clinic, although the models they advocate and describe are not necessarily confined to the clinic alone. Cunningham and Alexander describe innovations in some American law schools following the Carnegie Report. What each of these approaches reveals is the potential to create new and exciting opportunities for learning through a variety of strategies to augment existing classroom and clinical courses, such as student ethics committees, practice groups, practicums and even partnerships with law students in other countries. In offering 'a replicable model of ethics education that is affordable and manageable within the financial and other realities of international legal education', Chavkin also emphasizes the strengths of experiential learning, through an 'integration of andragogical experiential learning in the law school environment'. What he presents is a hybrid model, 'in between a clinic and a classroom course'. Nicolson provides a very persuasive account of the potential value of experiential learning through student involvement in a particular kind of live client clinic, and goes on to present evidence, gleaned from his own students' reflective diaries, which suggests that this kind of clinical exposure – even though limited to a relatively small cohort of students – 'may encourage the development of an attitude of ethical professionalism'.

Like Chavkin, Crowley-Cyr sees the relevance of andragogical theory in developing a better understanding of learning possibilities in this special area. She draws simultaneously on both pedagogical and andragogical theories to suggest practices that encourage students into what she refers to as 'ethical literacy and reflexive professionalism'. Sharp, in her close examination of how 'television's legal narratives' provides law students with a 'resource for talking through their moral positions', calls for 'legal educators . . . [to] place a high value on fostering student awareness of their developing personal ethics and identity projects'. Webb, in his discussion of the notion of 'democratic intellect' and his argument for taking more seriously 'the values and principles that underpin the discipline of law', calls for more 'discussion of values and value conflicts in lectures and large groups'. But he also thinks that 'legal education has to become more experiential, both in terms of its receptiveness to students' prior experiences, and in using experiential techniques of learning'. For Webb, a combination of problem-based learning, group work, exercises and role-plays 'can powerfully explore value dilemmas in depth and get "below the skin" of legal rules and traditional professional ethics'.

McQuoid-Mason, writing from the perspective of a scholar in a developing nation, in which international journals and other resources are often scarce or absent, argues that law students in developing countries, if not elsewhere, could learn much from four basic bioethical principles: client autonomy, beneficence, non-maleficence, and justice or fairness. He shows how the use of scenarios that draw upon these principles can be used to encourage the kind of learning that would enhance students' professional legal identities. Kruuse, who emphasizes the need to develop law students' deliberative capacities through what she refers to as substantive second-level reasoning, sees valuable opportunities in the study of South African constitutional cases involving the interpretation of constitutional rights. This is because this court has itself had to 'commit to substantive reasoning' in its interpretation of the Bill of Rights. Haller, too, sees valuable learning opportunities residing within case law if cases are analyzed in a particular way. Using an Australian case to illustrate her argument, Haller shows that students can be led to a far richer understanding of lawyers' roles and ethical responsibilities by reading cases through a legal ethics lens.

Finally, some of the chapters engage with the important matter of assessment in this area. Webb, for example, considers 'whether, and if so how, we assess students' legal or professional values *per se*', and suggests that there may be a way forward on this issue if we are willing to move away from traditional assessment practices and try others about which we may as yet have little direct experience. Chavkin, noting the Carnegie Report's criticisms of typical law school assessment practices, offers a detailed account of how he has attempted to address the criticisms. This approach includes strategies 'to get students to integrate the cognitive, practical and formative goals' of his teaching. Nicolson describes the role that clinical students' reflective diaries play in his assessment of their performances, but also how these, on a rereading, have provided a potential source of evidence of students' 'moral development and its influences'.

The contribution by Rogers focuses specifically on ethics assessment, in particular the vitally important part that assessment in general plays as a driver of student learning. Noting that for the most part 'legal ethics assessment remains an unimaginative and tentative enterprise . . . [and is also] beset by huge challenges and limitations' (including widespread cynicism about legal ethics assessment itself), Rogers is nevertheless optimistic about the potential for substantial improvement in this area. Drawing on lessons that can be learned from assessment practices in the field of medical ethics, Rogers explains in some detail how the 'experience of the medical profession provides several possibilities for progress at each phase of legal education and training'. In so doing, she also makes the argument that many contributors to this volume implicitly share: that legal education is lagging far behind other professions in being willing to engage progressively with ethics teaching and learning, including assessment.

In this chapter we have endeavoured to draw attention to some of the important themes that we detect in the chapters that follow, but emphasize that each chapter makes its own original contribution to an area of legal education that is likely to become even more significant in the years to come. Together, the contributions in this volume add substantially to our understanding of the ethics project in legal education, which includes what Nicolson in this volume refers to as 'the debate over whether and how best teaching can influence [law] student moral development'.

Notes

1 W.M. Sullivan, A. Colby, J. Welch Wegner, L. Bond and L.S. Schulman, *Educating Lawyers: Preparation for the Profession of Law* (2007) San Francisco: Jossey-Bass, 2007, p. 140.
2 J.R. Savery and T.M. Duffy, 'Problem based learning: An instructional model and its constructivist framework' *Educational Technology* 35, 1995, 31–8.

2 Taking values seriously: the democratic intellect and the place of values in the law school curriculum

Julian Webb

2.1 Introduction

Values matter because they are both constitutive of a mature moral identity and an attribute necessary for effective citizenship. In *Democracy and Education*,[1] John Dewey's belief in education as a fundamentally social practice led him to argue that all meaningful education is in fact moral education, and that moral education is what prepares us to take our place in a democratic society. Dewey thus saw a critical role for schools as the laboratories within which our values are not just shaped, but tested. As Larry May similarly asserts, 'the self matures by becoming committed to certain values and beliefs as a result of critical reflection, not merely as a result of being socialized to accept certain values and beliefs.'[2]

In this light, it is hardly radical to argue that one of the functions of legal education should be to provide an opportunity to develop[3] that kind of critical evaluation of and reflection on one's values within a legal context. Nevertheless, this suggestion will seem heresy to some. Even if we do accept the point, the hard work then only just begins. What are the values about which we should be talking? What kinds of learning experience will enable values elicitation and moral maturation – and, even more fundamentally, what is the kind of values talk in which we can and should be engaging at law school? These are the big issues I wish to explore within this chapter.[4]

My sense that this very complexity is important has been put into relief by my experiences as a teacher and legal ethicist in English law schools. In England and Wales, there has been a marked reluctance to address that complexity in a systematic fashion at any stage of legal education and training. What we therefore have is a segmented and incomplete picture. Attempts to sow the seeds of professional legal ethics within the law degree curriculum have tended, so far at least, to fall on stony ground,[5] while the professional ethics and conduct teaching that takes place at the vocational postgraduate stage of training has tended to be of a highly instrumental rule-based character.[6] By contrast, there are signs of a growing interest and awareness – at least in the textbook literature[7] – of the role of broader legal values in understanding substantive law subjects, and of a small, but possibly growing interest in and scholarship on the values of the law school itself as an avowedly liberal educational institution.[8] It is primarily in that context, then, that

I consider the issues raised in developing a more values-based legal education, and some of the challenges involved in taking values seriously.

My position also assumes that the law school is a social institution in which, to put it rather crudely, a variety of 'value systems' potentially come into play and into conflict.[9] Chief among these are broadly what we might call the values of 'society' at large; the values of law as a social and political construct; the ethics and values of legal professionalism, and those of liberal higher education itself. It is the latter with which we begin, rather than the more obvious issues of definition and scope, because in a sense they constitute a first hurdle if we are to get this particular show on the road.

2.2 Values in liberal (legal) education

This is a topic that my colleague Roger Burridge and I have recently discussed elsewhere at some length,[10] though it is one that also benefits from being located in the context of a growing renaissance in debate about educational values more generally in higher education.[11]

The law school has become characterized as relatively inhospitable ground for discussions of values and the moral content of law. Its dominant perspective has been described variously as 'technocentric',[12] a new 'philistinism',[13] a moral 'wasteland'[14] and even, in Harry Arthur's evocative phrase, 'So near to Wall Street, so far from god'![15]

This has not always been the case, however. As Wes Pue has demonstrated,[16] the current state of legal education reflects a rupture both in values and in the perceived importance of values. In its turn to technocentrism, it is hard to reject the view that legal education has become less self-aware of its own educational values. So what are these values? Some are obvious, others less so. Intellectual autonomy and integrity are clearly prized by the liberal tradition, as is the idea of knowledge as an end in itself, together with the development of general cognitive capacities – such as the ability to produce reasoned argument – and the capacities for reflection and creativity.[17] In many respects, these values will seem largely unobjectionable, if not positively desirable. Nevertheless, it is my argument here that some of these ideals have actually played an important role in limiting the capacity of legal education to take values seriously. I suggest that, for our present purposes, the key problematic tenets of most modern versions of liberal legal education are as follows:

- Intellectual development and the pursuit of knowledge are valuable ends in themselves, and separate from any process of character formation.
- University (legal) education serves as a preparation for life (or 'citizenship'), not just for work (either in general or more specifically – for example, as a legal practitioner).
- University legal education must be essentially 'value-free'; while it may be an education *about* values, it must maintain moral neutrality and not advance specific values.

Why should this be? I suggest there are at least three key reasons.

The first, and most obvious, of these is the myth of value-neutrality itself. All human activity is value laden, and teaching and learning are no exception. No pedagogy is or can be entirely value free so, as a matter of practice, values in supposedly value-free teaching can only disappear to a certain extent. The formal curriculum thus – almost by default – tends to emphasize technical-rational knowledge and skills while paying little or no attention to the (moral) purposes to which these may be put, or else reduces matters of ethics and values to processes of legalistic rule application. Values also become part of a hidden curriculum, which tends to be strongly individualistic and pragmatic in its approach to the law and to learning, and sometimes cynical in outlook.[18]

Second, it might also be asserted that the liberal university has actually not made a very good job of being liberal. There is an argument that liberalism's roots, in fact, have never run as deeply as we might like to think through academic life:

> [A]cademics' own values have never been straightforwardly in favour of autonomy or even of universalism. They have acceded to political pressure for over a century, not only because it brings funds, but also because they have not been averse to sharing the rooted local, regional or state values that the political system and the social demands articulate. The debate about academic values in Scotland and England since the mid-nineteenth century illustrates the multifarious character of academic identity quite well.[19]

Modern pressures on the traditional ideal of higher education as primarily a public rather than an economic good only add to the uncertainties. As Sheila Slaughter has observed:

> At one time, the boundaries between the professional world, at the heart of which was the university, and the business world, whose [goal] was profit, were fairly clear. Scientists and professionals were supposed to seek objective knowledge, foster the free flow of such knowledge, enhance learning and discovery, and use their expertise in the service of the common good. In return, they received public trust and subsidy.
>
> That bargain began to break down in the second half of the twentieth century, as intellectual property, found readily and cheaply in universities, became central to the market strategies of multinational corporations. Professionals outside the universities – physicians, lawyers, computer scientists – contributed to the breakdown of the social contract by forgoing altruism and miming corporate practices that focused on the bottom line. Within universities, administrators entered into multiple and complicated relationships with corporations, as did some faculty members. The lines between professional and corporate values, public and private support, the commons and the market became more and more difficult to discern.[20]

These tensions may also become reflected in pedagogic practices, particularly in a context where the role of student is steadily being transformed into that of client or consumer of services. For example, while we may pay proper lip service to the ideals of intellectual growth, and of the student as an autonomous and self-directed learner, the realities of massification, of student passivity *and* anxiety, and perhaps a certain authoritarianism in the law school culture, may all serve to reduce the liberal aspiration to something much more mundane.

Third, there is also the question of the 'dark side' of valuing. We have not thus far said anything much about the disvalues of legal education, but these are also significant. As Daicoff concludes, research in the United States has shown that lawyers tend to demonstrate behaviours such as competitiveness, dominance and aggressiveness (mixed with insecurity in law students) and are driven by material-ism and a desire to achieve.[21] Work by Sheldon and Krieger[22] also demonstrates that US students experience a loss of autonomy during their time at law school, and changes in valuing away from intrinsic helping and 'community' values towards extrinsic appearance and image values. Not only are such changes in valuing almost certainly undesirable in terms of community (and, we might hope, professional) expectations; they also have negative consequences for the well-being and motivation of the individuals concerned.

In sum, then, for law schools to participate in a conspiracy of silence about values does not bring us closer to understanding the normativity of law. It does not acknowledge either the value-laden character of the formal or the hidden curriculum, or the subjectivity involved in our (the teachers') selection and inter-pretation of legal materials.[23] It probably does nothing for student well-being, and does little to support students to engage more effectively in a world in which real decision-making is invariably value laden.

So, if we are to overturn our general reluctance to engage with values, what will that mean? Which values matter, and how might we go about bringing them back into the law school?[24]

2.3 What values are, and why they matter

Any attempt at cogent 'values talk' is made more difficult, once one tries to move beyond a lay understanding, by the relative absence of any common language and 'general theory of value' across disciplines. As Sherif observed as long ago as 1936, 'philosophers, psychologists and sociologists . . . have had a tendency to build up their own concepts, giving little or no attention to what their colleagues in other fields have been doing on the same problem'.[25] Nevertheless, by drawing on insights from a range of these disciplines, I think we can build a reasonably coherent picture of values that will work, at least for our present purposes. In other words, what I will do here is attempt to offer a brief but nonetheless 'natur-alistic account' of values that fits reasonably well with our growing understanding of human cognitive and emotional function and development. There is, of course, a danger that the picture I draw here is too broad brush in nature, and steps over some quite fundamental issues and distinctions within and between the different (disciplinary) perspectives on values. Where possible, I have sought in what follows to indicate major points of uncertainty, and to identify also those points where I have made quite specific choices from among competing theories.

The picture with which I begin is a relatively individualistic one. Values are essentially personal to us. While we may draw on the many familial and wider cultural influences to help shape our own value system, the ultimate construct is our own, and each of us ultimately builds our own set of value priorities out of our life experience. This is not to say all values are purely personal values: we can also legitimately talk about 'institutional values' as those values which a person may be expected to adopt having, in Brad Wendel's terms, ' "opted in" to a particular social role'[26] – as a lawyer, say, or even a law teacher. We will return to the importance of institutional values later in this chapter.

In thinking about values, it is sometimes said that the simplest point to start at is to consider what values are *not*. Accordingly, values are not the same as norms, attitudes, traits or needs,[27] though these all play some part in constructing identity in what Flanagan calls its 'thick, rich sense',[28] and have points of similarity and connection. Nevertheless, there are material differences which point to values having a special place in the processes of both identity construction and, possibly, behaviour change.[29]

While both possess, as Rokeach observes,[30] an element of 'oughtness', values differ from norms in that the latter tend to be defined in a way that is more situational, and at a lower level of abstraction. Values sit behind norms and serve as 'more generalized ideological justifications for roles and norms, and express the aspirations that allegedly inform the required activities'.[31] In language that is more common to legal analysis, we could reframe this in terms of the difference between values, rules and principles, though this is neither an easy, nor by any means a complete and perfect, distinction. Nevertheless, in theory values are highly abstract, pervasive and aspirational. Rules, at the other extreme, tend to be concrete, highly situational and deontological. Principles may be understood as sitting between rules and values. They share the deontological character of rules,[32] but tend to be more abstract than rules properly so called, and to have more of the pervasiveness of values.[33]

Attitudes are also regarded as more situational than values, and more concrete; however, unlike norms or values, they consist primarily of an emotional valence linked to a particular object, person or action.[34] For these reasons, values are thought to play a stronger role than attitudes in the construction of self-identity.[35] Traits, by contrast, are generally seen as far more fixed or enduring features of a personality, whereas values may be more fluid and changing over time. There is also no evidence of a strong correlation between traits and values. As Hitlin and Piliavin observe, it is quite possible to have a disposition towards aggression, while not highly valuing aggression.[36] The relationship between needs and values is perhaps more complex. Basic needs for things such as food, shelter and sex are essentially biological, and so to some degree predetermined or 'hard-wired' (though even this statement needs to be treated with some caution). Values, however, are much more culturally defined, and often serve to set socially acceptable limits on the way one expresses needs. Nerlich thus talks of *subjective values* as those values which a person derives from submitting their lower order desires, including basic needs, to evaluation in the light of higher (or second) order desires for self-construction and self-realization.[37] A need for sex, for example, may be socially reconstituted in terms of the value of love, or its inhibition (in certain circumstances) rationalized in terms of the values of self-denial, the sanctity of marriage, and so on.[38] As these examples show, however, the need is never the value.

So what does this enable us to say, more positively, about values? First, it is clear that all accounts treat values as representations of our commitment to certain human ideals, and thus cognitively distinct from our commitments to other specific human beings as such.[39] Values, in simple terms, are aspirational. As we have seen, they provide a way of mediating basic needs and desires – and, more positively, of expressing the moral and aesthetic highpoints of a shared culture.[40] They are the outcome of a complex interplay between nature and environment, though shaped predominantly by the latter.[41] In other words, they are not purely cognitive constructs, but are grounded in biology and sentiment, and are a product of language and culture.[42] Values can provide both a *post-hoc* rationalization of conduct and be motivational, the drivers by which we each cultivate our humanity and pursue projects that are, in most accounts, consistent with our notions of human flourishing.[43] It is also in this motivational respect that the affective dimension of values is particularly important.[44]

Of course, values don't just matter at the level of individual identity construction; they matter because they have a wider social role. They provide much of what defines and holds our communities together.[45] They help us to negotiate the complex web of social roles and commitments that lie in our path. They are important in understanding why people respond to morally complex or challenging situations in a particular way – even those situations that are apparently governed by formal ethical rules or guidance.[46] They may even help us to understand why people may act in ways that are seemingly contrary to what many of us would consider fundamental, universal beliefs and principles.[47]

This leads us to another issue. While the process of valuing is widely regarded as universal,[48] whether there are specific universal values is less certain – and, of course, this is a question that is surrounded by both philosophical and more empirical (methodological) difficulties.

Here is not the place to try to summarize the vast amounts of ink that have been spilled in trying to map the world of values. Nevertheless, there tends to be a strong core of agreement that certain broad values elicit sufficiently strong levels of agreement to create at least a prima facie claim to widespread acceptance, at least as they are understood within the Western tradition.[49] Such values tend to include benevolence, the pursuit of pleasure and happiness for all, self-directed goals of universal power and freedom, justice, unselfish personal love, aesthetic sensibility and the pursuit of knowledge as both an instrumental and terminal value.[50]

Whether or not Schwartz's account – or indeed any other account of social values – has strong empirical validity is not a primary concern of this chapter.

Rather, I intend to use these broad categories more to reflect briefly on the ways in which different value systems interact, and particularly to acknowledge and discuss how problems of potential value conflict might then emerge and need to be addressed in legal education. The move here to talking about 'value systems' as a feature of the social structure rather than of an individual mind is entirely deliberate. It suggests that we must at least consider the possibility of two related problems: first, that in complex societies values are likely to be functionally differentiated within and between different social systems, so that law, for example, functions as an at least semi-autonomous value system; and second, that genuine value conflicts can never be entirely resolved at the level of values because such values may be incomparable, both within and between value systems.[51] To get some sense of the problem, it is necessary to turn our attention to both legal and liberal educational values.

2.4 Thinking about the values of law and legal practice

Without doubt, law touches on some of the most fundamental of human values, albeit often hidden behind the masks of 'public policy' and 'moral neutrality'. However, relatively little effective mapping of the terrain has been undertaken. Consequently, if we turn our attention to the values of law, we see an increasingly rich, but nonetheless confusing, vista. This, of course, is one of the reasons why the values dimension is such an important subject for academic study: the conceptual complexity of legal values may be a problem for law, but it is also a central question and a resource for legal education.

Traditionally, order, justice and individual freedom have been considered three of the most basic, terminal values of law.[52] Utility and/or efficiency are also increasingly seen as strong contenders, particularly with the rise in some jurisdictions – notably the United States – of economic analysis of law within judicial as well as academic reasoning.[53] These are distinct, of course, from a whole variety of instrumental values and/or principles that give effect to these other terminal values, and which, as a collective whole, probably remain underdetermined in legal thought. Good examples of such things would be the 'due process' values/principles of certainty, neutrality, objectivity, and so on.[54]

Moreover, a number of modern trends – in particular, the growth in domestic and international human rights law, with its focus on 'fundamental legal values', and the emergence of 'outsider discourses' such as feminism and critical race theory – have introduced a range of newer candidates as potential terminal values in their own right. Examples of these might include human dignity,[55] equality,[56] care[57] and self-development.[58] These approaches have also served to make values, or the absence of values, more visible in legal discourse, and to move the discussion of values beyond its traditional home in jurisprudence or philosophy of law. As the Canadian Charter jurisprudence, and to a much lesser extent UK case law following the Human Rights Act, show, such fundamental legal values can serve to set principled limits on positive law, mostly by prescribing what the courts can and can't do in the name of law.[59]

The functional relationship between law and values also needs to be considered. Not surprisingly, functionality can also be viewed from a number of different – and possibly complementary – perspectives. Thus law itself can be seen as a means of realizing value. From this angle, law serves primarily as one of the institutions of civil society dedicated to human flourishing. Alternatively, values may be considered as external concepts against which the goodness or rightness of law may be evaluated.[60] From this perspective, any radical reassessment of fundamental values should lead to an equally radical reconstruction of law. From yet another viewpoint, certain values may be categorized as discrete 'legal values', which operate as internal standards of legal criticism. Indeed, if we take Luhmann's notion of the normative closure of systems seriously, then we might go further and say law is cognitively incapable of applying a genuinely external standard to itself. There will always be a process of translation, and so the value of justice, or equality, cannot but take on a specifically 'legal' meaning within the legal system, different from that employed in the political system and so on. This last perspective may be helpful in understanding the various gaps that emerge and create not just inter-systemic misunderstanding, but perhaps a form of trans-systemic incommensurability as well as more obvious disjunctures between 'professional' and lay discourses (e.g. in both lawyer–client, and judicial–lay conceptions of what is fair or just in a given cause) that may have consequences for the social legitimacy of law and legal decision-making.[61]

This leads us relatively neatly into the question of legal professional values. While this may seem a far more discrete and manageable field to consider than the realm of legal values per se, it is still not an easy area to map. Lawyers potentially promote multiple 'social' values through their practice:

> including not only preserving individual liberty, speaking truth to power, showing mercy, and resisting oppression, but also enhancing order and stability in opposition to the 'ill-considered passions' of democracy, aligning individual action with the public good, and shaping disputes for resolution by particular institutions such as courts and agencies.[62]

They are also expected to uphold a range of institutional values. The list may vary somewhat between jurisdictions, but integrity, loyalty, independence, competence, civility and a commitment to both individual and collective improvement and professional development are common components.[63] Others, such as a commitment to the rule of law or the promotion of access to justice, also appear in the literature.[64]

One problem with professional legal ethics, however – both as it is represented in the literature and as it is taught – is that this values dimension is often represented solely (or at least primarily) via the medium of discrete rules of conduct. This not only disguises the extent to which such a rule-centred paradigm may be quite differently represented among the range of legitimate value positions articulated by professional legal ethics,[65] but also potentially underplays the distinctive role of values and value conflict in ethical decision-making.

Value conflict is, we might argue, endemic in professional decision-making. Thus, for example, the pull of even the institutional values will not always be unidirectional and consistent – for example, loyalty to the client and professional independence obviously exist in, at best, a creative tension. Likewise – and perhaps increasingly with the segmentation of professional work – different practice settings may engage different value priorities, and justify different responses by individual agents.[66] A lawyer may thus be faced with a range of 'right answers' which they must evaluate in the light of their own value priorities and, as Wendel argues: 'As long as both ideals are indeed expressions of strands that we consider valuable and worthy of respect within our ethical tradition, either course of action must be regarded as permissible, and neither agent may be criticized in moral terms.'

Significant tensions will also arise between these special-purpose institutional values and the lawyer's own personal value commitments. Thus, as Rhode observes, 'doing good and doing well do not always push in similar directions',[67] and lawyers may commonly be confronted with conflicts between their professional values or duties and their own self-interest, or the interests of the firm. Similarly, professional obligations can conflict with loyalties to friends and family who may place the lawyer in a position that creates not just a conflict of interests but a real conflict of values.[68] These kinds of conflicts may appear less defensible, perhaps because such a clash of values is not seen as an incommensurability problem in the manner discussed by Wendel and others. There is an assumption – often implicit – here that institutional (moral) values must trump any inconsistent personal values; however, as Evans and Palermo's work indicates, that assumption may well be psychologically naïve, and certainly the emotional pull may well be towards the personal rather than institutional values.[69]

At the same time, we must take care that we don't present value conflict as somehow entirely pathological. Value conflict is a normal fact of life and, as Bernard Williams has argued, an ethical life inevitably involves compromising one's principles.[70] One's integrity is shaped in and by the attempt to balance the many things that are valued by the individual – and it is worth noting here that lifestyle and aesthetic choices may be as constitutive of the self as are moral values.

In this context, it is unsurprising that a number of writers on professional ethics, from within a range of different traditions,[71] have argued that an ethics that emphasizes rule application cannot be enough; they maintain that an 'ethics of obligation' (to use May's term) does not draw a sufficiently strong connection between our conceptions of who we are and what we do, and does not really pay attention to the power of the conflicted *feelings* that moral dilemmas evoke. As Christine Parker and Adrian Evans conclude:

> Inside lawyers' ethics in practice there are many very personal dilemmas. Feelings about what is right and wrong can lurk beneath the surface without being expressed. Many people find it difficult to recognise the importance of their often confused feelings for ethical decision-making, and lawyers can be particularly poor at this skill. We often gloss over the personal dimensions of

ethical conflicts by using only the rules as our guide, ignoring the fact that rules are often like cryptic crosswords full of overriding principles, qualifications, and provisos, and discounting our gut feelings about what is right.[72]

For the present purposes, of course, the central question that remains is what legal education can and should be doing to address this problem. In the remainder of this chapter, I will argue that this question raises a number of important but also difficult challenges, which need to be considered not just in terms of seeking to make better lawyers, but in more general terms of supporting our graduates to be better citizens.[73]

2.5 Developing the democratic intellect: bringing values home to legal education

In the final section of this chapter, I identify a number of conceptual and practical steps – some relatively simple and non-contentious, others much more challenging – as a way of engaging more deeply and effectively with values in the law school. In framing these steps, I first intend to resurrect the notion of the *democratic intellect* as a useful label for capturing the ideal type for this endeavour – the *praxis*, if you like, for what Burridge and I have described as a 'post-liberal' conception of legal education.[74]

The 'democratic intellect' was a term coined by George Davie[75] to describe the nineteenth-century tradition of Scottish university education. As Paterson observes, this tradition bore closer links to the dominant epistemology of France, Germany and the United States than the ancient universities of England. It was a tradition in which the university demonstrated a commitment to civic values, and regarded knowledge itself as a public good, 'a matter of clarifying and making rigorous the "common sense" of society'.[76] In arguing that we must pay attention to the ideal of the democratic intellect, I want to breathe new life into this concept. This is not least because my reconceptualization, in many respects, actually turns it *against* Davie. I suggest that this is not merely desirable, but necessary to better reflect the challenges represented by the complexity of modern society and the greater value pluralism of the early twenty-first century.[77]

2.5.1 Rethinking the ambit of the law school

The idea of the democratic intellect implies an education of humane breadth, grounded in the liberal arts and with a strong philosophical footing. It is perhaps best understood as a commitment to understanding the first principles that both bridge and bound the disciplines. But it was originally also more than that, insofar as it regarded the question of how we should live our lives as both an intently philosophical and also deeply social, practical question.[78] At a bare minimum, it means that students are indeed enabled to learn *about* the values and principles that underpin the discipline of law – a step that, in itself, requires us to take values much more seriously than we do now. As I have sought to show, there is still significant theoretical work to be done on the nature and scope of legal values. Although the broad concept-mapping developed in this chapter demonstrates a fair degree of common ground, a sense of gaps, discontinuities and incomparabilities is also readily apparent. I would argue in particular that we have generally failed to address the gaps between philosophy and professional ethics, or to take the complexity of value systems seriously as part of either academic or vocational legal education.

Without that kind of grounding, I am concerned that the processes of value identification and valuation may operate as little more than folk concepts or subjective preferences, reinforcing for ourselves and our students the sense that law operates only according to pragmatic precepts shaped, perhaps at best, by a kind of easy-going relativism. Equally, however, philosophy by itself has its limits. I would broadly endorse these recent comments by Seow Hon Tan:

> I want students to engage not just their minds, but their hearts, and to come up with their own theory about the legal process, and decide what role they will play in it in future. Philosophical musings are only the baby steps; I do not want students to stop with them. Philosophical conclusions must translate into politics and religion in the figurative sense of these words – politics in the sense of practical changes in the world in which my students will work, and religion in the sense of their personal worldviews that affect the conduct of their lives.[79]

However – and this is where my argument becomes more controversial – if this is what we want to achieve, conventional learning *about* values will not by itself be enough. To go back to where this chapter began, if we are convinced not only that values matter, but that they matter because they go some way towards shaping – positively – the manner of our being in the world, then mere teaching about values will not be enough. As we have seen, values are slippery, difficult customers. They are vulnerable to attack and easily overturned where there is insufficient scaffolding to maintain them. The liberal tradition, framed as it is around the Cartesian *cogito*, separates mind from body, individual from environment and thinking from being in ways that actively prevent us from taking values seriously. A more holistic, or what I have latterly come to call 'ecological', conception[80] of learning places those boundaries very much in question, and has the potential to open up the capacity of legal education to engage in more meaningful values talk.

Fundamentally, we need to support students in developing what Swanton[81] calls 'modes of moral responsiveness', of honouring value, in the sense of not 'dirtying one's hands'[82] in respect of that value. This itself involves the development of a number of capacities: the technical ability to identify and distinguish between plural value claims, a sensitivity to the complexity of human relationships, and a responsiveness to value conflict.[83] At the least, this implies some refocusing of the curriculum on both the identification of value issues (e.g. in typical 'Blackacre' or 'Janet and John Doe' problems), and on developing in students both the cognitive and soft skills necessary to respond effectively to the values dimension.

However, I would also go further than this and argue that law teachers should be prepared to advance certain value positions. Paradoxical though this may at first sound, this leads us to the second element of the democratic intellect: its emphasis on democracy.

2.5.2 *Taking democracy seriously*

While the recovery of the philosophical and wider intellectual dimension is important, we particularly need to take the democratic side of the democratic intellect far more seriously. This takes our attention away from what we teach to how we organize our universities as moral and political communities. This is increasingly seen by commentators as a necessary corrective to the more corrosive effects of neo-liberalism on the academy, whereby corporatization and com-modification, here as elsewhere, threaten to override the democratic impulses and practices of civil society through the new hegemony of market forces.[84]

Ernesto Laclau has argued that a strongly democratic society is one that accepts 'the contingent and radically open character of all of its values'.[85] This is, of course, itself a values position – it implies a commitment to and engagement with moral argument, and a belief that the very process of engaging in 'civilised conversa-tion'[86] across political and cultural divides can make a difference. On the other hand, we know also that institutional structures can enact powerful forms of oppression and acts of symbolic violence that chill genuine debate, and foster passivity and conformity of belief. In this light, I would repeat the argument that Burridge and I have adopted:[87] that we need to take our liberalisms more seriously, but their neutrality less so. Liberalism needs to be more open about its own lack of neutrality. As a self-sustaining social and political system, it does not (and perhaps logically cannot) ultimately require us to adopt a standard of persuasive neutrality[88] towards the values and practices of its core institutions, including the university itself. Jettisoning this kind of strong claim to neutrality would not have a chilling effect on discussion about values – indeed, its effect should be quite the reverse, since it counters the seeming laissez-faire-ness of liberalism and calls us to engage in 'real' debate about values, and to take value pluralism itself seriously as a meaningful, but problematic, project for our society, rather than an unexamined assumption. It must be desirable that uni-versities and their law schools, as moral and political institutions, 'walk the talk', and may be seen to honour the values that they claim underpin their educational mission. Arguably, this is particularly important in the context of law. Law matters in the real world. Its values and the values of its practitioners make a material difference to the lives of citizens. It is tempting, in this con-text, to make out a case for law as occupying a special (though not peculiar) sphere as one of the 'socio-practical' fields of knowledge – a term coined by de Castell and Freeman[89] in relation to education. To take the socio-practical character of law seriously would mean treating it as a field in which real-world problems (and problem-solving) are central to an understanding of the field, and one in which practice itself should be developed as a site of praxis – of critical theory and knowledge-construction – and not just applied academic knowledge.

Acceptance of this premise should also strengthen our ability to develop a values education that has the potential to make a real difference. Dewey wrote that education 'is learning the meaning of what we are about and employing that meaning in action'.[90] In other words, values education has to combine (abstract) knowledge and experience. Attacks against fundamental values can have dramatic effects on an individual's motivations and beliefs. If values are to be a meaningful basis for action, students need to have both a proper understanding of and affective commitment to developed value positions. Evidence suggests that an affective commitment by itself is not very effective at defending a persuasive (reasoned) attack on that value. On the other hand, the development of cognitive resources in support of a value has been shown to make that value more resistant to attack, particularly where such support is developed *actively* over time.[91] Moreover, there is also evidence from the same research that the provision of support for even a single value may not only strengthen the motivational force supporting that value, but may bolster other relevant attitudes and values.[92]

Taking democracy seriously also implies a modified role for (many) academics. It implies that it is an important part of our function to support democratic social and discursive practices within, and also perhaps outside, the university. This is not intended to impose some kind of corporatist uniformity on academia. Again, I would suggest that the reverse is true. Values positions will become stronger and more meaningful if they are subject to open, robust debate.[93] What I anticipate here is the need for a greater commitment to something closer to the role of public intellectual,[94] and a willingness among academics to see their work as inherently publicly and politically engaged, and the academic career as one that positions us both in and, where morally necessary, against the institutions of which we are part.

2.6 Finally: thinking about process

The arguments I have advanced in this chapter have important ramifications not just for the curriculum, but for the ways in which we teach and facilitate learning.

First, we should not overlook the extent to which value issues can be uncovered through much relatively traditional teaching and learning. It is not an impossible stretch to include discussion of values and value conflicts in lectures and large groups, and even quite conventional 'John Doe' or 'Blackacre' problem questions can be extended to include discussion of the underlying values and value conflicts that are engaged by the problem and its potential resolution(s).

Second, it will be readily apparent from what I have already said that Oliver Wendell Holmes' famous aphorism that 'the life of law is not logic but experience' has real relevance to the law school classroom.[95] If it is to take values seriously, legal education has to become more experiential, both in terms of its receptiveness to students' prior experiences and in using experiential techniques of learning. This does not just translate to 'more clinical legal education', though there is an undoubted place for clinic in developing ethical understanding and reflection on legal values.[96] There is also scope to develop a more 'holistic' form of problem-based learning, as well as other group work, exercises and role-plays that can powerfully explore value dilemmas in depth and get 'below the skin' of legal rules and traditional professional ethics. There is also no reason why existing traditional teaching methods cannot also play a part. But what is more important in this context is perhaps the creation of an over arching ethos. If values are to be taken seriously, we need to consider what it will take in our own law schools (again, I would hesitate to offer a general prescription – much will depend on local conditions) to foster an environment of 'critical morality in which individuals can debate, discuss and criticize majority views, internalizing their own values and acting on them'.[97]

Third, we need to explore ways to acknowledge and give appropriate space to the feelings and motivations that will arise in learning, since these too are integral to processes of valuation. The traditional separation between the formal intellectual work of the classroom and the informal processes of social learning that also characterize university life has to be recognized as unhelpful here. 'Self-work' – the development of confidence, interpersonal skills, the capacity for mature reflection, greater autonomy, and enhanced imaginative and empathic capacities – is rightly prized by students.[98] Students need to be viewed more consistently by academics as central to the development of themselves as actualized, reflective and emotionally intelligent citizens, and such a perspective must be a legitimate concern of higher education. Within this concept of self-work, we might also include the need to support students explicitly to engage with issues of self-identity associated with their value choices. Exercises can be developed to encourage students to confront value discrepancies and build self-knowledge about their own value priorities and the kinds of situational factors that will shape both their value priorities and their decision-making. These kinds of exercises may have particular relevance to the process of professional identity-formation.[99]

Space probably also needs to be found to take issues of social identity and place more seriously, both in terms of content and process. Social identity is a loaded and often problematic concept. Ideas of a shared culture and identity can readily be used to justify the *status quo* – often interpreted in terms of 'insiders = good' and 'outsiders = bad' – and these attitudes can commonly 'infect' the learning environment in subtle ways. That is precisely why it is important for the law school to address these issues, most obviously in the context of themes such as human rights, migration and asylum-seeking, and criminal justice – and yes, in terms also of the history and meanings of legal professionalism, as well as of learning relationships and processes in the law school itself.

Place is another important part of the story that has been neglected by much legal scholarship and pedagogy. In his book *Place: A Short Introduction* (2004), the cultural geographer Tim Cresswell argues that understanding somewhere as a place is to recognize the complexity of the lives of its inhabitants: 'Place is the raw material for the creative production of identity rather than an *a priori* label of identity . . . Place provides the conditions of possibility for creative social practice.'[100] Thinking about place in this way opens up the possibilities of a 'geo-jurisprudence' – and perhaps new ways of exploring and understanding the meaning and value of law in different social spaces.[101] Equally, experimenting with the places and spaces within which our students learn may also help us to engage with their values, and at the same time develop new fora for creative thinking and understanding about law and legal values – for example, creating opportunities within the curriculum where law students can work collaboratively with students of other disciplines, or engage in activities such as drama.[102]

We cannot really leave the practicalities without saying something about assessment, though this could generate a whole other chapter in its own right. Assessment, we know, sends out powerful messages about those parts of the curriculum and the learning process that are important. We know also that, while there are significant pockets of innovation, law schools still tend to draw on a relatively narrow range of assessment practices. As long ago as 1990, David Boud pointed to the problem of the inconsistency between established assessment practices and those principles – such as autonomy, critical analysis and reflection – that are among the espoused values of higher education.[103] But that is only part of the story. In taking values more seriously, we are in fact faced with two issues: this one, which involves creating assessments that better capture the range of students' achievements corresponding to those espoused *educational* values; and another, which is the far thornier issue of whether – and if so, how – we assess students' legal or professional values per se.

Boud's criticism may still have validity as a critique of educational practice, but there is no reason in theory why we cannot create assessment tools that test capacities such as autonomy, critical analysis and even creativity. These involve – to an extent, at least – higher level cognitive skills that can be assessed (so far as anything can) with some degree of reliability and objectivity. Some quite conventional tools may already do so, at least inferentially: an individualized research project can demonstrate aspects of autonomy in learning and critical analysis, for example – perhaps even creativity, if we deconstruct that to mean something like the original synthesis or transformation of a set of ideas or concepts.[104] Techniques that assess process as well as product, including tools of supervised practice, and/or self- and peer assessment, may be better at doing the job more directly.[105]

Assessing values development is a rather different ball game, though – one that, quite properly, remains contentious.[106] Assessment and evaluation in higher education still differ substantially from workplace practices, where the 'assessment' of hard-to-measure skills and attributes – such as teamwork and networking skills, or personal alignment with organizational or professional values – is increasingly commonplace. We should not be in a hurry to emulate business. The plasticity of the concepts involved naturally leads to a reluctance to assess anything beyond domain knowledge: it might be quite reasonable to ask someone to write an essay on some aspects of the concept of equality, but we might pause (to say the least) if asked formally to assess a student's conduct according to a standard of integrity, and for that evaluation to count towards their degree or diploma. Let's take another simple example to test the issues. What if, alternatively, we suggested incorporating psychometric integrity testing into (professional) higher education? This might generate some rather different responses, perhaps depending on whether or not we are persuaded of the value of psychometrics, or feel we can identify curriculum interventions that would enable students to develop their values in a way that could be captured by such a test.

These two examples in themselves help us to get closer to some of the likely roots of our concerns. The first is that values assessment itself can raise ethical issues – we should consider whether the very practice actually infringes student autonomy at quite a deep level. More specifically, issues of honesty and integrity in particular can be difficult to deal with in any properly reflective and personalized fashion, precisely because breaches of academic or professional standards could have disciplinary consequences for the individual concerned. Second, it has to be acknowledged that it is, objectively, harder to measure performance in the affective domain.[107] Finally, there remains some feeling that education should only assess that which is within its purview to influence or change. Many academics (and others) are likely to have strong doubts that matters of 'character' come into that category. The consequent problem of constructive (non-)alignment is obvious. We may want our students to receive an education in values, but we fear we will struggle to assess anything beyond their learning about values.

Part of the solution may lie in moving away from assessment as we traditionally understand it, towards evaluation – a process of negotiated 'assessment' that does not 'count' in a traditional summative sense, but that may provide other valuable (e.g. career or personal developmental) feedback on processes and outcomes.[108] Ipsative assessment, emphasizing the use of self-assessment, self-reflection and personal-professional development tools such as portfolios, may offer a way forward here, though it remains an area in which we still have relatively little direct experience in terms of legal higher education.

The introduction of these and other developments would necessarily have an impact on the balance of the curriculum, and the amount of substantive law focus. This in itself would constitute some corrective to the technocentrism of the modern law school. Such changes are likely to be resisted by some legal academics, who – understandably – see their own values and identity bound up in their substantive teaching and scholarship. The objections may be made that meaningful values discourse is not easy in the context of multiculturalism and value pluralism,[109] and that effective interventions may be hard to introduce in the face of massification and the under funding of law schools; however, these practical constraints are not, in my view, insurmountable. There is a need for education, support and advocacy among faculty if this agenda is to move forward, and not be ignored or marginalized. There is a need for creativity in thinking about how these wider objectives might be achieved in the classroom. And we must not expect to change everything tomorrow. Transformation is a long-term game.[110] The challenges are not insignificant, but likewise the rewards are great. In schools that are prepared to take the opportunity, the values agenda offers the chance to move beyond a rather degraded liberal technical-rationalism, to open up new fields of scholarship, to encourage forms of teaching and learning that may energize faculty and students alike, and above all else to get us talking about things that really *matter*.

Acknowledgements

I would like to thank Paul Maharg, Roger Burridge and Tracey Varnava for their helpful comments on an earlier draft of this chapter.

Notes

1 J. Dewey, *Democracy and Education*, Mineola, NY: Dover, 2004 (first published 1916).
2 L. May, *The Socially Responsive Self: Social Theory and Professional Ethics*, Chicago: University of Chicago Press, 1996, p. 20.
3 Arguably this may be regarded as a critical function for higher education, since much secondary education is still, *contra* Dewey, locked within a broadly 'transmission' model of learning.
4 This is the third in a series of four essays explicitly addressing the issue of 'values' in legal education. The first two, with my colleague Roger Burridge (discussed below), seek to locate the importance of values within what we call a 'post-liberal' theory of legal education. This chapter follows on from these, undertaking some of the preliminary mapping of the values terrain, and developing some further pedagogical principles. The fourth (in progress) was first presented in April 2009 at a workshop at the Oñati International Institute for the Sociology of Law and continues the pedagogical theme by considering the role of 'legal values' as potential 'threshold concepts' in legal education. (On threshold concepts in general, see J. Meyer and R. Land (eds), *Overcoming Barriers to Student Understanding: Threshold Concepts and Troublesome Knowledge*, London: Routledge, 2006.)
5 At the time of writing, a new set of recommendations, contained in K. Economides and J. Rogers, *Preparatory Ethics Training for Solicitors* (London: The Law Society, 2009), have gained the support of the Law Society Education and Training Committee and are under consideration by the Education and Training Committee of the profession's regulatory body, the Solicitors' Regulation Authority. For formal changes to be introduced at the academic stage of training, these recommendations would also need the support of the Bar Standards Board and, based on past practice, the university law schools.
6 J. Webb, 'Conduct, ethics and experience in vocational legal education: Opportunities missed', in K. Economides (ed.), *Ethical Challenges to Legal Education and Conduct*, Oxford: Hart, 1998.
7 See F. Cownie, 'Alternative values in legal education', *Legal Ethics* 6, 2003, 159; and '(Re)Evaluating values: A response to Burridge and Webb', *Law Teacher* 42, 2008, 306–8 for examples.
8 See, for example, the special issue of the *Law Teacher*, on 'The values of common law legal education', *Law Teacher* 42, 2008, discussed below.
9 The idea of a value system is recognized in both sociological and psychological models to reflect the idea that values may be linked or 'hang together' (whether in the mind of an individual actor or in social structures) to create 'value orientations' or integrated sets of 'value priorities'. See, for example, J.L. Spates, 'The sociology of values', *Annual Review of Sociology* 9, 1983, 31; S. Schwartz, 'Value priorities and behavior: Applying a theory of integrated value systems', in C. Seligman, J.P. Olson and M.P. Zanna (eds), *The Psychology of Values: The Ontario Symposium*, vol. 8, Mahwah,

NJ: Lawrence Erlbaum, 1996. The extent to which values within such a system are relatively static or dynamic and situational remains an issue of some contention: cf. C. Seligman and A. Katz, 'The dynamics of value systems', in Seligman et al., *The Psychology of Values*.

10 See R. Burridge and J. Webb, 'The values of common law legal education: rethinking rules, responsibilities, relationships and roles in the law school', *Legal Ethics* 10, 2007, 72; and R. Burridge and J. Webb, 'On liberal neutrality, the value of experience, and the loneliness of the long-distance academic: Further reflections on the values of a common law legal education', *Law Teacher* 42, 2008, 339.

11 See, for example, D. Bok, *Universities in the Marketplace: The Commercialization of Higher Education*, Princeton, NJ: Princeton University Press, 2003, Ch. 9; G. Graham, *The Institution of Intellectual Values: Realism and Idealism in Higher Education*, Exeter: Imprint Academic, 2005; M. Nussbaum, *Cultivating Humanity: A Classical Defense of Reform in Liberal Education*, Cambridge, MA: Harvard University Press, 1997.

12 M. Thornton, 'Technocentrism in the law school: Why the gender and color of law remain the same', *Osgoode Hall Law Journal* 36, 1998, 372. Thornton defines this as an approach that treats law as autonomous, and as separate from morality and other disciplines. It involves a pedagogy that is strongly focused on legal rules and their application.

13 I. Duncanson, 'The end of legal studies', *Web Journal of Current Legal Issues* 3, 1997. See http://webjcli.ncl.ac.uk/1997/issue3/duncan3.html (accessed 10 September 2009).

14 A. Evans, 'Southern exposure: Post-liberalism and moral recovery in Australian legal education', *Law Teacher* 42, 2008, 329.

15 H. Arthurs, 'Poor Canadian legal education: So near to Wall Street, so far from God', *Osgoode Hall Law Journal* 38, 2000, 381.

16 W. Pue, 'Educating the total jurist', *Legal Ethics* 8, 2005, 218.

17 See A. Bradney, *Conversations, Choices and Chances: The Liberal Law School in the Twenty-First Century*, Oxford: Hart, 2003, esp. Ch. 2; Burridge and Webb, 'The values of common law legal education', 75, 77–80.

18 See K. Economides, 'Cynical legal studies', in J. Cooper and L. Trubek (eds), *Educating for Justice: Social Values and Legal Education*, Aldershot: Dartmouth, 1997. The other side of this, of course, is the high level of altruism displayed by many students in undertaking charity work or pro bono activities, though these are often largely divorced from the academic part of their lives.

19 L. Paterson, 'The survival of the democratic intellect: Academic values in England and Scotland', *Higher Education Quarterly* 57, 2003, 69.

20 'Professional values and the allure of the market', *Academe*, September–October 2001. See www.aaup.org/AAUP/pubsres/academe/2001/SO/Feat/slau.htm (accessed 10 September 2009).

21 S. Daicof, 'Lawyer know thyself: A review of empirical research on attorney attributes bearing on professionalism', *American University Law Review* 46, 1997, 1427.

22 K. Sheldon and L. Krieger, 'Does law school undermine law students? Examining changes in goals, values, and well-being', *Behavioural Sciences and the Law* 22, 2004, 261; 'Understanding the negative effects of legal education on law students: A longitudinal test of self-determination theory', *Personality and Social Psychology Bulletin* 33, 2007, 883.

23 See, for example, Duncan Kennedy on the ways in which 'value-neutral' teaching in US law schools is politically loaded: D. Kennedy, 'Liberal values in legal education', *Nova Law Journal* 10, 1986, 608–10.

24 A note of caution: I do not, in this chapter, draw clear functional distinctions between the respective roles of academic and vocational training in this regard. I make the assumption that there is a need for values engagement in both, but treat the precise division and distribution of responsibilities as a matter of local detail rather than general principle.

25　M. Sherif, *The Psychology of Social Norms*, New York: Harper, 1936, cited in S. Hitlin and J.A. Piliavin, 'Values: Reviving a dormant concept', *American Sociological Review* 34, 2004, 360.

26　W.B. Wendel, 'Personal integrity and the conflict between personal and institutional values', *Cornell Law School Legal Studies Research Papers*, 2007, No 08-010, 2. See http://scholarship.law.cornell.edu/lsrp papers/97 (accessed 10 September 2009).

27　Hitlin and Piliavin, 'Values', 360–1.

28　O. Flanagan, *Varieties of Moral Personality*, Cambridge, MA: Harvard University Press, 1991, p. 135.

29　While there is some evidence of causal relationships between values, attitudes and behaviours, this remains difficult territory and common heuristic assumptions of causality are, at the risk of over simplifying, often misleading: see, for example, B. Reich and C. Adcock, *Values, Attitudes and Behaviour Change*, London: Methuen, 1976, pp. 129–33.

30　M. Rokeach, *The Nature of Human Values*, New York: The Free Press, 1973, pp. 9ff.

31　D. Katz and R.L. Kahn, *The Social Psychology of Organizations*, 2nd edn, New York: Wiley, 1978, p. 43.

32　See J. Habermas, *Between Facts and Norms*, Cambridge: Polity Press, 1996, p. 255.

33　N. MacCormick, *Institutions of Law: An Essay in Legal Theory*, Oxford: Oxford University Press, 2007, pp. 29–30.

34　Spates, 'The sociology of values', p. 30; W.A. Cunningham and P.D. Zelazo, 'Attitudes and evaluations: A social cognitive neuroscience perspective', *Trends in Cognitive Science* 11, 2007, 97; M.J. Rohan, 'A rose by any name? The values construct', *Personality and Social Psychology Review* 4, 2000, 255.

35　S. Hitlin, 'Values as the core of personal identity: Drawing links between two theories of self', *Social Psychology Quarterly* 66, 2003, 118.

36　Hitlin and Piliavin, 'Values', 361.

37　G. Nerlich, *Values and Valuing: Speculations on the Ethical Life of Persons*, Oxford: Clarendon Press, 2000, pp. 13–17 and Ch. 5. In some theoretical work, the distinction between needs and values breaks down once we move beyond the idea of basic needs. For example, in Maslow's well-known (but controversial) articulation of a hierarchy of needs, self-actualization itself is presented as the highest level of human need rather than a value to which people aspire.

38　See Rokeach, *The Nature of Human Values*, p. 13.

39　See H. Joas, 'Morality in an age of contingency', *Acta Sociologica* 47, 2004, 396. Though commitment to values such as family loyalty may be hard to disentangle from personal commitments to individual family members.

40　Nerlich, in *Values and Valuing*, develops this into a distinction between *subjective values* (above) and *objective values*, which are those values that are deeply embedded in a culture 'understood as an engineering programme for producing persons': pp. 13–17. This chapter, in framing the argument in these terms, assumes that what philosophers call the 'social dependence thesis' has validity for *at least some if not most* values. The social dependence thesis takes the view that values require sustaining by, and get their legitimacy from, actual social practices in a community. This is not the same as saying that the only plausible account of values involves taking a relativist position – cf. Joseph Raz's work on constructing a socially dependent but non-relativist account of values in J. Raz, *The Practice of Value*, Oxford: Oxford University Press, 2003.

41　Joas thus observes 'our value-commitments are not the result of rational-argumentative justifications, but of experiences of self-formation and self-transcendence': Joas, 'Morality in an age of contingency', 396. See also more generally H. Joas, *The Genesis of Values*, Cambridge: Polity Press, 2000.

42　D.C. Dennett, *Elbow Room: The Varieties of Free Will Worth Wanting*, Cambridge, MA: MIT Press, 1984, pp. 43–9; cf. also R. Rorty, *Contingency, Irony, and Solidarity*, Cambridge: Cambridge University Press, 1989, pp. 50–8 (specifically on the role of language in moral deliberation and moral education). Recent research by Maio and others indicates that many values, and particularly those values that individuals regard as very important, function as 'truisms' based more upon feelings and emotions than on reasons and beliefs: see G.R. Maio and J.M. Olson, 'Values as truisms: Evidence and implications', *Journal of Personality and Social Psychology* 74, 1998, 294, and G.R. Maio and G. Haddock, 'Implicit and explicit bases of values: Implications for behaviour change', RES-000-22-0519. See www.esrcsocietytoday.ac.uk/ESRCInfoCentre/Plain_English_Summaries/social_stability_exclusion/trust_cohesion/index49.aspx (accessed 10 September 2009). For examples of a growing body of philosophical work that emphasizes the emotional basis of moral judgment, and treats emotion as an alternative rationality rather than an inferior or irrational basis for action, see Nerlich, *Values and Valuing*, Ch. 3; M.C. Nussbaum, *Upheavals of Thought: The Intelligence of Emotions*, Cambridge: Cambridge University Press, 2003; J. Prinz, *The Emotional Construction of Morals*, Oxford: Oxford University Press, 2007.

43 See Hitlin and Piliavin, 'Values', 380
44 Maio and Olsen, 'Values as truisms'; S. Schwartz, 'Are there universal aspects in the structure and content of human values?', *Journal of Social Issues* 50, 1994, 19.
45 This is not to advance an over determined notion of community, nor to underplay the problems that may be associated with value pluralism. At the same time, this should not lead us either to infer the impossibility of community, or to overlook the extent to which communities are themselves constructed and a constant work in progress – I address this more extensively in the final paper in this series, 'Dealing (with) uncertainty: Values as threshold concepts in legal education' (forthcoming).
46 See A. Evans and J. Palermo, 'Zero impact: Are lawyers' values affected by law school?', *Legal Ethics* 8, 2005, 240.
47 See, for example, Hannah Arendt's famous illustration of the way the Nazis, in building the bureaucratic apparatus of Nazism, consciously sought out solid, reliable family men whose values of loyalty and desire for security could be exploited by the machinery of the state to ensure that they acted with 'horribly painstaking thoroughness in the execution of the final solution': H. Arendt, *Eichmann in Jerusalem*, New York: Viking, 1964, p. 137.
48 See, for example, Nerlich, *Values and Valuing*, pp. 1ff. Also Hugh MacDonald's claims for the 'universality of value' and the view that no areas of human endeavour, including philosophy itself, are 'value-free': H. MacDonald, *Radical Axiology: A First Philosophy of Values*, Amsterdam: Editions Rodopi, 2004, Ch. 4, esp. p. 202. For arguments that the postmodern turn in theorizing has actually reinvigorated the debate about values, see J. Fekete (ed.), *Life After Postmodernism: Essays on Value and Culture*, London: Macmillan, 1988, p. i; J. Squires (ed.), *Principled Positions: Postmodernism and the Rediscovery of Value*, London: Lawrence & Wishart, 1993.
49 Schwartz, 'Are there universal aspects'; and S. Schwartz and A. Bardi, 'Values hierarchies across cultures: Taking a similarities perspective', *Journal of Cross-Cultural Psychology* 32, 2001, 268.
50 See, for example, J.N. Findlay, *Axiological Ethics*, London: Macmillan, 1970, pp. 85–7.
51 This is another enormous issue that we must simply acknowledge in the process of mapping out the territory. The incommensurability problem is widely discussed in the literature on values. Luhmann summarizes the core of the problem thus: '[N]othing follows from values to aid in the adjudication of value conflicts. There is, as is often said, no firm hierarchical (transitive) order of such a type that certain values are always preferable to certain other ones.' N. Luhmann, 'Are there still indispensible norms in our society?', *Soziale Systeme* 14, 2008, 29. In the absence of any definitive tests of validity or even hierarchy, as Paterson provocatively argues in the same volume, we are thus forced back on to the simple fact that there *are* values as providing as much protection as we can hope for when law performs its function of stabilizing normative expectations: see J. Paterson, 'The fact of values', *Soziale Systeme* 14, 2008,

81–2. My thanks to John Paterson for alerting me to the existence of these papers. There is, I suggest, at the very least a linkage here to Dewey's rejection of the thesis that we can know *a priori* what we value independently of action – that is, it is Dewey's argument that our ethics and values need to be understood not just as situated in but created through our engagement in a course of action: see J. Dewey, 'The logic of judgments of practice', in J. Boydston (ed.), *The Middle Works of John Dewey: 1899–1924*, vol. 8, Carbondale, IL: Southern Illinois University Press, 1979, pp. 14–82.

52 See, for example, P. Stein and J. Shand, *Legal Values in Western Society*, Edinburgh: Edinburgh University Press, 1974. Stein and Shand note also that distinct legal theories have tended to concentrate on one of these values over the others; thus positivism focuses on order, natural law on justice, and natural rights theory on freedom: pp. 5–13.

53 See, for example, R.A. Posner, *The Economics of Justice*, Cambridge, MA: Harvard University Press, 1983; cf. J.L. Coleman, 'Efficiency, utility and wealth maximization', *Hofstra Law Review* 8, 1979, 509.

54 MacCormick, *Institutions of Law*, pp. 29–30 seems to indicate that these are principles rather than values.

55 See Luce Irigary's conception of human dignity and human identity as special rights that, *inter alia*, would prevent the commercial use/abuse of women's bodies: L. Irigary, *Thinking the Difference*, trans. K. Montin, London: Athlone Press, 1994. Within human rights discourse, compare, for example, O. Schachter, 'Human dignity as a normative concept', *American Journal of International Law* 77, 1983, 848; D. Feldman, 'Human dignity as a legal value' (Part 1), *Public Law* 60, 1999, and (Part 2) *Public Law* 61, 2000; C. McCrudden, 'Human dignity and judicial interpretation of human rights', *European Journal of International Law* 99, 2008, 655. In the context of legal ethics itself, see D. Luban, *Legal Ethics and Human Dignity*, Cambridge: Cambridge University Press, 2007 – but note also Bill Simon's powerful critique of Luban's use of human dignity as a substitute for 'justice': W.H. Simon, 'The past, present and future for legal ethics: Three comments for David Luban', *Cornell Law Review* 93, 2008, 1365.

56 Though this might more traditionally be regarded as an instrumental value in the pursuit of justice.

57 See, for example, J. Baier, *Our Lives Before the Law: Constructing a Feminist Jurisprudence*, Princeton, NJ: Princeton University Press, 1999; L. Bender, 'From gender difference to feminist solidarity: Using Carol Gilligan and an ethic of care in law', *Vermont Law Review* 15, 1990, 1.

58 T. Campbell, 'Human rights, humane values and positive law', in J. Tasioulos (ed.), *Law, Values and Social Practices*, Aldershot: Dartmouth, 1997.

59 See, for example, M. Moran, 'Time, place and value: *Mack* and the influence of the charter on private law', in M. Moran and D. Dyzenhaus (eds), *Calling Power to Account*, Toronto: University of Toronto Press, 2005. Cf. M. Hunt, 'The *Human Rights Act* and legal culture: The judiciary and the legal profession', *Journal of Law & Society* 26, 1999, 86.

60 See F.S. Cohen, *Ethical Systems and Legal Ideals*, Westport, CN: Greenwood Press, 1976 (first published 1933); R.M. Unger, *The Critical Legal Studies Movement*, Cambridge, MA: Harvard University Press, 1986.

61 See, for example, J. Finkel et al., 'Everyday life and legal values: A concept paper', *Law and Human Behavior* 25, 2001, 120–1.

62 W.B. Wendel, 'Value pluralism in legal ethics', *Washington University Law Quarterly* 78, 2001, 116–17.

63 See, for example, the statement of fundamental values in the MacCrate Report: American Bar Association, *Legal Education and Professional Development – An Educational Continuum: Narrowing the Gap*, Chicago, IL: ABA, 1992, p. 140.

64 Lord Chancellor's Advisory Committee on Legal Education and Conduct, *First Report on Legal Education and Training*, London: ACLEC, 1996, para 2.4.

65 See, for example, C. Parker and A. Evans, *Inside Lawyers' Ethics*, Melbourne: Cambridge University Press, 2007, who characterize these as adversarial advocacy, responsible lawyering, moral activism and ethics of care.

66 D. Rhode, *In the Interests of Justice: Reforming the Legal Profession*, New York: Oxford University Press, 2000, p. 50.

67 ibid., p. 23.

68 Evans and Palermo, 'Zero impact'.

69 ibid., pp. 243–4, 264.

70 See B. Williams, 'Persons, character and morality', in *Moral Luck: Philosophical Papers 1973–1980*, Cambridge: Cambridge University Press, 1981.

71 See, for example, May, *The Socially Responsive Self* (communitarian ethics); D. Nicolson, 'Making lawyers moral? Ethical codes and moral character', *Legal Studies* 25, 2005, 601 (virtue ethics); J. Webb, 'Being a lawyer/being a human being, *Legal Ethics* 5, 2002, 130 (ethics of alterity).

72 Parker and Evans, 'Zero impact', 245.

73 Cf. J. Webb, 'Ethics for lawyers or ethics for citizens: New directions for legal education', *Journal of Law & Society*, 25, 1998, 134.

74 Burridge and Webb, 'The values of common law legal education'.

75 G. Davie, *The Democratic Intellect: Scotland and Her Universities in the Nineteenth Century*, 2nd ed., Edinburgh: Edinburgh University Press, 1964. See also Paterson, 'The survival of the democratic intellect'; N. MacCormick, 'The democratic intellect and the law', *Legal Studies* 5, 1985, 172.

76 Paterson, 'The survival of the democratic intellect', 69.

77 The paternalistic and patrician dimensions of Davie's democratic intellect have been highlighted by a number of commentators, notably Jean Barr, who has argued for a rethinking of the democratic intellect in the light of recent debates within feminism and about globalization: see G. Davie, 'Re-framing the democratic intellect', *Scottish Affairs* 55, 2006. See www.scottishaffairs.org/onlinepub/sa/barr_sa55.spr06.html (accessed 6 November 2009); and G. Davie, *The Stranger Within: On the Idea of an Educated Public*, Rotterdam: Sense, 2008, esp. Ch. 12.

78 Cf. Paul Maharg's discussion of the philosophy of Adam Ferguson in P. Maharg, *Transforming Legal Education*, Aldershot: Ashgate, 2007, pp. 107–10.

79 S.H. Tan, 'Teaching legal ideals through jurisprudence', *Law Teacher* 43, 2009, 35.

80 See J. Webb, 'The "ambitious modesty" of Harry Arthurs' humane professionalism', *Osgoode Hall Law Journal* 44, 2006, 144–7.

81 C. Swanton, *Virtue Ethics: A Pluralistic View*, Oxford: Oxford University Press, 2003, pp. 21, 48–55, 220–1.

82 Drawing on Philip Pettit's notion of honouring in 'Consequentialism' in P. Singer (ed.), *A Companion to Ethics*, Oxford: Blackwell, 1991.

83 Swanton, *Virtue Ethics*, pp. 21–4.

84 See, for example, H. Giroux, 'Neoliberalism, corporate culture, and the promise of higher education: The university as a democratic public sphere', *Harvard Educational Review* 72, 2002, 425; J. Kelsey, 'Privatizing the universities', *Journal of Law & Society* 25, 1998, 58–62; also Thornton, 'Technocentrism in the law school', and S. Boyd, 'Corporatism and legal education in Canada', *Social and Legal Studies* 14, 2005, 287.

85 E. Laclau, *New Reflections on the Revolution of Our Time*, London: Verso, 1989, p. xiv.

86 Z. Bauman, *Legislators and Interpretors*, Cambridge: Polity Press, 1989, p. 143.

87 Op. cit. Burridge and Webb, 2007, 85; 2008, 344–6.

88 Put simply, this is the privilege of taking and advancing a value position, provided one does not then behave in a way that breaches the principle of permissive neutrality – that is, the idea that liberalism must ultimately be tolerant of value positions that are not the same as its own.

89 S. de Castell and H. Freeman, 'Education as a socio-practical field: The theory/ practice question reformulated', *Journal of Philosophy of Education* 12, 1978, 13; see also

J. Webb, 'Extending the theory-practice spiral: Action research as a mechanism for crossing the academic/professional divide', *Web Journal of Current Legal Issues*, 1995. See http://webjcli.ncl.ac.uk/articles2/webb2.html (accessed 12 September 2009).

90 J. Dewey, *Human Nature and Conduct*, 1922, reprinted in Boydston (ed.), *The Middle Works of John Dewey 1899–1924*, vol. 14, p. 194.

91 G. Maio, J. Olson, L. Allen and M. Bernard, 'Addressing discrepancies between values and behaviour: The motivating effect of reasons', *Journal of Experimental Social Psychology* 37, 2001, 294; M. Bernard, G. Maio and J. Olson, 'The vulnerability of values to attack: Inoculation of values and value-relevant attitudes', *Personality and Social Psychology Bulletin* 29, 2003, 63. Similar conclusions have been drawn on the efficacy of direct intervention in studies of moral development: see, for example, W. Penn, 'Teaching ethics – a direct approach', *Journal of Moral Education* 19, 1990, 124; J. Rest, *Moral Development: Advances in Research and Theory*, New York: Praeger, 1986, Ch. 3. As a side issue, whether this kind of cognitive scaffolding also bolsters the relevant value against an emotive attack remains a moot point.

92 Bernard et al., 'The vulnerability of values to attack'.

93 Though if it is to be effective, such debate should itself be shaped by values that will promote engagement and transcend narrow instrumentalism and self-interest.

94 Cf., for example, the work of M. Gibbons et al., *The New Production of Knowledge: The Dynamics of Science and Research in Contemporary Societies*, London: Sage, 1994. Note that William Twining in a recent but so far unpublished Centenary Lecture for the (United Kingdom-based) Society of Legal Scholars has also called for legal academics to pay greater attention to their public role and the need to increase public understanding of law: W. Twining, 'Punching our weight? Academic law and public understanding', lecture presented at The Society of Legal Scholars Centenary, the London School of Economics, 29 May 2009. See www.legalscholars.ac.uk/centenary-lecture (accessed 10 September 2009).

95 Cf. 'the vast majority of human choices are made in the labyrinthine structure of coupled feedback loops guided more by the events in one's life than the logician's syllogisms': W. McWhinney, 'The white horse: A reformulation of Bateson's typology of learning', *Cybernetics and Human Knowing* 12, 2005, 34–5. Work in neurobiology both supports this contention and indirectly undermines many of the assumptions underlying classical dualism (discussed above): see, for example, R. Cotterill, 'On the unity of conscious experience', *Journal of Consciousness Studies* 2, 1995, 290; and R. Cotterill, 'Cooperation of the basal ganglia, cerebellum, sensory cerebrum and hippocampus: Possible implications for cognition, consciousness, intelligence and creativity', *Progress in Neurobiology* 64, 2001, 1. See also D. Hofstadter, *I am a Strange Loop*, New York: Basic Books, 2007.

96 See, for example, A. Evans, 'The values priority in quality legal education', *Law Teacher* 32, 1998, 274.

97 C. Sampford with C. Parker, 'Legal regulation, ethical standard setting, and institutional design', in S. Parker and C. Sampford (eds), *Legal Ethics and Legal Practice: Contemporary Issues*, Oxford: Clarendon Press, 1995, p. 16. The emphasis on 'majority views' in this quote is, I suggest, not entirely misplaced, since there is an argument that, by definition, perceived majority views may be more likely to be treated as common sense or received wisdom, and perhaps more prone to the influence of 'groupthink', though I would also accept that any views, regardless of their perceived popularity or otherwise, should be subject to the same standards of ethical evaluation.

98 See, for example, M. Houston and Y. Lebeau, 'The social mediation of university learning', Working Paper 3, SOMUL Project, 2006. See www.open.ac.uk/cheri/pages/CHERI-projects-SOMUL.shtml (accessed 10 September 2009).

99 See Seligman and Katz, 'The dynamics of value systems', pp. 67–71 for evidence that what they call the 'value confrontation method' can generate changes in attitudes and related behaviours. For examples of exercises designed to generate value conflict

and debate in the context of legal ethics, see C. Maughan and J. Webb, *Lawyering Skills and the Legal Process*, Cambridge: Cambridge University Press, 2005, Ch. 6.

100 T. Cresswell, *Place: A Short Introduction*, Oxford: Blackwell, 2004, p. 39.

101 This has, of course, long been a feature of legal anthropology, a generally rather neglected dimension of legal scholarship; however, it is in the more conceptual work of writers like Bonaventura de Sousa Santos, notably in B. De Sousa Santos, *Toward a New Legal Common Sense*, 2nd edn, London: Butterworths, 2002, that we can see the kind of emancipatory geo-jurisprudence that I particularly have in mind.

102 An example would be the work of my colleague, Paul Raffield, who uses performance-linked teaching spaces at Warwick to teach courses in 'Origins, Images and Cultures of English Law' and 'On Trial: Shakespeare and the Law'. Paul has recently described his approach thus: 'Fundamental to the achievement of my object-ives is the strong emphasis I place on the development of a communitarian ethos within the class. Group work, in which students engage jointly in an assessed project, is the primary means through which individuals bond into an interdependent community of scholars.' See www.ukcle.ac.uk/directions/people.html (accessed 10 September 2009).

103 D. Boud, 'Assessment and the promotion of academic values', *Studies in Higher Education* 15, 1990, 101.

104 That the work demonstrates some element of newness and significance appropriate to that level of learner.

105 See, for example, Boud, 'Assessment and the promotion of academic values'; J. Cowan, 'How should I assess creativity?', in N. Jackson, M. Oliver, M. Shaw and J. Wisdom (eds), *Developing Creativity in Higher Education: An Imaginative Curriculum*, London: Routledge, 2006.

106 Cf. J. Fanghanel, 'Capturing dissonance in university teacher education environ-ments', *Studies in Higher Education* 29, 2004, 575.

107 A point acknowledged in D. Krathwohl, B. Bloom and B. Masia, *Taxonomy of Educational Objectives. Handbook II: Affective Domain*, New York: David McKay, 1956.

108 Cf. K. Shepard, 'E is for exploration: Assessing hard-to-measure learning outcomes', *British Journal of Educational Technology* 43, 2009, 386.

109 Though I would argue that this diversity should be seen as a resource rather than part of the problem.

110 Cf. Maharg, *Transforming Legal Education*, pp. 271–83.

3 'Represent a murderer . . . I'd never do that!' How students use stories to link ethical development and identity construction

Cassandra Sharp

3.1 Introduction

As active viewers of legal popular culture, law students are constantly interpreting, transforming and producing meaning in relation to the images and stories presented in fiction.[1] They are using this process not only to make sense of the law, but also to analyse and reflect on their personal values in light of their understandings. They are then transforming these into projections (both professional and personal) of the path that lies ahead. In this way, first-year law students are on a transformative journey. I have argued previously that, during this transformative time at law school, students use images of lawyers on television to identify with what they perceive to be positive and negative aspects of lawyering, and that part of the students' developing legal identity is a recognition that to be a lawyer requires ethical considerations.[2] By actively engaging in the (re)interpretation of law stories as played out on the small screen, students antithetically show both a lack of ethical knowledge and a substantial capacity for ethical reflection. The challenge for legal educators is to harness this ability for ethical self-reflection in teaching legal ethics.[3] Certainly, the body of literature surrounding ethical legal education is increasing rapidly, and is staunchly concerned with the best methods for teaching legal ethics.[4] This chapter suggests that one starting point may be to first acknowledge that when students articulate and discuss the stories of law that are told on fictional television, they simultaneously give themselves the chance to critically evaluate what it is they value and believe.

Take, for example, a student named Tara, who commented that in order to respond effectively to human problems, the practice of lawyering required some measure of 'inside values'.[5] This statement was made within the context of students discussing what they believed was admirable about television lawyers. As a group, the students agreed that being a lawyer must necessarily involve a basic interest in humanity (for example, helping your 'fellow people').[6] While Tara's comment reflects an understanding that inside values are something more than simply interpreting and applying the law, and in essence implies the need for some kind of internalized sense of ethics, her reference is somewhat vague and amorphous, and remains completely undefined. While students in their first year of law at times appear to lack clarity in assessing what is in and of itself an ethical issue,[7] this chapter focuses on how the students' use of stories reflects an important connection between ethics and identity that is a crucial aspect of the transformative process within legal education. In particular, this chapter suggests that stories are a useful catalyst to stimulate law students' self-reflection and awareness of ethics.

Drawing from the analysis of some focus group discussions conducted with a sample of first-year law students,[8] a selection of student comments will highlight the ways in which law students are using stories to decipher the actions of television lawyers as ethical or otherwise, and to imagine how they would react in similar circumstances. The chapter therefore first defines ethics as constitutive of identity, and as a basis upon which to articulate and justify ethical decision-making, and contrasts this with an understanding of morality that recognizes the cultural marking out of moral discourses. Within such a context, the chapter then illustrates that first-year law students use the resources of the wider community to make ethical judgments as part of their evolving subjectivity. The chapter posits that students should be encouraged to be self-reflective about their ethical and identity construction, and it concludes with a discussion of the use of stories in their development of ethical identity.

3.2 The need for 'inside values': what is 'ethics'

Over time, within legal discourse, terms like 'ethics', 'morality', 'values' and 'professionalism' are far too often left undefined. Indeed, Tranter argues that despite repeated calls from the legal profession for a more 'ethical' practice of law, a conception of ethics is rarely given any substance or clarity in definition.[9] He further argues that this lack of delineation within the 'advocate literature', as he calls it, is the result of a positivist legacy within the legal profession that is keen to retain a distinction between objective law and a more personal, subjective moral character.[10] Nevertheless, Tranter suggests that at the heart of this literature there is actually a desire for the classical conception of the ethical – where 'ethics deals with the public accountability to the Good for the practical values and judgments an individual makes in their daily life'.[11]

This chapter seeks to build on this conception of ethics by arguing that it is the public accountability for decisions that is central to the formation of identity within culture. Using student discussions as a stimulus, this research illustrates a differentiation between the terms 'morality' and 'ethics' within the context of culturally marking identity. As students develop an understanding and appreciation of their own ethical stance, so too they construct identity and provide a basis from which to justify both personal and professional decisions.

3.2.1 Ethics vs morality in the context of culture

The word 'ethics' derives from the Greek word *èthos*, referring to both 'custom' and 'character'.[12] 'To conform to the customs and character of the community meant that you were acting ethically.'[13] Often these two derivations have formed the basis for a dualistic approach to an account of ethics in terms of either 'duty' or 'virtue'. In the first account, ethics of duty, the focus is on morally evaluated actions, with a particular concern to locate the action or types of actions that people have an obligation to do or to avoid doing. In Foucauldian terms, this is what actually lies at the heart of 'morality'. That is, to Foucault morality is interested in those moral discourses that are concerned with prohibition, and culturally sanctioned rules.[11] In this sense, morality is not of the individual, but rather of the culture.

In contrast, the focus of the second account, ethics of virtue, 'is not the detached actions of people but the moral agent who performs the actions'.[15] That is, virtue ethics is based on a human's moral experience of character, or identity. It is not about *doing*, but about *being*, and a person's character (rather than action) is the object of analysis. In this second account, ethics therefore regards identity as the 'basis of human existence and the manner in which the formation of the self takes place', shaping the nature and content of the self.[16] It is in this account that it can be argued that ethics is seen as constitutive of identity. That is, ethics is crucial to the construction of the self and is concerned with how individuals negotiate the rules of morality (or moral discourse) in order to arrive at personal ethically sound judgments.[17]

Although they are often seen as rivals, it is appropriate to argue that these two accounts are intricately linked within culture. It is hard to believe that a conception of morality could only be concerned with the rules and outward acts – you cannot have the *doing* without the *being*. To deny their complementary status does not allow for the individual's ethical development,[18] nor does it acknowledge that ethical negotiations as part of identity construction occur within the boundaries marked out by various discourses. Yet it is useful, when discussing the transformation of legal identity among law students, to highlight the distinction between morality and ethics along the lines of this twin conception. That is, it should be understood that when referring to ethics in this chapter, I am actually pointing to that which gives rise to identity – that is, the process through which it is possible for individuals to construct their selves as they negotiate within the more rigid and collectively based moral discourse or 'morality'.

The key emphasis is that ethics are seen as cultural and not universal or metaphysical. Ethical judgments are therefore sourced from cultural warrants and norms such that individuals can justify ethical decisions within the context of community. This argument recognizes that individuals exist in relationship with others in the community, and that rather than complying with a universal benchmark of ethics, individuals must provide justifications for their actions within the bounds of culture. Such a theory of ethics thus differs from moral relativism, 'which implies that no rational agreement on ethical principles can be reached'.[19] Focusing on the idea of community, the conception of ethics proposed here emphasizes that 'individual identities and mutual interests are situated or embedded within the institutions or social groups' to which a person belongs.[20]

Viewing 'ethics', then, as the study and analysis of how individuals negotiate morality and construct identity, it is argued that personal ethics can be conceived of as providing the opportunity to be attentive to one's individual sense of judgment and decision-making. In this sense, ethics is one of the processes through which it is possible for individuals to construct their selves as they negotiate within the more rigid and collectively based moral discourse or 'morality'.

This means that, as students develop ethical awareness through which they can have an articulated justification for their ethical choices, they are concomitantly constructing identity. Such awareness is not to be seen, however, as a fixed pro forma that, once an individual has worked out their particular value system, can be applied successfully to any ethical dilemma. Rather, it is intended to be viewed as the broad basis from which an individual can begin to understand, articulate and justify their ethical decisions. By attending to ethics as constitutive of identity, it is acknowledged that ethical judgment does not spring into existence from the mere contemplation of rules, but rather is a matter of becoming.[21] Viewing legal ethics in this vein requires an attention to 'not so much the isolated moments of moral decision and action, as it [should] to the cumulative effect of many such moments'.[22]

3.3 Ethical awareness and first-year law students

Having argued that ethics gives rise to identity construction, it is important to recognize that a student, upon entering law school, is 'not entering a seminary or political organization. Although anticipating exposure to new ideas and views, he or she does not agree to take on any new system of values.'[23] A central aspect of university life is the access that students have to a multiplicity of views, and it is certainly not the role of the university lecturer to inculcate any one set of values in their students.[24] On this basis, it is of vital importance to make possible the enhancement of student capacity for self-determination, rather than seeking to 'mould their personal or political views in any particular way'.[25] Requiring students to develop ethical awareness is not about ensuring that they implement the 'right' values or morals, but is instead an opportunity to provide a basis for effective and appropriate personal and professional decision-making, enabling them to develop and evaluate their values and attitudes in a self-reflective manner.

Although we could say that it is possible that everyone has a sense of morality, 'it is certainly not true that everyone has given explicit thought to seeing that the moral standards and rules they operate on are consistent or justifiable'[26] – that is, it cannot be said that everyone has a self-reflexive[27] understanding of their ethics. To argue this in another way, we can have moral positions or beliefs without ever having analysed how they fit together or how they will be applied in any given situation. This is a synthetic knowledge of ethics without the accompanying analytic knowledge:

> People might have an intuitive apprehension of how their morals fit together, without being able to explicitly state how. What is more, people can operate quite adequately without this analytic knowledge until they are faced with a

conflict of values or until their morality is challenged . . . We must have an ethic as well as a morality.[28]

So we can operate within a culturally sanctioned and constituted morality without personal ethical awareness. But this can leave us confused when we are faced with moral dilemmas and have no basis from which to make decisions. This is exactly where first-year law students are positioned, and it is made obvious through the retelling of popular cultural stories. The focus group discussions revealed that while students were evaluating the decisions and actions of television lawyers based on personal standards of morality, the students did not yet have an articulated justification for their choices – that is, personal ethics from which to justify their decisions.

This was most evident when the students made ethical assessments about defence lawyering without any justified basis for their assessment. For example, the students' use of evocative language to describe what they perceived as 'bad' television lawyering indicated the passing of moral judgment. Operating from within community-bounded norms, students consistently connected the representation of guilty clients (especially murderers) with those lawyers who were unethical – both from the perspective of an ethics of duty (compliance within a moral discourse) and an ethics of virtue (a reference to character). Although students did not recognize the distinction between these two aspects,[29] they would interchangeably refer to elements of unethical practice and unethical character. Take, for example, the following discussion, which highlights the students' placement of moral evaluation on a lawyer's tasks:

Jess: Yeah you never see lawyers on television being like sly or underhanded.
Rob: And if they are, they're the bad lawyers like they're . . .
Jess: Yeah.
Rob: Representing a murderer or something . . . or the big corporation.
Tara: And you go I'd never be like that.[30]

It has previously been argued in relation to this interaction that there is a big distinction here between 'lawyers' and 'bad lawyers'.[31] Students seem to place positive meaning on the term 'lawyer' as a divergent position from that of the 'bad lawyer' (from whom they are quick to disassociate themselves). To them, it is the 'bad' lawyer who will represent the guilty. It is the use of the evocative descriptor 'murderer' that indicates the students' passing of legal and ethical judgment on a client charged with murder, and subsequently the ethical judgment passed on the lawyer: guilty murderers are in need of representation from those lawyers who are 'sly' and 'underhanded'.

Yet if this analysis were taken even further, it could be argued that, although the students seem to be in agreement about what a bad lawyer is, there is a distinction between the examples given by Jess and Rob. While Jess attributes elements of deceit and therefore professionally unethical practices, Rob argues that bad lawyers also make ethically reprehensible decisions by representing murderers (and corporations!). In this way, one could argue that Jess is making a comment about the rejection of culturally sanctioned moral rules in contradistinction to Rob's more specific evaluation of character, and how it reflects standards of personal ethics.[32] This suggests that while students on the one hand are clearly trying to distinguish between good and bad legal practice, they are at the same time inadvertently expressing the tension that exists between understanding their personal ethics and applying it within a professional legal context that is bounded by community morality. The students' talk reveals that their concern is to 'focus attention on themselves' and use ethics as a mode of self-production – that is, as an active construction of identity.[33] Indeed, student comments reflect the very nature of an identity project – that is, that their understanding of their own personal ethics is an ongoing work in progress.

Interestingly, the 'work in progress' can be seen in this representative comment that the only necessary element of being a 'good' lawyer is a high standard of ethics:

Ava: There's being good at what they do and the ones you actually think is a good person, I mean all of them in *The Practice* are really good at what they do *but I wouldn't necessarily want to be like all of them* are because I don't think that their motivations or their values, I don't agree with, so they might not be like good lawyers but they are good at what they do.[34]

There is a nice simpatico here with the way Asimow defines good lawyers as portrayed in the movies. He argues that a 'good' lawyer is 'one that you want *both* as your friend (meaning you see the lawyer as a good human being) *and* as your lawyer (meaning the lawyer appears to be competent, ethical, and dedicated to clients)'.[35] In critiquing the lawyers in *The Practice*, it appears that Ava's identification lies with those lawyers who comply with Asimow's definition. Yet there is uncertainty in her articulation, and in one sense this is what is most exciting about the transformative process of law school. By using fiction as a stimulus for discussion, the students are actively contributing to their own identity projects.

This identity project is again evident in the way students talk about the recurring narrative that television lawyers are often personally conflicted when representing clients they know to be guilty, and it is through this critique that they begin to imagine themselves in the same situation:

Donny: Just like . . . with Bobby [from *The Practice*] he's always . . . defending the people who have done something wrong and they're always trying to get these people off, like just having to, knowing someone's guilty and to still have to try and find some way because *you're* employed by them to get them off, is just, you can see how hard it is for those guys that have to do it.[36]

Kylie: . . . especially on *The Practice* where you see the defence lawyers where . . . they're trying to defend a murderer, but then they find out that they did it, and they've still got to get up in court and put up a defence for them and try and win, and the moral issue of sort of do you let your enthusiasm slide, and try and get them convicted or still go for the win?[37]

In both these examples, the students describe the difficulties television lawyers must face when they are representing the guilty (especially when dealing with the charge of murder). Here, the students are sympathetic to the plight of the defence lawyer, yet their language reveals a lack of understanding of what legal representation actually involves. By discussing the prevalent theme of morality in television legal dramas, the students are identifying what they consider to be a morally confronting situation of defending a 'murderer' who is actually guilty. Interestingly, Kylie questions the options that would be available if the truth about a client's guilt were to be discovered. The alternatives she presents are to 'lose enthusiasm' and relinquish effort, or to still try for the 'win'. Kylie does not seem to acknowledge the more appropriate alternative of fulfilling professional responsibility by working to the best of her ability, regardless of guilt or innocence.

Undoubtedly, *The Practice* provided a rich source of ethical dilemmas for the students to critically evaluate – and interestingly, despite the students' clearly polarized identification with the lawyers on the basis of guilt or innocence, students also recognized that some dilemmas are not so easily delineated. Complying with Simon's argument that audiences identify with 'hero' lawyers in popular culture who display a transgressive 'moral pluck', students seemed to indicate that some questionable practices of television lawyers were not necessarily unethical. That is, students believed that to serve the ultimate good, sometimes lawyers required 'moral pluck' to 'actively and ingeniously confront difficult issues'.[38] Indeed, students' comments reflected that, as a means to an end, transgressive lawyering was seen not only as acceptable but also as important. This was most evident to the students in *The Practice*, a show that derives most of its dramatic tension from ethical challenges faced by its protagonists: Bobby Donnell, Jimmy Berluti and Helen Gamble. It is the goal of pursuing justice that leads students to deploy justifications of transgression based in the 'rule of man' rather than the 'rule of law'.[39] In the following extract, two students discuss the various ethical dilemmas facing television lawyers, and focus on the ways in which lawyers in *The Practice* convince clients to produce confessions:

Megan: . . . informing your client of offers knowing that they're guilty . . . like they'll be allowed to go free for certain information or something, like I think there was something on *The Practice* a while ago where he made up an offer – he got somebody to call him for 30 seconds or so and he made up saying that they had this offer, and the guy confessed for it when of course the offer wasn't really there, so it was absolutely wrong, *but you know* . . .

Ava: There are different ways, especially like the prosecution side . . . that they'll go around getting people to admit to stuff, like the one in *The Practice* [the character of Helen] . . . once this teenage girl was pregnant and she did something to herself, I don't know, if it was specifically killed her baby or something and then she denied [it] . . . so she [Helen] got in the room and she sat down and said look 'I know what it's like, I got pregnant when I was your age and I had to go for an abortion', and got this woman all upset and then [she] confessed, and then [Helen] walked out and said 'I never really had an abortion – I was never pregnant'. *And you go* 'you lied to her' . . .[40]

It would seem that the students are using television narratives like those of *The Practice* to evaluate the ways in which lawyers act ethically. Megan, in yet another reference to the difficulty that defence lawyers face when representing 'guilty' clients, provides an example of the type of action television lawyers might take when negotiating plea bargains. Although used as an example of what the students represent as an understandably difficult situation, her evaluation is that such action by the lawyer was 'absolutely wrong'. Students seem to place a value on the importance of honesty in dealing with clients, as is seen in the comment from Ava who views the actions of prosecutor Helen Gamble in *The Practice* as inappropriate. Yet, in a way, that ameliorates the definitive nature of Megan's moral absolutism, and her statement 'but you know . . .' is an indication that, although lying to a client to procure a confession is wrong per se, perhaps there are some circumstances in which lawyers would be entitled to do the wrong thing.

This acceptance of some of television lawyers' more questionable actions further illustrates the argument that students look forward to seeking justice in the community by representing only the innocent. When lawyers on television bend the rules, or act outside certain legal boundaries, students view these actions as morally justifiable as long as they are for the cause of protecting the innocent. This is evidenced in the following comment from Margaret:

Margaret: I think Jimmy from *The Practice* . . . seems to have more of a conscience even if it goes *against what you're supposed to do as a lawyer*, like I remember this one show that there was some sick boy [and] he wasn't supposed to let him know he was dying. I don't know what the medical thing behind it was and he wasn't supposed to breach confidentiality . . . but he did because it was the right thing to do.[41]

Margaret referentially agrees with Jimmy's actions. Even though she believes legal professional regulations would not permit such a breach of confidentiality, Jimmy's disclosure was apparently the 'right' course of action. This student is relying on a personal intuitive[42] sense of ethics to interpret the validity of the actions of these fictional television lawyers. Without yet having a real understanding of legal professional obligations, the students can only rely on their personal ethics (validated by television) to evaluate what would be appropriate ethical responses to such difficult situations. The narratives provided by the legal dramas offer the students an opportunity for reflection and interpretation of their own ethical stance. Interestingly, one student, Emily, expressed a slight annoyance at the way in which television lawyers appear to always be engaged in a personal battle over ethical matters:

> So you feel like lawyers suffer the daily grind a lot like . . . cause that's what I think comes out in, in the shows, like they've always got some moral dilemma or some spiritual crusade going on inside their soul . . . Lara Flynn Boyle in *The Practice* is always arguing that . . . [in] her position as a Prosecutor that she has to do something underhanded in order to . . . be able to catch the criminals, and she's always in this massive malaise as to whether or not she can live with herself and the job that she does and whether she should cross over to the defence attorney just so she can win a case. And . . . I get bored of it, I mean . . . like yes that is the job you went into you should just deal with it.[13]

In this comment, Emily first critically draws attention to how television productions frequently depict lawyers as suffering the daily grind – and not because of tedious, mechanical work but because of intensely affecting 'spiritual crusades' and 'massive malaise'. But then it is interesting to note the easy slippage into a referential assessment that lawyers should expect such ethical dilemmas to be a natural part of legal work. By relating to Lara Flynn Boyle as if she were real, the student makes a judgment that lawyers should be able to deal with these dilemmas because they have chosen to work in the ethically challenging environment of the legal profession. Notice the use here of the actor's name (Lara Flynn Boyle) rather than that of the character she plays in *The Practice* (Helen Gamble), which might indicate that, despite mixing fact and fiction, there is a personal expectation being transformed and presented of what would actually occur within the reality of legal practice. This expectation involves an understanding that transgressive practice is a necessary aspect in the business of 'catching criminals'.

Another student presents the argument that admirable lawyers within popular culture are those who manipulate the law in order to achieve the desired outcome of upholding a certain ethical standard in society:

Heather: I admire the ones that . . . uphold moral good and all that kind of thing . . . like I kind of have this idealistic admiration of Atticus Finch from *To Kill a Mockingbird* like I don't know, he just does the right thing and I like that, I'd like to be able to do that . . . To go against what other people are saying and *use the law for your good purposes* . . . But use the law to support that . . . manipulated the system for good ends.[44]

Although this statement initially begins with a fairly straightforward view that admirable lawyers are those who act morally and do the 'right thing' in order to achieve 'good purposes', the student finishes with an articulation that manipulation of the law is an acceptable part of this. The implication from this comment is that an admirable lawyer is to be judged not necessarily by the success with which he or she is capable of effecting that manipulation, but instead by the purpose for which that manipulation is practised. It might be interesting to note that the purpose served here is not the law itself, but rather some sort of higher moral code.

Time and time again, the students articulate the notion that transgressive legal practices are permissible only within endeavours that seek to protect the innocent,[45] and this is most evident in their discussions of a particular strategy that was employed by the lawyers in *The Practice*. 'Plan B' was a strategic move developed by the partners as a trial tactic intended to shift blame from their client to any other person, even though they lacked reasonable grounds for suspecting them. Although it was discouraged and condemned as unprofessional by their colleagues within the legal community, the use of 'Plan B' was not always deemed illegal by the judge. The following interaction reflects the level of interest raised in the students by the deployment of such a strategy:

Emily: . . . I like watching *The Practice* like 'cos there's always some . . . there's always like sick and twisted character[s] and I like to see how they're going to get them off . . . it doesn't mean that I'm immoral and that I side with the way they do it . . . But I guess [it's] just a fascination with what they do and how they do it.

Molly: Yeah, I'd have to agree with that, the way they 'Plan B' to come up with sort of the alternatives . . . I find interesting.[46]

Watching *The Practice* gives students a window into the ways in which the law can be manipulated. Although they are quick to articulate a distance from any morally questionable practices, students nevertheless seem fascinated by transgressive actions. Later in the discussion, the students were asked whether they considered the 'Plan B scenario' to be an unethical practice and Molly responded with the following statement that encapsulates the acquiescence of transgression only on behalf of the innocent:

Molly: I think only if you're certain of your client's guilt or innocence, if you're uncertain . . . either because you don't know or because you're uncertain then I don't think that it would be acceptable to point to another person and say its possible that they did it . . . but if you are certain that your client is guilty . . . then I find that completely abhorrent and I wouldn't be doing it.[47]

As a defence lawyer, if you are certain of your client's innocence, then it is acceptable to adopt underhanded or devious tactics in order to save them from unjust punishment. In this way, the students see the means as justified by the end result. But, in line with the students' strict moral stance observed so far, if you are certain of your client's guilt, or simply unsure, then it would be completely immoral to call into question the innocence of a third party for the sake of saving a potentially guilty client. This student firmly believes that such questionable practices are immoral if the client is actually (or possibly) guilty, but implies that using a 'Plan B' type strategy is acceptable transgressive behaviour when fighting for the innocent. Although of course it may not completely resolve the issue, there is again no recognition that professional ethics requirements could provide some guidance.

Clearly a demarcation of ethical and professional practice is not easy. Students simply do not know what professional responsibility norms would require of them as lawyers, and they lack the confidence to work out how they would react in those types of situations. Yet, through their critique of television lawyers, and even despite their burgeoning legal knowledge, they are able to use these stories to contribute to the process of identity construction. Take, for example, this comment from a student who takes the critique of *The Practice* a step further by referentially building a picture of what makes a good lawyer:

Molly: . . . [Helen Gamble on *The Practice*] sort of grapples with issues that I . . . imagine *you* would actually have to grapple with at some point, like you know how far do *you* go in questioning a child for their testimony . . . that sort of thing I can sort of see coming up in day to day so I can relate to that and say that makes a good lawyer.[48]

It would seem that students are very keen to create for themselves an ethical position on which to base their future legal identities, even despite lacking sufficient understanding of the essence of legal representation or the nature of ethical awareness. By evaluating the storied actions of fictional characters on television, these first-year students take part in the process of assembling a picture of the legal identity they will assume. In the next extract, while displaying a clearly deficient understanding about the defence/prosecution distinction, one student, Dan, also self-referentially articulates a fervent desire towards effecting social justice:

Dan: . . . one of the things that TV has directly influenced me in [was] . . . I'd be very interested in prosecution because that way I can kind of decide whether I'd prosecute someone, you know and or not to, you know if it was obvious that they were, they were innocent then you could let them go you know or you wouldn't push it or whatever, but you would, you would if it was if it seemed on the face of it that they were obviously guilty . . . Whereas in defence you know you'd have to take any, any scumbag that came along so to speak.[49]

Dan is interested in taking on the identity of a prosecutor because of a belief that, unlike defence lawyering, this position would involve a generous exercise of discretion. In this way, Dan could ensure that the 'innocent' were protected and only those who were 'obviously guilty' were actually prosecuted. It is fascinating to note again that there is no acknowledgement that the law has any part to play in the decision of whether to prosecute criminal defendants.[50] In Dan's interpretation of being a prosecutor, it is the application of a personal and arbitrary moral judgment that drives discretion, rather than the specific legal requirements set out in detailed legislation and learned in legal training. In his story, the position of the prosecutor is juxtaposed with that of the defence lawyer who, according to Dan, must take on any morally questionable character ('scumbag') that comes their way.[51] He so keenly wants to take on the legal identity of a lawyer who works only with and for the innocent that he adopts an incorrect assumption about the discretion available to defence lawyers when choosing whom they will represent. Although there is much more discretion available to private practitioners in their selection of clients than there is for prosecutors, Dan articulates a firm desire to disassociate from all that is morally questionable. In reversing the discretionary roles generally accredited to defence lawyers and prosecutors when 'choosing' clients, Dan reflects not only a lack of understanding about these roles in practice but also his adoption of a polarized ethical identity that seeks to ensure the protection of the innocent.

One interesting aspect of this dichotomy was the frequent reference by many of the students to corporate lawyers as inherently unethical. Take this next interchange as an example:

Dave: . . . you've got [lawyers that are] usually defending the underdog and then you see these just nondescript people who are the lawyers defending like the corporation or something and you think yeah those are obviously you know immoral, bad people [and] they like to view the changing lawyers, . . . lawyers who were like sort of like blood-sucking ideology and then changed to the moral side . . .

Kylie: Actually I watched *The Secret Life of Us* . . . And he was working in the community service and then he became a corporate lawyer and he was saying 'I hate it, I wanted to go back', and I thought oh well that's going to probably be a good image to portray to people that he actually doesn't want to work [in corporate law] and his soul is restored if he went back.[52]

Dave clearly makes a contrast between two types of lawyers: those defending the 'underdog' or the 'moral side', and corporate lawyers who are 'obviously' immoral and 'bad'. He uses intriguing terminology to describe this second type of lawyer – in contrast to those on the 'moral side', corporate lawyers are of a 'blood-sucking ideology'. The implication is that immoral lawyers, like those representing corporations, are parasites who feed on other people's problems.[53] Kylie makes a similar argument by using religious and morally redemptive imagery to indicate that working for corporations necessarily results in the loss of your soul – although it is retrievable upon re-entry into a more morally appropriate position within the legal profession, such as community service.[54]

By telling stories about the ethical stance displayed by television lawyers, the students are demonstrating the very process of identity construction that is taking place as they concurrently begin their law studies and watch the practices of lawyers on television. On the one hand, they are keen to uphold high ethical standards, and do not want to contemplate dealing with those who might be guilty: one student clearly stated that she would have trouble representing 'rapists'.[55] Another student argued that a 'big ethical question' for her would be: 'How can you get up and try and get a murderer or a rapist on a lesser charge or off altogether? That's something that would bother me.'[56] On the other hand, their comments reveal that they don't yet fully understand or appreciate the relationship between ethics, morality and legal representation. This was most evident in the following comment: 'A defence lawyer itself is an ethical thing because you're defending someone who is accused of a crime and . . . that's an ethical stance that you're taking to prove that they're not guilty.'[57] There is simply no clarity in the knowledge they currently possess about legal ethics – to defend someone is seen by these students as constituting, in and of itself, an ethical dilemma. Again, it would seem that they are projecting a legal identity where to *be* a lawyer is to inescapably be embroiled in an ethical situation. Within this context, the last section of the chapter shows the diverse benefits to be gained within legal education by allowing students to work through the various ethical issues they identify in popular culture and further emphasizing this connection of ethics and identity through an exploration of storytelling.

3.4 Linking identity and developing ethical judgment through storytelling

The examples spotlighted above indicate that students use legal narratives on fictional television as one resource for talking through their moral positions. It is through their talk about television lawyers and the various ethical approaches these characters employ that students illustrate the deep connections between personal ethics and identity.[58] That is, placed at the intersection of law, society and popular culture, students discuss and (re)tell the stories of popular culture, and in so doing are articulating their own process of ethical judgment and identity-construction.

Self-identity is constituted not by the possession of traits but rather as a reflexively sustained narrative of the self.[59] Thus, although students identify specific characteristics to which they aspire, it is not the final attribution of these that will constitute students' self-identity. As students reflect on the embodiment and enactments of their personal ethics, they must decide whether the rationalizations they make for their legal decision-making will fit with the kind of self-identity they envision for themselves. As these ethical deliberations are constitutive of their identity, it is important to recognize that reflexivity is an integral part of the identity project. For legal education in the first year, this means acknowledging that individuals have the capacity to reflexively understand themselves and construct coherent narratives that assist in the interpretation and understanding of the self.[60] Reflexivity is a continual monitoring of an individual's activities as a natural feature of being human, and enables the constant revision of social activity in the light of new knowledge.[61] Significantly, then, reflexive law students could reflect on their own experiences, as well as those of television lawyers, and actively construct identity in light of those reflections.

It is argued that law students, at the commencement of their studies, are unaware or unsure of their personal ethics and have only begun the process of developing self-identity within the discourses of law. It is within this great trans-formative stage that students will experience a surge of understanding about their self-identity, thereby enabling them to build on what they experienced in the past, and draw from the experiences of the present, to form an identity project.[62] Therefore, the key argument is that the ongoing process of identity development is taking place whether the student is aware of it or not. Students cannot help but participate in the continuing transformation. Yet how much more would they learn about the law and themselves if they were given the opportunity within legal education to become aware of this process and be actively reflexive? The students in this research have shown that by talking about what it is they value, and 'about how matters of value are shared and disputed in the world we inhabit with others',[63] they can be pushed to evaluate, defend and sometimes reconstruct their self-identity in relation to the way they view the world of law.

In recognizing this process of discursive construction, legal educators could place a high value on fostering student awareness of their developing personal ethics and identity projects. 'The aim of all education, even in law school [*sic!*], is to encourage a process of continuous self-learning that involves the mind, spirit and body of the whole person.'[64] If legal education can engage its students in a reflexive focus on ethical approaches to lawyering, then it can positively contribute to the identity projects students are building in relation to a career in law.

The role of stories, then, is crucial to the students' reflexive ability and concur-rent development of ethical identity, and completes a triangle of exchange occur-ring within the law student. That is, students have shown that there are substantial connections between their interpretation of popular legal stories, their ethical development and their identity construction. Figure 3.1 was devised to illustrate this unique interactive exchange of the first-year law student.

The focus of Figure 3.1 is on the ways in which ethics, identity and stories are triangularly connected through the law students' transformed understanding and (re)production of stories of law. It was earlier argued that students were showing in their talk the connection between developing ethical judgment and the mark-ing of identity. As a part of the process of *becoming* in their developing identity, students were formulating an awareness of their personal ethics, and this is the interaction that forms the base of the triangle in Figure 3.1. The right side of the triangle was also illustrated in the extracted interactions, with the argument that, through the students' talk, there is a clear link between popular fiction and iden-tity. That is, popular legal narratives on television are used by students to interpret and explore legal practices and behaviours, and they not only construct meaning about the law through these stories but actively use them to construct identity. In this last section of the chapter, it is important to complete the discussion of the triangular exchange by showing that fiction has a further function in the develop-ment of personal ethical judgment (the left side of the triangle), and that ethics, identity and fiction are each constitutive of stories. In particular, it is argued that within the law student, stories comprise a central link between ethics and identity.

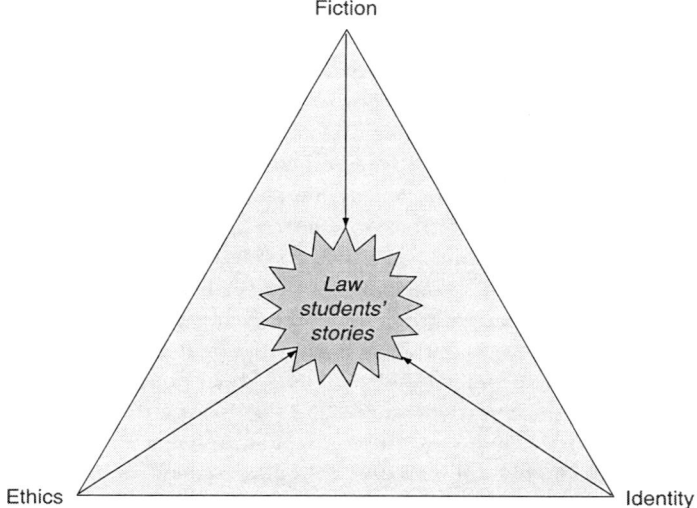

Figure 3.1 The exchange process within the first-year law student.

So, to return to the ideas of both Aristotle and Giddens, we develop a character, or identity, through a process of becoming. Ethics is concerned with the way in which individuals negotiate moral discourses and so there are ethical implications in the stories we tell each other about the law and our lives. We learn, argue and contest what is right and wrong through the construction of self-identity, which 'as a coherent phenomenon, presumes a narrative'.[65] In this way, stories are essential to the transformative power of identity construction. In the context of first-year law students, while the television texts offer various moralities, it is the students' stories that actually become the site for ethical development. The students' talk about the moral discourses produced in and through television is an integral part of the formation of their ethics and identity.

'Stories do not prescribe behaviour; they do not lay down laws for us. Instead, they inscribe behaviour: they lay down ways of being in us.'[66] Students are thus utilizing stories in two ways: to develop a sense of what it means to 'be' a lawyer through a deployment of television stories; and to articulate who they are and what they are becoming through the telling of their own stories. It is the combination of these two uses of stories that helps students to construct identity. That is, the articulation of students' stories about their ethical development is more than just an integral part of identity construction: it *is* identity in construction. Through stories, students are reflexively speaking to what they are doing when they study law, what path they are travelling on, and the bases from which they will justify legal and ethical decisions. This means, to highlight the triangular exchange, that the transformative journey of becoming a lawyer sets students on a path of story production and identity construction that will form the basis of ethical development and justifiable decision-making.

3.5 Conclusion

This chapter illustrates that students are readily deploying television narratives to picture the way they want to see themselves as lawyers. Using the students' discussions, it was argued that television helps to reinforce the positive view students have of their chosen careers. By listening to the stories the students tell of their interpretations of television fiction, we can better understand their motivations, expectations and the simultaneous construction of legal identity.

Without the benefit of practical experience or study in legal and professional ethics, first-year law students are constructing professional identities from a position where what is 'ethical' behaviour has not yet been evaluated, tested and delineated. While students are picking up on the theme (as presented in television fiction) that ethical dilemmas are an everyday aspect of lawyering, their discussions reveal an extremely blurred understanding about morality and legal ethics. Nevertheless, it is important to recognize that they do use these fictional actions and behaviours – both virtuous and immoral – to transform and shape their ideas about professional identity and practice. As a part of their process of becoming, students are reflexively formulating an awareness of their personal ethics, and thus it is argued that within the law student, stories comprise a central link between ethics and identity.

Notes

1 C. Sharp, 'Changing the channel: What to do with the critical abilities of law students as viewers?', *Griffith Law Review* 13, 2004, 185.

2 C. Sharp, 'Scarlet letter or chastity belt? What legal dramas of the twenty-first century are "telling" law students about a career in law', *Legal Ethics* 5, 2002, 90.

3 Tranter also argues that 'students must be made aware of the ethical as a legitimate realm for the discussion and evaluation of human action': K. Tranter, ' "Ethical, ooh, yeah ethical is yeah, what's right yeah": A snapshot of first year law students' conception of ethics', *Legal Ethics* 7, 2004, 102.

4 See, for example, D. Rhode, 'Into the valley of ethics: Professional responsibility and educational reform', *Law and Contemporary Problems* 58, 1995, 139; D. Rhode, 'Ethics by the pervasive method', *Journal of Legal Education* 42, 1992, 31; C. Parker, 'What do they learn when they learn legal ethics?', *Legal Education Review* 12, 2001, 175; F. Armer, 'The reaching of ethics in Australian law schools', *Journal of Professional Education* 16, 1998, 247.

5 The data are reported by focus group number, student identification letter (if needed) and page of the transcript where information occurs (on file with author). FG 7, Tara, 10. Within the context of the surrounding discussion, she is clearly referring to the internal or personal values, as distinct from any professional or external community values.

6 See generally Sharp, 'Scarlet letter or chastity belt?', 90.

7 A key finding of Tranter's study is also that 'law students do not have a clear conception of the ethical': Tranter, ' "Ethical, ooh, yeah ethical is yeah" ', 106. Of course, this is not to say that students lack ethical values, or that there isn't an ethical position implicit in what they say and do. Individuals spend a lifetime sorting through ethical views that are constantly being challenged and modified. Students should not be expected to come to law school already aware of how they will meet the particular responsibilities, obligations and obstacles that they will face as lawyers.

8 These data originate from research conducted over the 2002 and 2003 academic years among Wollongong University first-year law students. This was part of doctoral research that focused on the role of television representations of lawyers on the transforming ethical identity of first-year law students: C. Sharp, *Becoming a Lawyer: The Transformation of Student Identity Through Stories*, PhD Thesis, University of Wollongong, 2006. The focus group discussions about popular stories on television provided an opportunity to observe part of the transformative process law students are experiencing. Methodologically, this research has a basis in cultural studies theory, which advocates the interpretive fluidity of making meaning and supports the 'active audience' paradigm, contending that audiences are not cultural dopes but instead are active producers of meaning from within a cultural context of their own: see D. Morley, *Television, Audiences and Cultural Studies*, London: Routledge, 1992, which centres on the notion of the active audience and responding to the 'assumption that watching television was passive in character with the meanings and messages of television unproblematically taken up by audiences'. For further explanation of the methodology or to read more of the analysis highlighted here, see C. Sharp, 'The "extreme makeover" effect of law school: Students being transformed by stories', *Texas Wesleyan Law Review* 12, 2005, 233; Sharp, 'Changing the channel', 185; Sharp, 'Scarlet letter or chastity belt?', 90.

9 Tranter, ' "Ethical, ooh, yeah ethical is yeah" ', 86.

10 ibid., 87.

11 ibid., 88. This research is situated within the context of empirical studies of first-year law students that Tranter argues have been lacking in recent years: see p. 91. Despite two significant projects that empirically explore graduate values (Evans) and learning legal ethics in final year law (Parker), very little has been achieved in understanding the way students learn at the start of their legal education: A. Evans, 'Lawyers' perceptions of their values: An empirical assessment of Monash University graduates in law, 1980–1988', *Legal Education Review* 12, 2001, 209; A. Evans and J. Palermo, 'Australian law students' perceptions of their values: Interim results in the first year – 2001 – of a three year empirical assessment', *Legal Ethics* 5, 2002, 103; and Parker, 'What do they learn?' This current research seeks to complement the work of Tranter (' "Ethical, ooh, yeah ethical is yeah" ') in specifically exploring first-year values and judgments – Tranter examines the ethical baseline of new law students and this current study seeks to explore the ongoing construction of ethical identity in first-year students as they embark upon a legal career.

12 Aristotle refers to *èthos*, meaning character, and *ethos*, meaning custom, as different aspects of the same root *eth–*. The adjective of *ethos* (*èthikos*) is the origin of our term *ethics*: Aristotle, *Ethics*, Harmondsworth: Penguin, 1976, pp. 90–1.

13 Y. Ross, *Ethics in Law: Lawyers' Responsibility and Accountability in Australia*, Sydney: Butterworths, 2001, p. 9.

14 M. Foucault, *The Care of the Self: The History of Sexuality Vol. 3*, London: Penguin, 1986; see also C. Barker, *Cultural Studies: Theory and Practice*, London: Sage, 2000, p. 239.

15 M. Hill, *The How and Why of Love: An Introduction to Evangelical Ethics*, Sydney: Matthias Media, 2002, p. 23.

16 ibid., p. 38.

17 Foucault, *The Care of the Self*; see also Barker, *Cultural Studies: Theory and Practice*, p. 239. Ethics is seen by Foucault as crucial to the construction of subjectivity (that which presents identity as the product of discourses and institutional practices). See further G. Danaher, T. Schirato et al., *Understanding Foucault*, Sydney: Allen & Unwin, 2000.

18 Hill, *The How and Why of Love*, p. 35.

19 L.M. Graham, 'Aristotle's ethic and the virtuous lawyer: Part one of a study on legal ethics and clinical legal education', *The Journal of the Legal Profession* 20, 1995/96, 9.

20 J. Webb, 'Ethics for lawyers or ethics for citizens? New directions for legal education',

Journal of Law and Society 25, 1998, 142. This is also reminiscent of Aristotle's approach to ethics, which views human beings as 'inherently social' and treats ethical judgment and conduct as social constructs. See further Aristotle, *Ethics*.

21　T.L. Hall, 'Moral character, the practice of law and legal education', *Mississippi* 60, 1990, 515–17; See generally, Aristotle, *Ethics*, p. 1103b.

22　ibid., 517.

23　D. Webb, 'Ethics as a compulsory element of qualifying degrees: Some modest expect-ations', *Legal Ethics* 4, 2001, 111.

24　ibid.

25　ibid.

26　Hill, *The How and Why of Love*, p. 21.

27　Reflexivity here refers to the way we reflect on information from our social context and incorporate it into our knowledge of the world in our subsequent actions. See generally, A. Giddens, *Modernity and Self-Identity*, Cambridge: Polity Press, 1991.

28　Hill, *The How and Why of Love*, pp. 21–2.

29　And why would they, if they have never been taught how to differentiate them?

30　FG 7, 13.

31　Sharp, 'Scarlet letter or chastity belt?'

32　Of course, Jess also makes a comment on character by her use of the adjective 'sly', but it is argued that she uses it more to relate to a culturally sanctioned judgment about deceitful lawyering practices.

33　Foucault, *The Care of the Self*.

34　FG 1, Ava, 21.

35　M. Asimow and S. Mader, *Popular Culture: A Course Book*, New York: Peter Lang, 2004, p. 53.

36　FG 6, Donny, 3.

37　FG 1, Kylie, 26.

38　W.H. Simon, 'Moral pluck: Legal ethics in popular culture', *Columbia Law Review* 101, 2001, 421. For a discussion on the idealistic altruism common among first-year law students, see Sharp, 'Scarlet letter or chastity belt?' and Tranter, ' "Ethical, ooh, yeah ethical is yeah" ', 94.

39　J. Thomas, 'Legal Culture and *The Practice:* A post-modern depiction of the rule of law', *UCLA Law Review* 48, 2001, 1495–517. Here Thomas argues that the law on *The Practice* is portrayed as arbitrary, subject to manipulation and 'post-modern'.

40　FG 1, 26–7.

41　FG 3, Margaret, 11.

42　Tranter argues from his study that law students regard ethical values as 'deeply per-sonal, possibly intuitive and ultimately subjective, varying with the person and their cultural context': Tranter, ' "Ethical, ooh, yeah ethical is yeah" ', 96.

43　FG 4, Emily, 4–5.

44　FG 6, Heather, 12.

45　Note how the students never directly discuss how they will evaluate who is innocent and who is not – it is just as if it will be self-evident to them – and this is just like it is on television (which gives us God-like knowledge of a person's character).

46　FG 4, 6.

47　FG 4, Molly, 7.

48　FG 4, Molly, 20–1.

49　FG 4, Dan, 28.

50　The *Prosecution Policy of the Commonwealth* is a public document that has been tabled in Parliament and sets out guidelines for the making of decisions in the prosecution process. Under the *Prosecution Policy*, there is a two-stage test that must be satisfied: (i) there must be sufficient evidence to prosecute the case; and (ii) it must be evident from the facts of the case (and surrounding circumstances) that the prosecution would be in the public interest. (Each state has equivalent policies providing consistent

guidelines.) See further the Commonwealth DPP website, www.cdpp.gov.au (accessed 21 January 2010).
51 Generally, solicitors are free to pick and choose whom they represent – there is no obligation to accept any particular case. Barristers, on the other hand, are bound by the 'cab rank' rule. This is formulated in Rule 85 of the *Australian Bar Association Model Rules* (ABA), 8 December 2002, and states that a barrister must accept a brief if: (a) it is within their capacity and skill; (b) there are no scheduling conflicts; and (c) the fee offered is acceptable. Of course, given these provisos, it is not too difficult for a barrister to avoid any particular client.
52 FG 5, 16.
53 Dave earlier had articulated his moral evaluation in this way: 'the bad lawyer I think would be the morally worse one, the one that doesn't have any problems with taking on, you know, a corporation taking out some poor people . . . you know, the cut-throat lawyer . . . which is contrasted with the good, moral, decent lawyer': FG 5, Dave, 8.
54 Interestingly, Granfield notes that a growing acceptance of and preference for corporate law practice by many law students over the course of their studies corresponds with the diminution of idealism that was commented on earlier in the chapter: R. Granfield, *Making Elite Lawyers: Visions of Law at Harvard and Beyond* (1992), cited in A. Goldsmith, 'Warning law school can endanger your health!', *Monash University Law Review* 21, 1995, 274.
55 FG 7, Beth, 11.
56 FG 9, Tara, 10. Another student made this argument in identification with the effects that working for the prosecution could have on personal morals: 'And if this guy gets off we'll be releasing a killer into the community and then he'll go murder someone and it will be on their conscience for ever that they got off this killer and he's gone and murdered someone and you know that happens every three weeks or something and then that would get to *you* I think.' (FG 1, Ava, 5) The students here are recognizing via television stories that there are moral consequences to a bad performance on the job. Losing a case means more than just losing!
57 FG 7, Craig, 19.
58 In his research into the moral discourse produced by British-Asian girls in relation to soap operas, Barker concludes that the ethics of 'relationships is crucial in the identity formation of young people': C. Barker, ' "Cindy's a slut": Moral identities and moral responsibility in the "soap talk" of British Asian girls', *Sociology* 32, 1998, 79.
59 See Giddens, *Modernity and Self-Identity*, p. 53: 'Self-identity is not a distinctive trait, or even a collection of traits, possessed by the individual. It is the self as reflexively understood by the person in terms of her or his biography.'
60 C. Barker, 'Television and the reflexive project of the self: Soaps, teenage talk and hybrid identities', *British Journal of Sociology* 48, 1997, 614; Giddens, *Modernity and Self-Identity*.
61 Giddens, *Modernity and Self-Identity*, p. 35.
62 See Giddens, *Modernity and Self-Identity*, p. 75; Barker, 'Television and the reflexive project of the self', 181.
63 Barker, 'Television and the reflexive project of the self', 127–9.
64 R. Cramton, 'The ordinary religion of the law school classroom', *Journal of Legal Education* 29, 1978, 262, quoted in K. Economides and J. Webb, 'Do law schools care about law students and legal values?', *Legal Ethics* 3, 2000, 9.
65 Giddens, *Modernity and Self-Identity*, p. 76.
66 D. Manderson, 'From hunger to love: Myths of the source, interpretation and constitution of law in children's literature', *Law and Literature* 15, 2003, 90.

4 Experience is the *only* teacher: bringing practice to the teaching of ethics

David F. Chavkin

4.1 Introduction

During my career as a law professor, I have had the opportunity to teach law students and to interact with law professors on every continent except Antarctica. And if the penguins had responded more favorably to my outreach, I might have ended up on that continent as well.

In all of these interactions, and despite the significant differences in settings and educational environments, I have been surprised by the common themes that transcend these different legal education systems. Whether legal education is an undergraduate degree, as in the continental system and those countries descended from that system, or a graduate degree, as in the United States and more recently in countries including Japan, legal education too often fails its students and the clients on whom they will depend. Perhaps in no area is legal education more deficient than in the teaching of professional responsibility.[1]

Because I teach students in both clinical[2] and classroom settings, professional responsibility is an everyday topic and clinic students grapple throughout their representation of clients with issues of their roles and responsibilities as advocates and advisers and with issues of their future identities as lawyers with broad personal and professional responsibilities. Perhaps most striking in the clinical setting is the virtually daily revelation by students that ethical rules first came alive and really meant something when they became personally responsible for their ethical actions (or inactions) and when their personal professional identity was on the line.[3]

It should probably come as no surprise that this is the case. Too often, learning is not the goal of education. Instead, education too often focuses on the transmission and temporary retention of information and not on the development of knowledge. I therefore adopt for the purposes of this chapter the following definition of learning:

> Learning involves change. It is concerned with the acquisition of habits, knowledge, and attitudes. It enables the individual to make both personal and social adjustments. Since the concept of change is inherent in the concept of learning, any change in behavior implies that learning is taking place or has

taken place. Learning that occurs during the process of change can be referred to as the *learning process*.[1]

In referring to 'habits, knowledge and attitudes', we might just as easily substitute the synonyms 'practice, doctrine and values'. In substituting these terms, I am anticipating and incorporating the terminology used in recent groundbreaking reports on and indictments of American legal education.

4.2 Impact of the Carnegie Foundation and Best Practices Reports

In 2007, the Carnegie Foundation for the Advancement of Teaching issued its report on American Legal Education – Educating Lawyers: Preparation for the Profession of Law.[5] Although I believe that their choice of certain language was unfortunate, the authors identified three 'apprenticeships'[6] for legal education:[7]

> The first apprenticeship . . . intellectual or cognitive, focuses the student on the knowledge and way of thinking of the profession . . . The . . . second apprenticeship is to the forms of expert practice shared by competent practitioners . . . The third apprenticeship, . . . identity and purpose, introduces students to the purposes and attitudes that are guided by the values for which the professional community is responsible.[8]

Critical to my thinking was the recognition in the Carnegie Foundation Report that experiential learning was necessary to achieve the goals of the second and third apprenticeships.[9] And, while the report did not mandate real-life client representation as the modality for the 'values' apprenticeship, it did acknowledge that: 'Much of the humanizing and inspiring aspects of the law have always resided in actual contact with clients and their needs.'[10]

Once real-life clients are brought into the equation, the opportunities for cognitive, practical and formative development are virtually unlimited. For example, in describing the educational model in the law school of the City University of New York, the authors note that 'clinics "teach a lot of law" '.[11] Perhaps most telling for me was the following description of how a clinical programme focused on substantive law necessarily must inculcate values of professional responsibility in its students:

> A Spanish-speaking client – a recent immigrant – brought her brother to an important case conference. The student handling the case was at first dismayed. Why was the brother there? Did he expect to be involved in the interview? Would his presence compromise confidentiality? How to explain this to the client? . . . In order to fulfill her fiduciary responsibility to her client, the student had to find ways to negotiate this conflict without, she hoped, either losing her client's trust or devaluing her client's dignity.[12]

One could teach most of the critical concepts covered in a legal ethics course from that single experience. In addition, students would be given the opportunity[13] to develop many of the cultural competencies they would need for effective and responsible lawyering in the years ahead.

At the same time that the Carnegie Foundation Report was being prepared by adult learning theorists, a group of legal educators and practitioners began working together to develop a statement of best practices in legal education. Chaired by Professor Roy Stuckey of the University of South Carolina, the steering committee prepared draft statements, posted those drafts for public comment, and incorporated suggestions over the next six years.[14]

Complementing the findings and recommendations of the Carnegie Foundation Report,[15] the Best Practices Report concluded that: 'While law schools help students acquire some of the essential skills and knowledge required for law practice, most law schools are not committed to preparing students for practice.'[16] To counteract this shortcoming, the report authors recommended that: 'Law schools should help students acquire the attributes of effective, responsible lawyers including self-reflection and lifelong learning skills, intellectual and analytical skills, core knowledge and understanding of law, professional skills, and professionalism.'[17] In order to achieve this result, law professors need to incorporate learning theory into their teaching and recognize that: 'Optimal learning from experience involves a continuous, circular four stage sequence of experience, reflection, theory, and application.'[18]

This observation parallels the work of David Kolb, a Professor of Organizational Behavior at Case Western Reserve University. Kolb defined 'learning' as 'the process whereby knowledge is created through the transformation of experience'.[19] Building on the work of Kurt Lewin,[20] Kolb adapted and enhanced the 'Lewinian Experiential Learning Model' shown in Figure 4.1.[21] I will use this model as I describe the blueprint for a very different vision of legal education.

4.3 The impact of the accreditation standards

The history of the requirement that American law schools teach professional responsibility is fairly well known because it is a relatively recent development.[22] Probably the central value of lawyers – professional responsibility or legal ethics – did not even become a fixture in American law schools until the Watergate scandal engulfed American society.[23]

One of the characteristics that nearly every individual who was criminally involved in the Watergate scandal shared, from the President down, was a legal education. This fact was extremely embarrassing to the legal community, and spurred it into action to rethink its underlying values and training in those values.[24] In response to the scandal, the American Bar Association amended its standards for legal education to require that every law school offer instruction in professional responsibility.[25] If smart lawyers from good law schools were so susceptible to breaking the law,[26] the thinking went, it must be because the ethical values of the profession had not been sufficiently inculcated in these individuals

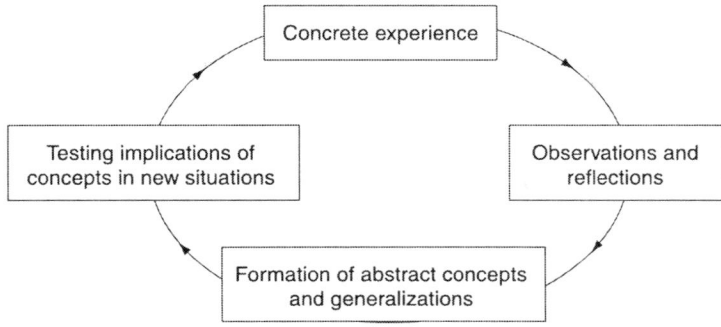

Figure 4.1 The Lewinian Experiential Learning Model.

when they were students. This was one of the first times that the accreditation standards actually defined the content of the instruction that law schools had to provide.

Perhaps in part because the teaching of ethics did not rise to the same perceived level of intellectual inquiry as contracts or torts, legal ethics classes have tended to be taught by adjunct professors or by professors with lower status than that enjoyed by most classroom teachers.[27] This phenomenon was also facilitated by the reference in an earlier version of the ABA standard that: 'A law school should involve members of the bench and bar in this instruction.'[28] This language was an open invitation for law schools to relegate the teaching of legal ethics to outsiders with little quality control or supervision over their teaching.[29]

The result of these two factors is that too often the teaching of ethics proceeds as a disjointed journey through a series of ethics rules without context.[30] Little use is made of simulations or exercises that could help give context, and ethics classes too often degenerate into a series of 'war stories' told to the younger generation.

Admittedly, there is nothing inevitable about this. Adjunct professors can be and sometimes are excellent teachers. However, they have other professional lives and identities, are primarily accountable to other employers, and may be forced to miss class and then reschedule due to other obligations.[31]

The result of this model has been an approach to ethics education that no one seems to believe actually 'works'. Students rate ethics courses near the bottom in evaluating how useful law school experiences were in their transition to real-life practice.[32] And, at least as long ago as 1996, the Professionalism Committee of the American Bar Association's Section of Legal Education and Admission to the Bar criticized the current model of ethics education for failing to adequately prepare graduates for practice.[33] The committee also identified the need for programmes that would support the development of a stronger sense of ethical integrity, civility and commitment to the profession's public mission. Despite these criticisms,[34] the current model continues to predominate.[35] The need to explore other approaches is therefore obvious.

4.4 Writing on a crowded slate

As I began to reconceptualize my course in professional responsibility, I was mindful of some of the efforts that had been undertaken previously.[36] For example, some of the available textbooks now provide an extensive variety of exercises that can be integrated into class discussions to provide a context for the discussion of particular issues of professional responsibility.[37] These exercises, or simulations, permit instructors to bring something approaching real life into the classroom without incurring the costs and other burdens of real-life client representation.[38]

As good as these new textbooks are, they still suffer from the limitations of simulations.[39] Students know that simulations are an exercise or game, and they do not invest themselves the same way they would in real life.[40] Simulations therefore have their place and they are a significant improvement over exclusive reliance on the case-dialogue method or on lectures. However, that place is limited by the very nature of the simulations. Role-plays are simply not the same as role assumption.

Although its programme is by no means unique, the University of Maryland School of Law helped pioneer a model of integrating theory and practice that is representative of some of the best efforts within legal education to bring the cognitive, practical and formative apprenticeship models together. As described by one member of the brain trust that developed the model,[41] the law school 'unite[d] the study of the substance and operation of law and legal systems, with the provision of legal assistance to real people in need'.[42] Within the experimentation encouraged within this legal theory and practice (LTP) approach, David Luban and Michael Millemann combined a traditional classroom course in ethics with a clinical course in which students would represent real clients. As described by Luban and Millemann, in this model 'the teachers and students continually use practice to criticize ethics theory and ethics theory to inform practice'.[43]

I part company with Luban and Millemann in a few of the areas they discuss.[44] However, the major elements of their model anticipated the critical challenges posed by the authors of the Carnegie Foundation Report. So, if that is the case, why did I not simply recreate their model at American University? There are two basic reasons for this.

First, clinical education is limited by the supervision ratios (ordinarily eight to one) that are necessary to ensure competent representation and critical reflection. While this approach is not as costly as some make it out to be, it is far more costly than a large ethics class. I was therefore looking to develop a model that would represent a hybrid structure – in between a clinic and a classroom course.

The second reason for departing from the model described by Luban and Millemann is that I did not want this course to substitute for the clinical experience, but rather to precede it. In this ethics course, my primary goal is to use client representation as a way to provide a meaningful context for students to grapple with issues of professional responsibility.[45] To achieve that goal, I can demand a much smaller commitment of student credits and time, and thereby encourage students to enrol who might otherwise be reluctant to take on the demands of our seven-credit-per-semester clinical courses.

4.5　The teaching of values

The important role that values play in the lawyering process has not always been a given.[16] Even the writings of someone as thoughtful as Professor Karl Llewellyn are sometimes interpreted as neglecting the importance of inculcating values in law students and lawyers. For example, in his commentary on the 'craft' of lawyering, Llewellyn wrote:

> [T]he essence of the lawyer's craftsmanship lies in skills, and wisdoms; in practical, effective, persuasive, inventive skills for getting things done, any kind of thing in any field; in wisdom and judgment in selecting the things to get done; in skills for moving men into desired action, any kind of man, in any field; and then in skills for *regularizing* the results, for building into controlled large-scale action such doing of things and such moving of men. Our game is essentially the game of planning and organizing management (not of running it), except that we concentrate on the areas of conflict, tension, friction, trouble, doubt – and in those areas we have the skills for working out results.[17]

However, it is important to continue reading that commentary to understand the place of values in the practice of law and in the betterment of the profession:

> Technique without ideals is a menace: and that, all men know, and laymen fear. The other half of the same truth which we could teach them reads: Ideals without technique are a mess. But to show what is not a mess, but a salvation, one needs to put technique to work upon ideals, with vision.[48]

So, in the Llewellyn model, in order to advance the profession we need both technique and ideals. We are thereby led inescapably back to the equation of the ABA Accreditation Standards – 'responsible and effective' or, in Llewellyn's language, technique coupled with ideals.

Although the current ABA Accreditation Standards reflect the dichotomy between 'skills' and 'values' advanced by the MacCrate Report,[49] many of us do not believe that it is helpful to distinguish between skills and values because of the interrelationship between skills and values. For example, most American professionals view 'client interviewing' as a skill that is important for effective lawyers.[50] However, many of us believe that it is not possible to be an 'effective' interviewer without also being a 'responsible' interviewer. We cannot effectively interview our clients if we are not respectful[51] of our clients; we cannot effectively interview our clients if we are not empathic[52] to our clients; we cannot effectively interview our clients if we are not genuine[53] in our dealings with our clients; and we cannot effectively interview our clients if we are not concrete[54] in our communications with our clients.[55]

For this reason, many of us blend the concepts of 'skills' and 'values' inseparably together as '*skillsandvalues*'. However, for the purposes of this chapter, I will embrace the dichotomy of the MacCrate Report and the ABA Accreditation Standards and focus on the role of legal education in producing 'responsible' lawyers – lawyers with the values necessary for appropriate representation of clients and continued improvement of the profession.

Although I began with, and have emphasized, the importance of values within the lawyer–client relationship, I do not mean to suggest that these are the only professional values worth teaching to students or worthy of developing in our future lawyers.[56] There are at least four types of values, three of which I believe are critical to the future of the profession and to which attention should be given during a student's law school experience.[57] Of the three values that I believe can and should be taught, the first might be described as a 'private' value; the second and third might be described as 'public' values.[58]

The first type of value focuses on the lawyer–client relationship.[59] It considers how lawyers will demonstrate respect for and communicate effectively with clients; how decisions will be made and implemented; and the role of the lawyer as helper and adviser.[60] It also includes such values as zealous advocacy on behalf of a client.[61] Many law professors agree with Professor Watson that there is no way to effectively teach these values unless and until the student has the opportunity to establish an attorney–client relationship and confront these issues of role definition.

The second type of value focuses on the lawyer's relationship to opposing counsel and to judges and other court and administrative agency. This arena includes such values as civility to opposing counsel and candour to tribunals. While some of these values may be developed as students watch attorneys, there is no substitute for the value of having students struggle with being civil to opposing counsel in the face of uncivil behaviours or being put in the situation of being honest with a tribunal when it risks a client's goals to do so. Here the experiential model is so far superior that it justifies the additional educational costs associated with this approach.

The final type of value that I believe can and should be taught to students involves the lawyer's relationship with the profession. These types of values include the obligation to provide pro bono representation and to consistently strive to improve the profession.[62] While students come to law school with some of these values, experiential education is critical to preserve and reinforce these values against the perverse and pervasive influences to the contrary.

Many ethics teachers have recognized that it is impossible to effectively teach professional ethics in a classroom.[63] I will analyse this shortcoming of classroom instruction in ethics and I will discuss the ways in which clinical legal education overcomes these shortcomings through further reference to the work of the late Professor Andrew Watson.[64]

Participating in one of the first public forums on the teaching of professional responsibility,[65] Professor Watson explained that 'lawyers of high professional caliber [do not] evolve from Sunday School lessons on proper behavior'.[66] Instead, he observed: 'The aspects of behavior that dictate how a person shall behave professionally derive from the internalized values that the person has incorporated from prior experiences with other people.'[67] To effectively examine these internalized values, Watson concluded that: 'Students need both the ongoing pressure of frequent demands to evaluate professional experiences objectively and then to integrate such learning into mature patterns of behavior.'[68]

If this is going to take place, Watson emphasized, it cannot be done by most law professors. He explained why most law professors have so little interest in teaching professionalism, and why they are so ill-suited to the task:[69]

> [P]rofessionalism is psychologically threatening to law professors because they have had little or no experience in dealing with these matters, nor have they resolved the personal problems that facilitate professional behavior. Never having suffered these conflicts directly, they cannot help those who are struggling with them.[70]

The result, Watson points out, is that: 'There appears to be a common attitude among many law professors that teaching the stuff of law practice is a low-status activity that should be left either to the drudges and incompetents or to such informal learning as may take place after graduation during the early years of practice.'[71]

Although Watson would later become even more specific in identifying the ways that experiential education overcomes these barriers, even at this early stage he emphasized that: 'The principal goal is to provide frequent opportunities for practicing this task.'[72] In practising this task of confronting professional responsibility issues, Watson also emphasized the importance of support by a qualified individual who could help the student to reflect on the feelings and emotions at play.[73]

Only when one assumes the role of a professional and is professionally responsible for one's actions do the ethical rules really have meaning.[74] This requires that the student assume the role of attorney – being bound by the code of professional responsibility applicable to lawyers – and own the experience so that he or she must grapple long and hard with professional obligations to a client and to the legal system. Or, as Watson explains, the experiential model succeeds because it has the following attributes:

- This method of teaching will place the student under some emotional pressure to delve into conflictual situations and to grapple with them.
- It will demonstrate to students that the teacher is aware of and cares about the difficult problems that are being dealt with, and that he or she is willing to lend (at least tacitly) full support to their exploration and solution.
- This kind of exploration will produce pressure that forces students to deal

with psychological defences that in the past have obscured the nature of their emotional conflict.

- The fact that these powerful and irrational feelings have risen to view provides and facilitates the utilization of rational controls and resolutions that were not previously possible or available.[75]

What is it about the opportunities presented by live client legal education that suggests that values can truly be inculcated in our students?[76] In large part, the answer revolves around the magical opportunities presented by the lawyer–client relationship – by the one-on-one interactions (or two-on-one interactions in clinics in which students work in pairs) between student attorney and client. In doing so, we necessarily correct the pervasive disappearance of clients and their stories in existing models of legal education in this country.[77]

Even the most zealous supporters of live client legal education would not claim that this connection between student and client is realized for every student in every opportunity. It would be unrealistic to expect every student to be transformed by even the best models of instruction. As acknowledged by Professor Homer La Rue:

> [Not] every student . . . has a transformative experience in which she moves from 'conventional moral reasoning' to a reasoning that emanates from a full integration of all dimensions of the person. Nor does every student understand the lawyer's role as translator as one of power, in which the client being served can be further silenced or assisted in obtaining her, his, or the community's own voice. However, there is anecdotal evidence that for some students, such a transformation does take place. Whatever the number of students affected may be . . . [such] courses legitimate the inquiry into how law can serve human needs.[78]

However, while education in values is by no means automatic, the heart of this adult learning experience is the processing of experience. At least as far back as 1926, the importance of experience was highlighted by learning theorists. In *The Meaning of Adult Education*, Eduard C. Lindeman wrote:

> [T]he resource of highest value in adult education is the *learner's experience*. If education is life, then life is also education. Too much of learning consists of vicarious substitution of someone else's experience and knowledge. Psychology is teaching us, however, that we learn what we do, and that therefore all genuine education will keep doing and thinking together . . . Experience is the adult learner's living textbook.[79]

With this perspective on adult learning in mind, what is the most effective model for an ethics course? As I answer that question, I am guided by the principle enunciated by John Dewey that: 'All genuine education comes about through experience.'[80]

4.6 Building a different model

I wanted to accept the challenge of the Carnegie Foundation Report[81] by building an 'apprenticeship' model for practice and formative goals that would look more like the clinical legal education model which I believe is the best model for inculcating skills and values.[82] And I wanted to pay heed to the warning sounded by Andrew Watson about the limitations of free-standing courses:

> The present practice of giving a single course seems about as logical as keeping a medical student in laboratories during the four years of medical school and then turning him out upon an innocent population after a one-hour course in 'medical practice'. He would assuredly be lost, and so would his patients.[83]

So what would this new model look like?

The first step was to decide on a model in which students would assist clients. Specifically, would they function as lawyers for their clients or as something less? Because, in my experience, the ethics rules only come to life when students are themselves on the ethics hot seat, I decided to implement a model in which students would function as lawyers for some population of clients.

This choice necessarily had other consequences, since it would be somewhat jarring to have students engage in the unauthorized practice of law in a course on professional responsibility.[84] That recognition necessitated locating the student practice in a jurisdiction in which second-year spring semester students could practise under the applicable student practice rule.[85] In Maryland, the student practice rule permits students who have completed one-third of their legal education to practise in the state.[86] This rule made certification of my target students a simple process.

The next question to answer would be the focus of the live client experience. In the clinic I direct, students represent clients in a general practice environment in which student teams might assist one client with a criminal matter, another client with a family law problem, another client with a consumer case, and a fourth client with a problem involving intellectual property.[87] My primary reason for this model of clinic design is that it encourages student attorneys to see clients as unique individuals rather than as 'cases', easily pigeonholed as an 'eviction case' or a 'divorce case'.

In my clinic, students earn seven credits for their work during the semester. In the fieldwork component, they earn four credits and must commit to between 15 and 20 hours per week. Since there was no space for fieldwork activities within the two credits allocated to the existing legal ethics course, I knew that I would need to obtain approval for an additional credit from the faculty. However, even with that additional credit, the representation and related tasks would need to be able to be completed within the 56 hours associated with the additional credit.[88] How should I spend those hours in the way most likely to yield formative benefits for students (and, to a lesser extent, practical benefits for clients)?

I decided to control the scope of the clinic by focusing on an area of substantive law that was relatively straightforward for this population.[89] Because I believe that the richest context for student exploration of their professional responsibilities is in the attorney–client relationship, I decided to choose an area of the law that presented rich opportunities for students to consider their role and responsibilities within that relationship. I ultimately chose wills and advance directives for these reasons.[90]

The next issue was to determine how large a student population could be served in this kind of setting. Two competing factors immediately came into play. The first factor was the need to ensure that clients served by the student attorneys received competent representation. Ensuring quality of representation would require ongoing supervision meetings and constant monitoring of student work product. These supervision meetings needed to take place at least bi-weekly, and they needed to last long enough to provide sufficient opportunities for feedback and to guide students through critical reflection of their experiences.[91] The second factor was the need to serve as many students as possible. Although most clinical programmes use an eight to one student to faculty supervision ratio, the nature of this kind of hybrid model seemed to permit a far higher student to faculty ratio.

I ultimately opted to limit enrolment to a total of 20 students during the first semester. Since I believe strongly in the benefits of teaming students in live client representation,[92] this meant that I would be working with 10 two-person teams, a fairly manageable structure.[93] This also meant that there would be a critical mass for classroom discussions of doctrine and for rounds,[94] while keeping the numbers small enough so that all students could participate.

Students would attend class twice each week for one and one half hours each class. Allocation of those hours would vary considerably from class to class between case-dialogue method (focusing on consideration of doctrine embodied in the Model Rules and cases), simulations and exercises (focusing on application of these principles to practice), and rounds (focusing on drawing both practical and formative lessons from the live client representation).

In this structure, all three academic apprenticeships identified in the Carnegie Foundation Report would be integrated so that students could internalize cognitive, practical and formative lessons. The next question was how to assess students in this model in a way that would measure student development and performance in each of these three apprenticeship areas.

4.7 Assessment and feedback

The Carnegie Foundation Report severely criticized the sole reliance in most law school classes on a final examination as the means of assessment, and also criticized the lack of meaningful feedback for students.[95] Two important observations were made by the report's authors. First, they noted that: 'What teachers value – what they deem important and essential for students to learn – can be ascertained most directly by what they assess – what they require students to know and be able to do.'[96] Second, they answered the question 'What should be the purpose of assessment in the preparation of legal professionals?' in the following way:

> From our observations, we believe that assessment should be understood as a coordinated set of formative practices that, by providing important information about the students' progress in learning to both students and faculty, can strengthen law schools' capacity to develop competent and responsible lawyers.

How could I design methods of assessment and feedback that would meet these challenges? I ultimately decided to establish three modes of assessment corresponding to the three apprenticeships identified in the Carnegie Foundation Report. In doing so, I recognized that evaluation would require a lot more effort on my part if it were to be effective.[97] And I would need to use techniques that would further the effort to get students to integrate the cognitive, practical and formative goals of my teaching.[98]

To assess student cognitive development and performance, I decided to use a two-step process. In order to measure the breadth of substantive issues discussed in the course, I decided to use 10 multiple-choice examinations,[99] administered each week starting after the second week and ending after the eleventh week. Since I use a course-management tool in most of my classes, the process of administering and grading these examinations would be almost automatic once the questions and answers were developed.[100]

I believe that assessment should play a *teaching* role and not merely a *sorting* role.[101] I therefore decided to provide students with immediate feedback regarding the 'right' answer, but also to allow students to take each quiz as many times as they wished in order to get a perfect score. Students would thereby be rewarded for wanting to 'get it right', and at the same time they would hopefully internalize the 'right' answer.

Another capability of the various course-management systems provided two other potential learning benefits. First, these course-management tools identify the frequency with which questions are 'missed' and the extent to which the 'wrong' answer is chosen. By monitoring these results, I could question my own choice of the 'right' answer and help validate the examination on the fly. Second, the frequency with which questions were 'missed' would provide *me* with valuable interim feedback on the extent to which students were grasping critical concepts in the course. I could use this information to return to these concepts in clearing up confusion.[102]

The second aspect of evaluation of cognitive development and performance would be based on a final examination – but a somewhat non-traditional final examination.[103] Instead of using a hypothetical written fact pattern, I decided to use film clips of lawyers in action.[104] Students would watch these clips at their leisure and as many times as they wished,[105] and would then evaluate lawyer actions and inactions against a framework of the Model Rules of Professional Conduct and broader issues of professional responsibility.

While students would have to demonstrate knowledge of the Model Rules and demonstrate ability to apply these rules (cognitive ability), they would also have to demonstrate competencies in practice and formative areas. In a simulated sense, students would be assuming the role of attorney and would be grappling with questions of how they would behave in these situations. And, because the examination instructions required students to consider issues of professional responsibility that went beyond a strict application of the Model Rules, students were forced to consider questions of professional identity and related values.

The next aspect of assessment and feedback was based on student journals.[106] I decided to require students to maintain weekly journals of professional responsibility issues that they encountered in their lives. These could include issues that arose in their cases, but it could also include issues that arose in their paid employment and externships. They could also include the nearly daily event on the Washington Metropolitan Area subway system (Metro) of seeing a lawyer breach client confidentiality by reviewing a client's file in public or by discussing confidential information with a client in a public setting.

I decided to have students submit these journals electronically. I agreed to provide written feedback on their entries electronically.[107] And I scheduled bi-weekly one-on-one meetings with all students to discuss the issues raised in their journals in a more interactive and spontaneous manner.

The final basis of evaluation related to student work on behalf of clients. This aspect of evaluation is very similar to that employed every day in clinical programmes across the country. Although the exact model may differ somewhat from programme to programme, the model I espouse rewards insight and reflective practice (learning) as opposed to overall quality of performance or outcome of efforts.[108]

Putting these various evaluation vehicles together, I needed to decide what weight to give to each of these elements. While there is no magic to the weighting of each factor, I wanted to give substantial weight to student performance in the cognitive, practical and formative arenas. I ultimately decided to allocate 20 points to the 10 multiple-choice examinations, 30 points to the final examination, 30 points for the client-representation component of student work, and 20 points for the student journals. Students would need to engage each evaluation element in order to get a high grade in the course, and each of the three apprenticeship elements would receive significant and relatively equal weight.

4.8 How well does the model work?

Because students are not randomly assigned to legal ethics sections, and since instructors and students know what instructional model is being used, it is not possible to assess achievement of educational outcomes scientifically. Self-selection is unavoidable, and this factor frustrates the creation of anything like a double-blind research model. However, much valuable anecdotal information has already been obtained from students and from my own experience in implementing this model.

First, students will take advantage of the opportunity to take an expanded ethics course, even though ethics teaching is still generally perceived as the 'dog' of the curriculum. They will expend a precious additional credit on a 'required' course even at a time when they are anxious to begin their exploration of elective courses in the curriculum.

Second, students can complete the fieldwork and assessment components within the credit allocations for the course. Even students who worked full-time during the day were able to schedule client meetings for weekends and evenings.

Third, the subject-matter of the fieldwork and the client population targeted proved to be good choices. The basic substantive law of wills and 'advance directives' was easily taught during a single class session. As a result, the course remained focused on issues of professional responsibility and not on wills, trusts and estates. Scheduling appointments with elderly clients was quite easy for students, and these clients tended to show up for appointments more regularly than do clients in our clinics generally.

Fourth, although the law that students would encounter was relatively straightforward, the issues of professional responsibility they would face proved to be extremely rich. Almost from the outset, students encountered issues of confidentiality as they confronted questions of what message they could leave on a client's answering machine, whether spouses or adult children could attend meetings with the clients, and whether the meetings could be held in client homes or in senior centres at which other persons were present. Similarly, issues of capacity were present in nearly every case as students recognized that capacity often is measured on a continuum that may vary with the day on which the client interaction takes place or even the hour of the day at which the interaction occurs.

Fifth, the discussions in 'rounds' regarding ethical issues that arose in student–client interactions were far richer and far more nuanced than the discussions of ethical issues that took place in the initial class discussions of ethical requirements. Even with the use of creative simulations with which the students engaged, discussions of topics like conflict of interest were very different when the students brought their client experiences into the classroom and brainstormed with other students about how to protect the integrity of the representational process when they had been brought in by an adult child to draft documents for a parent and over whom the child seemed to be exerting substantial influence, even if that influence was well intentioned.

There is still much more evaluation to be done as the course is repeated by me and replicated by others. For example, do students in this kind of course engage in more or less future pro bono representation than their contemporaries who have not been exposed to such experiential learning? However, even in the short run, there are many strong reasons to go forward with this experiment.

4.9 The shortcomings of apprenticeships

The final question is why we cannot simply leave the development of responsible and effective lawyers to the profession in apprenticeships or articles.[109] There are several answers to that question. All of those answers argue for the integration of andragogical[110] experiential learning in the law school environment.

First, the law graduate experience in apprenticeships or articles is too uneven. Some students have excellent educational experiences in their postgraduate work. However, far too many students describe hours spent photocopying or delivering documents, or writing memoranda no different in content and with less effective feedback than the students experienced in law school.

Second, the postgraduate experience is supervised by lawyers or judges who may not be effective educators. Law school professors are selected for their ability to teach, in addition to their responsibilities to develop scholarship and provide service. By contrast, lawyers or judges supervising students in apprenticeships or articles may not be effective teachers in providing guidance and facilitating self-reflection.

Third, the priority within the law school experience is on the education of the student. In apprenticeships or articles, the focus is on the delivery of services, whether in the form of legal representation by lawyers or rendering decisions by judges. This inherent conflict means that maximizing education of the law graduate may be – and indeed will often need to be – sacrificed to realize other goals.

Fourth, as we know from the andragogical model, autonomy and personal responsibility are critical elements of adult learning. In most apprenticeship or articles settings, with the possible exception of law graduates placed in state prosecutor offices, autonomy and personal responsibility are necessarily sacrificed because of the setting. Clients have retained lawyers, not law graduates, and judges may not delegate their professional responsibility to their clerks. Education is therefore necessarily compromised.

Fifth, the comment that 'First year they scare you; Second year they work you; Third year they bore you' is all too true. In too many law schools and for too many law students, legal education is a repetitive and relatively unproductive experience of drawing theory from the reading of appellate cases or the learning of doctrine that will change over the course of a career. Over and over again, the same skills are tested, even as the subject-matter changes. There is significant movement in the United States to reducing the length of the law school experience or to use the time that is spent more productively. In the continental system, students would be far better served by requiring them to take psychology courses and courses from similar disciplines as opposed to learning doctrine that will be forgotten almost as soon as it is learned.

One could go on with criticisms of the apprenticeship model. However, the point has probably been made by these five areas of focus. These reasons explain, at least in part, why American legal education largely abandoned the apprenticeship model starting in the late 1800s, and why American legal education brought experiential learning into law schools starting widely in the late 1960s.

4.10 Conclusion

In the section on 'Professional Identity and Purpose', the authors of the Carnegie Foundation Report posed the following question: 'How can law schools best teach that sense of public responsibility, indeed, public service that the American Bar Association uses to frame its own discussion of model rules?'[111] They ultimately answered that question by proposing 'an integrative model for law schools' in which 'students [could] fit together the various elements of their educational experience, preparing them for the varied demands of professional legal work'.[112]

In this chapter I have described a replicable model of ethics education that is affordable and manageable within the financial and other realities of international legal education. The authors of the Carnegie Foundation Report have thrown down the gauntlet, challenging legal educators to improve on our model of developing lawyers, and I have tried to respond to that challenge. To paraphrase the CUNY administrators interviewed for that report,[113] we cannot afford to not respond to that challenge and seize this opportune moment for educational reform.

Notes

1 I am using the term 'professional responsibility' here instead of the word 'ethics' because of the importance of developing a sense of professionalism in our students that goes beyond mere compliance with the applicable ethical rules.

2 My clinical experiences have included teaching in a Women and the Law Clinic, a Criminal Justice Clinic, a Health Law Clinic, a Mental Health Law Clinic, a Family Poverty Clinic, a Civil Practice Clinic and a General Practice Clinic.

3 Students in my clinical courses are certified to practise pursuant to the applicable student practice rules in the jurisdictions in which they provide representation. In my current incarnation, the General Practice Clinic at the Washington College of Law, those jurisdictions include the State of Maryland, pursuant to Rule 16 of the Maryland Rules Governing Admission to the Bar, and the District of Columbia, pursuant to Rule 48 of the Rules of the District of Columbia Court of Appeals. In both of these jurisdictions, students must certify knowledge of the applicable rules of professional responsibility and must comply with those rules.

4 L.D. Crow and A. Crow, 'Meaning and scope of learning', in L.D. Crow and A. Crow (eds), *Readings in Human Learning*, New York: McKay, 1963, p. 1.

5 W.M. Sullivan, A. Colby, J.W. Wegner, L. Bond and L.S. Shulman, *Educating Lawyers: Preparation for the Profession of Law*, Carnegie Foundation for the Advancement of Teaching, 2007. The Carnegie Foundation for the Advancement of Teaching has conducted numerous studies of professional education. In 1910, the Carnegie Foundation issued the landmark Flexner Report on medical education (hereinafter Carnegie Foundation Report). It then conducted other pioneering studies of education in engineering, architecture, teaching and law as part of a research agenda to influence improvement of education for the professions. Sullivan et al., *Educating Lawyers* is part of a series of reports on professional education issued by the Foundation through its Preparation for the Professions Program. *Educating Clergy* was the first in this series, which will also include reports on the education of engineers, nurses and physicians.

6 As the authors explain: '[T]he metaphor of apprenticeship sheds useful light on the practices of professional education . . . [W]e . . . extend it [the metaphor] to the whole range of imperatives confronting professional education. So we speak of three

apprenticeships. The signature pedagogies of each professional field all have to confront a common task: preparing students . . . to think, to perform, and to conduct themselves like professionals.' Sullivan et al., *Educating Lawyers*, p. 27.

7 My quarrel is with the choice of the word 'apprenticeship'. I worry that the term will conjure up the kind of postgraduate apprenticeship still used in many countries, in which law school graduates spend up to two years in legal practice settings.

8 Sullivan et al., *Educating Lawyers*, p. 28. In the report, the authors later define the cognitive apprenticeship as '[t]he teaching of legal doctrine and analysis, which provides the basis for professional growth': p. 194. The authors define the practice apprenticeship as '[a]n introduction to the several facets of practice included under the rubric of lawyering, leading to acting with responsibility for clients': p. 194. They define the formative apprenticeship as '[a] theoretical and practical emphasis on inculcation of the identity, values, and dispositions consonant with the fundamental purposes of the legal profession': p. 194. The authors also expand on the scope of the formative apprenticeship in the following language: 'This apprenticeship of professional identity should encompass issues of both individual and social justice, and it includes the virtues of integrity, consideration, civility, and other aspects of professionalism. The values that lie at the heart of the apprenticeship of professionalism and purpose also include conceptions of the personal meaning that legal work has for practicing attorneys and their sense of responsibility toward the profession.': p. 132.

9 Sullivan et al., *Educating Lawyers*, p. 28. ('In this second apprenticeship, students learn by taking part in simulated practice situations, as in case studies, or in actual clinical experience with real clients . . . [The] lessons [of the third apprenticeship] are also ideally taught through dramatic pedagogies of simulation and participation.') Although the report's authors promote the notion that the intellectual or cognitive apprenticeship can be achieved through the existing classroom model (p. 28), I am far less accepting of this belief. I find the powerful socialization referred to by the report's authors, especially during the first year of law school, too often dehumanizing and devaluing of the values that will become necessary to further the second and third apprenticeships – the practical and formative apprenticeships: p. 33. I also question the extent to which students who are 'passively' involved in the case-dialogue method actually engage in the intellectual and cognitive process theorized by advocates of the case-dialogue method. To be fair, the Carnegie Foundation Report authors do acknowledge that: '[W]e found two missing complements to the case-dialogue method. The first and more significant of the two is something that is the natural concomitant of most lawyers' activity: experience with clients. It is noteworthy that throughout legal education, the focus remains on cases rather than clients . . . The second "shadow" that emerged from our conversations with students (and occasionally with faculty) is the worry that the profession itself lacks ethical substance.': pp. 56–7.

10 ibid., p. 33.

11 ibid., p. 37.

12 ibid., p. 37.

13 I use the phrase 'given the opportunity' because not every student develops the skills and values that we might hope. In large classroom courses, we hope that every student learns, but we accept the fact that some will not. And, although it is far less tolerable and far less frequent for that result to occur in a real-life clinical setting, there are successes and failures in that setting as well.

14 R. Stuckey et al., *Best Practices for Legal Education: A Vision and a Road Map*, Washington, DC: Clinical Legal Education Association, 2007 (hereinafter Best Practices Report). A description of the process used in preparing the report is available online. See www.cleaweb.org/resources/bp.html (accessed 24 February 2009). A copy of the report may also be downloaded from that site.

15 There was considerable cross-fertilization between the two reports. See Best Practices Report, Acknowledgments, p. x.
16 Best Practices Report, Executive Summary and Key Recommendations, p. 5.
17 ibid., p. 25.
18 ibid., p. 136.
19 D.A. Kolb, *Experiential Learning: Experience as the Source of Learning and Development*, Englewood Cliffs, NJ: Prentice Hall, 1984, p. 38.
20 ibid., p. 8, Kolb describes Lewin as the founder of American social psychology.
21 ibid., p. 21.
22 One commentator described the situation in these terms: 'In the too recent past, ethics-legal profession teaching was not merely a weakness in legal education but a farce. As recently as 1966, one prominent law school's offering (or non-offering as it turned out) consisted of three one-hour lecture meetings for which neither credit nor grade were given; as it turned out, even the lectures were never actually given.' J.E. Moliterno, 'An analysis of ethics teaching in law schools: Replacing lost benefits of the apprentice system in the academic atmosphere', *University of Cincinnati Law Review* 60, 1991, n.p. (footnotes omitted).
23 The Watergate scandal involved a break-in by Republican operatives into the headquarters of the Democratic National Committee in the Watergate Hotel in Washington, DC and the cover-up of that break-in by members of the Administration of President Richard Nixon. It culminated in the resignation of Richard Nixon from office and his subsequent pardon by President Gerald Ford. See C. Bernstein and B. Woodward, *All the President's Men*, New York: Simon and Schuster, 1974. That is not to say that American legal educators completely ignored the issue of professional responsibility prior to the Watergate scandal. See, for example, Council on Education in Professional Responsibility, *Proceedings: The Asheville Conference of Law School Deans on Education for Professional Responsibility*, 1966; E.W. Kitch (ed.), *Clinical Education and the Law School of the Future*, Chicago: University of Chicago Law School, 1970; J. Stone (ed.), *Legal Education and Public Responsibility: Report and Analysis of the Conference on the Education of Lawyers for their Public Responsibilities*, Washington, DC: Association of American Law Schools, 1959; D.T. Weckstein (ed.), *Education in the Professional Responsibilities of the Lawyer: Proceedings*, Charlottesville, VA: University of Virginia Press, 1970. In 1992, at its annual meeting, the Association of American Law Schools presented a round-table discussion of 'Education for Professional Responsibility'. See, for example, T.A. Smedley, 'The pervasive approach on a large scale – 'the Vanderbilt Experiment', *The Journal of Legal Education* 7, 1963, n.p. Professor Andrew Watson commented that: 'The recent events of Watergate have demonstrated the high vulnerability of lawyers to professional educations of one sort or another. At least a part of this must be attributed to an inadequacy in legal education.' A.S. Watson, 'Lawyers and professionalism: A further psychiatric perspective on legal education', *University of Michigan Journal of Law Reform* 8, 1975, 3. In 1956, a committee of the Association of American Law Schools sponsored a conference in Boulder, Colorado (known as the Boulder I Conference) to discuss the education of law students in the public responsibilities as lawyers. For a history of the teaching of legal ethics in American law schools, see M.J. Kelly, *Legal Ethics and Legal Education*, New York: The Hastings Centre, 1980, pp. 5–21.
24 For example, many states now require completion of a course in professional responsibility as a precondition for admission to the Bar. This occurs after the passage of the Bar exam and after the passage of the Multistate Professional Responsibility Examination (MPRE) developed by the National Conference of Bar Examiners. See www.ncbex.org/multistate-tests/mpre (accessed 18 July 2007).
25 Standard 302(a), *Standards for Approval of Law Schools of the American Bar Association Section of Legal Education and Admissions to the Bar*, 2007 provides as follows: 'A law school shall require that each student receive substantial instruction in: (1) the substantive law

generally regarded as necessary to effective and responsible participation in the legal profession; . . . (5) the history, goals, structure, values, and responsibilities of the legal profession and its members.'

26 Graduates of some of the best American law schools were included among the Watergate defendants. For example, Donald Segretti graduated from my alma mater, the University of California at Berkeley (Boalt Hall School of Law). His presence at Boalt was captured in a series in 'Doonesbury' describing the imposition by the American Bar Association of the requirement that law schools teach ethics to students and the role that such a course might have played in helping Segretti avoid his fate. G. Trudeau, *Doonesbury*, Miami, FL: American Heritage Press, 1971.

27 R.G. Pearce, 'Teaching ethics seriously: Legal ethics as the most important subject in law school', *Loyola University of Chicago Law Journal* 29, 1998, 720: 'Despite lip service given to the importance of legal ethics, most law schools (with a few notable exceptions) fail to give legal ethics the same respect and attention given to most other courses, let alone a central role in the curriculum.' See also R.M. Pipkin, 'Law school instruction in professional responsibility: A curricular paradox', *American Bar Foundation Research Journal* 1979, 248.

28 *ABA Standard 2004*, 302(b).

29 *ABA Standard 2004*, 403(b) requires that: 'A law school shall ensure effective teaching by all persons providing instruction to students.' Anyone who has ever done a site inspection knows how little actual monitoring actually takes place.

30 As emphasized throughout the Best Practices Report, context-based education is essential for effective adult learning.

31 Even these shortcomings can be contested, however. Starting in the 2006–07 academic year, faculty teaching professional responsibility courses (and those interested in the teaching of professional responsibility) at the Washington College of Law, American University began meeting on a regular basis. Consistent with the principles of academic freedom, the goal was not to have all instructors teaching the same course in the same way. Instead, the goal was to ask the same questions, even if particular instructors came up with different answers to those questions. So topics ranging from teaching goals, syllabi, choice of textbooks, teaching techniques, use of technology, simulations and exercises, and testing were discussed. By the end of the first academic year, a community had been created of very disparate individuals using very disparate approaches. Participants shared successes and failures, and engaged the topics in creative and thoughtful ways that revealed what can be achieved with institutional support.

32 R. Dinovitzer et al., *After the JD: First Results of a National Study of Legal Careers*, Washington, DC: National Association for Law Placement Foundation for Law Career Research and Education and American Bar Foundation, 2004, p. 81. See www.nalpfoundation.org/webmodules/articles/articlefiles/87-After_JD_2004_web.pdf (accessed 24 June 2007).

33 American Bar Association, Section of Legal Education and Admissions to the Bar, *Teaching and Learning Professionalism: Report of the Professional Committee*, Washington, DC: American Bar Association: 1996, p. 5: '[L]awyer professionalism has declined in recent years and increasing the level of professionalism will require significant changes in the way professionalism ideals are taught.'

34 Another commentator has criticized the current situation in the following language: 'The law student who merely takes a variety of pure theory courses, and learns that "practitioners [a]re sell outs", will be woefully unprepared for legal practice. That student will lack the basic doctrinal skills: the capacity to analyze, interpret and apply cases, statutes, and other legal texts. More generally, the student will not understand how to practice *as a professional*. He or she will have gained the impression that law practice is necessarily grubby, materialistic, and self-interested and will not understand, in a concrete way, what professional practice means.'

'Law students need concrete ethical training. They need to know why *pro bono* work is so important. They need to understand their duties as "officers of the court". They need to learn that cases and statutes are normative texts, appropriately interpreted from a public-regarding point of view, and not mere missiles to be hurled at opposing counsel. They need to have great ethical teachers, and to have *every* teacher address ethical problems where such problems arise.

'The schools' failure to enhance the teaching of ethics is occurring at a time when that training has become all the more important. In the past, new lawyers might have learned law "on the job". But as law firms have become increasingly materialistic – as *pro bono* work has been displaced by profit-maximization, and the "officers of the court" by the "hired guns" – we can no longer count on the law firms to be "law schools". New lawyers need to know, before they enter full-time employment, what ethical practice means. Otherwise, their only model of the practicing lawyer may well be crudely materialistic.' H.T. Edwards, 'The growing disjunction between legal education and the legal profession', *Michigan Law Review* 91, 1992, 38.

35 In the Carnegie Foundation Report, the authors describe the efforts by two law schools to create an integrated approach to legal education that is attentive to the development of values: 'Recognizing the limitations of exclusive reliance on the case-dialogue method to teach law, these programmes resisted the common tendency in higher education to respond by simply adding a special course to "fix" the problem. (Mandated courses on such topics as "professional responsibility" are typical attempts.)' Sullivan et al., *Educating Lawyers*, p. 58.

36 Among the new efforts in this area is the approach undertaken by Drake University Law School: M.H. Weresh, 'An integrated approach to teaching ethics and professionalism', *Professional Lawyer* 18, 2007, n.p. Under this approach, students are exposed during the first year to a variety of learning opportunities, including observation of a real trial (the First-Year Trial Practicum). These activities are designed to supplement the required upper level course in professional responsibility. Although proponents argue that these changes respond to both the Best Practices Report and to the Carnegie Foundation Report, it is hard to see how these lectures and field trips provide either the context or the personal experiences advocated by both reports.

37 I adopted the textbook authored by Lisa Lerman and Philip Schrag for the range of problems provided and for the excellent support in the Teacher's Manual: L.G. Lerman and P.G. Schrag, *Ethical Problems in the Practice of Law*, 2nd edn, New York: Aspen, 2008. However, this book is not unique in its approach.

38 The lower costs associated with simulations are part of the reason that some commentators are willing to accept the trade-offs of simulations within the law school curriculum. See Moliterno, 'An analysis of ethics teaching in law schools', 122–33.

39 In making this statement, I am not unmindful of the value that some of my contemporaries place on simulations. For example, Angela McCaffrey has written of the role that she thinks simulations can play in transforming the values of her students: A. McCaffrey, 'Transforming Minnesota nice law students into vigorous, yet respectful advocates: The value of simulations in preparing clinical law students for ethical and effective client representation', *Thomas M. Cooley Journal of Practical and Clinical Law* 7, 2004, 91. I do not claim that simulations are valueless. However, I do believe that their value pales in comparison to the benefits of role assumption in a live client context. Perhaps the place where Angela and I part company most clearly is in her statement that: 'Persons interested in the law enter as students and leave some three years later transformed into attorneys.' (p. 91) I think that it is far more accurate to state that: 'Persons interested in the law enter as students and leave some three years later transformed into law graduates.' They do get transformed, often in negative ways, but they are seldom transformed into attorneys.

40 In describing her work teaching a simulation course, Professor Barbara Bennett

Woodhouse acknowledged these limitations: '[T]he kind of simulations I suggest incorporating in traditional courses are no substitute for real client representation and I have live client too great a respect for the craft of clinical teaching to pretend that such "learning experiences" are a substitute, much less a match, for supervision by skilled and experienced clinical professors.' B.B. Woodhouse, 'Mad midwifery: Bringing theory, doctrine, and practice to life', *Michigan Law Review* 91, 1993, 1982–3.

As described by another legal educator: 'The strengths of simulation over experiential learning are considered to be uniformity of experience among students, simplification of difficult problems with an orderly progression to the more complex, repetition of student performance when necessary, susceptibility to interruption and videotaping, lack of costliness, and a higher student-teacher ratio.

'On the other hand, simulation is considered to lack the factual complexity and uncertainty of real cases. Furthermore, students do not become as emotionally involved. Because the emotional investment is less, motivation and level of leaning decreases as well. Also, real cases present students with ethical dilemmas in their emotional context. Many consider this necessary for teaching professional responsibility. To be *truly* effectual, simulation is seen to require the same level of supervision, making it just as expensive as live client learning.' G.S. Laser, 'Educating for professional competence in the twenty-first century: Educational reform at Chicago-Kent College of Law', *Chicago-Kent Law Review* 63, 1992, 265–6.

41 These included Dean Michael Kelly and Professors Barbara Bezdek, Richard Boldt, Marc Feldman, Homer LaRue and Michael Millemann.

42 B.L. Bezdek, 'Legal theory and practice development at the University of Maryland: One teacher's experience in programmatic context', *Washington University Journal of Urban and Contemporary Law* 42, 1992, 127.

43 D. Luban and M. Millemann, 'Good judgment: Ethics teaching in dark times', *Georgetown Journal of Legal Ethics* 31, 1995, 64.

44 For example, they argue that students cannot provide competent representation in certain types of cases: Luban and Millemann, 'Good judgment', 65. To the extent that this observation may be true, I believe that it leads to the conclusion that these cases have no place in the context of a law course whose primary goal should be the education of students. Law professors may provide this representation as part of their service obligations. However, such representation should not be confused with legal education of students.

45 In the legal theory and practice course that I developed at the University of Maryland School of Law during my time there, my focus was similarly on the use of client representation as a way of helping students better understand issues in health law or issues in mental health law. See D.F. Chavkin, 'Training the Ed Sparers of tomorrow: Integrating theory and practice', *Brooklyn Law Review* 60, 1994, 303.

46 In discussing the teaching of values (or professional responsibility), I will use the description developed by Professor Andrew S. Watson, MD: 'Whenever we discuss professional responsibility, we refer directly or indirectly to the creation of an internalized self-image that incorporates complex value judgments about what shall and what shall not be done with clients or patients, and includes some concrete notions about the process of Professional Activity.' A.S. Watson, 'Some psychological aspects of teaching professional responsibility', *Journal of Legal Education* 16, 1963–64, 1. There are numerous other ways of describing the values that make up a profession. See, for example, L.D. Brandeis, *Business – A Profession*, Boston: Hale, Cushman and Flint, 1933.

47 K.N. Llewellyn, 'The crafts of law re-valued', *Rocky Mountain Law Review* 15, 1942, 3.

48 ibid., 5.

49 In 1989, the Section of Legal Education and Admissions to the Bar of the American

Bar Association established the Task Force on Law Schools and the Profession: Narrowing the Gap to examine the extent to which law schools were actually preparing students for the profession. Chaired by Robert MacCrate, the ABA President in 1987–88, the Task Force issued its report in 1992. ABA Section of Legal Education and Admissions, *ABA Task Force on Law Schools and the Profession: Narrowing the Gap, Statement of Fundamental Lawyering Skills and Professional Values*, 1992 (hereafter MacCrate Report).

50 See F.K. Zemans and V.G. Rosenblum, *The Making of a Public Profession*, Chicago: American Bar Association, 1981, p. 137. The authors conducted a survey of practising lawyers to determine the skills and values most needed in the practice of law and the ways that lawyers developed those skills and values.

51 By 'respect', I mean caring about clients and their needs and communicating that respect to our clients.

52 By 'empathy', I mean understanding our clients and their lives and communicating that understanding to our clients.

53 By 'genuine', I mean being honest with our clients and communicating that honesty to our clients.

54 By 'concrete', I mean communicating orally and in writing in a manner that is both respectful of and accessible to our clients.

55 In a recent article, Jane Aiken and Stephen Wizner criticized the American legal profession for not incorporating enough of these values. As they have emphasized: 'Except in law school clinical programmes, lawyers typically do not receive instruction in the skills of interacting with clients, particularly those from different economic, social, racial, ethnic, or religious backgrounds. There is no professional expectation or ethical rule that requires a lawyer to learn these professional skills, other than the general rule requiring lawyers to be "competent".' J. Aiken and S. Wizner, 'Promoting justice through interdisciplinary teaching, practice, and scholarship: Law as social work', *Washington University Journal of Law and Policy* 11, 2003, 66.

56 The MacCrate Report identified four fundamental values: provision of competent representation; striving to promote justice, fairness and morality; striving to improve the profession; and professional self-development. MacCrate Report, p. 140.

57 This trinity of values in part is drawn from the Preamble to the ABA, *Model Rules of Professional Conduct*, 1983. In that Preamble, the Model Rules describe 'a lawyer's responsibility' in the following terms: 'A lawyer is a representative of clients, an officer of the legal system and a public citizen having special responsibility for the quality of justice.' American Bar Association, *Model Rules of Professional Conduct*, 1983, Preamble. The one type of value that I do not believe it is appropriate to instil in students is the self-protection by the profession of its own well-being. In the United States, this type of value has included the imposition of fee schedules (to protect the livelihood of lawyers and to artificially inflate fees) and prohibitions on lawyers advertising. *See Bates v State Bar of Arizona* 433 US 350; 97 S. Ct. 2691; 53 L. Ed. 2d 810 (1977) (invalidating a state's blanket prohibition against all attorney advertising as unconstitutional under the First Amendment); *Goldfarb v Virginia State Bar* 421 US 773; 95 S. Ct. 2004; 44 L. Ed. 2d 572 (1975) (invalidating minimum fee schedule for lawyers promulgated by state and county Bar associations as violative of the federal antitrust laws as anticompetitive conduct by lawyers).

58 While I think this division between 'public' and 'private' values is useful, I do not want to suggest that questions of professional responsibility can always be so neatly divided.

59 Many other commentators have analysed important aspects of the lawyer–client relationship. See, for example, M.A. Silver, 'Love, hate, and other emotional interference in the lawyer/client relationship', *Clinical Law Review* 6, 1999, 259. However, in focusing on the centrality of the lawyer–client relationship, I do so with a different goal from that sometimes advanced by others. I view the lawyer–client relationship

as the door through which all progressive legal values enter. By exploring the micro-relationship of lawyer to client, a clinical professor and student attorney can develop most of the themes underlying values in the macro-relationship of lawyers to society.

60 This is often referred to as the client-centred model of representation. See D.A. Binder, Paul Bergman, Susan C. Price and Paul R. Tremblay, *Lawyers as Counselors: A Client-Centered Approach*, 2nd edn, St Paul, MN: West Publishing, 2004; see also D.F. Chavkin, *Clinical Legal Education: A Textbook for Law School Clinical Programs*, Sydney: LexisNexis, 2002, pp. 51–7.

61 Everett Hughes concluded that the central feature of the attorney–client relationship was *credat emptor* – let the buyer trust – instead of *caveat emptor* – let the buyer beware (the common warning in the commercial marketplace). E.C. Hughes, 'Professions', *Daedalus* Fall, 1963, 656.

62 In 1908, the American Bar Association adopted *Canons of Professional Ethics*. The Preamble to these Canons provided as follows: 'The future of the Republic, to a great extent, depends upon our maintenance of Justice pure and unsullied. It cannot be so maintained unless the conduct and the motives of the members of our profession are such as to merit the approval of all just men.'

63 For example, Professor Andrew Watson has written that: 'Professionalism relates to behavior and, therefore, it must be approached through some kind of *experiential process* . . . [A]ny method which draws the emphasis away from actual involvement in the operations of professionalism is to be seriously questioned.' A.S. Watson, 'The quest for professional competence: Psychological aspects of legal education', *Cincinnati Law Review* 37, 1968, 144–5. The consequences of failing to utilize such a method, Watson points out, can be dire for both the individual lawyer and for the profession: 'If a lawyer does not have the personality equipment to resolve such stresses [those associated with legal practice], he may surrender to a cynical attitude of unconcern about such matters as his emotional attitude toward his clients. *Only guided experience in dealing with such stresses can develop a belief that it is possible to face and overcome such anxious events*' (p. 132, emphasis added).

64 Professor Watson was a Professor of Law and a Professor of Psychiatry at the University of Michigan. Although not strictly a clinical law teacher himself, his writings provide much guidance on the importance of guided role assumption – student practice – as a tool for developing professional values in students.

65 Watson, 'Some psychological aspects', 4.

66 ibid. Although he was not aware of it, one student anticipated the warning by Professor Watson when he told his ethics instructor: 'I don't need to take this course; I went to Sunday School.' B.A. Green, 'Less is more: Teaching legal ethics in context', *William and Mary Law Review* 39, 1998, 387 n. 22 (quoting a former student).

67 ibid., 4.

68 ibid., 6.

69 In many American law faculties, candidates are selected because they have been chosen for law reviews while in law school. After law school, they have clerked for an appellate judge and/or for a US Supreme Court justice. Legal practice is often not only not valued; it is a barrier to hiring for an otherwise impressive candidate. As critiqued by Watson: 'In my opinion, the faculty's psychological bias, both conscious and unconscious, tends to create immediately a split in the student's orientation. If he is to become a top-notch student and identify himself with the professor, he will tend to avoid the mundane problems of law practice. [Footnote omitted.] He will deal with law primarily as a series of intellectual abstractions that permit him to avoid unpleasant emotions and result in a barrier between himself and all truly professional operations. On the other hand, if a student retains concern with the 'people' part of law practice (which is the area where all professional questions lie), then he must resist identification with the professor. He will need to depreciate the importance of the

intellectual tasks placed before him and will often develop serious goal conflicts as he studies law.' Watson, 'Some psychological aspects', 12.

70 ibid., 12.

71 ibid., 16.

72 ibid., 17.

73 Watson warns that: 'If a student senses cynicism or criticalness in the teacher regarding the emotions he expresses, he will swiftly learn to obscure them from visibility as well as awareness. This reinforces the very defenses we wish to obviate. It is just at the point when students freely express themselves that they hang in precarious balance. If feelings and emotions are treated as acceptable whatever they are, then and only then may they be kept in awareness long enough to test their rationality and validity . . . This is the reason why one of the goals in professional education should be to help students re-examine their feelings and attitudes in light of the impending role of lawyer. So far as education for professionalism is concerned, this is the moment of truth.' ibid., 17.

74 William Pincus has described this phenomenon in the following terms: '[T]here is no substitute for personally living through the circumstances which create the ethical dilemma and for having personally to face the consequences of the action or inaction which is used as a response to the moral challenge.' W. Pincus, 'One man's perspective on ethics and the legal profession', *San Diego Law Review* 12, 1975, 285.

75 Watson, 'Some psychological aspects', 19–20.

76 From a somewhat more Aristotelian perspective, James Moliterno argues that: 'In order to develop virtue, one must do virtuous things, preferably under the guidance of a moral teacher. One cannot develop morally by study alone. This practicing of virtuous lawyering can occur, and probably better occurs, in an academic setting than in the office.' Moliterno, 'An analysis of ethics teaching in law schools', 116.

77 A. Shalleck, 'Constructions of the client within legal education', *Stanford Law Review* 45, 1993, 1740–1.

78 H.C. La Rue, 'Developing an identity of responsible lawyering through experiential learning', *Hastings Law Journal* 43, 1992, 1148–9.

79 E.C. Lindeman, *The Meaning of Adult Education*, New York: New Republic, 1926, pp. 9–10.

80 J. Dewey, *Experience and Education*, New York: Macmillan, 1938, p. 13.

81 The authors of the report conclude that: '[W]e think that practice-oriented courses can provide important motivation for engaging with the moral dimensions of professional life – a motivation that is rarely accorded status or emphasis in the present curriculum.' Sullivan et al., *Educating Lawyers*, p. 88. They also conclude that: '[L]egal educators will have to do more than shuffle the existing pieces. The problem demands their careful rethinking of both the existing curriculum and the pedagogies that law schools employ to produce a more coherent and integrated initiation into a life in the law' (p. 147). In adopting the model proposed in this chapter, I am suggesting a very different model along the 'continuum of teaching and learning' than the ones identified by the report authors.

82 In using the term 'clinical legal education', I mean the following: 'Clinical education is first and foremost a method of teaching. Among the principal aspects of that method are these features: students are confronted with problem situations of the sort that lawyers confront in practice; the students deal with the problem in role; the students are required to interact with others in attempts to identify and solve the problem; and, perhaps most critically, the student performance is subjected to intensive critical review.' 'Report of the Committee on the Future of the In-House Clinic', *Journal of Legal Education* 42, 1992, 511. The essence of this model is learning by doing, with critical reflection of both the learning and doing steps. This resonates with the ancient Chinese proverb: 'I hear, and I forget. I see, and I remember. I do, and I understand.' Kenneth Kreiling has described the process of clinical education in the

following way: 'Traditional classroom legal education is concerned with the process of learning through information assimilation. Usually the information to be assimilated is applied within the narrowly circumscribed confines of the instructor-defined class-room. In contrast, clinical education is primarily concerned with the process of learning from actual experience, learning through taking action (or observing someone else taking action) and then analyzing the effects of the action. The data of learning are provided primarily by the students' actual performances and experiences with clients who have legal problems. Such performances arise in a world where some facts cannot be ascertained, where personal qualities and interpersonal relationships are often critical, where the 'problem-solver' must take action and choose solutions while faced with unpleasant contingencies. Clinical education provides a model of the multi-dimensional world of practice that traditional classroom education simply cannot provide.' K.R. Kreiling, 'Clinical education and lawyer competency: The process of learning to learn from experience through properly structured clinical supervision', *Maryland Law Review* 40, 1981, 285–6.

83 Watson, 'Some psychological aspects', 20. Others have contrasted medical education and legal education. See, for example, E. Egan, K. Parsi and C. Ramirez, 'Comparing ethics education in medicine and law: Combining the best of both worlds', *Annals of Health Law* 13, 2004, noting that medical education mandates hands-on experience with patients while legal education makes activities, such as clinic and pro bono, electives. Law students spend much of their time in a classroom compared with medical students. Professional socialization seems to be lacking in legal education, in part because students rarely if ever observe their professors in practice. Alternatively, medical students model themselves after practitioners who are trying to pursue their own research and a profitable practice. This paper argues that legal ethics targets behaviour and results, whereas medical ethics targets character, virtue and judgment.

84 For example, Rule 49 of the *Rules of the District of Columbia Court of Appeals* prohibits the unauthorized practice of law and defines the term 'practice' broadly in Rule 49(b)(2) to include 'the provision of professional legal advice or services where there is a client relationship of trust or reliance'.

85 Student practice rules vary significantly from jurisdiction to jurisdiction. See D.F. Chavkin, 'Am I my client's lawyer: Role definition and the clinical supervisor', *Southern Methodist University Law Review* 51, 1998 (containing a national compendium of student practice rules).

86 Rule 16 of the *Rules Governing Admission to the Bar* in Maryland authorizes legal assistance by law students.

87 This range of experiences is a great attraction to potential students who have not yet decided on their future fields of practice. However, it also has other significant peda-gogical benefits.

88 The ordinary calculation is that four hours per week is required for each credit. Since the fall and spring semesters each run for 14 weeks, that means that students would allocate 56 hours (14 weeks × 4 hours per week = 56 hours per semester).

89 Before professors and practitioners working in this area I have chosen (wills and advance directives) attack me too ferociously for suggesting that this area of the law is 'relatively straightforward', let me try to deflect those attacks in advance. Our client population consists of indigent clients whose estates are quite limited. They do not require complex trust arrangements, for example. And, since the number of clients represented would be quite small, I could be alert to complex estate planning requirements and shift those cases to the clinical programme.

90 This is also an area of legal assistance in which there is a large and unmet need. Most low-income clients in the metropolitan area in which we would provide representation die intestate. Expanding services would therefore help meet a large unmet need and there were ready pools of clients seeking assistance, from which clients could be culled. These organizations include Legal Services for the Elderly, a project of the AARP.

91 Andrew Watson criticizes those forms of experiential learning in which critical reflection does not take place: 'My own assessment of their value [clinical programmes] as part of professional education relates directly to the amount of interpreted experience which the student encounters. Mere contact with these professional situations may do little more than stir anxiety – anxiety traced to its source and analyzed creates growth potential.' Watson, 'The quest for professional competence', 157.

92 See D.F. Chavkin, 'Matchmaker, matchmaker: Student collaboration in clinical programs', *Clinical Law Review*, 1, 1994, 199.

93 In addition to my services, I utilized the services of a dean's fellow (research assistant). Since the legal ethics course is customarily taught in the spring semester, it was relatively easy to find a clinic student from the fall semester to serve in this capacity.

94 'Rounds' is a process in which student teams present their experiences in working with clients to the rest of the class. This process serves two educational goals. First, students learn from the experiences of others. Second, students can bring troublesome tactical, ethical and counselling issues to the entire class so that the student teams can benefit from the collective wisdom of the group. For a comprehensive discussion of the role of 'rounds' in clinical legal education, see S. Bryant and E. Milstein, 'Rounds: A "signature pedagogy" for clinical education', *Clinical Law Review*, 14, 2007, 195.

95 Sullivan et al., *Educating Lawyers*, pp. 162–71. The authors are especially critical of the fact that most law school assessment is 'summative', at the end of the course. As the authors note: '[A]lthough it measures achievement, its after-the-fact character forecloses the possibility of giving meaningful feedback to the student about progress in learning' (p. 164).

96 ibid., p. 163.

97 This is, of course, no surprise for those who have taught classes based on models other than the case-dialogue approach. As noted in the Carnegie Foundation Report: 'Compared to the efficiency of the large case-dialogue classroom, the formats that lend themselves to clinical and lawyering activities, including legal writing, are highly labor-intensive.' Sullivan et al., *Educating Lawyers*, p. 175.

98 'It is not enough to develop analytical knowledge plus merely skillful performance. The goal has to be integration into a whole greater than the sum of its parts.' Sullivan et al., *Educating Lawyers*, p. 178.

99 The Carnegie Foundation Report refers to such examinations as 'objective' examinations. That term would suggest only one answer is objectively correct. However, like beauty, the 'correct' answer is often in the eye of the beholder.

100 I generally use TWEN (The West Educational Network) as a course-management tool in my classes. However, other course-management tools have this capability as well. These course-management tools grade examinations automatically based on the instructor's key. They also automatically compile a gradebook for each student and for each question.

101 The Carnegie Foundation Report reaches the same conclusion in somewhat different language. The authors use the term 'formative assessment' to describe 'feedback [that] is provided primarily to support students' learning and self-understanding rather than to rank or sort'. Sullivan et al., *Educating Lawyers*, p. 189.

102 In the words of the Carnegie Foundation Report, this would put 'two kinds of assessment together – linking feedback *to* students with feedback *from* students about how well they are achieving the learning goals of a course'. Sullivan et al., *Educating Lawyers*, p. 180.

103 Because it is somewhat non-traditional, we devote a class to this model. The students watch a series of clips from the movie *Class Action*, a film rich in ethical issues. They are told to make notes to themselves of the ethical issues that they see in the film. Then they are placed in groups to share these issues, brainstorm additional issues and flesh out their positions on the issues identified. After that, we reconvene as a class to discuss these topics.

104 For example, I have sometimes used a short interaction between the president of a corporation and the general counsel of the corporation that was developed some time ago as part of the ABA series *Dilemmas in Legal Ethics*. I have also used a far lengthier set of sequences from the pilot episode of *LA Law* involving choices confronted by criminal defence attorneys.

105 In order to make this possible, film clips were digitized and made available to students as streaming video on the web.

106 See J.P. Ogilvy, 'The use of journals in legal education: A tool for reflection', *Clinical Law Review* 3, 1996, 157 (providing an excellent description of the many ways to use journals to further student self-reflection and learning).

107 I use the Microsoft Word 'Review and Comment' function to facilitate this process. Electronic submission avoids the necessity of deciphering student handwriting and the Microsoft Word capability makes it far easier and time-efficient to submit even extensive comments.

108 I have described my basic criteria and method of evaluation in S.L. Brustin and D.F. Chavkin, 'Testing the grades: Evaluating grading models in clinical legal education', *Clinical Law Review* 3, 1995, 299.

109 Even some reports critical of the current state of legal education, like the Best Practices Report, speak almost nostalgically about articles and apprenticeships. See Best Practices Report, p. 25.

110 The term 'andragogy' refers to the education of adults, while the term 'pedagogy' refers to the education of children. As described by Malcolm Knowles, ' "Pedagogy" is derived from the Greek words *paid*, meaning "child" (the same stem from which "pediatrics" comes) and *agogus*, meaning "leader of".' M.S. Knowles, E.F. Holton III and R.A. Swanson, *The Adult Learner*, 6th edn, New York: Butterworth-Heinemann, 2005, p. 36. Pedagogy therefore literally means 'the art and science of teaching children' (p. 36). As described by Knowles, 'adults have by and large been taught as if they were children until fairly recently' (p. 61). Of course, it may turn out that the pedagogical approach to teaching and learning is as corrupt for children as it has proven to be for adults. For a discussion of the application of andragogical principles in the context of legal education, see F. Bloch, 'The andragogical basis of clinical legal education', *Vanderbilt Law Review* 35, 1982, 321.

111 Sullivan et al., *Educating Lawyers*, p. 129. The report referenced the following language in the Preamble to the American Bar Association's *Model Rules of Professional Conduct*: 'A lawyer, as a member of the legal profession, is a representative of clients, an officer of the legal system and a public citizen having special responsibility for the quality of justice' (p. 29).

112 ibid., p. 194.

113 When asked by the authors of the Carnegie Foundation Report how they could afford to provide a context-based small-class environment for first-year classes 'when their more affluent competitor institutions obviously seek the economy of scale afforded by large first-year classes, CUNY administrators answered: "We cannot afford not to do it" ', ibid., p. 36.

5 Developing professional judgment: law school innovations in response to the Carnegie Foundation's critique of American legal education*

*Clark D. Cunningham and
Charlotte Alexander*

5.1 Introduction

On 29 June 2006, the US Supreme Court issued one of its most important decisions of the past decade in the case of *Hamdan v Rumsfeld*,[1] holding that detainees at the Guantanamo Bay military prison were entitled to the protections of the Geneva Conventions. The successful plaintiff, Salim Ahmed Hamdan, is most frequently identified as the personal driver for Osama Bin Laden prior to the events of 11 September 2001. That case would never have reached the Supreme Court but for the exemplary professional judgment exercised by Lieutenant Commander Charles Swift, the military lawyer assigned to Hamdan at the prison at Guantanamo Bay, who defied the terms of his appointment – which was limited for the purpose of negotiating a guilty plea. Here is Swift's explanation, given to an interviewer for National Public Radio, for why he acted as he did:

Swift:	I was surprised when the letter conditioned my access to Mr. Hamdan on a guilty plea . . . [T]he letter made quite plain that you would see the prosecutor to get access, and that if for some reason you were unable to negotiate a guilty plea, [then] that access could be cut off.
Interviewer:	And at that point, once you've read this letter, are you allowed to say hey wait a minute, this is not what I learned in law school . . .?
Swift:	You know, that's exactly what I thought about . . . This is not how I view myself as an independent lawyer when I represent an individual; and I'm being asked to represent him, not the government . . .
Interviewer:	Let me ask you Commander Swift, when you decided to file the lawsuit [that led to the Supreme Court decision] . . . did you think, oh boy, this might be a career killer?
Swift:	. . . I didn't think about it in those terms. I thought about it as this is the ethical way that I can do my job.[2]

A year later, in 2007, the highly regarded Carnegie Foundation for the Advancement of Teaching issued a book-length report on American legal education, *Educating Lawyers: Preparation for the Profession of Law* (the Carnegie Report). The central message of the report is that law schools should, and can, do much more to produce lawyers who will exercise the type of professional judgment exemplified by Lt Commamder Swift, who readily identified a moral dilemma that implicated his professional ethics, reasoned through conflicting values to choose a course of action, committed himself to that action as 'the ethical way to do my job' despite risk to his career, and then effectively implemented the decision.

This chapter first summarizes the Carnegie Report, its call for reform in American legal education and its focus on the development of professional judgment. It then discusses concepts from the field of moral psychology that have been used in other American professional schools to assess how schools teach and students learn professional judgment, and applies those concepts to the report's critique of the conventional US approach to teaching legal ethics. The chapter concludes by highlighting innovative approaches to teaching ethics and professionalism that three American law schools have implemented since the Carnegie Report, and analyses them using these concepts from moral psychology.

5.2 The Carnegie Report's focus on the development of professional judgment

The Carnegie Foundation for the Advancement of Teaching was founded in 1905 by the philanthropist Andrew Carnegie. Over the past century, it has prompted many important changes in higher education. The Foundation's 1910 critique of medical education, known as the Flexner Report, is widely credited for establishing the standards for modern medical education.[3] Since 2004, a major initiative of the Foundation has been the Preparation for the Professions Program, which has overseen a series of multi-year comparative studies of the education of clergy, engineers, lawyers, doctors and nurses.[4]

There have been a number of critiques of American legal education that both laid a foundation for the Carnegie Report and foreshadowed many of its conclusions, but all were from within the legal academy or the profession; the Carnegie Report, in contrast, offers an independent, external perspective. One of the co-authors is a distinguished legal educator, but the other four come from other disciplines. Three are social scientists, including the Carnegie Foundation's president at that time, and the other is a moral philosopher. Their methodology was to focus on how teaching and learning really happens through classroom observations and interviews with teachers and students at 16 law schools. As the authors explain:

> We adopted an unusual angle of vision . . . by focusing on the daily practices of teaching and learning . . . We compared these practices with those in other professions . . . [and] also looked at them through the lens of contemporary understanding of how learning occurs.[5]

The report begins with the observation that the modern American law school is heir to 'a history of unfortunate misunderstandings and even conflict between defenders of theoretical legal learning and champions of a legal education that includes introduction to the practice of law'.[6] Probably the signal contribution of the report is the way it draws upon comparative study of other forms of professional education and upon recent social science research to propose 'hope for healing [these] old rifts'.[7] And the keystone of the bridge it would build between these opposing views of legal education is a revitalized approach to teaching legal ethics.

The Carnegie Foundation's extensive comparative study of various professions leads the authors of the report to an understanding of 'professional practice as judgment in action':[8]

> Skillful practice, whether of a surgeon, a judge, a teacher, a legal counselor, or a nurse, means involvement in situations that are necessarily indeterminate from the point of view of formal knowledge. Professional practice . . . [therefore] depends on judgment in order to yield an outcome that can further the profession's intended purposes . . . The mark of professional expertise is the ability to both act and think well in uncertain situations.[9]

Research in the social sciences has helped identify the components that comprise professional judgment and demonstrates that it is possible to promote the development of such judgment through university-based professional education.

By focusing on the development of professional judgment, the report is able to insist that knowledge, skill and ethics – and the teaching of them – are inseparable. 'In practice, knowledge, skill, and ethical comportment[s] are literally interdependent: a practitioner cannot employ one without involving the others at the same time.'[10] Thus, 'the goal of professional education cannot be analytic knowledge alone or, perhaps, even predominantly. Neither can it be analytic knowledge plus merely skillful performance.'[11]

The report concludes that 'this is a propitious moment for uniting, in a single educational framework, the two sides of legal knowledge: (1) formal knowledge and (2) the experience of practice.'[12] This new approach to legal education would 'combine . . . conceptual knowledge, skill, and moral discernment . . . into the capacity for judgment guided by a sense of professional responsibility'.[13] The authors of the report 'believe that if legal education had as its focus forming legal professionals who are both competent and responsible to clients and the public, learning legal analysis and practical skills would [*both*] be more fully significant to both the students and faculty'.[14]

5.2.1 *Moral psychology applied to professional education*

The Carnegie Report's focus on the development of professional judgment draws on insights from the field of moral psychology into how students learn and how schools teach ethical decision-making. These insights, which have been applied in other professional schools, provide a useful framework for understanding the development of professional judgment and assessing law schools' innovations in response to the Carnegie Report.

Moral psychology's inquiry into ethical and moral decision-making began with Lawrence Kohlberg's hypothesis that there are stages of development of moral judgment over the course of an individual's lifespan.[15] Subsequently, James Rest built on Kohlberg's work in several important ways. First, he created an easily administered assessment instrument, the Defining Issues Test (DIT), which presents ethical dilemmas and then measures the proportion of times an individual selects arguments to resolve the dilemma that appeal to each of three conceptually different moral frameworks.[16] The DIT has been extensively validated, including studies showing links between high DIT scores and actual behaviour such as clinical performance in nursing, medicine and dentistry;[17] likelihood of fraud detection by auditors;[18] and willingness to inform superiors or law enforcement of wrong-doing.[19] Low DIT scores have been shown to correlate with disciplinary action in dentistry,[20] and both disciplinary action and malpractice claims in medicine.[21]

The moral reasoning measured by the DIT is not, however, a conclusive determinant of actual behaviour. Rest therefore articulated what is known as the Four Component Model for explaining how cognition, affect and social dynamics interact to influence moral behaviour.[22] He began by identifying four different possible reasons for moral failure:

1   missing the moral issue;
2   defective moral reasoning;
3   insufficient moral motivation; and
4   ineffective implementation.

He then defined four corresponding capacities for moral action, each of which is necessary, but none by itself sufficient:

1   moral sensitivity that can interpret the need for a moral decision;
2   clear ethical reasoning that can reach a morally defensible decision;
3   identity-formation that will support the prioritization of the moral decision over competing interests; and
4   competence to implement the moral decision.

The Carnegie Report's call for development of law students' professional judgment echoes Rest's first three capacities for moral action:

> Law school graduates . . . need the capacity to recognize the ethical questions their cases raise, even when those questions are obscured by other issues and therefore not particularly salient [Rest's first capacity]. They need wise judgment when values conflict [Rest's second capacity], as well as the

integrity to keep self-interest from clouding their judgment [Rest's third capacity].[23]

Dr Muriel Bebeau, a colleague of Rest, has developed a number of practical applications of Rest's Four Component Model for professional education. In fact, we have found that becoming familiar with Bebeau's work has greatly enhanced our understanding of both the critiques and the recommendations found in the Carnegie Report. Accordingly, in the balance of this chapter we will be using Rest's Four Component Model as applied by Bebeau to explicate the report's critique of the conventional American approach to teaching legal ethics and to analyse American innovations in teaching professional judgment now being implemented in the wake of the report.

Bebeau's work indicates that a well-designed curriculum can promote each of the four capacities in ways that are connected to professional behaviour. Such educational programmes:

1   create sensitivity to ethical issues likely to arise in practice;
2   build the capacity for reasoning carefully about conflicts inherent in practice;
3   establish a sense of personal identity that incorporates professional norms and values; and
4   develop competence in problem-solving, including necessary interpersonal skills.

Some of the best evidence that these capacities can be effectively taught is found in the ethics curriculum developed by Bebeau at the University of Minnesota School of Dentistry in 1985 and widely adapted throughout American dental education.[24] Bebeau's work confirms that the capacity to identify issues that require professional judgment requires much more than just a mastery of professional conduct rules (although such knowledge is, of course, necessary). Equally critical is the ability to engage imaginatively as a situation unfolds, constructing various possible scenarios – often with limited cues and partial information – combined with the ability to foresee realistic cause–consequence chains of events.[25] Empathy and role-taking skills are often required, involving both cognitive and affective processes. Therefore, both teaching and assessment strategies must avoid reliance on what Bebeau calls 'predigested' or already interpreted fact scenarios (of which the appellate cases used for conventional classes in American law schools are a prime example).[26] Significant increases in students' scores on a dental ethical sensitivity test (similar to the DIT) provided evidence that profession-based ethical sensitivity – Rest's first capacity for moral action – can be enhanced through instruction along the lines of Bebeau's model.[27]

Bebeau's research also provides evidence that ethical sensitivity – the first capacity – is distinct from the second capacity, moral reasoning. Research has shown a great deal of variability among professional students in their ability to reason about moral issues, regardless of their level of ethical sensitivity.[28] In 33 studies of the effects of professional education, none showed significant increases in DIT scores without a carefully validated ethics curriculum.[29] However, significantly increased DIT scores are produced by the use of small-group dilemma discussions that require students to present criteria for well-reasoned arguments, exercising Rest's second capacity, moral reasoning.[30]

There is ample evidence that professionals are sometimes aware of the ethical implications of a situation, yet either fail to act or act in ways inconsistent with that awareness – evidencing a deficiency in Rest's third moral capacity, prioritizing the ethical decision over other interests.[31] Research in moral psychology suggests that, for professionals, the key to the development of this third capacity is identity-formation. Research indicates that differing levels of professional identity-formation can be distinguished. Studies of professionals identified by their peers as moral exemplars reveal a common theme: these exemplars feel that actions that prioritize the needs of clients and society over the self are obligatory rather optional because of the unity of their sense of self with the profession's moral values.[32] Research has also shown that, although a professional's moral identity-formation can be facilitated during professional school, students do not internalize the norms of a profession from an educational environment simply by osmosis. Deliberate teaching about professional norms is required, combined with examples of exemplary professionals and a system to promote student self-reflection about their own professional identity-formation over the course of their education.[33]

Although the ability to identify ethical issues (the first capacity), to reason to the contextually appropriate decision in the face of conflicting values (the second capacity) and to internalize professional identity to motivate moral commitment (the third capacity) are all necessary to the exercise of professional judgment, actual and effective implementation – the fourth capacity – is also required. Bebeau points out that the professional cannot stop with 'what is happening' (the first capacity) and 'what ought to be done' (the second capacity), but must always consider questions such as 'what should I say' and 'how should I say it?' Therefore, the teaching strategies developed by Bebeau for addressing the fourth capacity, implementation, require students to develop action plans and even specific dialogue for resolving tough problems.[34]

5.3 Illustrating Rest's model of moral behaviour with the story of Charles Swift

The unscripted reflections in the National Public Radio interview of Lt Commander Charles Swift on his representation of Hamdan illustrate vividly the interconnected dynamics of Rest's four capacities of ethical sensitivity, moral reasoning, professional identity and effective implementation. The transcript excerpt that begins this chapter illustrates how Swift's ethical sensitivity was immediately alerted when he learned of the unusual conditions of his appointment. Swift also realized that difficult moral reasoning was required: 'I asked myself some very hard ethical questions. And I came back with the answer that (a) maybe he wants to plead guilty, and I don't know; and (b) . . . if I can offer him another choice, if there's something else other than plead guilty . . . then I see that I can do this ethically.'[35]

Swift could have followed orders, ignoring the insights of his ethical sensitivity and moral reasoning, or could have declined to represent Hamdan at all, passing the dilemma on to the next military lawyer assigned to Hamdan. Instead, Swift's internalized professional identity powerfully motivated him to act on the results of his moral reasoning. When Swift tells the interviewer that he did not think about the consequences to his career but rather that 'this is the ethical way that I can do my job', the interviewer seems almost startled as he echoes back Swift's words:

Interviewer: Ethical way you can do your job?
Swift: Exactly. I mean, I couldn't sit down there – as a defense attorney, if I'd been assigned to zealously represent somebody, if I was going to be their defense counsel, I couldn't be there to force a man to plead guilty when he didn't want to plead guilty . . . [F]ollowing an order that you believe to be absolutely unconstitutional without challenging it when you're in a position to do so, I saw as simply wrong. This was the ethical way to carry out my duties.[36]

To implement his professional judgment, Swift not only needed to develop a litigation strategy that could address the extraordinary constraints of his client's detention at Guantanamo Bay but, even perhaps more challenging, he needed superb client relationship skills in order to gain the trust of his client:

And so when I went down to meet with Hamdan, I went down and said . . . they would like you to plead guilty. They haven't said to what, and they haven't said what kind of time you'd do. And they have said they can keep you after you plead guilty and that you by no means would ever be released. But I can offer you an alternative, and that is to sue in federal court. And I explained why I thought the law of war, the Constitution and other law applied here, and his answer to me was that the guard said there was no law in Guantanamo. It didn't exist. And I said to him, you know, I don't believe that, but perhaps . . . we're going to have to go the United States Supreme Court and win that. And you know, he ultimately agreed to that level of representation, and that began a three-year odyssey that got us to the Supreme Court, where we won.[37]

5.4 The Carnegie critique and Rest's model of moral behaviour

Before the Carnegie Report, the typical approach to ethics and professionalism by US law schools was to require students to take a single course on 'professional responsibility' that covered the American Bar Association's Model Rules of Professional Conduct.[38] At many law schools, this was the only required course after the first year. The report describes this typical ethics course as teaching 'the law of lawyering':[39]

> [S]tudents learn the profession's ethical code as represented in the [ABA] Model Rules, how those rules have been interpreted and applied, and the circumstances under which sanctions have been imposed . . . Often these courses are structured around legal cases that concern alleged violations of the Model Rules. Students apply their analytical skills to these cases, approaching them in much the same way they have learned to approach challenging legal cases in torts or contracts.[40]

Although courses on the law of lawyering might seem adequate to teach the students sensitivity to ethical issues (the first capacity for moral action in Rest's model), the report echoes Bebeau's view that ethical sensitivity cannot effectively be taught using only 'pre-interpreted' factual scenarios such as presented in decided cases:

> [Teaching ethics through the law of lawyering] misses an important dimension of ethical development – the capacity and inclination to notice moral issues when they are embedded in complex and ambiguous situations, as they usually are in actual legal practice.[41]

The report raises an even more serious concern that the 'law of lawyering' approach may actually be counter-productive to the formation of the capacity for ethical sensitivity required for professional judgment:

> When legal ethics courses focus exclusively on teaching students what a lawyer can and cannot get away with, they inadvertently convey a sense that knowing this is all there is to ethics . . . [Thus by] defining 'legal ethics' as narrowly as most legal ethics courses do, these courses are likely to limit the scope of what graduates perceive to be ethical issues.[42]

The conventional 'law of lawyering' course also failed to engage with the second capacity: moral reasoning. The report cites several studies showing that students who completed a traditional ethics course did not show significantly more sophisticated moral reasoning, as measured by DIT scores, at the end of the course than at the beginning. The most thorough of these studies, however, indicates that a law school course built around small-group discussions of realistic ethical dilemmas that cannot be resolved by legalistic application of the Model Rules *can* produce very significant increases in DIT scores.[43] The report thus concludes that 'research makes quite clear that higher education can promote the development of more mature moral thinking', and that specially designed courses on professional responsibility and legal ethics do support that development. However, for most students traditional legal ethics courses did not contribute to greater development of moral reasoning.[44]

The report concludes its critique of American law schools' traditional Model Rules-based ethics courses with a focus on the third and fourth capacities required for moral action: formation of professional identity and competence to implement a moral decision. Once again, the authors summarize what has been learned in other professions and from the social sciences to set an aspirational standard for legal education:

> [W]hat kinds of pedagogies and assessment procedures are effective in developing professional dispositions and good judgment [?] . . . [C]ritical analysis of students' own experience in both simulated and actual situations of practice, including expert feedback, is a pedagogical process with enormous power . . . [C]ross-professional comparison indicates that, although difficult, it is not impossible to systematically provide feedback to students about both their understanding of and performance with regard to the ethical norms of the profession. The analogous clinical training in the health professions and for the clergy offers useful models . . . The key components are close working relationships between students and faculty, opportunity to take responsibility for professional interventions and outcomes, and timely feedback. Unless law schools can provide the proper opportunities, however, little such formation is likely to occur.[45]

Unfortunately, the conventional legal ethics course, by focusing on whether conduct could result in discipline or civil liability, unintentionally appeals primarily to narrow self-interest – the desire to avoid punishment – rather than encouraging development of a mature professional identity in which lawyers feel they must act consistently with sound professional judgment because their professional and personal identities have become intertwined.

In addressing Rest's fourth capacity, effective implementation, the report provides this concise paraphrase: 'the "bottom line" [is] . . . not . . . what [students] know but what they can do. They must come to understand thoroughly so they can act competently, and they must act competently in order to serve responsibly.'[46] Students in the traditional legal ethics course take the role of observer rather than actor. According to the report, to build the fourth capacity, teaching and assessment must instead 'take place in role rather than in the more detached mode that the law-of-lawyering courses typically foster'.[47]

For the authors of the report, the development of the professional judgment required of all lawyers cannot be left to a single course, but should be the motivating goal of the entire three-year curriculum that allows development of all four of Rest's capacities for moral action:

> The framework we propose seeks to mediate between the claims for legal theory and the need of practice, in order to do justice to the importance of both while responding to the demands of professional responsibility . . . [The process of developing both theoretical and practical knowledge in a mutual relationship] will progress best when it is directed by a focus on the

professional formation of law students . . . In short, we propose an integration of student learning of theoretical and practical legal knowledge and professional identity.[48]

The report suggests that such an integrated programme of legal education could begin in the first phase with 'well-designed lawyering courses . . . taught as intentional complements to doctrinal instruction'. Then 'this experience of complementarity would continue in the second and third years as a gradual development of practice knowledge and skill, beginning in simulation and moving into actual responsibility for clients'.[49] Put another way, a reformed law school curriculum would require students to spot issues and develop ethical sensitivity; would then require them to engage in moral reasoning, in role; and finally would require them to take on the professional identity of attorney and implement their moral judgment in the carefully supervised representation of actual clients.

5.5 Innovations in American legal education after the Carnegie Report

In December 2007, nine months after publication of the Carnegie Report, '[b]elieving that this is a critical moment for the future of legal education', deans and faculty representatives from 10 American law schools gathered in Palo Alto, California for a meeting convened by the lead author of the report, William Sullivan, and Associate Dean Lawrence Marshall of Stanford Law School.[50] Out of that meeting, three working groups were formed. Eighteen months later, in March 2009, this consortium of law schools – now named the Legal Education Analysis and Reform Network (LEARN)[51] – announced a detailed programme of action intended to 'maintain and enhance the momentum for law schools across the country' to create a 'wider array of learning environments', including simulations and clinical work, and to further integrate the teaching of substantive knowledge, legal skills and professional values.[52] Noting that 2010 is the 100th anniversary of the Carnegie Foundation's Flexner Report, which helped transform medical education, the LEARN group concluded that 'now, one century later, again with the involvement of the Carnegie Foundation for the Advancement of Teaching, we have a spectacular opportunity to effect dramatic and much-needed changes in legal education'.[53]

5.5.1 Clinical education at Stanford Law School

At the time of the LEARN meeting, Stanford, under the leadership of Dean Larry Kramer, was in the midst of a major reshaping of its upper level curriculum with a strong focus on expanding and deepening clinical teaching.[54] In a 2006 press release describing the new approach as the '3DJD', Dean Kramer had said:

Talk to any lawyer or law school graduate and they will tell you they were increasingly disengaged in their second and third years. It's because the second and third year curriculum is for the most part repeating what they did in their first year and adds little of intellectual and professional value. They learn more doctrine, which is certainly valuable, but in a way that is inefficient and progressively less useful.[55]

Stanford has not only added two new clinics and created a dean-level position for 'Public Interest and Clinical Education', but has developed a 'clinical rotation' where students take only a clinic during a particular term – with no competing exams or classes. This innovation is intended to 'mirror the way that medical students have been trained as doctors for the past century [and] deliver a much more intensive experience, including a better professional ethics component . . .'.[56]

It is significant that Stanford has chosen to justify its new clinical rotation as modelling medical education in providing a more 'intensive' experience that provides 'a better professional ethics component' than those currently offered by most American law schools. The Carnegie Report also emphasizes the value of clinical education, not merely in terms of skills development, but in the formation of professional identity, and does so by reference to medical education: '[where] beyond the inculcation of knowledge and the simulation of skills, it proves to be the assumption of responsibility for patient outcomes that enables the student for the first time to fully enter and grasp the disposition of a physician'.[57] The report views such guided 'real world' experience as providing genuine content to hortatory lessons about professional purpose, fuelling the motivation to give greater priority to the client than one's own self and forcing students to reflect on their own identity as lawyers:

> Compassion and concern about injustice become much more intense when students develop personal connections with those who have experienced hardship or injustice. This has been a persistent theme among students in some of the clinical courses we observed.[58]

Well-taught, intensive clinical experiences are designed not only to promote the third ethical capacity of Rest's model – moral commitment – in ways and to a degree not found elsewhere in the law school curriculum; but, as pointed out by the report, they can also develop the critical fourth capacity – moral implementation. 'It is in these situations of intensive analysis of practice that the fundamental norms and expectations that make up professional expertise are taught. They are reinforced by the feedback that students receive as they attempt various approximations to expert practice.'[59]

The effectiveness of traditional law school clinics has been questioned, though, as to the development of ethical sensitivity:

> A problem with the clinical setting for addressing ethical and moral issues . . . is that the primary focus of clinic activity is solving the client's legal problems rather than examining ethical questions. Students often miss these questions

in the hurly-burly of drafting a complaint or getting ready for a hearing. Ethical issues in the clinic setting arise haphazardly and cannot be anticipated, so the clinic course cannot be relied upon to raise specific ethical questions.[60]

Stanford's new clinic initiative offers an unusual solution to this critique by offering a parallel course on ethics and professional responsibility exclusively for students enrolled in nine of the law school's clinics. These students act as the clinics' collective ethics committee – much in the same way that many law firms have an ethics committee to resolve issues referred by members of the firm. Each week, the course's teacher, Associate Dean Lawrence Marshall – who is also the co-convenor of the LEARN consortium – presents a real ethical issue that has arisen in the clinics. Students must work through the issue, applying the rules of professional conduct when appropriate, and come to an actual decision, which the clinics then implement. When a useful ethical problem has not arisen during a particular week, the students tackle an ongoing policy question facing the clinics – concerning the clinics' conflict-of-interest rules or intake guidelines, for example. Because Marshall draws on a pool of nine clinics for real-life ethical dilemmas, and because he has prepared a set of policy issues as fallbacks, the course exposes students to a broad range of ethical questions, not limited by the haphazard nature of clinical practice, and provides structured guidance for students as they reason to a moral conclusion.

To the extent that Marshall is not also directly supervising the clinical case under discussion, his separate role also addresses a concern that the clinical setting may not promote moral reasoning, Rest's second component. Steven Hartwell, who is both an experienced clinical teacher and one of the few US law professors to apply principles of moral psychology to teaching ethics,[61] has pointed out the danger of the 'persuasion mode' of instruction in clinics, in which the clinical supervisor 'attempt[s] to convince [his or her] students' to take the course that the instructor deems ethical, rather than guiding the students through their own process of moral reasoning.[62] Marshall's separation from the role of supervisor, and explicit responsibility for promoting class deliberation over difficult issues, creates superb opportunities for blending moral reasoning with issues of professional identity and effective implementation.[63]

A number of other US law schools are experimenting with ways to integrate the teaching of professional judgment with real-life educational experiences. One such experiment is described in Chapter 4 of this book by David Chavkin – an experienced clinical teacher at American University's Washington College of Law. Rather than add a legal ethics class to accompany one or more existing clinical courses, Chavkin has expanded his professional responsibility course by one credit hour to add a modest client representation component in which students provide assistance in drafting wills and advance directives regarding end-of-life medical treatments.[64] At Mercer University's law school, an upper-level externship course has been restructured to make 'formation of professional identity the primary educational goal through readings, reflections, discussions, and exercises'.[65] A new law school at the University of St Thomas in Minneapolis has developed a very ambitious programme in which every student is required to participate in a Mentorship Externship Program, involving more than 550 lawyers and programmes, which is also specifically focused on professional identity-formation.[66]

5.5.2 Legal ethics in the first year at Indiana University School of Law

At the November 2007 meeting that founded the LEARN Consortium, the law school at Indiana University (Bloomington) announced that, effective from the 2008–09 academic year, it would move the required legal ethics course into the core first-year curriculum with the same four credit hours as such venerable subjects as Torts, Contracts and Property. In making this significant change to the almost canonical first year of US legal education, the Indiana faculty wanted to 'send a clear and unambiguous signal . . . that the ethical practice of law is a foundational value that will affect [students'] long-term job satisfaction, reputation, and career advancement . . . instill a deep appreciation for ethics and professional values, and equip our students with the perspective and judgment to eventually become leaders in the profession'.[67] The faculty also hoped that their innovative course 'could become the gold-standard through[out] the legal academy'.[68] The Carnegie Report's critique of conventional teaching of legal ethics was explicitly cited as a justification for this innovation.

At least 50 per cent of the curricular content of this new first-year course goes beyond doctrinal analysis of legal ethics,[69] focusing primarily on precisely those pedagogic strategies identified by Bebeau for developing professional identity-formation: deliberate teaching about professional norms, examples of exemplary professionals and a system to promote student self-reflection about their own identity-formation. Building on Indiana's strong tradition in social science approaches to the study of law, the course begins with 'an accurate, systematic, and factually rich introduction to the structure and substance of the modern legal profession.'[70] Distinctive to this overview of the legal profession is careful analysis of a variety of specific practice settings – for example, family law, criminal defence, personal injury, large law firm, in-house counsel, prosecution, public interest – using carefully edited ethnographies, with an exploration of 'the ethical problems that can predominate in each form of practice'.[71] Woven into this review and analysis of specific practice settings is exposure to theories of professionalization, as well as a comparative study of the legal profession in other countries.[72]

Each student is assigned to a 'Practice Group', a unit of six or seven students who are assigned to several group projects during the course of the semester, which culminate in formal presentations to the entire class.[73] Indiana reports that it designed these complex group projects in consultation with experts at the Carnegie Foundation in particular to teach 'professionalism'.[74] The course website informs students that, although 'careful, precise legal analysis is an important element of effective lawyering ... success as a lawyer – or more broadly, as a professional – also requires a wider array of abilities and perspectives'.[75] The website continues: 'Virtually every law firm partner, government agency supervisor, public interest lawyer, or corporate general counsel can recount examples of lawyers who, despite stellar "law review" credentials, failed to progress professionally and eventually left the organization. Conversely, when lawyers reflect upon truly great lawyers who have influenced their careers, descriptions often encompass traits such as character, integrity, diligence, discretion, kindness, judgment, wit, communication, empathy, and creativity.'[76]

The first project requires each group to distill from a series of readings up to three attributes of a successful young lawyer, and to propose ways that those attributes could be acquired or fostered during law school. The pedagogical method not only requires students to talk about such traits as diligence, communication and creativity, but to put them into practice through the group dynamics of the activity. Each student is required to reflect critically about both the student's own role within the group and the performance of other group members. In particular, students must discuss noteworthy contributions of individual group members that contributed to the success of the group, such as 'displays of . . . humility, intellectual courage ... empathy ... perseverance ... and fair-mindedness'.[77]

A variety of different topics is assigned for the second and third group projects. Common to all third group projects is the presentation of a detailed hypothetical problem that requires students to identify ethical issues and propose an appropriate course of action; all of these projects are 'imbedded in a practice environment that students have just learned about'.[78] As discussed above, such small-group discussion of moral dilemmas that go beyond legalistic application of the 'law of lawyering' have been shown to develop moral reasoning, as measured by DIT scores, whereas other pedagogical methods – including conventional legal ethics courses – have no measurable effect.[79]

The final group project involves interviewing a practising lawyer and preparing a group report to the class on that lawyer's professional development and experience in handling challenging problems of professional judgment. These interviews are then reinforced by 'Practice Forums', in which lawyers who represent the various practice areas studied in the course appear as guest speakers to the entire class.

In the academic year following the introduction of Indiana's first-year course, two other American law schools added required courses on the legal profession to their first-year curriculum. The new law school at the University of California at Irvine – intended to be 'the first top-tier American law school founded in more than 50 years'[80] – requires all first-year students to take two credits of 'Legal Profession' in both the first and second semesters. This course, like the class at Indiana, not only teaches legal ethics but also provides instruction on the economics and sociology of the legal profession.[81] The law school at the University of Minnesota has added a required course on 'Practice and Professionalism' to the second semester of the first year, but the course differs from both the courses at

Indiana and Irvine in that it does not take the place of an upper-level required course in legal ethics and incorporates a number of simulation exercises.[82]

Also noteworthy is the first-year course on the legal profession added to the required curriculum at the Mercer Law School in 2004; this three-credit course, which does not replace the upper level course in legal ethics, is designed to enable to students to learn: (1) a vocabulary and structure for understanding 'what professionalism means for lawyers'; (2) about the pressures that lead lawyers to engage in unprofessional conduct; (3) how expectations of professionalism are promoted and enforced; and (4) the connection between professionalism and students' own personal sense of fulfilment.[83]

5.5.3 The experiential third year at Washington and Lee School of Law

Probably the most ambitious educational innovation that has been implemented in the United States since the publication of the Carnegie Report is taking place at a law school that is not a member of the LEARN consortium. In March 2008, the Washington and Lee University School of Law – more than 150 years old and ranked by *US News & World Report* among the top 30 law schools in the United States – announced that it was 'embarking on a dramatic revision of its law school curriculum, entirely reinventing the third year to make it a year of professional development through simulated and actual practice experiences'.[84] In that announcement, Dean Rodney Smolla described the new third-year curriculum as 'a creative blend of intellectually rigorous study of legal theory and doctrine . . . with the development of professional identity, ethical sensibilities, problem-solving, and the exercise of judgment in action'. He also explicitly invoked the Carnegie Report as 'forcefully explain[ing]' that the traditional American legal education provides 'an incomplete vision of what it should need to prepare a lawyer for the profession'. When later interviewed by the American Bar Association in September 2009, Smolla provided the following explanation for this initiative:

> We thought we were superb at teaching students to think like lawyers. But to be like lawyers? We were only scratching the surface. Extremely bright students had very little sense of the complexities of client counseling, of working with opposing counsel – and they had no sense of judgment.[85]

In an article he authored for *Legal Times*, when Smolla described the 'core intellectual experiences in the third-year', the first attribute he ascribed to the new curriculum was that it 'will require students to exercise professional judgment'.[86]

The new third year consists of two 12-week semesters consisting of 14 credit hours each. Each semester begins with a two-credit course that takes up the entire first two weeks, immersing students in practice-intensive training in both transactional and dispute-resolution skills. The remaining 10 weeks of each semester consist of two five-credit experiential courses – practicums, clinics or externships – plus one credit for a professionalism programme that extends over both semesters (for a total of two credits) and one credit for 'law-related service' such as working on student-edited law reviews, moot court, community service or pro bono representation.

Although students will have already taken a course in professional responsibility during their second year, the third-year professionalism programme (currently taught by Dean Smolla) continues to 'develop ethical judgment in context and in action' by presenting students 'with simulated practice conundrums in which ethical judgment must be exercised in simulated, real-world environments'.[87] The professionalism programme also seeks to promote the development of professional identity 'beyond mere adherence to disciplinary ethics rules' and to address the challenges that 'arise in managing one's life as a lawyer'.[88]

Washington and Lee's catalogue lists three ten-credit, year-long clinics and one five-credit clinic that could be taken for either one or both semesters, as well as one ten-credit, year-long externship and four one-semester five-credit externships. (Thus, like Stanford, Washington and Lee is creating a number of more intensive clinic experiences than typically found at an American law school.) Although some students may spend the majority of their third year in a combination of clinic and externship, it appears that for most students the heart of the third-year experience will consist of taking a number of the 23 practicums listed in the 2009–10 law catalogue. Announcing the new programme, Washington and Lee insisted that any course subject typically taken in the third year of a traditional law school curriculum could be offered 'through a practicum course with no fall off in breadth of coverage or intellectual depth or rigor'.[89] Indeed, 19 of the practicums listed in the catalogue appear to correspond with traditional subject-matter topics.[90]

Nonetheless, the school appears to be making a serious effort to teach both practical skills and professional judgment while also providing subject-matter coverage.[91] The advanced family law practicum, for example, is described as involving seven different simulated lawyering activities,[92] and thus in the process 'emphasizes the art of lawyering . . . and explore[s] the roles and relationships between attorneys and clients – and between attorneys, senior partners, judges, and opposing counsel'. The course description further states that students 'will consider the potential effects of . . . ethical rules' and will specifically consider 'how ethical doctrines like confidentiality may constrain their choices in representing a client'. By embedding ethical issues in realistic and complex fact patterns, set in a variety of subject-matter courses, these practicums offer great potential for developing sophisticated ethical sensitivity, described by Bebeau as 'the ability to engage imaginatively as a situation unfolds, constructing various possible scenarios, often with limited cues and partial information, combined with the ability to foresee realistic cause-consequence chains of events'.[93]

In addition to the 19 'subject-matter' practicums, the catalogue also identifies four one-semester, five-credit courses in 'transnational' human rights that combine elements of practicums, externships and clinics. For example, students in the Transnational Access to Justice course will partner with a law school in Liberia, including two weeks spent in that country, working on access to legal aid in the criminal justice system. Students in the European Court of Human Rights course will work with a law school in Serbia, representing disadvantaged persons there, and will travel to Belgrade and the Court of Human Rights in Strasbourg as part of the course. These courses, along with the more traditional clinics and externships in the third-year curriculum, can provide important experience in implementing professional judgment and in development of moral commitment.[94]

Enthusiasm for the new programme among current students is high. Even though the new third-year programme is not scheduled to become mandatory for all students until the 2010–11 academic year, as early as the 2009–10 academic year two-thirds of the students had voluntarily chosen the new curriculum.[95] The innovation also apparently appeals to prospective students. Applications to the law school are up by 33 per cent, a 'remarkable' increase that Dean Smolla attributes entirely to the new third-year curriculum.[96]

5.6 Conclusion

In 1905, the famous Boston lawyer Louis Brandeis – later to become one of the most distinguished justices of the US Supreme Court – was asked to address the Harvard Ethics Society on the topic 'The Opportunity in the Law'. He told his audience that although the 'ordinary man thinks of the Bar as a body of men who are trying cases . . . by far the greater part of the work done by lawyers is done not in court, but in advising men on important matters'.[97] Therefore, the 'whole training of the lawyer leads to the development of judgment'.[98] However, as Karl Llewellyn – one of the greatest of America's law teachers – told a group of beginning law students several decades later, the first year of law school has the effect of knocking 'your ethics into temporary anesthesia'.[99] Llewellyn then said, with fine irony: 'It is not easy thus to turn human beings into lawyers. Neither is it safe. For a mere legal machine is a social danger. Indeed, a mere legal machine is not even a good lawyer. It lacks insight and judgment.'[100] Llewellyn promised those students that, in the subsequent years of law school, their teachers 'shall then duly endeavor' to restore the capacity for ethical judgment that had been anaesthetised in the first year.[101]

The Carnegie Report powerfully makes the case that Llewellyn's promise to develop the judgment that Brandeis considered to be 'the whole training of the lawyer' has not been fulfilled in contemporary American legal education. But the serious reception the report has received among legal educators, and the concrete innovations already taking place in response to its critique, give hope that the vision of Brandeis and the promise of Llewellyn may both begin to be more fully realized as the twenty-first century enters its second decade.

Notes

  * Many of the references cited herein can be downloaded from the website of the International Forum on Teaching Ethics & Professionalism at www.

teachinglegalethics.org/. The authors thank those who have reviewed and commented on earlier drafts, including Muriel Bebeau, Anne Colby, William Henderson, Lawrence Marshall, Rodney Smella and William Sullivan.

 1 *Hamdan v Rumsfeld*, 548 US 557 (2006).
 2 National Public Radio, 'Navy Lawyer Discusses Hamdan, Guantanamo', *Talk of the Nation*, 15 February 2007. See www.npr.org/templates/transcript/transcript.php?storyId'7422513 (accessed 22 January 2010).
 3 A. Flexner, *Medical Education in the United States and Canada*, New York: Carnegie Foundation for the Advancement of Teaching, 1910.
 4 Carnegie Foundation for the Advancement of Teaching, Preparation for the Professions Program, 2009. See www.carnegiefoundation.org/programs/sub.asp?key'30 (accessed 10 August 2009).
 5 W. Sullivan, A. Colby, J. Welch Wegner, L. Bond and L. Shulman, *Educating Lawyers: Preparation for the Profession of Law* (Carnegie Report), Stanford, CA: Carnegie Foundation, 2007, pp. 1–2.
 6 ibid., p. 8.
 7 ibid., p. 8.
 8 ibid., p. 9.
 9 ibid., pp. 8–9.
10 ibid., p. 172.
11 ibid., p. 160.
12 ibid., p. 12.
13 ibid., p. 12.
14 ibid., p. 14.
15 J. Rest and D.F. Narvaez (eds), *Moral Development in the Professions*, Hillsdale, NJ: Lawrence Erlbaum Associates, Inc., pp. 1–3; see also L. Kohlberg. *The Psychology of Moral Development: Moral Stages and the Life Cycle*, San Francisco: Harper Row, 1984. One of the co-authors of the Carnegie Report, Anne Colby, was a co-author of Kohlberg's: A. Colby and L. Kohlberg. *The Psychology of Moral Judgment*, New York: Cambridge University Press, 1987.
16 These three frameworks are: a personal interests (PI) framework; a maintaining norms (MN) framework; and a post-conventional (P) framework that is based upon moral ideals or principles. DIT scores indicate which framework predominates for the individual, whether the person is consolidated on a particular moral framework, or the extent to which an individual has difficulty distinguishing among arguments that represent each framework.
17 M.J. Bebeau, 'The defining issues test and the four component model: Contributions of professional education', *Journal of Moral Education* 31, 2002, 279–81.
18 L.A. Ponemon and D.R.L. Gabhart, 'Ethical reasoning research in the accounting and auditing professions', in Rest and Narvaez (eds), *Moral Development in the Professions*, pp. 101–18.
19 D. Arnold, and L. Ponemon, 'Internal auditors' perceptions of whistle-blowing and the influence of moral reasoning: An experiment', *Auditing: A Journal of Practice and Theory* 10, 1991, 1–15; R.A. Bernardi, 'Suggestions for providing legitimacy for accounting ethics research', *Issues in Accounting Education* 19, 2004, 145–6.
20 M.J. Bebeau, 'Enhancing professionalism using ethics education as part of a Dental Licensure Board's disciplinary process. Part I: An evidence-based process', *Journal of the American College of Dentists* 76, 2009, 38–50.
21 D.C. Baldwin Jr, T.E. Adamson, J.T. Sheehan, D.J. Self and A.A. Oppenberg, 'Moral reasoning and malpractice: A pilot study of orthopedic surgeons', *American Journal of Orthopedics* 25, 1996, 481–4. The phrases 'high DIT scores' and 'low DIT scores' in the text refer to scores indicating the proportion of times an individual indicates a preference for post-conventional moral arguments (called 'the P score').
22 M.J. Bebeau and V.E. Monson, 'Guided by theory, grounded in evidence: A way

forward for professional ethics education', in D. Narvaez and L. Nucci (eds), *Handbook on Moral and Character Education*, Hillsdale, NJ: Routledge, 2008, pp. 557–82.

23   Sullivan et al., *Educating Lawyers*, p. 146

24   This curriculum requires 44 contact hours (the equivalent of a one-semester, three-credit American law school course) spent primarily in small group instruction with an emphasis on performance, self-assessment and personalized feedback. Both high-status professionals and full-time faculty are involved in teaching the curriculum.

25   M. Bebeau, J.R. Rest and C.M. Yamoor, 'Measuring dental students' ethical sensitivity', *Journal of Dental Education* 49, 1985, 225–35.

26   Bebeau and Monson, 'Guided by theory, grounded in evidence'.

27   M. Bebeau, 'Evidence-based character development', in N. Kenny and W. Shelton (eds), *Lost Virtue: Professional Character Development in Medical Education, Volume 10 (Advances in Bioethics)*, Oxford: Elsevier, 2006, pp. 47–86.

28   Bebeau, 'The defining issues test and the four component model'.

29   ibid.

30   ibid., p. 282.

31   For example, while approximately 40 per cent of Scottish medical students in one study said they should report misconduct, only 13 per cent of the same group said they actually would do so. Bebeau and Monson, 'Guided by theory, grounded in evidence'. Some 65 per cent of US medical students in another study expressed discomfort at challenging other members of the medical team over wrongdoing. Bebeau and Monson, 'Guided by theory, grounded in evidence'.

32   J.T. Rule and M.J. Bebeau, *Dentists Who Care: Inspiring Stories of Professional Commitment*, Chicago, IL: Quintessence, 2005. Carnegie Report co-author Anne Colby has written one of the leading studies of such moral exemplars. A. Colby and W. Damon, *Some Do Care: Contemporary Lives of Moral Commitment*, New York: Macmillan, 2002. Rule and Bebeau patterned their study of moral exemplars in the dental profession on the Colby and Damon study.

33   For a review of this research, see M.J. Bebeau and V.E. Monson, in A. McKee and M. Eraut (eds), *Professional Learning Over the Life Span: Innovation and Change*, New York, Springer, forthcoming 2010.

34   Bebeau & Monson, 'Guided by theory, grounded in evidence'.

35   National Public Radio, 'Navy lawyer discusses Hamdan, Guantanamo'.

36   ibid.

37   ibid.

38   The American Bar Association (ABA), which serves as the accrediting agency for most law schools in the United States, requires that during the three years of post-graduate law school which constitute American legal education, students take a course in professional responsibility. This requirement has been in place since the mid-1970s. Course coverage must include the ABA's Model Rules of Professional Conduct (Model Rules or 'MRs'), approved by the ABA's governing body, the House of Delegates, with the intent that the states, which actually regulate attorney conduct, will adopt them. In addition to the influence of the ABA accreditation standards, all but one state require as a condition of law licensure that the applicant pass the Multistate Professional Responsibility Examination (MPRE), a 60-question multiple-choice test administered by the National Conference of Bar Examiners largely based on the Model Rules.

39   However, a number of law schools have either developed alternative curricular methods for meeting the ABA's requirement or teach considerably more than just 'the law of lawyering' in their legal ethics course.

40   Sullivan et al., *Educating Lawyers*, p. 148.

41   ibid., p. 149.

42   ibid., p. 149; B. Green, 'Less is more: Teaching legal ethics in context', *William and Mary Law Review* 39, 1998, 362 n. 29: 'Students have a tendency to think that insofar

as professional obligations are left to be interpreted and enforced by individual lawyers at the level of conscience, these obligations are not taken seriously by the law or the legal profession, and so need not be taken very seriously by lawyers or law students.'

43 S. Hartwell, 'Promoting moral development through experiential teaching', *Clinical Law Review* 1, 1994–95, 505.

44 Sullivan et al., *Educating Lawyers*, p. 149, p. 134.

45 ibid., pp. 177–8.

46 ibid., p. 23.

47 ibid., p. 178.

48 ibid., pp. 12–13.

49 ibid., p. 195.

50 The 10 law schools represented were the City University of New York, Georgetown, Harvard, Indiana University (Bloomington), New York University, Southwestern, Stanford, University of Dayton, University of New Mexico, and Vanderbilt. Several of these schools are routinely listed among the top 10 in the United States. A number of consultants on legal education, including one of the authors of this chapter, were also invited to the meeting.

51 The March 2009 announcement acknowledged that the list of 10 schools comprising the LEARN consortium was 'substantially under-inclusive' and that 'many other law schools are also deeply engaged' in rethinking their curricula in light of the Carnegie Report. The announcement indicated the expectation that the network would grow to include more schools who are also committed to the goals articulated by the LEARN group. Legal Education Analysis and Reform Network (LEARN) (2009). See www.law.stanford.edu/display/images/dynamic/events_ media/LEARN_030509_lr.pdf (accessed 14 August 2009).

52 ibid.

53 ibid.

54 Several of the other schools in the LEARN consortium have been at the vanguard of the clinical education movement for decades. New York University and Georgetown have long distinguished themselves among top-ranked law schools in terms of the number of faculty members involved in clinical teaching and the variety and range of offerings. The City University of New York and the University of New Mexico are among the few law schools that require all students to take a clinical course before graduation. According to data collected in 2001–02, approximately 35 per cent of students at ABA-accredited US law schools participated in an in-house clinical course before graduation. P.A. Joy, 'The ethics of law school clinic students as student lawyers', *South Texas Law Review* 45, 2003–04, 822.

55 Stanford Law School, 'A "3D" JD: Stanford Law School announces new model for legal education', 28 November 2006. See www.law.stanford.edu/news/pr/47 (accessed 15 January 2010).

56 ibid.

57 Sullivan et al., *Educating Lawyers*, p. 160.

58 ibid., p. 146.

59 ibid., pp. 10–11.

60 D. Turner, 'Infusing ethical, moral, and religious values into a law school curriculum: A modest proposal', *University of Dayton Law Review* 24, 1998–99, 292–93.

61 Hartwell, 'Promoting moral development through experiential teaching', 505.

62 S. Hartwell, 'Moral development, ethical conduct, and clinical education', *New York Law School Law Review* 35, 1990, 131.

63 In the mid-1990s, there were also experiments with having a legal ethics teacher offer a parallel course to clinic students to analyse ethical issues arising from their cases. See, for example, T. Shaeffer, 'On teaching legal ethics in the law office', *Notre Dame Law Review* 71, 1995, 613 (describing an ethics seminar at Notre Dame Law School in which students in the school's legal aid clinic were asked to decide whether

to reveal information to a lawyer on the other side, or the child protective office in the welfare department, or the judge. Revelation or silence may become irrevocable within hours of the time the seminar adjourns: D. Luban and M. Millemann, 'Good judgment: Ethics teaching in dark times', *Georgetown Journal of Legal Ethics* 9, 1995–96, 64–85 (describing in particular the role of the ethics teacher, Luban, in enabling students to openly discuss ethical issues raised by various courses of action proposed by the professor supervising the clinical work, Millemann).

64 D.F. Chavkin, 'Experience is the *only* teacher: Bringing practice to the teaching of ethics', in M. Robertson, L. Corbin, K. Tranter and F. Bartlett (eds), *The Ethics Project in Legal Education*, London: Routledge-Cavendish 2010.

65 T.W. Floyd, 'Moral vision, moral courage, and the formation of the lawyer's professional identity', *Mississippi Law Review* 28, 2009, 351. This externship course builds upon Mercer's innovative first-year course on the legal profession, described below at text accompanying note 85.

66 N. Hamilton, and L.M. Brabbitt, 'Fostering professionalism through mentoring', *Journal of Legal Education* 57, 2007, n.p.

67 Indiana University Maurer School of Law, 'Proposal for new one legal profession course', Memorandum from Committee on Professionalism in the Curriculum, 4 April 2007, 6, 10.

68 ibid., p. 10.

69 ibid., p. 2.

70 ibid., p. 2.

71 ibid., p. 3.

72 ibid., p. 3. This approach is consistent with the following advice from Bebeau: 'In my experience, one needs to begin an ethics curriculum by exploring the role of the lawyer in society. Without developing some kind of ground rules on ethical expectations, working on ethical reasoning can become a very time-consuming process as much time can be spent on whether or not professionals have particular duties.' Email correspondence with authors, 16 December 2009.

73 Indiana University Maurer School of Law, 'The legal profession: Spring 2009'. Course website available at www.law.indiana.edu/instruction/profession (accessed 15 January 2010).

74 ibid.

75 ibid.

76 ibid.

77 ibid.

78 ibid.

79 Hartwell, 'Promoting moral development through experiential teaching'.

80 R.M. Zahorsky, 'Irvine by Erwin: Can a top legal academic create a law school that is both innovative and elite?', *American Bar Association Journal* 46, August 2009, 47.

81 University of California at Irvine School of Law, First Year Curriculum. See www.law.uci.edu/registrar/curriculum.html (accessed 22 January 2010).

82 N. Cook, 'University of Minnesota Law School's Practice and Professionalism course: Story exchange exercise', presented at Fall 2009 Workshop of the National Institute for Teaching Ethics and Professionalism. See http://law.gsu.edu/niftep/WorkshopF09-Program.htm (accessed 22 January 2010). See also B. McDonnell, 'Curricular reform', presented at 2008 International Conference on the Future of Legal Education. See http://law.gsu.edu/FutureOfLegalEducationConference/Papers/McDonnell.pdf (accessed 22 January 2010).

83 P.E. Longan, 'Teaching professionalism', *Mercer Law Review* 60, 2009, 659, 664. Another important experiment has been the Legal Skills course taught over the first two years at the William and Mary Law School since 1988, in which legal ethics, legal writing and a number of lawyering skills are integrated. J.E. Moliterno, 'Teaching

legal ethics in a programme of comprehensive skills development', *Journal of the Legal Profession* 15, 1990, 145.

84 Washington and Lee, 'Third year reform. Washington & Lee School of Law'. See http://law.wlu.edu/thirdyear (accessed 15 January 2010).

85 L.A. Gordon, *Rodney Smolla: Running a New Play*, Washington: American Bar Association, 2009. See www.legalrebels.com/profiles/rodney_smolla_running_a_new_play (accessed 15 January 2010).

86 R. Smolla, 'We're preparing 3Ls for professional life: New curriculum at Washington and Lee aims to give students practical experiences'. See http://law.wlu.edu/news/storydetailpr.asp?id'420 (accessed 15 January 2010).

87 Washington and Lee, 'Third year reform'.

88 ibid.

89 ibid.

90 The subject areas addressed by these 19 practicums are appellate advocacy, bankruptcy, business planning, business tax planning, civil litigation, corporate counsel, criminal practice, e-commerce, entertainment law, family law, federal energy regulation, fiduciary litigation, higher education, intellectual property, jury advocacy, labour and employment law, patent law, sports law, and torts and insurance.

91 A number of other law schools are experimenting with the use of simulation-based teaching to develop professional judgment. A new law school in Arizona, the Phoenix School of Law, has introduced a six-credit, one-semester course required of all third-year students that integrates the teaching of professional values with 13 different professional skills. S. Gerst and G. Hess, 'Professional skills and values in legal education: The GPS model', *Valparaiso University Law Review* 43, 2009, 513. The Pierce Law School in New Hampshire has collaborated with the Supreme Court, Bar association, and Bar examiners in that state to develop a two-year 'honours' curriculum for selected students that combines simulation, externship and clinical teaching; 'issues of ethics and professionalism are integrated into the fact pattern' of the simulations. J.B. Garvey and A.F. Zinkin, 'Making law students client-ready: A new model in legal education', *Duke Forum for Law & Social Change* 1, 2009, 123. Students who successfully complete the programme are admitted to practice in New Hampshire immediately upon graduation without being required to take the conventional Bar examination. L.S. Dalianis and S.M. Sparrow, 'New Hampshire's performance-based variant of the Bar examination: The Daniel Webster Scholar Program', *The Bar Examiner*, November 2005, 23–26. For other examples of using skills simulation exercises to teach professional judgment, see R.P. Burns, 'Teaching the basic ethics class through simulation: The Northwestern Program in Advocacy and Professionalism', *Law & Contemporary Problems* 58, 1995, 126–8; C.B. Liebman, 'The profession of law: Columbia Law School's use of experiential learning techniques to teach professional responsibility', *Law & Contemporary Problems* 58, 1995, 73–86; C.D. Cunningham, ' "How can we give up our child?" A practice-based approach to teaching legal ethics', *The Law Teacher: The International Journal of Legal Education* 42, 2008, 312; C.D. Cunningham, 'How to explain confidentiality?', *Clinical Law Review* 9, 2003, 579.

92 These activities are negotiating a prenuptial agreement, representing the intended father in a surrogate parenting arrangement, oral argument in a contested custody proceeding between a biological father and a surrogate mother, representing a surviving family member before the federal fund established for the victims of 9/11, preparation of a legal memorandum to characterize stock funds as marital property, preparation of affidavit in support of a motion for support, and negotiation of a divorce settlement.

93 Bebeau et al., 'Measuring dental students' ethical sensitivity'. Such practicum courses can be seen as fulfilling the vision of one of America's leading experts on legal ethics, Deborah Rhode, who has advocated for more than two decades the 'pervasive teaching of legal ethics throughout the curriculum and developed extensive

materials for use in a wide variety of subject matter courses'. See, for example, D.L. Rhode, *Professional Responsibility: Ethics by the Pervasive Method*, New York: Aspen Law & Business, 1998.

94 It is reported that every student is required to have at least one experience in representing a real client. K. Sloan, 'Reality's knocking: The recession is forcing schools to bow to reality', *National Law Journal*, 7 September 2009. See www.law.com/jsp/nlj/PubArticleNLJ.jsp?id'1202433612463 (accessed 15 January 2010). All third-year students participating in the programme are required to obtain a third-year practice certificate, enabling students to handle real client matters in Virginia courts, the state where the law school is located. Also, all students are assigned an alumni mentor. Washington and Lee, 'Third year reform'.

95 Sloan, *Reality's knocking*.

96 Gordon, *Rodney Smolla: Running a new play*.

97 L.D. Brandeis, 'The opportunity in the law', speech presented to the Harvard Ethical Society at Phillips Brooks House, 4 May 1905. See www.law.louisville.edu/library/collections/brandeis/node/222 (accessed 22 January 2010).

98 ibid.

99 K. Llewellyn, *The Bramble Bush*, 10th edn, New York: Oceana Publications, 1996, p. 116. Quoted in Sullivan et al., *Educating Lawyers*, pp. 77–8.

100 ibid.

101 ibid.

6 A South African response to ethics in legal education

Helen Kruuse

6.1 Introduction

In a recent statement by the South African Law Deans Association (SALDA),[1] the association identified that socio-economic factors such as the rising levels of fraud, corruption, criminality, social instability and poverty in South Africa affected the way in which law in that country is both studied and practised. The association identified further that the study and practice of law were made more difficult by the pressures under which the justice system had to work – that is, issues around diversity, over burdened court rolls and case backlogs of several years. These pressures have resulted in what some have called a crisis of social justice in South Africa, with a lack of access to justice, poor results in litigation, high costs and long delays as its hallmarks.[2]

In the context of such factors, this chapter explores the place and importance of the legal ethics education project in South Africa today. This exploration briefly focuses on how historic and social conditions affect legal education in South Africa, particularly the teaching of legal ethics. The chapter follows the premise that the capability and functioning of law students not only depend on their individual circumstances, but also on the social conditions and contexts within which they operate.[3] Similarly, the chapter takes it as axiomatic that any legal ethics teaching must include an awareness of the structural conditions in which lawyers operate (or create) in order to adequately prepare aspirant lawyers for their role in society.[4] As a point of departure, the chapter focuses on the adoption of a Legal Services Sector Charter ('the Charter') in South Africa as a 'social arrangement' that attempts to address the current crisis alluded to by SALDA. In discussing the Charter, I consider whether its provisions provide an appropriate basis for the teaching of ethics to future legal practitioners. Finding this questionable, the chapter explores an alternative basis for teaching ethics – that is, second-level substantive reasoning. While this concept is usually punted in legal interpretation, I argue that such reasoning can be very powerful in the context of teaching legal ethics – especially when the kind of reasoning suggested is imagined as fundamentally about the spirit of the law, and requiring lawyers to act accordingly.

Taking into account the highly contextual nature of the law teacher's work, the remainder of the chapter is divided into three sections: (1) teaching legal ethics in the context of social phenomena; (2) the adoption of a Charter to address issues of access to justice and access to legal services; and (3) an alternate vision for teaching ethics.

6.2 Teaching legal ethics in the context of social phenomena

As already mentioned, when teaching legal ethics the context of justice in any particular society cannot be ignored.[5] A nuanced appreciation of the social context is essential to our understanding of how lawyers in a particular society operate, and what is – and might be – expected of them.

SALDA's statement highlights the conditions within which lawyers in South African society operate. Despite the phenomenal transformation of the legal system as it existed under apartheid to one based on a constitutional democracy, it is still affected by what Budlender and Latsky describe as:

> Generations of legal tinkering, of piecemeal and painstaking technical embellishments of structures created, on the one hand, in the service of the grand apartheid plan and on the other hand, in response to ideological, development and economic realities from time to time and from area to area.[6]

What, then, is expected of lawyers in these conditions – or, put another way, what is their responsibility in this context? The expectation in South Africa is, as in most societies, that lawyers should play a central role in the attainment of justice.[7] However, such expectations are given extra significance in South Africa because of its choice of a constitutional democracy over the supremacy of Parliament in the early 1990s. By choosing a constitutional democracy, it is clear that the courts, and those who appear in them, are expected to act as the main vehicles to protect and realize rights. Since the South African Constitution contains justiciable socio-economic rights, the public must turn to the legal system to remedy social inequality and injustice instead of relying on centrally directed radical interventions of social policy.[8]

In South Africa, then, lawyers are seen as especially responsible for what might happen to South Africa's constitutional democracy over the next few years.[9] South African lawyers are called upon to advise and represent persons in a wide range of socially significant instances, and their role[10] often touches the daily lives of South Africans, from accessing basic services to uncovering fraud and corruption in both government and private corporations.[11]

This complex set of social conditions requires that we consider the standards by which lawyers should behave, together with their conduct in the light of these standards. These standards are important, as they are likely to influence the way in which law develops and whether as many people as possible have access to the law.[12] Considering the profession's standards and its conduct is also important because it probes the link between the perceived crisis of social justice in South Africa and the standards adopted by the legal profession.

This crisis is perceived (rightly or wrongly) to be heavily influenced by the practices and procedures of the legal profession, particularly the conduct of lawyers who are the very people entrusted with securing social justice in South Africa.[13] This perception is exacerbated by increasingly reported cases in the media of indolence, if not outright fraud, by lawyers – especially in motor vehicle accident and social assistance cases – and in charging excessive costs. The gap between lawyers – and by implication, the law – and the community seems to be growing wider.

While there is no empirical data on this phenomenon, the problem does not appear to be simply a public perception issue. Increasingly, concerns are being raised about the conduct of lawyers in courtrooms outside the usual forum of a law society or society of advocates' application for a member to be struck from the side-Bar or Bar. For instance, courts have begun criticizing the way in which lawyers have represented their clients,[14] commenting on fees that, in the court's opinion, were undeserved and/or excessive,[15] and commenting negatively on delay tactics.[16] In several cases[17] the courts have queried the competence and effectiveness of legal representation. In one such case, the Supreme Court of Appeal warned that, should it find legal representation incompetent, this would violate an accused's fair trial right and would necessarily vitiate any conviction or sentence in respect of a 'victim' of such incompetent lawyering.[18] Increasingly, South African courts are using a variety of mechanisms to protect clients from their own lawyers. In what may be interpreted as a lack of trust in the ability of law societies in South Africa to regulate conduct, the Witwatersrand Local Division High Court (renamed South Gauteng High Court in terms of the Renaming of High Courts Act 30 of 2008) went so far as to issue a directive to a provincial law society to submit to it a report about its proposed actions against a lawyer who had appeared before it in a particularly unethical fashion.[19] In another demonstration of protection, the Constitutional Court recently required a lawyer to file an affidavit to explain her inefficiency in representing her client.[20] And in another matter, a court introduced Lord Woolfe-type pre-trial procedures in an effort to avoid lawyers issuing proceedings prematurely and without sufficient information, ostensibly as a means of driving up the costs payable in the matter.[21] Of importance is the fact that many of these cases involved indigent or near-indigent plaintiffs. While these cases represent isolated incidences of unethical conduct, and cannot be said to be indicative of the profession as a whole, it can be accepted that they undermine faith in the system and those who operate within it. There is no doubt that we need more historical/empirical data on the subject. Of course, the problem remains as to whether it is possible, after the fact, to accurately record whether and how the legal profession's actions have contributed to (or averted) South Africa's perceived crisis of social justice.[22]

6.3 The adoption of the Legal Services Sector Charter to address issues of access to justice and access to legal services

In response to the perceived lack of access to justice and the need to facilitate transformation,[23] the legal profession (inclusive of the General Bar Council and the Law Society of SA) and the government recently adopted a Legal Services Sector Charter. This Charter was the subject of extensive debate and consultation over two years, and was finally adopted on 10 December 2007. It is seen as the precursor to a Legal Practice Bill, which is expected to radically change the legal profession in South Africa. Central to the Charter is access in two senses: access to justice for the people, and the issue of access to the legal profession itself.[24]

It is the provisions relating to access in the first sense – that is, access to justice – which are the focus of this chapter. In particular, the focus is on how such provisions can provide a compass for law teachers to prepare students to adequately fulfil the Charter's purpose of access to justice within the context of the ethical dilemmas that they will inevitably face in practice.

Notably, while the principal aim of the Charter is on access to justice, it says very little about the actual development of ethical conduct for practitioners,[25] despite its centrality in any access to justice debate.[26] Notwithstanding, the Charter adopts two main ways in which access to justice is to be achieved. It seeks to achieve access to justice first by including a provision for mandatory pro bono work for every legal practitioner,[27] and second by the stated intention to produce 'competent' legal practitioners who will be regulated by a common set of rules that will govern their conduct. Interestingly, the penultimate draft of the Charter set out the need to produce 'ethical practitioners', but this term was subsequently replaced by 'competent practitioners'. The meaning of 'competence' is far-ranging, but its replacement value over the term 'ethical' is intriguing. One implication is that any set of rules drafted will be proscriptive rather than aspirational (inherent in the concept of 'rules' as opposed to a 'code').[28] This implication also follows on from the type of terminology used in provisions regarding the proposed conduct of practitioners, namely 'codes', 'regulation', 'regulatory bodies', 'complaints-mechanisms' and 'discipline'.[29] Since nothing more is said about the development of an ethical practice by lawyers in the Charter, the implication is that regulation by a proscriptive common set of rules is sufficient to ensure the ethical conduct of practitioners in South Africa.[30]

The Charter's reference to 'competency' certainly reflects the goal of 'performativity' echoed by the professional bodies of the legal profession, who demand that students be equipped for a life of practice. The South African legal profession puts pressure on university law faculties to emphasize skills related to numeracy, administration, and so on, rather than on what it calls 'esoteric theorizing'. In turn, this emphasis has been strongly resisted by most South African law teachers.[31] This is not simply a national issue – it has been the subject of debate in the United States since the early 1990s.[32] However, the problem in this debate is its very trajectory – that is, the belief that practice can ever be devoid of theory.

More problematic is the idea that lawyers can and do operate with abstract and universal concepts.[33] Barnett, for instance, describes the shift to performativity in higher education as one that 'implies doing, rather than knowing, and performance, rather than understanding'.[34]

The reading of the Charter can be said to be premised along the same lines. The drafters see the rule-based approach as the solution to the issue of ethical behaviour. For law teachers, this approach is deeply concerning, as it reveals the danger of conflating the concept of a common set of rules with the conditions necessary for the exercise of ethical conduct. We know that rules do not self-generate their meanings; they must be interpreted. In any event, these rules themselves are often ambiguous and conflict with each other.[35] Faced with these ambiguities and conflicts, it is unrealistic to expect students who have rote-learnt such rules to apply them to a particular situation, since the correct ethical stances will very infrequently come readily labelled.[36] Consequently, it is important to note that the rules do not and cannot relieve lawyers of the continuing responsibility to exercise their own judgment about the appropriate course to follow.

In criticizing the emphasis on a common set of rules, it is not disputed that there should be rules (or a code of conduct), and that such rules (or code) should be taught. Indeed, a code can and does act as an important reference point and/ or guide. However, what is disputed here is the way in which the rules are presented in the Charter: as a potential solve-all and a mechanism which, by its very presence, will ensure ethical conduct. Instead, this is the very point for which we need to prepare our students: that rules and codes often cannot give a straight answer to the dilemmas they face, and that unthinking compliance with rote-learnt rules does not guarantee that lawyers will develop a sense of ethical judgment. At best, a code is a rudimentary framework within which students can debate and develop in their own ethical practice.[37]

In moving away from the idea of rules and codes as a solve-all, law teachers need to provide students in South Africa with a 'framework of reasoning' to resolve difficult questions. When the student has long forgotten the specific rule applicable,[38] the student should have the capacity to place the situation (the ethical dilemma) within a framework of individual, community and social interests wider than just a rule or a code which is deemed to govern the situation. Students must also know how to treat rules or codes – that is, that they cannot accept it as automatons because of its supposed inherent authority or its supposed inherent superior value or logic.

But how does one teach this capacity or 'framework of reasoning'? Commentators have emphasized the importance of teachers providing law students with access to different vantage points and perspectives – practical as well as theoretical – on the law. Some commentators suggest that students should be exposed to applied philosophy,[39] others to the work of political theorists, sociologists and social ethicists.[40] One of the most interesting approaches is that of Nussbaum, who places great emphasis on the literary imagination. If she had her way, every student in every law school would be compelled to read *Hard Times* and the works of Walt Whitman![41]

All of this may be necessary. However, the problem remains that the South African law student in the ethics classroom, having been exposed to these materials outside the normal law curricula, is still educated in the traditional private-law 'habits of mind' and 'intellectual reflexes' that induce him or her to routinely accept or reject particular views of how the law works and what arguments are and are not convincing.[12] This is true in many, if not most, law subjects where students are taught the value of cultivating rule-craft[13] – that is, the ability to identify the extant rules of the legal system and apply them to particular situations.[14] Thus, the concern here is that students could very easily adopt the same reasoning in the ethics classroom and in practice, despite their access to different vantage points and perspectives.

This concern is very real in South Africa, where the legal culture has been called conservative – not in political outlook, but rather in jurisprudential approach.[15] Following this approach, students are predisposed to think about law in terms of rules developed, interpreted or applied by the courts. This practice is confirmed by both those within and outside the South African legal profession. South Africa's former Chief Justice, Pius Langa,[16] has acknowledged that most South African lawyers, including himself, have a traditional legal education that focuses on and rewards the rational deduction of inevitable conclusions from unquestionable principles.[17] In his seminal work on legal culture in South Africa, visiting US Professor Karl Klare confirmed former Chief Justice Langa's view by stating:

> US lawyers are often struck by their South African colleagues' relatively strong faith in the precision, determinacy and self-revealingness of words and texts. Legal interpretation in South Africa tends to be more highly structured, technicist, literal and rule-bound than in the States . . . South African lawyers appear more prepared than their US counterparts to deduce relatively specific conclusions from general and abstract premises, with fewer intermediate steps than Americans would look for. There is a bit more reverence for law among South African lawyers.[18]

It is not suggested in these comments that analytical argument is not important. However, if this is the only kind of argument or reasoning, it may simply perpetuate the myth that analytical reasoning on a common code of conduct is enough to prepare lawyers to deal with ethical dilemmas seriously, and that ethics is simply about following a shopping list. The challenge then is this: what can teachers in South African law schools do to ensure that the Charter's emphasis on regulation by a common code does not encourage students to adopt a purely formalist and rule-based approach to it, potentially turning students into what Nicholson and Webb have termed 'amoral ciphers'?[19] The suggestion here is simple: students should be encouraged to adopt a particular *mode of reasoning* when faced with ethical dilemmas in practice within the broad framework of a code.[50] This type of reasoning has come to the fore in a number of court decisions in South Africa, and has been given various names, the best description of which is 'substantive second-level reasoning' as coined by Judge Froneman of the Constitutional Court of South Africa.

6.4 An alternate vision for teaching ethics

This 'substantive second-level reasoning' is based largely on Atiyah and Summer's influential work on legal reasoning which requires the 'reasoner' – the student, in our case – to state his or her substantive reasons for following a particular rule or conducting him or herself in a particular way. The proposed mode of reasoning necessarily makes students acutely aware of their agency in choosing to follow a particular course of conduct. In this way, students cannot and may not rely on unquestioned obedience to authority (being a code of conduct in this setting), since the reasoning process itself requires that students declare what substantive reasons lie behind their conduct and/or behind any provision in the code of conduct on which they wish to rely.

A substantive reason, according to Atiyah and Summers, is a moral, economic, political, institutional or other social reason.[51] These reasons are roughly divided into 'rightness reasons' or 'goal reasons'. Good 'goal' reasons are justified when the rule or decision they support can be predicted to have effects that serve a good social goal such as the promotion of safety or the facilitation of democracy.[52] Thus, in stating his or her 'goal' reasons, a student needs to state why his or her preferred conduct serves society or democracy best. 'Rightness' reasons do not depend on expected consequences for justification, but on the way the decision accords with norms of rightness, such as equity, fairness, good faith or the like. Thus students must state why their preferred conduct, in their personal opinion, is just or equitable.[53] Importantly, the goal of this method is the *process of ethical deliberation* rather than the particular answer given by the student. This is simply because it is not, and cannot be, assured that such process will produce the 'right' kind of ethical conduct when the students enter practice.[54] However, in providing those reasons, students lay bare their views on how law should work in (and for) a society. The student here cannot see the ethical problem as just another set of legal issues in which a premium is placed on being able to argue around or otherwise 'game' the rules in order to reach a desired result.[55] Thus students are forced to identify that ethical conduct/reasoning is a conscious structured process[56] that does not allow them to absolve themselves from the responsibility of making the actual ethical decisions. By adopting this reasoning, student values cannot be hidden from scrutiny, and their actual social and political choices on contested issues come to light. In a similar vein, Dodek[57] encourages an openness in the ethics classroom setting where, instead of learning to 'think like a lawyer', students are encouraged to 'think like who they are'. In the context of substantive second-level reasoning, such openness would enable students to 'own' their chosen conduct, thereby accepting not only the external but also the internal consequences of their decisions.[58]

How can this type of reasoning be imparted in the ethics classroom? The first step in the process is to identify a particular moment as a decision point, through

simulations, role-plays or the like. The appropriate question, then, is to ask something along the lines of: 'What courses of conduct will you or would you have
followed at this decision point?' Each student then has to list his or her goal or
rightness reasons in identifying a course of conduct. Where the student wants to
list compliance to a provision in a code, such student must consider why such
provision formally became part of a code, and whether it should remain so in the
context of the simulation. The process of looking behind a provision in a code is
especially useful in getting students to see the value of articulating their own
beliefs and choices in following a particular course of conduct.[59] This, then, would
lead to a more deliberative educational process and a more reflective ethical
orientation. In educational literature, Bruner[60] aptly summarizes the intended
outcome of this method:

> We teach a subject not to produce little libraries on that subject, but rather to
> get a student to think mathematically [supplant mathematics with 'about
> law'] for himself, to consider matters as an historian does, *to take part in the
> process of knowledge-getting.*[61]

In finding examples of both formal and substantive reasoning, a case-study
approach is advocated. While case studies are often criticized as a method of
instruction,[62] it is one method that could be very powerful here. This method
does not imply studying cases that deal with whether a lawyer's conduct was
unethical, violated a prohibition or was otherwise actionable. Instead it is the
study of the *process of deliberation* in cases where the facts may have nothing to do
with a lawyer's conduct.[63] The important discovery to be made in this examination is that blinding reliance on rules cannot *by itself* provide the justification
needed when making a particular decision. What may provide justification for the
use or non-use of a rule is the substance or merit in the reasons used to reach a
particular decision.[64]

Court decisions involving constitutional rights are particularly appropriate for
this sort of exercise, particularly those of the South African Constitutional Court.
This is because the South African Constitution directs that the court *must* (not *may*)
apply or develop the law to give expression to the Bill of Rights; the Bill of Rights
must be interpreted to promote the values of an open and democratic society; and
the development of the common law should take place by taking into account the
interests of justice.[65] In articulating what those values are and what the interests of
justice require, the courts have had to commit to substantive reasoning, at least in
principle, in coming to any decision.[66] So, for example, some of the Constitutional
Court decisions reveal that supposedly abstract, universal concepts to which lawyers cling often hide the social and political choices behind those concepts made
in earlier times. These decisions include concepts such as:

- *ownership* in the law of property – especially when a court is faced with
  evicting squatters who were never allowed to own land under the previous
  regime, or whose land was taken away from them in the first place;[67] and

- the definition of *marriage* – especially when a court is faced with denying rights to couples such as same-sex partnerships and polygynous customary and/or Muslim marriages that fall outside of that definition.[68]

In going through a judge's process of deliberation, then, one can tease out the type of reasoning employed, whether formal or substantive, and the consequent results. Having examined examples of these processes of deliberation, the ethics student cannot approach issues such as client confidentiality, conflicts of interest, contingency fees, disclosure and the like with simple reference to a rule or code that exonerates him or her from the responsibility for that decision. Here we come back to the notion of the capability of the individual agent to critically reflect and make worthwhile choices from the alternatives available to him or her.[69] One can see this type of decision-making in the dissenting judgment of the SCA when dealing with the retention of the referral rule (the requirement of a divided Bar in South Africa is that a client may only approach an advocate through an attorney). In exploring the rationale for the retention of the referral rule in South Africa, Cameron JA (as he then was) required not only evidence of a professional rule or practice of referral, but also a justification as to whether the rationale for that rule (*viz.* the public interest) still applied.[70] He required that the rule be scrutinized to ensure that it was 'not loosely or over-broadly made'. Cameron JA goes on to say:

> The crisis of legal services in South Africa is too acute, and the threat this crisis represents to the administration of justice too grave, for the Courts to enforce tradition without there being compelling reason in the public interest for doing so.[71]

In the same way, for each decision that a student takes in resolving whether he or she can use a civil procedure rule to delay a trial, accept a mediocre settlement to ensure payment in a contingency fee setting, or fail to disclose material information to the court or the opposing party, the student needs to state his or her 'goal' reasons and why his or her preferred conduct serves society or democracy best. This reasoning may not lead to 'justice', but it may lead to a more reflective practice by law students who cannot escape their responsibility in shaping a legal system that urgently needs ethically reflective practitioners.

6.5 Conclusion

Substantive second-level reasoning in ethics is not a novel concept. One can certainly find variations of this kind of reasoning in both the United States and the United Kingdom. However, with South Africa's particular background of social injustice, law teachers (and students) need to take additional care. Given the current conditions around access to justice in South Africa, this consideration is urgent. The Charter proposed by the government and the legal profession is indeed a welcome recognition of the need to address problems around access to justice in South Africa. However, the lack of reference in the Charter to the kind of conduct required by practitioners is inadequate for the purposes of preparing students for the world of practice in South Africa. What is needed is for law schools in South Africa to recognize the importance of ethics in the LLB programme. In particular, this recognition should take the shape of developing capacity, agency and accountability in students in choosing a course of action. Substantive second-level reasoning can go some way to advancing this cause.

Notes

1   SALDA press statement issued 23 May 2008.
2   E. Cameron, 'Shared norms of conduct', *The Advocate* 21, 2008, 36.
3   This idea draws on Amartya Sen's capability approach, but in the context of education. See generally M. Walker and E. Unterhalter, 'The capability approach: Its potential for work in education', in M. Walker and E. Unterhalter (eds), *Amartya Sen's Capability Approach and Social Justice in Education*, Basingstoke: Palgrave Macmillan, 2007.
4   See D. Rhode, 'Ethics by the pervasive method', *Journal of Legal Education* 42, 1992, 32, 47. In educational literature, Barnett confirms that a teacher in *any* discipline should situate his or her curricula in the wider social context. See R. Barnett, *The Limits of Competence: Knowledge, Higher Education and Society*, Buckingham: Open University Press, 1994, p. 257.
5   See R. Grimes, 'Learning and practising law in the South Pacific – the ethical dimension', in K. Economides (ed.), *Ethical Challenges to Legal Education and Conduct*, Oxford: Hart, 1998, p. 188. This context is necessarily informed by the political, social and economic issues in a country. In *The Investigating Directorate: Serious Economic Offences v Hyundai Motor Distributors (Pty) Ltd* 2001 (1) SA 545 (CC); 2000 (10) BCLR 1079 (CC) para 21, the Constitutional Court of South Africa commented on the fact that South Africa's history 'involves a transition from a society based on division, injustice and exclusion from the democratic process to one which respects the dignity of all citizens, and includes all in the process of governance'. See also *President of the Republic of South Africa and another v Modderklip Boerdery* 2005 (5) SA 3 (CC) paras 39–40, where the same court highlighted the importance of section 34 of the Constitution of the Republic of South Africa, 1996 (access to courts provision) in the light of this context.
6   G. Budlender and J. Latsky, 'Unravelling rights to land and to agricultural activity in rural race zones', *South African Journal of Human Rights* 6, 1990, 155.
7   See, for example, Nicolson and Webb's comments on legal practitioners in the United Kingdom that: 'As key actors in the legal system, lawyers are particularly well placed to promote justice and hence serve society.' (see D. Nicolson and J. Webb, *Professional Legal Ethics: Critical Interrogations*, Oxford: Oxford University Press, 1999, p. 1). Grimes also comments on legal practitioners in the South Pacific, especially focusing on the fact that the South Pacific is a country 'dominated by the legacy of the common law and consequently an adversarial legal system' (see Grimes, 'Learning and Practising Law in the South Pacific', p. 187). See also Hutchinson on Canadian lawyers: 'Mindful of the special responsibility that lawyers have for the quality of justice in society, lawyers . . . must support efforts to ensure that the legal profession fulfils its civic and public calling.' A. Hutchinson, *Legal Ethics and Professional Responsibility*, 2nd edn, Toronto: Irwin Law, 2006, p. 15.
8   In this way, K. Klare, 'Legal culture and transformative constitutionalism', *South African Journal of Human Rights* 14, 1998, 146 makes the general point that the new social order in South Africa is dependent on the country's adjudicative practices and those operating in that setting. In particular, Klare comments at p. 147 as follows: '[T]hat South Africans opted to accomplish a significant portion of their law-making

through adjudication is a decision fraught with institutional consequences. At the most superficial level, South Africans have chosen to compromise the supremacy of Parliament, and correspondingly to increase the power of judges, each to an as yet unknowable extent.' In similar terms, D. Kennedy, *A Critique of Adjudication: (fin de siècle)*, Cambridge, MA: Harvard University Press, 1997, p. 2 comments that: 'The diffusion of law-making [in adopting a constitutional democracy] . . . empowers the legal fractions of intelligentia to decide the outcomes of ideological conflicts amongst themselves, outside of the legislative processes.'

9 Cameron, 'Shared norms of conduct', p. 36 illustrates this point by emphasizing the responsibility of lawyers (and judges) in preventing social injustice, even extending this responsibility to institutions associated with the legal system, such as prisons: '[F]or a gross social injustice that should press upon the conscience of every lawyer in this country, and especially the conscience of judges, we need merely look at our prisons. They are desperately overcrowded. And malpractice and corruption in them are rife. *No lawyer can sleep complacent practising law in a legal system with prisons such as ours*' (my emphasis). Cameron J is currently a judge of the Constitutional Court of South Africa, and formerly a judge of the South African Supreme Court of Appeal.

10 Cramton's views in the United States can be similarly applied here. He notes at p. 1118 that citizens are denied their constitutional rights to access the legal system and those rights cannot be returned without the help of the people who have the knowledge, training and expertise to make the legal system work, namely lawyers. See R. Cramton, 'Mandatory *pro bono*', *Hofstra Law Review* 19, 1990–91, 1113.

11 This role is explicitly mandated by the South African Constitution, particularly sections 34 and 35. These sections give every person the right to have access to courts and to legal representation (in criminal matters) respectively. During 2008–09, lawyers and judges operating within the legal system played a significant role in politics. This reference alludes to the criminal investigation and attempted (but eventual withdrawal of the) prosecution of Jacob Zuma, the president of the ruling party of the country (the African National Congress) and recently elected President of South Africa. Three pivotal points bear reference: first, a Judge President of a provincial division was on suspension for allegedly attempting to improperly influence two Constitutional Court judges in making a favourable finding for Zuma; second, while overturned on appeal due to evidential issues, the High Court found that the lawyers for the state were improperly influenced by the erstwhile President of South Africa in their decision to prosecute Zuma (*Zuma v National Director of Public Prosecutions* (unreported case no: 8652/08 NPD, 12 September 2008); and third – of particular interest to law students – the acting head of the National Prosecuting Authority acknowledged that his statement giving reasons for dropping charges against Jacob Zuma was sourced from the judgment of a Hong Kong High Court without acknowledgement (since overturned). The acting head called it 'an oversight', the media called it plagiarism and the judge of the judgment in question (Judge Seagroatt) called it 'sloppy and undisciplined'. See A. Basson, 'Mpshe's big Fong Kong', *Mail & Guardian*, 19 April 2009.

12 Nicolson and Webb, *Professional Legal Ethics*, p. 1.

13 For example, Navsa JA of the South African Supreme Court of Appeal states: 'There is a growing perception that in spite of SA having one of the best Constitutions in the world, its legal practitioners are losing their social consciousness' (quoted by J. Eksteen, 'Enforcing quality and the ethics of the Bar', *The Advocate*, 20, 2007, 2).

14 The South African Constitutional Court has particularly criticized the 'bureaucratic bungling' by lawyers acting on behalf of the state. For example, in *South African Liquor Traders Association and Others v Chairperson, Gauteng Liquor Board and Other* 2006 (8) BCLR (CC), the court at para 52 stated: 'It is serious [i.e. the attorney's bungling] because as a matter of common practice it is the State Attorney who is briefed by the government when it is involved in litigation. Given the government's responsibility to assist the work of courts, a lapse of this sort in the State Attorney's office gives cause for grave

concern.' See also *Nyathi v MEC for Department of Health, Gauteng and Another* 2008 (5) 94 (CC) at para 64ff.

15 See, for example, *Cele v South African Social Security Agency and 22 Related Cases* 2009 (5) SA 105 (D). This is quite a radical change since, traditionally, courts in South Africa rarely criticize those who appear in them, except for the rare occasion when a court will award costs against the lawyer personally (i.e. costs *de bonis propriis*).

16 *Thint (Pty) Ltd v National Director of Public Prosecutions and Others, Zuma and another v NDPP and Others* [2008] ZACC 13.

17 *S v Ntuli* 2003 (4) SA 258 (W); *Beyers v Director of Public Prosecutions, Western Cape* 2003 (1) SACR 164 (C); *S v Mofokeng* 2004 (1) SACR 349 (W); *S v Chabedi* 2004 (1) SACR 477 (W); *Fhetani v The State* [2007] SCA 113 (RSA); *S v Tandwa and Others* 2008 (1) SACR 613 (SCA).

18 *S v Tandwa and others* 2008 (1) SACR 613 (SCA) para 7.

19 *Ulde v Minister of Home Affairs and Another* 2008 (6) SA 483 (W) paras 36–42, 44(3) and (4). In this matter, the lawyer failed to bring adverse case law to the attention of the court despite having argued the precedent-setting case himself and despite its binding nature on the court. The latter paragraphs of the judgment direct that: 'The transcript of these proceedings is to [be] made available as soon as possible and is to accompany a referral to the Law Society of the Northern Provinces of the complaints articulated by me [i.e. Sunderland AJ] . . . The Law Society is directed to report the outcome of such enquiry to the Deputy Judge-President of the Witwatersrand Local Division.'

20 *Nyathi v MEC for Department of Health, Gauteng and Another* 2008 (5) 94 (CC). At para 112 of the case, it is recorded that the Chief Justice of the Constitutional Court directed the State Attorney to file an affidavit 'fully explaining the reason for the failure by her staff to take instructions adequately from the respondents . . . as well as the manner in which her staff has generally conducted the litigation on behalf of the respondents in this matter'. The State Attorney was also called upon 'to set out what steps she is taking to prevent the recurrence of unprofessional conduct in the future'. The court also directed the State Attorney to be present at the next hearing of the matter.

21 In social grant matters, the courts have increasingly recognized that lawyers have acted improperly or negligently for sheer financial gain, to the detriment of both their clients and the courts – creating, as a court has put it, a 'a mini-industry' in cases of that type (*Cele v South African Social Security Agency and 22 Related Cases* 2009 (5) SA 105 (D) para 8).

22 In arguing the other way, Stephen Pepper, in his famous paper on the amoral role of lawyering, asked for historical and empirical data to show: 'How would a moralistic as opposed to amoral role of lawyers have affected a 20th-centry American history?' See S. Pepper, 'The lawyer's amoral ethical role: A defence, a problem and some possibilities', *American Bar Foundation Research Journal*, 1986, 620.

23 See the address by Adv J. de Lange, MP, Deputy Minister for Justice and Constitutional Development (as he then was), at the Annual General Meeting of the Gauteng Law Council, South Africa, 16 September 2006. See www.info.gov.za/speeches/2006/07052211151002.htm (accessed 4 September 2008).

24 While these two purposes are seen as complementary, critics of the Charter have suggested that the Charter's focus on access to the legal profession – that is, the empowerment of the black segment of the legal profession – has overshadowed the more pressing issue of access to justice and quality legal services for the majority of the country's poor, marginalized and vulnerable people (for example, see Y.A. Vawda, 'The Legal Services Charter debate: Where are the people?', *De Rebus*, December 2006). Various organizations have also raised this concern in their submissions to the drafters of the Charter. For example, the AIDS Law Project (in its submission to the Department of Justice and the Legal Services Charter Steering Committee) commented at para 24 that, while the transformation of the legal profession is an important and necessary step in the creation of a non-racist and non-sexist society, it is

problematic to think that transformation itself will necessarily result in greater access to legal services – and *ethical* legal services at that: AIDS Law Project submission on the Draft Legal Services Sector Charter. See www.alp.org.za/index.php?option=com_content&task= view&id=6&Itemid=3 (accessed 15 June 2008). Put another way, it does not automatically follow that increasing the base of ownership, management and control of the legal profession will necessarily enhance access to justice. The Centre for Applied Legal Studies in South Africa (CALS) similarly submitted to the Department of Justice in its submission at 3 that 'CALS is concerned that the draft charter appears to focus more on transforming the racial and gender composition than on transforming the content of legal services, i.e. widening access to the poor and other vulnerable groupings. In fact, provisions . . . may do serious damage to the transformation project.' CALS submission on the Draft Legal Services Sector Charter. See http://web.wits. ac.za/Academic/Centres/CALS/AccessToJustice (accessed 15 June 2008). The provisions to which CALS referred (in the penultimate draft of the charter and now excised) drastically reduced the number of years of practical training required for entry to the profession and required that graduates with no experience in providing legal services should service people in poor and under-resourced communities in a six-month community service requirement. On this issue, see also the AIDS Law Project submission at para 34.

25 In a last-minute amendment to the Charter, the drafters included a clause (para 2.5.2(iii)) that reads: 'The legal profession undertakes to ensure that legal training and education includes social awareness training.' Law Society of South Africa, *Legal Services Sector Charter*, 2007. See www.doj.gov.za/LSC/LSSC_Dec%2007.pdf (accessed 7 January 2010). This is a fascinating and positive step for legal education; however, the undertaking is made in respect of the 'access to the legal profession' provisions rather than the 'access to justice' section. Thus, simply considering the location of such a clause implies that this training is aimed at lawyers accepting those of a different racial and gender composition into their flock, rather than addressing the issue of lawyers' responsibilities to a diverse society.

26 A recent comment of a Chief Executive Office (CEO) of one of the largest banks in South Africa displays the public's perception of how lawyers actually obstruct access and process. This CEO was asked in 2003 how the banks and financial firms had managed to draw up the financial sector charter so quickly. The CEO is reported to have said that they had 'chucked all the lawyers out [of] the room, hauling them in at the last minute only to check the fine print' (quoted by J. Strachan, 'The Legal Services Charter – the devil's in the detail', *Without Prejudice* 6, 2006, 4).

27 The issue of whether mandatory pro bono work will ensure proper access to justice is beyond the scope of this chapter; suffice to mention the continued debate in the United States as to its advantages and disadvantages. Notably, Australia has adopted a voluntary model of pro bono work organized and monitored by the National Pro Bono Resource Centre in Sydney (see www.nationalprobono.org.au). Given a constitutional provision guaranteeing the right to a fair trial (s 34) and the right to a legal representative in criminal trials where 'substantial justice would otherwise result' (s 35) in South Africa, I believe there is an obligation for legal practitioners to perform pro bono work – with pragmatic qualifiers. For my views, see 'Mandating *pro bono* in South Africa', *National Pro Bono News*, May 2009. See www.nationalprobono.org.au/page.asp?from=1&id=235&preview=true (accessed 26 June 2009).

28 Education specialists may be interested in the change in terminology from the penultimate to final version of the Charter. The simplistic use of 'competence' in this context seems to ignore increasing literature on education – specifically in the United Kingdom – that questions whether the goal of 'competence' (admittedly, narrowly construed) can adequately prepare students for the ethical dilemmas they will inevitably face in practice. In this regard, Barnett notes that: '*Competences* remain behaviours and capacities to act as desired and defined by others. They reduce the authenticity of human action'

(my emphasis). If we understand competence in this sense, then, it is implied by the Charter that legal educators will produce Dworkin's 'unreflective athletes'. See R. Barnett, *The Limits of Competence: Knowledge, Higher Education and Society*, Buckingham: Open University Press, 1994, p. 81.

29 See, for example, paras 2.1(ii) and (v), 3.2(iii)(e) and 3.3 (ii)(d) of the Law Society of South Africa, *Legal Services Sector Charter*.

30 Charter provisions (relating to the 'quality' and continuing education (e.g. para 1.1.1 (iv)(a)) presumably follow this premise in the absence of any reference to the contrary: Law Society of South Africa, *Legal Services Sector Charter*.

31 See the South African Law Deans Association (SALDA) *Position Paper on Legal Education*, August 2008 as well as the SALDA Resolution in December 2008 that resolves to institute a systematic appraisal of all aspects of training and legal education at universities. The former document sets out (at para 1.5.1) SALDA's views that '[a] university degree primarily serves to equip graduates with a particular disciplinary lens through which they can approach opportunities, issues and problems that they may confront in their lives. The greater the disciplinary background of an individual, the greater the variety of approaches open to him or her.'

32 This debate was largely initiated by Judge Harry Edwards in a widely cited article in the *Michigan Law Review*, where he lamented 'the growing disjunction between legal education and the legal profession' claiming that 'many law schools . . . have abandoned their proper place, by emphasizing abstract theory at the expense of practical scholarship and pedagogy'. See H.T. Edwards, 'The growing disjunction between legal education and the legal profession', *Michigan Law* Review 91, 1992, 34. See also K. Abramson, ' "Art for a better life": A new image of American legal education', *Brigham Young University Education and Law Journal*, 2006, 227, specifically at pp. 283–4 where she describes this disjuncture.

33 The fact that legal concepts are not sent from a celestial being on high can at times offend students. This relates back to the Palinscar's notion of the 'interdependence of social and individual processes in the co-construction of knowledge': see A. Palinscar, 'Social constructivist perspectives on teaching and learning', *Annual Review of Psychology* 49, 1998, 345, 352). The notion really requires students to develop the capacity for extended abstract thinking – for them to develop the capacity to see connections between things, facts, ideas and ultimately law.

34 See R. Barnett, G. Parry and K. Coate, 'Conceptualizing curriculum change', *Teaching in Higher Education* 6, 2001, 436, where the authors bemoan the fact that performativity is associated with an increased emphasis on 'efficiency', 'outputs' and 'use-value' for the same reasons as those discussed above. In a recent acerbic attack in the *New York Times* on higher education goals, Stanley Fish also reflected on this aspect: see S. Fish, 'The last professor', *New York Times*, 18 January 2009. He berates higher education institutions that produce graduates who have the skills 'to gain employment' but who do not value the activity of understanding or explaining for its own sake (unless, of course, it is directly linked to a skill or output). He continues: 'The for-profit university is the logical end of a shift from a model of education centered in an individual professor who delivers insight and inspiration to a model that begins and ends with the imperative to deliver the information and skills necessary to gain employment. In this latter model, the mode of delivery – a disc, a computer screen, a video hook-up – doesn't matter so long as delivery occurs. Insofar as there are real-life faculty in the picture, their credentials and publications (if they have any) are beside the point, for they are just "delivery people".'

35 A common example of this might be the responsibilities to one's clients with respect to confidentiality. A provision in a code might be unclear in itself, and recommend a different course of action from a similar provision in a code recommended by the responsibilities as an officer of the court. See Hutchinson, *Legal Ethics and Professional Responsibility*, p. 15.

36 A. Goldsmith and G. Powles, 'Lawyers behaving badly: Where now in legal educa-
    tion for acting responsibly in Australia?', in Economides (ed.), *Ethical Challenges to
    Legal Education and Conduct*, p. 141. See also Hutchinson, *Legal Ethics and Professional
    Responsibility*, p. 15, who confirms that: 'In hard cases, there is rarely an obvious or
    incontestable path to follow.' Monroe Freedman's perjury trilemma is the classic
    example of a lawyer's competing interests.

37 Hutchinson, *Legal Ethics and Professional Responsibility*, p. 15.

38 See Rhode, 'Ethics by the pervasive method', p. 43.

39 Goldsmith and Powles, 'Lawyers behaving badly', 142 and M. Nussbaum, *Poetic Justice:
    The Literary Imagination and Public Life*, Boston: Beacon Press, 1995, p. 1627.

40 J. Callahan (ed.), *Ethical Issues in Professional Life*, Oxford: Oxford University Press, 1988,
    p. 219.

41 Nussbaum, *Poetic Justice*. For ideas on novels appropriate for the South African
    context, see E. Holland, ' "How to fix a life": Lessons on *ubuntu* and restorative justice
    from Alexander McCall Smith's *The No. 1 Ladies' Detective Agency*', *Speculum Juris*
    22, 2008, 123. Holland suggests that Alexander McCall Smith's *The No. 1 Ladies'
    Detective Agency* would be an appropriate text, with its emphasis on restorative justice and
    ubuntu.

42 Chief Justice P. Langa, 'Transformative constitutionalism', *Stellenbosch Law Review* 17,
    2006, 351. See also Klare, 'Legal culture and transformative constitutionalism', 168.
    Put another way, Van der Walt comments that such an approach determines (1) what
    constitutes a legal problem, (2) an authoritative rule or principle for solving the prob-
    lem, and (3) a valid legal argument in applying the principle or rule to the problem. See
    A. Van der Walt, 'Legal history, legal culture and transformation in a constitutional
    democracy', *Fundamina* 12, 2006, 36.

43 See Hutchinson, *Legal Ethics and Professional Responsibility*, p. 25.

44 ibid.

45 Klare, 'Legal culture and transformative constitutionalism'; Langa, 'Transformative
    constitutionalism'; van der Walt, 'Legal history, legal culture and transformation in a
    constitutional democracy'.

46 Langa CJ retired in October 2009.

47 Langa, 'Transformative constitutionalism', 355.

48 Klare, 'Legal culture and transformative constitutionalism', 168.

49 Nicolson and Webb, *Professional Legal Ethics*, p. 279. Frenkel terms this 'the pedagogy of
    legal ethics-as-code compliance' See D.N. Frenkel, 'On trying to teach judgment', *Legal
    Education Review* 12, 2001, 24.

50 The rationale behind adopting this type of reasoning is to challenge the traditional
    'habits of mind' and 'intellectual reflexes' of South African law students. This reason-
    ing attempts to get them away from the idea that law is stable, determinate and insti-
    tutionally distinct from other disciplines.

51 P.S. Atiyah and R.S. Summers, *Form and Substance in Anglo-American Law: A Comparative
    Study of Legal Reasoning, Legal Theory, and Legal Institutions*, Oxford: Clarendon Press,
    1987, p. 5.

52 J.C. Froneman, 'Legal reasoning and legal culture: Our "vision" of law', *Stellenbosch
    Law Review* 16, 2005, 6.

53 According to Froneman, ibid., p. 16, the point of departure for such reasoning is that,
    at university, a student is typically taught to analyse the whole body of law into com-
    partments and concepts in order to make sense of the whole. This is understandable in
    the context of trying to make a curriculum workable. So the law is divided into public
    and private law, into contract, delict, family law, succession and the like. Then concepts
    are created in each category to explain the workings of the categories. Froneman tells
    us that this is necessary, but there is a danger too: that we forget that our compartalizing
    and conceptualization are in the end mere constructs of our own reason. We begin
    to think that the compartments and concepts actually have lives of their own, that

somehow they exist outside of our construction of them. They become autopoietic, having as their main purpose their own self-perpetuation.

54 This process is similar to 'ethical discretionary judgment' proposed by Simon in his seminal article: W.H. Simon, 'Ethical discretion in lawyering', *Harvard Law Review* 101, 1987–88, 1139. Importantly, Simon points out that this process does not exclude the possibility of a student choosing 'aggressive advocacy' or a similar strategy, subject to the qualification that aggressive advocacy must be part of a lawyer's good faith effort to vindicate legal merit.

55 Frenkel, 'On trying to teach judgment', p. 24.

56 ibid., p. 41. This type of reasoning avoids the danger of seeing the law, and consequently the code, as an imposing and imposed structure that is operationally determinate in the guidance it extends to the training lawyer, and institutionally distinct from the more open-minded debates around ideological politics. See comments on this in Hutchinson, *Legal Ethics and Professional Responsibility*, p. 25.

57 A. Dodek, 'Canadian legal ethics: A subject in search of scholarship', *Toronto Law Journal* 50, 2000, 129.

58 This type of reasoning process also addresses the 'problem of responsibility' raised by G. Postema, 'Moral responsibility in professional ethics', *New York Law Review* 55, 1980, 74. In terms of this problem, the process does not allow the student to simply rely on responses like 'because I am a lawyer' or, in this context, 'because the rules explicitly don't forbid it'. The student needs to close the gap between private and public moralities.

59 For example, the student would need to provide a goal or rightness reason if he or she decided on whether to disclose in the course of negotiations material facts unknown to the other side.

60 Quoted in P. Ramsden, *Learning to Teach in Higher Education*, 2nd edn, New York: Routledge/Falmer, 2002, p. 115.

61 My emphasis. This is especially difficult to achieve in the discipline of law when the traditional association between law and adjudication is reflected in more than just the substance of what is taught. It has been hard-wired into the process used to transmit knowledge, validate learning, evaluate performance and reward achievement. See in general, S. Sturm and L. Guinier, 'The law school matrix: Reforming legal education in a culture of competition and conformity', *Vanderbilt Law Review* 60, 2007, 515.

62 Two critiques of the case method stand out. First, it is argued that the case method focuses on the principles of doctrine and not behaviour, thereby promoting moral relativism. Second, case studies tend to focus on the most egregious sorts of misconduct with the attendant risk that teaching the minimum level of ethical sensitivity is in fact the desired level, or at least the accepted level. See D. Turner, 'Infusing ethical, moral and religious values into a law school curriculum: A modest proposal', *Dayton Law Review* 24, 1999, 296; and J. Moliterno, 'An analysis of ethics teaching in law schools: Replacing the lost benefits of the apprentice system in the academic atmosphere', *Cincinnati Law Review* 69, 1991–92, 109 respectively. These problems are not fatal if attention is paid to the type of cases studied (see above).

63 Simon, 'Ethical discretion in lawyering', 1125 notes that one of the lessons of legal realism for legal ethics is that rules are indeterminate and must be elaborated in the process of application to various controversies. Seen in this light, studying the process of deliberation becomes important *vis-à-vis* a code of conduct, since lawyers effectively determine the meaning of clauses within the code of conduct.

64 Goldsmith and Powles, 'Lawyers behaving badly', 147.

65 Sections 8(3)(a), 39(1) and 173 of the *Constitution of the Republic of South Africa*, 1996 respectively.

66 This is confirmed by Langa CJ (as he then was), who has stated that: 'At the heart of a transformative constitution is a commitment to substantive reasoning, to examining the

underlying principles that inform laws themselves and judicial reaction to those laws.'
Langa, 'Transformative constitutionalism', p. 357.

67 For example, *Jaftha v Schoeman; Van Rooyen v Scholtz* 2005 (2) SA 140 (CC); and *Port Elizabeth Municipality v Various Occupiers* 2005 (1) SA 217 (CC).

68 *Minister of Home Affairs and Another v Fourie and Another* 2006 (1) SA 524 (CC); and *Hassam v Jacobs NO and Others* (CCT83/08) [2009] ZACC 19. Notably, the Constitutional Court has also engaged in formal reasoning that hides social and political choices – for example, *Volks NO v Robinson and Others* 2005 (5) BCLR 446 (CC), where the court denied benefits to the 16-year-old unmarried partner of a deceased person on the basis that marriage as an institution should be protected. Or the *UDM United Democratic Movement v President of the Republic of South Africa and Others* 2003 (1) SA 488 (CC) case where the court was at pains to point out that decisions regarding floor-crossing were not political choices but legal choices. In these decisions, then, the Constitutional Court has committed the same thought crime.

69 See note 3 above.

70 *De Freitas and Another v Society of Advocates of Natal and another* 2001 (3) SA 750 (SCA).

71 ibid., para. 5 of Cameron JA's judgment.

7 Can the bioethical principles provide simple signposts for ethical legal practice? Some thoughts on using the bioethical principles as broad guidelines for ethical conduct in developing Commonwealth countries in the context of the English *Solicitors' Code of Conduct* and other ethical rules

David McQuoid-Mason

7.1 Introduction

This chapter is aimed at practitioners, aspiring lawyers, vocational law school instructors and university law teachers concerned with legal ethics in the developing world, particularly in British Commonwealth countries. It is not aimed at developed world legal practitioners, or legal ethicists and legal philosophers teaching in a developed world environment. The teaching of legal ethics in developing countries at both universities and vocational schools usually takes the form of recitation of the local Bar Association rules with very little emphasis on ethical principles – and in many instances, the latter are completely avoided.[1] There are probably very few full credit legal ethics courses at Commonwealth university law faculties in developing countries, and the position is likely to be similar in some developed Commonwealth countries as well.[2] It has been suggested that, instead of stand-alone legal ethics courses, a 'pervasive ethics'[3] or 'whole-of-curriculum'[4] approach should be adopted at universities, in which ethics learning and teaching occur across the law school curriculum.[5]

Legal practitioners and legal ethics instructors in developing Commonwealth countries usually operate within a resource-starved environment. They often do not have access to the international journals in which the academic debates about the nature and function of lawyers and the legal profession in the context of ethics occur. Very few of these journals – if any – are available to them online free of charge. The result is that many of the developing country Commonwealth law teachers and practitioners have not been exposed to the different approaches to legal ethics. Very few have probably heard of the 'zealous advocacy within the bounds of the law'[6] approach, (often called the 'dominant view'[7] or the 'standard conception'[8]); the 'libertarian-positivist view';[9] the 'neutral partnership approach';[10] the 'loyalty approach';[11] the 'autonomy approach';[12] the 'authority conception'[13] approach; or the need to see legal ethics as a branch of moral philosophy[14] and not just a set of rules to govern the legal profession.

For the purposes of developing world legal practitioners, aspiring lawyers and legal ethics instructors, the four basic bioethical principles of client autonomy – beneficence, non-maleficence, and justice or fairness[15] – were chosen as simple signposts for ethical legal practice because of the similarities between the legal and medical professions. These similarities have been recognized by clinical law teachers for decades, and are self-evident: (1) both professions assist clients in trouble; (2) both recognize the importance of respecting the rights of their clients to make decisions for themselves; (3) both require confidentiality between practitioners and their clients in order to build trust; (4) both may give rise to conflicts of interest between practitioners and their clients because of duties owed to third parties; (5) both bind their members by detailed ethical rules; and (6) both require aspiring practitioners to undergo theoretical and practical training.

The four bioethical principles used in this chapter as simple guidelines for legal practice are not intended to supersede the ethical rules of conduct of the legal profession. Nor are they offered as an alternative to the different ethical theories developed by legal ethicists and legal philosophers – indeed, some of the bioethical principles track aspects of these ethical theories, for instance the 'autonomy approach'.[16] The principles are merely offered as a simple tool for busy practitioners and aspiring lawyers and resource-starved legal ethics instructors in developing Commonwealth countries to navigate their way through their local professional rules of conduct.

The approaches adopted to the scenarios in this chapter may seem somewhat naïve and simplistic to legal ethicists, but they are designed to show how busy practitioners or aspiring lawyers in the developing world who are faced with a dual loyalty situation can quickly and simply come up with a solution that will be consistent with their professional rules of conduct. The purpose is to simplify rather than complicate ethical issues for legal practitioners and aspiring lawyers, so that they do not feel overwhelmed and disempowered by them. In short, the aim is to provide simple guidelines to assist practitioners and aspiring lawyers in developing countries to make morally right decisions when dealing with clients.[17]

Lawyers and law teachers in developing Commonwealth countries hold the English legal profession in very high esteem. Therefore, legal instructors with access to the internet may sometimes refer to developments in the English professional rules of conduct where they are available online – as in the case of the English *Solicitors' Code of Conduct*.[18] It was for this reason that the *Solicitors' Code of Conduct* was chosen as a point of reference for this chapter, rather than one of the local developing country codes of professional conduct for lawyers.

As a general rule, lawyers in developing Commonwealth countries, as in developed countries, owe a duty to their clients, and to others such as the courts and society. Lawyers have to observe a host of intricate professional rules of conduct to guide them in the practice of law.[19] For the reasons mentioned above, a useful lesson can be learned from bioethics, which tends to crystallize many of its ethical rules under four basic bioethical principles. As previously mentioned, these principles are client autonomy, beneficence, non-maleficence, and justice or fairness,[20] and they could be adapted by the legal profession to provide practical guidelines to ensure that lawyers adopt an ethical and client-centred approach to their clients.[21]

While it is not recommended that the current ethical rules of the legal profession be replaced, or that the current ethical theories of legal ethicists[22] be disregarded, it is suggested that the four basic principles of bioethics may provide some simple signposts for ethical legal practice by lawyers in developing countries. The principles could be adapted by the legal profession by requiring lawyers to ask themselves the following questions when dealing with their clients: How can I recognize the autonomy of my client? How can I do good for my client? How can I prevent harm to my client? How can I treat my client justly and fairly?

In the light of a lawyer's other duties, such as the duty the court and to society in general, in conflict of interest situations the client autonomy principle may sometimes have to give way.[23] However, the other principles of beneficence, non-maleficence, and justice or fairness should continue to be applied to the client. The principles of beneficence, non-maleficence, and justice or fairness may also be applied to the lawyer's duties outside of the lawyer–client relationship, such as those to the court and society. This can be done by lawyers asking themselves the following questions: How can I do good for the interests of the court (or society)? How can I prevent harm to the interests of the court (or society)? How can I treat the interests of the court (or society) justly or fairly?

Two scenarios are used here to illustrate the conflict of interest dilemmas that lawyers may face and how the modified bioethical principles may assist in resolving them. As this chapter is aimed at lawyers practising in developing countries, the scenarios are based on practical situations that may face legal practitioners, rather than esoteric hypotheticals.

Selected rules of professional conduct, primarily from the *English Solicitors' Code of Conduct*,[24] that will resonate with many developing Commonwealth countries, will be used to illustrate the types of duties lawyers owe to their clients, the court and society in general. Occasional reference will also be made to other professional codes of conduct.

7.2 The bioethical principles

As has been mentioned, the bioethical principles that govern the health professions are client autonomy, beneficence, non-maleficence, and justice or fairness.[25]

Client autonomy means that health care workers should respect the right of patients to make their own decisions about treatment, based on full information concerning the available options.[26] Beneficence means that health care workers should always do good for their patients.[27] Non-maleficence means that health care workers should not harm their patients.[28] The principle of justice or fairness means that health care workers should always treat their patients justly and fairly – without discrimination.[29]

In the context of the lawyer–client relationship in legal practice, the bioethical principles can be modified to mean that lawyers should: (1) respect the autonomy of their clients; (2) do good for their clients; (3) not harm their clients; and (4) treat all their clients justly and fairly. However, once lawyers are confronted with conflict of interest situations, such as where the lawyer's duty to the client clashes with the lawyer's duty to the court or society, client autonomy may have to give way. In these circumstances, the other principles of beneficence, non-maleficence, and justice or fairness should continue to be applied to the lawyer–client relationship to protect the client's interests.[30]

The ethical principles of beneficence, non-maleficence, and justice or fairness may also be applied to other duties faced by lawyers outside the lawyer–client relationship – for instance, the lawyer's duty to the court (or society), by requiring lawyers (1) to do good for the interests of the court and society; (2) not to harm the interests of the court and society; and (3) to treat the interests of the court and society justly or fairly.

7.3 The ethical duties of lawyers

Lawyers owe ethical duties, *inter alia*, to their clients, the courts and society in general. These are encapsulated in the ethical rules of conduct of the legal profession in different countries. Some examples from the English *Solicitors' Code of Conduct*, together with occasional references to other professional rules governing lawyers, will be used to illustrate the kinds of ethical rules to which lawyers may be subjected regarding their duties to their clients, the court and society. The list of professional rules provided below has is also aimed at giving lawyers and legal ethics instructors in developing Commonwealth countries an idea of some of the new approaches to ethical rules of practice adopted by the English solicitor's profession and elsewhere.

7.3.1 The lawyer's ethical duty to clients

According to the English *Solicitors' Code of Conduct*, the South African General Council of the Bar *Uniform Rules* and the International Bar Association *International Code of Ethics*, some of the ethical duties that lawyers owe to their clients are the following:

- the duty to act with integrity;[31]
- the duty to provide a good standard of service to their clients;[32]
- the duty to provide proper client care;[33]
- the duty to provide clients with the best information possible about the likely overall cost of the matter at the outset and as it progresses;[34]

- the duty to act in the best interests of their clients;[35]
- the duty to fearlessly uphold the interests of their clients;[36]
- the duty not to allow their independence to be compromised;[37]
- the duty to keep the affairs of clients or former clients confidential except where disclosure is required or permitted by law or by the client or former client;[38]
- the duty to disclose to a client all information of which the lawyer is aware which is material to the client's case regardless of the source of the information;[39]
- the duty not to put their claim for compensation before their client's interests or the interests of justice.[40]
- the duty to consult with client when choosing an appropriate method of presenting the client's case;[41]
- the duty not to cease acting for a client except for good reason and on reasonable notice;[42]
- the duty not to act if there is a conflict of interest;[43] and
- the duty not to discriminate against clients on the grounds of race or racial group, sex, sexual orientation, religion or belief, age or disability.[44]

7.3.2 The lawyer's ethical duty to the court

According to the English *Solicitors' Code of Conduct*, the English Bar Standards Board *Code of Conduct*, the South African General Council of the Bar *Uniform Rules* and the International Bar Association *International Code of Ethics*, some of the ethical duties that lawyers owe to the courts are the following:

- the duty to uphold the rule of law and the proper administration of justice;[45]
- the duty to assume personal responsibility for their conduct before the court;[46]
- the duty not to give personal opinions unless asked to do so by the court;[47]
- the duty to disclose all relevant decisions or legislative provisions to ensure that the court is fully informed;[48]
- the duty to bring any irregularity to the attention of the court;[49]
- the duty not to mislead the court;[50]
- the duty to act courteously at all times;[51]
- the duty not to waste the court's time;[52]
- the duty to obey court orders;[53]
- the duty not to be in contempt of court;[54]
- the duty to disclose documents notionally within the knowledge of the court where such documents have not been brought to the attention of the court;[55] and
- the duty not to construct facts supporting a client's case or to draft documents containing contents that are not properly arguable.[56]

7.3.3 *The lawyer's ethical duty to society in general*

According to the English *Solicitors' Code of Conduct*, the South African General Council of the Bar *Uniform Rules* and the International Bar Association *International Code of Ethics*, some of the ethical duties that lawyers owe to society in general include:

- the duty to uphold the rule of law and the proper administration of justice;[57]
- the duty not to behave in a way that is likely to diminish the trust the public places in the legal profession;[58]
- the duty not to take unfair advantage of people;[59]
- the duty, when called upon, to assist the state or legal aid authorities with legal aid;[60]
- the duty, when called upon, to assist the state as a prosecutor in a criminal case; and[61]
- the duty not to assist clients to commit crimes.[62]

7.4 Applying the bioethical principles to the lawyer's duty to their clients

All four of the modified bioethical principles of client autonomy, beneficence, non-maleficence, and justice or fairness can usually be applied to the duty of lawyers to their clients. As previously mentioned, this can be done by lawyers asking themselves the following questions: How can I recognize the autonomy of my client? How can I do good for my client? How can I prevent harm to my client? How can I treat my client justly and fairly?

Sometimes the ethical principles overlap with each other (e.g. the duty to respect the client's confidence – client autonomy – may overlap with the duty not to breach the client's confidence – non-maleficence). Furthermore, sometimes when the lawyer also owes a duty to some person or body outside the lawyer–client relationship, the client autonomy principle may be in conflict with the others. For example, where recognition of the client autonomy principle may result in the lawyer undermining his or her duty as an officer of the court, as occurs in conflict of interest situations, client autonomy may have to yield to the lawyer's duty to the court.[63] In such cases, the remaining ethical principles should be applied to the client–lawyer relationship to safeguard the interests of the client. Thus, where the lawyer has to withdraw from representing the client because client autonomy clashes with the lawyer's duty to the court, the client autonomy principle falls away. However, the lawyer should then apply the other ethical principles of beneficence, non-maleficence, and justice or fairness to protect the client.[64] These limitations should be borne in mind when applying the bioethical principles to the lawyer–client relationship.

7.4.1 Applying the autonomy principle to the duty of lawyers to their clients

Client autonomy means that legal practitioners recognize that clients have the right to decide for themselves on their course of action by adopting a client-centred approach, and presenting clients with each option and its consequences, and then inviting the clients to choose which they prefer.[65] This is consistent with the rule that, before deciding on a strategy, a lawyer should give his or her client an idea of the available options concerning a particular course of conduct and then seek the client's approval for the method chosen.[66]

Examples of professional legal rules that acknowledge client autonomy include (1) the duty to respect the confidentiality of client communications;[67] (2) the duty to provide clients with the best information possible about the likely overall cost of the matter at the outset and as it progresses;[68] (3) the duty to disclose to a client all information of which the lawyer is aware which is material to the client's case regardless of the source of the information;[69] (4) the duty to consult with client when choosing an appropriate method of presenting the client's case; [70] and (5) the duty to provide proper client care.[71]

The autonomy principle manifests in the lawyer's duty to respect the client's right to confidentiality because it allows the client to decide who may have access to personal information about them, and under what circumstances. The duty to provide clients with the best information possible about the likely costs of their case enables clients to decide whether or not they wish to proceed. Disclosure of material information to their clients by lawyers enables clients to be fully informed when making decisions about their cases. The duty to consult with clients before engaging in a particular course of action is a clear reflection of the client autonomy principle. The provision of proper client care also embodies the autonomy principle, as it requires lawyers to adopt a client-centred approach to their clients.[72] However, it also overlaps with the principle of beneficence – to do good for one's clients.[73]

Client autonomy, however, will be limited in conflict of interest situations where clients wish their lawyers to undermine their duty to the court (e.g. by asking the lawyer to mislead the court) or society (e.g. by seeking advice on how to commit illegal acts).[74] In such situations, client autonomy gives way to the lawyer's duty to the court or society. However, the lawyer should still apply the other principles of beneficence, non-maleficence, and justice or fairness to protect the interests of their client.[75]

7.4.2 Applying the beneficence ('do good') principle to the duty of lawyers to their clients

Beneficence means that lawyers should always do good for their clients by taking positive steps to act in the best interests of their clients. Thus the interests of clients must be promoted above those of other persons within the constraints of the law. For example, lawyers should do good for their clients by (1) acting with integrity;[76] (2) acting in the best interests of their clients;[77] (3) fearlessly upholding the interests of their clients;[78] (4) providing a good standard of service to their clients;[79] and (5) providing proper client care.[80]

The requirement that lawyers must act with integrity emphasises the need for lawyers to do good for their clients by being honest in all their dealings with their clients and others.[81] In order to do good for their clients, lawyers should always act in their best interests and fearlessly uphold the clients' interests.[82] The provision of a good standard of service is a clear example of the principle of beneficence, as is the duty to provide proper client care. The latter is also an illustration of the principle of autonomy where it requires a client-centred approach to be used in dealings with clients.[83]

In situations of conflicts of interest where a lawyer owes a duty to both the client and the court or society, the beneficence principle may require the lawyer to withdraw from representing the client. Where this is necessary, the withdrawal must be done in a manner that does good by protecting the client's interests[84] (e.g. by ensuring that another competent lawyer takes over the client's case).

7.4.3 Applying the non-maleficence ('do no harm') principle to the duty of lawyers to their clients

Non-maleficence means that lawyers should not harm their clients. Where there is a danger that a client's interests may be harmed, lawyers should uphold the principle of non-maleficence by (1) not allowing their independence to be compromised;[85] (2) not breaching their client's confidentiality without consent from the client;[86] (3) not putting their right to compensation before their client's interests or the interests of justice;[87] (4) not to cease acting for a client except for good reason and on reasonable notice;[88] and (5) not acting if there is a conflict of interest.[89]

The duty of lawyers not to breach their client's confidentiality without consent from the client is the converse of respecting their client's confidences, and is an example of non-maleficence that overlaps with the client autonomy principle.[90] Likewise, the lawyer's duty not to put their right to compensation before their client's interests or the interests of justice is another illustration of the 'do no harm' principle,[91] as is the duty not to cease acting for a client except for good reason and on reasonable notice.[92] The duty not to act if there is a conflict of interest arises where there is a conflict between the duty the lawyer owes to the client and the duty the lawyer owes to some other person, or where there is a conflict between the lawyer's interests and those of their client.[93]

7.4.4 Applying the justice or fairness principle to the duty of lawyers to their clients

The justice or fairness principle means that lawyers have a duty not to discriminate against their clients (or anyone else), without lawful cause, on the grounds of race or racial group, sex, sexual orientation, religion or belief, age or disability.[94]

In addition, all clients should be treated equally and fairly, irrespective of the nature of the alleged crime or civil wrong committed by them or whether the clients are rich or poor.[95]

7.5 Applying the bioethical principles to the lawyer's duty to the court

Lawyers as officers of the court should take all reasonable steps to assist in the smooth running of the court, but only insofar as it is consistent with their duties to their client.[96] The principles of beneficence, non-maleficence, and justice or fairness may be applied to the lawyer's duty to the court to ensure that justice is done. This can be done by lawyers asking themselves: How can I do good for the interests of the court? How can I prevent harm to the interests of the court? How can I treat the interests of the court justly or fairly?

7.5.1 *Applying the beneficence principle to the duty of lawyers to the court*

The beneficence principle requires lawyers to do good for the court (1) by upholding the rule of law and the proper administration of justice;[97] (2) by assuming personal responsibility for their conduct when addressing or interacting with the court;[98] (3) by acting courteously at all times;[99] and (4) by obeying court orders.[100]

The duty of lawyers to do good by upholding the rule of law and the proper administration of justice is reinforced by the additional duties requiring them (1) to disclose all relevant decisions or legislative provisions to ensure that the court is fully informed;[101] (2) to bring any irregularity to the attention of the court;[102] and (3) to disclose to the court documents notionally within its knowledge where such documents have not been brought to the attention of the court.[103] These duties ensure that lawyers do good for the court by ensuring that the presiding officer is provided with full information and can make decisions in accordance with justice. For this reason, these duties also fall under the justice or fairness principle.[104]

Lawyers must take responsibility for what they say and do in court, and cannot simply act as 'hired guns'[105] should their clients instruct them to act unethically or illegally (e.g. by misleading the court or undermining the authority of the presiding officer). Courteous behaviour ensures that the court proceedings are conducted in an appropriately objective manner by the presiding officer and counsel, and that all parties get a proper hearing. Lawyers are also expected to do good by obeying court orders, as a failure to do so undermines the dignity of the court and amounts to contempt of court.

7.5.2 *Applying the non-maleficence principle to the lawyer's duty to the court*

The non-maleficence principle requires lawyers (1) not to give personal opinions unless asked by the court;[106] (2) not to mislead the court;[107] (3) not to waste the court's time;[108] (4) not to be in contempt of court;[109] and (5) not to construct facts supporting a client's case or to draft documents containing contents that are not properly arguable.[110]

The giving of personal opinions may result in a lawyer losing his or her objectivity, and is likely to result in an admonition from the court.[111] Misleading the court prevents the presiding officer from making rulings based on true information. Unwarranted wasting of the time of the court undermines the administration of justice, and may result in justice being delayed. As previously mentioned, contempt of court undermines the dignity of the court. The duty on lawyers not to construct facts supporting a client's case and not to draft documents containing contents that are not properly arguable is a manifestation of the non-maleficence principle because it undermines the court's ability to administer justice.

7.5.3 Applying the justice or fairness principle to the lawyer's duty to the court

The justice or fairness principle overlaps with the beneficence principle in the context of the court because it requires lawyers to act for the good of the administration of justice.[112] Thus the justice or fairness principle requires lawyers to disclose (1) all relevant decisions and legislative provisions;[113] (2) all irregularities;[114] and (3) all documents notionally within the knowledge of the court.[115]

The disclosure of all relevant decisions and legislative provisions is essential for the proper administration of justice. This applies even if case authority is against the lawyer's contentions – in such a situation, he or she should seek to distinguish their case from the case before the court. All irregularities and documents notionally within the knowledge of the court should also be disclosed to ensure that the court makes a decision that is consistent with the fair administration of justice.

7.6 Applying the bioethical principles to the lawyer's duty to society in general

In conflict of interest situations where the duty of the lawyer to their client clashes with their duty to society, it is suggested that the public interest – especially the public interest in the administration of justice – should take precedence.[116] The principles of beneficence, non-maleficence and justice or fairness may assist in this regard. This can be done by lawyers asking themselves: How can I do good for the interests of society? How can I prevent harm to the interests of society? How can I treat the interests of society justly or fairly?

7.6.1 Applying the beneficence principle to the lawyer's duty to society

The principle of beneficence in the context of society in general requires lawyers to uphold the rule of law and the proper administration of justice[117] – for instance, when called upon (1) to assist the state or legal aid authorities with legal aid;[118] and (2) to assist the state as a prosecutor in criminal cases.[119]

It is axiomatic that lawyers do good by upholding the rule of law and respecting the laws of their country, and this is often included in the oath that lawyers take on being admitted to practice. The beneficence principle is reflected in countries where the legal profession maintains a strong tradition of pro bono work and where such pro bono work is subsumed into legal aid schemes or used to supplement them. The beneficence principle is also apparent when private lawyers comply with requests by the state to assist in the administration of justice by acting as prosecutors.

7.6.2 Applying the non-maleficence principle to the lawyer's duty to society in general

The principle of non-maleficence in the societal context requires lawyers (1) not to behave in a way that is likely to diminish the trust the public places in the legal profession;[120] (2) not to take unfair advantage of people;[121] and (3) not to assist clients to commit crimes.[122]

Behaviour within or outside a lawyer's professional practice that undermines the trust the public has in the legal profession damages the ability of the profession to serve society.[123] Lawyers should not use their position to take unfair advantage of anyone, either for their own benefit or for the benefit of others.[124] Assisting clients in the commission of crimes undermines the administration of justice and is a violation of a lawyer's duty to assist with the administration of justice.[125] This duty complements the duty of lawyers to uphold the law, and overlaps with the beneficence principle. A failure to uphold the law would amount to maleficence, which is a violation of the principle of non-maleficence.

7.6.3 Applying the justice or fairness principle to the lawyer's duty to society in general

The lawyer's duties to society that reflect the justice or fairness principle are (1) the duty not to take unfair advantage of anyone;[126] (2) the duty to uphold the rule of law and the proper administration of justice;[127] and (3) the duty not to assist clients to commit crimes.[128] These duties also overlap with the principles of beneficence and non-maleficence.[129]

The justice or fairness principle requires the lawyer not to take advantage of anyone by finding a balance between the lawyer's duty to his or her client and treating the other person fairly.[130] For example, where an unrepresented opponent provides badly drawn documentation, the lawyer should recommend that the person finds legal representation.[131]

7.7 Conflicts of interests and the duty of lawyers to their clients

Conflicts of interest arise where lawyers are required to balance their duty to the client with their duty to someone else, such as to the court or to society. The bioethical approach is to put the interests of patients or clients before those of other parties.[132] However, in the legal profession the lawyer's duty as an officer of the court is to assist the court insofar as it is consistent with their duties to their client.[133]

Where the lawyer has to limit the client's autonomy because of a conflict of interest, it should be done in such a manner as to apply the other principles of beneficence, non-maleficence, and justice or fairness to the lawyer–client relationship. For example, if a lawyer is faced with a conflict of interest between the lawyer's duty to their client and their duty to the court or society that requires the lawyer to withdraw from acting for the client, such withdrawal should be done in a manner that is consistent with the principles of beneficence, non-maleficence, and justice or fairness, so that the client's interests are not compromised. This is consistent with the lawyer's duty not to cease acting for a client except for good reason and on reasonable notice.[134] Therefore, when the lawyer abandons the client autonomy principle in order to comply with their duty to the court or to society in general, the lawyer should do good for the client and not harm the client by providing reasonable notice, and acting justly or fairly by having a good reason for ceasing to act.

The following scenarios illustrate how dual-loyalty situations may be resolved using the principles of client autonomy, beneficence, non-maleficence, and justice or fairness. The scenarios and their analysis have been deliberately simplified to demonstrate how the bioethical principles can be used as simple guidelines for busy practitioners in the developing world. It is beyond the scope of this chapter to compare how the decisions reached using the proposed modified bioethical guidelines would measure up against decisions based on the different legal ethics theories developed by legal ethicists and philosophers.

7.7.1 Scenario 1: The hit-and-run driver

A lawyer hears a radio report that a hit-and-run driver has run over and killed 15 school children outside a primary school. The police have appealed for anyone with information about the driver to contact them urgently. Two hours later, a person consults the lawyer and says that he is the hit-and-run driver and wants to know how he can avoid reporting the incident and being arrested.

1   What is the lawyer's duty to the hit-and-run driver?
2   Does the lawyer owe any duty to society? If so, what should she do?

7.7.1.1 Application of the ethical principles

7.7.1.1.1 DUTY TO CLIENT

If the lawyer agrees to take on the hit-and-run driver as a client, she must ask herself the following questions reflecting the ethical principles of client autonomy, beneficence, non-maleficence, and justice or fairness: 'How can I recognize the autonomy of my client?' She should recognize the autonomy of her client by explaining to him the consequences of a hit-and-run offence and the chances of his avoiding arrest, and then allowing him to make an informed choice regarding the action he wishes to take. This would be consistent with the lawyer's duty in the English *Solicitor's Code of Conduct* to provide proper client care by giving the client a clear explanation of the issues involved and the options available to the client.[135] She might convince the client to surrender to the police, and if he accepted her advice, her questions would then be: 'How can I do good for my client?' She should do good for her client by assisting him with the process for surrendering himself and represent him in court. This would also accord with the legal duty to provide proper client care required by the English *Solicitors' Code of Conduct* by agreeing with the client the next steps to be taken.[136] The next question would be: 'How can I prevent harm to my client?' She should try to prevent further harm to her client by advising him not to continue avoiding the police. Here she would be acting in accordance with the English *Solicitor's Code of Conduct* requirement that she act in the 'best interests' of her client,[137] because if he were to continue avoiding the police and were then arrested, he would face even more severe charges regarding his failure to stop and report the accident. She should ask: 'How can I treat my client justly and fairly?' She should treat him justly and fairly by continuing to treat him like any other client – despite the fact that he may have been responsible for failing to stop after killing 15 school children. The General Council of the Bar of South Africa *Uniform Rules* require that lawyers may not discriminate against their clients because of the nature of the crimes committed by them.[138]

If the client refuses to follow her advice, the lawyer would be faced with a conflict between her duty to the client and her duty to society. In such circumstances, she would be justified in abandoning the client autonomy principle by refusing to act for the client because she is faced with a conflict of interest, as she cannot be party to criminal conduct by her client and cannot undermine the rule of law by conniving with him to avoid reporting a fatal accident. This is in line with the English *Solicitors' Code of Conduct* rule that requires lawyers not to assist clients to commit crimes,[139] and to uphold the rule of law and the proper administration of justice.[140] It also satisfies the English *Solicitors' Code of Conduct*[141] and the International Bar Association's *International Code of Ethics*[142] rules, stating how lawyers should act in conflict of interest situations. However, she must still apply the other principles of beneficence, non-maleficence, and justice and fairness, and ask herself the other questions: 'How can I do good for my client?' She should do good for her client by referring him to another lawyer. This is consistent with the

English *Solicitors' Code of Conduct* rule that imposes a duty on lawyers to act in the best interests of their clients and not to cease acting for them except for good reason and on reasonable notice.[113] It is submitted that this would include giving them sufficient time and the opportunity to obtain other legal assistance. 'How can I prevent harm to my client?' She should prevent harm to her client by not breaching the confidentiality of the discussions between her and the client if the client consults another lawyer. 'How can I treat my client justly and fairly?' She should treat him justly and fairly by treating him like any other client and not disclosing to the police or anyone else what her client had told her. Both of these actions would comply with the English *Solicitors' Code of Conduct*,[114] the General Council of the Bar of South Africa *Uniform Rules*[115] and the International Bar Association *International Code of Ethics*[116] rules that lawyers keep the affairs of their clients or former clients confidential except where disclosure is required or permitted by law or the client or former client.

7.7.1.1.2 DUTY TO SOCIETY

If the client follows the lawyer's advice to surrender to the police, the lawyer will also have carried out her duty to society. The lawyer can check this by asking herself the following questions that relate to the principles of beneficence, non-maleficence and justice or fairness: 'How can I do good for the interests of society?' She should do good for the interests of society by trying to persuade the client to report the accident to the police. 'How can I prevent harm to the interests of society?' She should prevent harm to the interests of society by recommending to her client that he surrender to the police so that the criminal justice system takes it course. 'How can I treat the interests of society justly fairly?' She should treat the interests of society justly and fairly by trying to ensure that the innocence or guilt of her client is tested in a court of law. By responding to these three questions in the manner mentioned above, she will be following the English *Solicitor's Code of Conduct* by upholding the rule of law and proper administration of justice.[147] She would also not be assisting her client to persist in his criminal conduct, which would also be against the English *Solicitor's Code of Conduct*.[148]

If the client refuses to follow her advice, the lawyer needs to ask the following questions: 'How can I do good for the interests of society?' She should do good for the interests of society by withdrawing from the case because she cannot be party to her client's attempt to undermine the rule of law. Here she would also be following the English *Solicitors' Code of Conduct* by upholding the rule of law and proper administration of justice.[149] 'How can I prevent harm to the interests of society?' She should prevent harm to the interests of society by refusing to assist her client to avoid reporting the fatal accident. This is consistent with the English *Solicitors' Code of Conduct* rule about lawyers not assisting clients to commit crimes.[150] 'How can I treat the interests of society justly and fairly?' She should treat the interests of society justly and fairly by referring her client to another lawyer who might be able to persuade the client to report the accident. Once again this would satisfy the English *Solicitors' Code of Conduct* requirement of upholding the rule of law and proper administration of justice,[151] by ensuring that the client gets a fair trial.

7.7.2 Scenario 2: The client who changed her mind

A lawyer interviews a client before the client gives evidence in a trial, in which she is charged with murder. When she gives her evidence in court, however, the client completely changes her evidence. The lawyer realizes that if he continues, he will be leading her through false evidence.

1   What is the lawyer's duty to his client? What should he do?
2   What is the lawyer's duty to the court? What should he do?

7.7.2.1 *Application of the ethical principles*

7.7.2.1.1 DUTY TO CLIENT

The client autonomy principle applies for as long as the client does not expect the lawyer to violate his duty to the court. In this instance, by expecting the lawyer to lead her through evidence that is false, the client will be compelling him to mislead the court. This would fly in the face of the rules of the English *Solicitors' Code of Conduct*,[152] the General Council of the Bar of South Africa *Uniform Rules*[153] and the International Bar Association *International Code of Ethics*,[154] which state that lawyers have a duty not to mislead the court. Faced with this situation, the client autonomy principle falls away. However, the lawyer must still apply the principles of beneficence, non-maleficence, and justice and fairness for his client. In this respect, the lawyer should ask himself the following questions: 'How can I do good for my client?' The lawyer should do good for his client by asking the court for an adjournment and, while acknowledging his client's autonomy to decide what she wants to do in court, he should explain to her the consequences of her conduct. He should state that, as an officer of the court, he cannot lead false evidence, and that if she continues to give untrue evidence, his duty to her as a client will have to yield to his duty not to mislead the court, with the result that he will have to withdraw from the case. This approach is consistent with the legal duty to provide proper client care required by the English *Solicitors' Code of Conduct* by agreeing with the client the next steps to be taken.[155] 'How can I prevent harm to my client?' The lawyer should prevent harm to his client by advising her that it is for her own good that she should tell the truth and that it will harm her case if she continues, because the falsity of her evidence is likely to be exposed in cross-examination. This approach accords with the English *Solicitors' Code of Conduct* rule that lawyers have a duty to consult with client when choosing appropriate methods of presenting their clients cases.[156] 'How can I treat my client justly and fairly?' The lawyer should ensure that when he withdraws, his client has enough time to consult another lawyer, and that he withdraws in circumstances that do not harm her case. Here the lawyer would be following the rule in the English

Solicitors' Code of Conduct that lawyers should not cease to acting for clients except for good reason and on reasonable notice.[157]

7.7.2.1.2 DUTY TO THE COURT

The lawyer's duty to the court is not to mislead it. This is provided for in the English *Solicitors' Code of Conduct*,[158] the General Council of the Bar of South Africa *Uniform Rules*[159] and the International Bar Association *International Code of Ethics*.[160] Therefore, if his client insists on giving false evidence, and the lawyer has to withdraw, he should ask himself the following questions in relation to his duty to the court: 'How can I do good for the interests of the court?' He should do good for the interests of the court by withdrawing from the case, to avoid leading false evidence from his client. This is required by the English *Solicitors' Code of Conduct*[161] and the English Bar Standards Board *Code of Conduct*,[162] which state that lawyers have a duty not to construct facts supporting a client's case. 'How can I prevent harm to the interests of court?' He should prevent harm to the interests of the court by withdrawing in circumstances that do not harm the administration of justice. 'How can I treat the interests of the court justly and fairly?' He should treat the interests of the court justly and fairly by withdrawing in a manner that enables the court to come to a decision based on truth instead of falsity. These actions are in accordance with the English *Solicitors' Code of Conduct* rule that lawyers have a duty to uphold the rule of law and proper administration of justice.[163]

7.8 Conclusion

The following conclusions may be drawn from the above discussion:

- In developing Commonwealth countries, the teaching of legal ethics at both universities and vocational schools often takes the form of recitation of the local Bar Association rules, with very little emphasis on ethical principles.
- Legal practitioners and legal ethics instructors in developing Commonwealth countries usually operate within a resource-starved environment and do not have access to the international materials reflecting the debates between legal ethicists about ethical principles.
- There are similarities between the medical and legal professions, and a modified version of the bioethical principles of client autonomy, beneficence, non-maleficence, and justice or fairness may provide simple signposts for the ethical duties of lawyers towards their clients, the courts and society in developing countries.
- All four ethical principles can be applied to the duty of lawyers to their clients by lawyers asking themselves the following questions: How can I recognize the autonomy of my client? How can I do good for my client? How can I prevent harm to my client? How can I treat my client justly and fairly?
- In the light of a lawyer's other duties – such as the duty to the court and

society in general – in conflict of interest situations, the client autonomy principle may have to give way. However, the principles of beneficence, non-maleficence, and justice or fairness should continue to be applied to the client to protect the client's interests.

- The principles of beneficence, non-maleficence, and justice or fairness may also be applied to the lawyer's other duties, such as those to the court and society. In such situations, lawyers should ask themselves the following questions: How can I do good for the interests of the court (or society)? How can I prevent harm to the interests of the court (or society)? How can I treat the interests of the court (or society) justly or fairly?

- The ethical principles of client autonomy, beneficence, non-maleficence, and justice or fairness provide simple signposts for lawyers in developing countries when navigating the ethical rules that govern the legal profession regarding their duties to their clients and to others, such as the court and society.

- Lawyers in developing countries who use the above ethical principles as basic guidelines for the practice of law are likely to find that in general they will be acting in harmony with the ethical rules of their particular branch of the legal profession, as illustrated by applying the ethical principles to two conflict of interest scenarios and comparing their application with that of some rules of the English *Solicitors' Code of Conduct*, the English Bar Standards *Code of Conduct*, the General Council of the Bar of South Africa *Uniform Rules* and the International Bar Association *International Code of Ethics*.

Notes

1 A good example is the standard text on legal ethics in South Africa, E.A.L. Lewis, *Legal Ethics: A Guide to Professional Conduct for South African Attorneys*, Kenwyn: Juta & Co., 1982, p. 1, where the author begins his first chapter as follows: 'Ethical philosophy is not part of this book. Fortunately it is no part of the purpose of this book to plunge into the philosophy of ethics and into discussion of what in modern terminology are . . . called the normative, the descriptive and ethics proper. Its purpose is entirely practical and concerned with the rules of conduct and precepts which the attorney is required to obey in the course of practising his [*sic*] profession, as well as extra-professional while he [*sic*] remains in the profession.'

2 See, for instance, in Australia, S. Ross, *Ethics in Law: Lawyers' Responsibility and Accountability in Australia*, Sydney: Butterworths, 1995, p. 3; and more recently, M. Robertson, 'Providing ethics learning opportunities throughout the legal curriculum', *Legal Ethics* 12, 2009, 59–66, where he remarks that: 'In Australia and elsewhere, the main focus of in compulsory courses on lawyers' professional and ethical responsibilities has most often been on the content of the formal law of lawyering. This means that the predominant course learning objectives have been directed to the knowledge of professional legal duties as they appear in statutes, the general law, and in professional codes of responsibility.'

3 D.L. Rhode, 'Ethics by the pervasive method', *Journal of Legal Education* 42, 1992, 31.

4 Robertson, 'Providing ethics learning opportunities', 60–2.

5 ibid., 60.

6 M.H. Freedman, 'The lawyer's moral obligation of justification', *Texas Law Review* 74, 1995, 111, 116–17.

7 W.H. Simon, *The Practice of Justice*, Cambridge: Harvard University Press, 1998, p. 7.
8 G.J. Postema, 'Moral responsibility in professional ethics', *New York University Law Review* 55, 1980, 63, 75; D. Luban, *Lawyers and Justice*, Princeton, NJ: Princeton University Press, 1988, p. 7.
9 R. W. Gordon, 'Why lawyers can't just be hired guns', in D.L. Rhode (ed.), *Ethics in Practice: Lawyers' Roles, Responsibilities and Regulation*, Oxford: Oxford University Press, 2000, pp. 42, 47.
10 N.W. Spaulding, 'Reinterpreting professional identity', *University of Colorado Law Review* 54, 2003, 1, 52.
11 C. Fried, 'The lawyer as friend: The moral foundations of the lawyer–client relation', *Yale Law Journal* 85, 1976, 1060, 1071–76.
12 S.L. Pepper, 'The lawyer's amoral ethical rule: A defense, a problem, and some possibilities', *American Bar Foundation Research Journal* 11, 1986, 613, 616–17; cf. M. H. Freedman and A. Smith, *Understanding Lawyers' Ethics*, 2nd edn, Philadelphia: Lexis Nexis, 2002, pp. 56–8, 69–70.
13 W.B. Wendel, 'Civil obedience', *Columbia Law Review* 104, 2004, 363, 368–9.
14 D.L. Rhode, *In the Interest of Justice*, New York: Oxford University Press, 2001, p. 58.
15 See generally, T.L. Beauchamp and J.F. Childress, *The Principles of Biomedical Ethics*, 3rd edn, New York: Oxford University Press, 1994.
16 Pepper, 'The lawyer's amoral ethical rule', pp. 616–17.
17 The author has tried this approach on practising lawyers at International Bar Association meetings in Singapore in October 2007 and Buenos Aires in October 2008, at an African Clinical Law Teachers Roundtable in Cape Town in November 2007, and on legal aid and other lawyers in South Africa over several years. In every instance, the practitioners concerned have remarked on how useful and practical it is. In April 2008, the author made the bioethical principles the subject of his DCL (*honoris causa*) Graduation Address at Windsor University, Ontario, where he also addressed graduands in other disciplines. The response to the address by the graduands and their parents on the usefulness of the approach was overwhelmingly positive, both during and after the graduation ceremony.
18 England and Wales Solicitors' Regulation Authority, *Solicitors' Code of Conduct*, 2007. See www.sra.org.uk/solicitors/code-of-conduct (accessed 22 August 2009).
19 See generally, for the purposes of this chapter, ibid.; England and Wales Bar Standards Authority, *Code of Conduct*, 8th edn, 2004; General Council of the Bar of South Africa, *Uniform Rules of Professional Conduct*, 2004; International Bar Association, *International Code of Ethics*, 1988.
20 See generally, Beauchamp and Childress, *Principles of Biomedical Ethics*, pp. 67–302.
21 Some of these – for instance, the 'client autonomy' approach – resonate with the 'autonomy' approach of Pepper, 'The lawyer's amoral ethical rule', pp. 616, 617, in respect of client autonomy, or the 'standard conception' mentioned by Postema, 'Moral responsibility in professional ethics', pp. 63, 75 and Luban, *Lawyers and Justice*, p. 7.
22 See above notes 6–14.
23 These situations are likely to fall under Pepper's exceptions to the 'autonomy' rule, including when lawyers are entitled to take a conscientious objector position: Pepper, 'The lawyer's amoral ethical rule', 628–35; cf. Ross, *Ethics in Law*, p. 24.
24 Solicitors' Regulation Authority, *Solicitors' Code of Conduct*, 2007.
25 See generally, Beauchamp and Childress, *Principles of Bioethics*, pp. 67–302.
26 Beauchamp and Childress, *Principles of Bioethics*, pp. 67–113. Autonomous action requires a person to act (1) intentionally; (2) with understanding; and (3) without controlling influences that determine the action (Beauchamp and Childress, *Principles of Bioethics*, p. 69).
27 ibid., pp. 194–249. The general principle of beneficence has two elements: (1) the provision of benefits; and (2) the balance of benefits and harms: ibid., p. 195.

28 ibid., pp. 120–84. The principle of non-maleficence includes (1) not imposing risks of harm; and (2) not inflicting actual harms: ibid., p. 125.
29 ibid., pp. 256–302. Justice is often equated to fairness and in simple terms means that everyone should be treated equally: ibid., pp. 257–59.
30 See below, section 7.7.
31 Solicitors' Regulation Authority, *Solicitors' Code of Conduct*, 2007, rule 1.02. Personal integrity is central to the role of a lawyer as a client's trusted adviser: rule 1.02, Guidance comment 6.
32 ibid., rule 1.05. This requires lawyers to act with competence, skill and diligence: rule 1.05, Guidance comment 9.
33 ibid., rule 2.02. Client care requires lawyers to (1) identify clearly the client's object-ives in relation to the work to be done for the client; (2) give the client a clear explanation of the issues involved and the options available to the client; (3) agree with the client the next steps to be taken; and (4) keep the client informed of progress, unless otherwise agreed: rule 2.02(1). They should also (1) agree an appropriate level of service; (2) explain their responsibilities; (3) explain the client's responsibilities; (4) ensure that the client is given, in writing, the name and status of the person dealing with the matter and the name of the person responsible for its overall supervision; and (5) explain any limitations or conditions resulting from their relationship with a third party (e.g. a funder, fee sharer or introducer) that affect the steps the lawyer can take on the client's behalf: rule 2.02(2).
34 ibid., rule 2.03. Clients are required to be given detailed information about costs including (1) the basis and terms of the charges; (2) whether the charging rates are to be increased; (3) the likely payments that may need to be made to others; (4) how the client will pay; and (5) such matters as whether the client may be eligible and should apply for public funding or whether the client's costs are likely to be paid by insurance or a third party such as an employer or trade union: rule 2.03(1).
35 ibid., rule 1.04.
36 General Council of the Bar of South Africa, *Uniform Rules*, rule 3.1; International Bar Association, *International Code of Ethics*, rule 6, which require advocates to uphold the interests of their clients fearlessly by rendering every argument which can be legitimately advanced on behalf of their clients – irrespective of any unpleasant consequences the advocate or others may experience.
37 Solicitors' Regulation Authority, *Solicitors' Code of Conduct*, rule 2.02; cf. General Council of the Bar of South Africa, *Uniform Rules*, rule 4.26; International Bar Associ-ation, *International Code of Ethics*, rule 3.
38 Solicitors' Regulation Authority, *Solicitors' Code of Conduct*, rule 4.01; General Council of the Bar of South Africa, *Uniform Rules*, rule 3.2; International Bar Association, *International Code of Ethics*, rule 14. The confidence belongs to the client and the client may consent to disclosure of such confidence provided he or she has full knowledge and appreciation of the consequences of the disclosure: R. Palmer and D. McQuoid-Mason, *Basic Trial Advocacy Skills*, Durban: Butterworths, 2000, p. 11.
39 Solicitors' Regulation Authority, *Solicitors' Code of Conduct*, rule 4.02, subject to excep-tions where (1) the duty of confidentiality in rule 4.01 overrides such disclosure; (2) such disclosure is prohibited by law; (3) it is agreed expressly that no duty to disclose arises or a different standard of disclosure applies; or (4) where the lawyer reasonably believes that serious physical or mental injury will be caused to any person if the information is disclosed to the client: rule 4.02(a) and (b).
40 The lawyer's right to demand payment of a deposit or out-of-pocket expenses, failing payment of which they may withdraw from the case or refuse to handle it, should never be exercised at a moment at which the client may be unable to find other assistance to prevent irreparable harm being done to the case: International Bar Association, *International Code of Ethics*, rule 17.
41 Solicitors' Regulation Authority, *Solicitors' Code of Conduct*, rule 2.02(2).

42 ibid.
43 Solicitors' Regulation Authority, *Solicitors' Code of Conduct*, rule 3.01 – for example, where the lawyer or the lawyer's firm (1) owes separate duties to act in the best interests of two or more clients in relation to the same or related matters, and those duties conflict, or there is a significant risk that those duties may conflict; and (2) the lawyer's duty to act in the best interests of a client in relation to a matter conflicts, or there is a significant risk that it may conflict, with the lawyer's own interests in relation to that or a related matter: rule 3.01(2). See also International Bar Association, *International Code of Ethics*, rule 13.
44 ibid., rule 6.01(1). Discrimination on such grounds may also not be made, without lawful cause, against employees, partners, members, directors, barristers, other lawyers or third parties, and the same applies to victimization and harassment of such persons or clients on the same grounds: rule 6.01(1).
45 ibid., rule 1.01. This is also a duty owed to society in general: see below section 7.6.3.
46 Bar Standards Board, *Code of Conduct*, Part VII, rule 708(a).
47 ibid., Part VII, rule 708 (b). For example, in England when Lord Erskine was defending Tom Paine, Erskine said: 'I will now lay aside the role of the advocate and address you as a man.' The judge replied: 'You will do nothing of the sort. The only right and licence you have is to appear in this court as an advocate.' R. Du Cann, *The Art of the Advocate*, London: Penguin, 1980, p. 40.
48 Solicitors' Regulation Authority, *Solicitors' Code of Conduct*, rule 11.02(2); Bar Standards Board, *Code of Conduct*, Part VII, rule 708 (c). For example, if one lawyer omits a case or provision, it is the duty of the other to draw attention to it even if it assists the opponent's case: Palmer and McQuoid-Mason, *Basic Trial Advocacy*, p. 8.
49 ibid., rule 11.01(2); Bar Standards Board, *Code of Conduct*, Part VII, rule 708(d).
50 ibid., rule 11.01(1); General Council of the Bar of South Africa, *Uniform Rules*, rule 3.2; International Bar Association, *International Code of Ethics*, rule 6. Lawyers may use only proper and lawful means to promote and protect the interests of their clients. Lawyers may not knowingly put forward false information with the intention to mislead the court. For example, they may not construct facts supporting a client's case or draft documents containing contents that are not properly arguable: Solicitors' Regulation Authority, *Solicitors' Code of Conduct*, rule 11.01(3); Bar Standards Board, *Code of Conduct*, Part VII, rule 704.
51 Bar Standards Board, *Code of Conduct*, Part VII, rule 701(a), which states that lawyers should at all times be courteous to the court and to all those with whom they have professional dealings.
52 ibid.
53 Solicitors' Regulation Authority, *Solicitors' Code of Conduct*, rule 11.02.
54 ibid., rule 11.03.
55 ibid., rule 11.01(2).
56 ibid., rule 11.01(3); Bar Standards Board, *Code of Conduct*, Part VII, rule 704.
57 Solicitors' Regulation Authority, *Solicitors' Code of Conduct*, rule 1.01.
58 ibid., rule 1.06.
59 ibid., rule 10.01.
60 General Council of the Bar of South Africa, *Uniform Rules*, rule 6.3.1; International Bar Association, *International Code of Ethics*, rule 17. The International Bar Association, *International Code of Ethics*, rule 17 states that attorneys are expected to assist in cases 'assigned by a competent body' which could be interpreted to mean a legal aid authority: Palmer and McQuoid-Mason, *Basic Trial Advocacy*, p. 21.
61 General Council of the Bar of South Africa, *Uniform Rules*, rule 2.1. This is in terms of the 'cab rank' rule which also applies to barristers in England, but does not apply to solicitors: cf. Solicitors' Regulation Authority, *Solicitors' Code of Conduct*, rule 11.04(2).
62 Assisting clients in the commission of crimes would undermine the administration of

justice and would be a violation of a lawyer's duty to assist with the administration of justice: cf. Solicitors' Regulation Authority, *Solicitors' Code of Conduct*, rule 1.01.

63 See below section 7.7.

64 See below paras 7.4.2, 7.4.3 and 7.4.4.

65 See above note 26.

66 Solicitors' Regulation Authority, *Solicitors' Code of Conduct*, rule 2.02. See above note 33.

67 ibid., rule 4.01; cf. General Council of the Bar of South Africa, *Uniform Rules*, rule 3.2; International Bar Association, *International Code of Ethics*, rule 14. See above note 38.

68 Solicitors' Regulation Authority, *Solicitors' Code of Conduct*, rule 2.03. See above note 34.

69 ibid., rule 4.02, subject to exceptions where (1) the duty of confidentiality in rule 4.01 overrides such disclosure; (2) such disclosure is prohibited by law; (3) it is agreed expressly that no duty to disclose arises or a different standard of disclosure applies; or (4) where the lawyer reasonably believes that serious physical or mental injury will be caused to any person if the information is disclosed to the client (rule 4.02(a) and (b)).

70 Solicitors' Regulation Authority, *Solicitors' Code of Conduct*, rule 2.02(2).

71 ibid., rule 2.02. See above note 33.

72 ibid., rule 2.02(2). See above note 33.

73 See below para 7.4.2.

74 See below section 7.7.

75 See Solicitors' Regulation Authority, *Solicitors' Code of Conduct*, rule 11, Guidance comment 5, which requires lawyers to assist the court only to the extent that it is consistent with their duties to their client.

76 ibid., rule 1.02. See above note 31.

77 ibid., rule 1.04.

78 General Council of the Bar of South Africa, *Uniform Rules*, rule 3.1; International Bar Association, *International Code of Ethics*, rule 6. See above note 36.

79 Solicitors' Regulation Authority, *Solicitors' Code of Conduct*, rule 1.05. See above note 32.

80 ibid., rule 2.02. See above note 33.

81 ibid., rule 1.02.

82 See above notes 35 and 36.

83 See above section 7.4.1 and note 26.

84 Solicitors' Regulation Authority, *Solicitors' Code of Conduct*, rule 2.01(2) and rule 11, Guidance comment 5.

85 ibid., rule 2.02; General Council of the Bar of South Africa, *Uniform Rules*, rule 4.26; International Bar Association, *International Code of Ethics*, rule 3.

86 General Council of the Bar of South Africa, *Uniform Rules*, rule 3.2; International Bar Association, *International Code of Ethics*, rule 14. See above note 38.

87 International Bar Association, *International Code of Ethics*, rule 17. See above note 40.

88 Solicitors' Regulation Authority, *Solicitors' Code of Conduct*, rule 2.01(2).

89 ibid., rule 3.01. See above note 43.

90 See above section 7.4.1.

91 International Bar Association, *International Code of Ethics*, rule 17. See above note 40.

92 Solicitors' Regulation Authority, *Solicitors' Code of Conduct*, rule 2.01(2).

93 ibid., rule 3.01. See above note 43.

94 ibid., rule 6.01(1). See above note 44.

95 General Council of the Bar of South Africa, *Uniform Rules*, rule 3.1.

96 Solicitors' Regulation Authority, *Solicitors' Code of Conduct*, rule 11, Guidance comment 5.

97 ibid., rule 1.01.

98 Bar Standards Board, *Code of Conduct*, Part VII, rule 708(a).

99 ibid., Part VII, rule 701(a). See above note 51.

100 Solicitors' Regulation Authority, *Solicitors' Code of Conduct*, rule 11.02.

101 Bar Standards Board, *Code of Conduct*, Part VII, rule 708 (c); Solicitors' Regulation Authority, *Solicitors' Code of Conduct*, rule 11.02(2). See above note 48.
102 Solicitors' Regulation Authority, *Solicitors' Code of Conduct*, rule 11.01(2); Bar Standards Board, *Code of Conduct*, Part VII, rule 708 (d).
103 Solicitors' Regulation Authority, *Solicitors' Code of Conduct*, rule 11.01(2).
104 See below section 7.5.3.
105 See generally, R. Lefcourt (ed.), *The Law Against the People: Essays to Demystify Law, Order and the Courts*, New York: Vintage, 1971.
106 Bar Standards Board, *Code of Conduct*, Part VII, rule 708 (b). See above note 47.
107 Solicitors' Regulation Authority, *Solicitors' Code of Conduct*, rule 11.01(1); General Council of the Bar of South Africa, *Uniform Rules*, rule 3.2; International Bar Association, *International Code of Ethics*, rule 6.
108 Bar Standards Board, *Code of Conduct*, Part VII, rule 701(a).
109 Solicitors' Regulation Authority, *Solicitors' Code of Conduct*, rule 11.03.
110 ibid., rule 11.01(3); Bar Standards Board, *Code of Conduct*, Part VII, rule 704.
111 Du Cann, *Art of the Advocate*, p. 40, citing the admonition by the judge of Lord Erskine in the Tom Paine case: see above note 47.
112 Solicitors' Regulation Authority, *Solicitors' Code of Conduct*, rule 1.01.
113 ibid., rule 11.02(2); Bar Standards Board, *Code of Conduct*, Part VII, rule 708(c). See above note 48.
114 ibid., rule 11.01(2); Bar Standards Board, *Code of Conduct*, Part VII, rule 708(d).
115 Solicitors' Regulation Authority, *Solicitors' Code of Conduct*, rule 11.01(2).
116 ibid., rule 1, Guidance comment 3.
117 ibid., rule 1.01.
118 General Council of the Bar of South Africa, *Uniform Rules*, rule 6.3.1; International Bar Association, *International Code of Ethics*, rule 17. See above note 60.
119 General Council of the Bar of South Africa, *Uniform Rules*, rule 2.1. See above note 61.
120 Solicitors' Regulation Authority, *Solicitors' Code of Conduct*, rule 1.06.
121 ibid., rule 10.01.
122 See above note 62.
123 Solicitors' Regulation Authority, *Solicitors' Code of Conduct*, rule 1.06, Guidance comment 10.
124 ibid., rule 10.01.
125 ibid., rule 1.01.
126 ibid, rule 10.01.
127 Cf. ibid., rule 1.01.
128 ibid. See above note 62.
129 See above sections 7.5.1. and 7.5.2 respectively.
130 Cf. Solicitors' Regulation Authority, *Solicitors' Code of Conduct*, rule 1.01, Guidance comment 2.
131 If the opponent does not seek legal representation, the lawyer must maintain a balance between doing the best for their client and not taking unfair advantage of the opponent's lack of knowledge and drafting skills: Solicitors' Regulation Authority, *Solicitors' Code of Conduct*, rule 1.01, Guidance comment 2.
132 See World Medical Association, *Declaration of Geneva*, adopted by the General Assembly of the World Medical Association, Geneva, Switzerland, September 1948: 'The health of my patient shall be my first consideration'; World Medical Association, *International Code of Medical Ethics*, adopted by the 35th General Assembly of the World Medical Association, Venice, Italy, October 1983: 'A physician shall owe his patients complete loyalty and all the resources of his science.'
133 Solicitors' Regulation Authority, *Solicitors' Code of Conduct*, rule 11, Guidance comment 5.
134 ibid., rule 2.01(2).
135 ibid., rule 2.02. See above note 33.

136 ibid.
137 ibid., rule 1.04. See above note 35.
138 General Council of the Bar of South Africa, *Uniform Rules*, rule 3.1. See above note 95.
139 Solicitors' Regulation Authority, *Solicitor's Code of Conduct*, rule 1.01. See above note 62.
140 ibid., rule 2.01(2). See above note 45.
141 ibid., rule 6.01(1). See above note 43.
142 International Bar Association, *International Code of Ethics*, rule 13.
143 Solicitors' Regulation Authority, *Solicitor's Code of Conduct*, rule 6.01(1). See above note 42.
144 ibid., rule 4.01. See above note 38.
145 General Council of the Bar of South Africa, *Uniform Rules*, rule 4.26.
146 International Bar Association, *International Code of Ethics*, rule 14.
147 Solicitors' Regulation Authority, *Solicitor's Code of Conduct*, rule 1.01. See above note 57.
148 ibid. See above note 62.
149 ibid. See above note 57.
150 ibid. See above note 62.
151 ibid. See above note 57.
152 Solicitors' Regulation Authority, *Solicitor's Code of Conduct*, rule 11.01(1). See above note 50.
153 General Council of the Bar of South Africa, *Uniform Rules*, rule 3.2. See above note 50.
154 International Bar Association, *International Code of Ethics*, rule 6. See above note 50.
155 Solicitors' Regulation Authority, *Solicitor's Code of Conduct*, rule 2.02. See above note 33.
156 ibid., rule 2.02(2). See above note 41.
157 ibid., rule 2.01(2). See above note 42.
158 ibid. See above note 50.
159 General Council of the Bar of South Africa, *Uniform Rules*, rule 3.2.
160 International Bar Association, *International Code of Ethics*, rule 6.
161 Solicitors' Regulation Authority, *Solicitor's Code of Conduct*, rule 11.01(3). See above note 56.
162 Bar Standards Board, *Code of Conduct*, Part VII, rule 704. See above note 56.
163 Solicitors' Regulation Authority, *Solicitor's Code of Conduct*, rule 2.01(2). See above note 45.

8 Towards ethical literacy by enhancing reflexivity in law students

Lynda Crowley-Cyr

8.1 Introduction

Legal ethics is typically taught as part of the undergraduate law degree in Australia. In this chapter, I share why I do what I do: the theories that inform my classroom practice, and my experiences in teaching legal ethics at James Cook University in North Queensland.[1] The teaching approach I have developed aims to better equip students to become reflexive, ethically literate professionals. Other teachers who may be seeking an approach to engaging students in a more authentic adult learning experience may find my reflections useful.

My core proposition is that legal education in general does not adequately prepare students for the pressures of legal practice. Today's practising lawyers must manage a seemingly irreconcilable tension between making a profit and providing ethically and technically appropriate professional service. Meanwhile, phenomena such as mental ill-health, substance abuse and apparent ethical blindness to or complicity in unethical conduct suggest a deficit in lawyers 'reflexive capacity'.[2] Such wider moral and ethical questions – which, as Giddens says, 'day-to-day life poses but which are denied answers' – form a key part of my teaching process.[3] In my experience, teaching legal ethics must include more than dictating professional rules and interpretive case law for students to memorize and regurgitate. Knowledge of the ethical rules associated with practising law is a requirement for admission as a legal practitioner in Australia. However, this knowledge alone does not provide students with the necessary tools to engage the moral self with the professional rules. The premise upon which reflexive ethical literacy is grounded is that law schools have a public duty to educate future professionals who have internalized an autonomous capacity to apply ethics in the practice of law.[4]

Traditional law school curricula emphasizes critical analysis of law and society. This preoccupation with the cognitive domain, however, means that students who have almost completed their law degrees may have had little opportunity to rigorously scrutinize their personal values or their knowledge of the values of the legal profession. In an attempt to address this lack, my approach to teaching legal ethics is embedded in the scholarship of modernity, critical literacy and adult education. It is influenced by clinical educators of various disciplines to provide an inter-professional knowledge base.

This chapter is presented in three parts. The first section discusses theories of modernity that help explain changes in the legal profession that impact on the ethical practice of law and the emotional and mental state of lawyers. Recent findings about similar problems experienced by graduating law students support my proposition that a teaching approach that enhances students' reflexive capacity is critical to enabling them to identify and manage ethical challenges. Emotional intelligence and moral courage are also paramount in enabling students to become more aware of how they (and the communities to which they belong, past and present) are engaged in an ongoing process of identity-construction.

The second part of the chapter briefly discusses some of the assumptions and shortcomings of pedagogy and andragogy in legal education in terms of preparing students for ethical practice. My goal is to build a bridge between what is an essentially pedagogical approach to curriculum and an andragogical one embedded in reflexivity. This 'hybrid', combining pedagogy and andragogy, is one way of assisting students to make the transition from university to professional life. Andragogical ideas, theories and methods for adult education, developed notably by Knowles[5] and Freire,[6] have specific benefits for teaching legal ethics. The students who take my subject are typically adults,[7] and a robust literature establishes that adults learn in a manner qualitatively different from that which suits pre-adult students.

The third section turns to the curriculum design of my legal ethics subject, and provides some reflections on the reflexive andragogic approach that I have taken. Some of the responses from students who have taken my subject, past and present, are included.

8.2 Malaise in the legal profession: a case for reflexivity

In 1996, the then Justice Kirby described the loss of tradition in the legal profession as a 'deep malaise' that is partly associated with the 'general rejection of any spiritual dimension whatever to life'.[8] For some lawyers, the modern legal profession's love of money over the love for fellow human beings exemplifies this malaise.[9] The so called 'tyranny of billable hours' illustrates this modern tension within the profession. John Briton, Queensland's Legal Services Commissioner, comments on the findings of a 2009 survey of young lawyers:[10]

> [B]illing pressure is pushing many young lawyers to fudge their time sheets. Only 38% of respondents said they always recorded their time accurately, citing billing pressure from senior staff. This means that if accurate, these findings show 62% of young lawyers in NSW admit to having lied at least once in a way that effectively defrauded a client. That will not have been an emotionally neutral event.

In a secular risk culture like Australia, there is radical doubt about the reliability of certain forms of social and technical systems that filters into most aspects of everyday life. Such doubt, Giddens says, causes feelings of restlessness, foreboding and desperation.[11] Individuals struggle to come to terms with who they are and who it is that society expects them to be. The incessant struggle for security experienced by all human beings, including lawyers, is a dimension of 'reflexive modernization'. It generates what Giddens describes as 'ontological insecurity'.[12] Reflexive capacity is dependent upon, among other things, managing such insecurities in the 'self'.[13]

Ontological insecurity is a hallmark of most conceptualizations of fundamental social change.[14] Nothing these days, not jobs nor relationships, 'comes fully equipped or with a life-time guarantee'.[15] Consequently, as Blackshaw writes, 'if absolute security eludes liquid moderns, absolutely anything else does too. It is as if today they are forced to live their lives when the overall effect is analogous to shifting-sand dunes; just when you think you have got a foothold on a track, it slips away'.[16]

I would suggest that recent findings about the impaired emotional and mental state of legal practitioners support ideas of malaise within the profession and the self. In 2007 and 2008, for instance, lawyers in Australia were found to be two and a half to four times more likely than other professionals to suffer from clinical depression.[17] One study reportedly found that 11 per cent of lawyers contemplated suicide every month.[18] Workplace bullying that occurs in some law firms, in mediation or in court has also been causally linked to emotional distress in young lawyers. In one study in Victoria, almost 70 per cent of lawyers surveyed reported having been humiliated by a colleague during the previous year.[19] Such humiliation resulted from sarcasm, criticism and often-defamatory condescending remarks from a colleague about age or relative inexperience. Lawyers tend to 'self-medicate' with non-prescription drugs and alcohol as a means of 'managing' their symptoms,[20] a tendency that is mirrored overseas.[21] Managing workplace pressures in dysfunctional and self-harming ways is symptomatic of ontological insecurity.

As with all professionals, emotional distress, depression and substance abuse can impact on the quality of the services provided by those affected. In March 2009, Briton estimated that emotional distress features in 30 per cent of the disciplinary matters dealt with in Queensland alone.[22] This is a conservative figure compared with general estimates of substance abuse, said to dominate up to 80 per cent of complaints against the Australian legal profession.[23] Any impairment to the intellectual functions of legal practitioners gives rise to significant professional and ethical risk. Briton openly states that his interest in this matter stems from his presumption that emotional distress among lawyers 'reveals itself in behaviours that fall short of the standards . . . that members of the public and the profession are entitled to expect of them'.[24] All too often, this leads to consumer and conduct complaints against impaired practitioners. Such dysfunctionality also brings into question the ethical leadership role of lawyers. As one senior practitioner in Australia remarked, 'excessive proximity to business clients, and their money, seems to have produced elements of imitation unlikely to enhance professionalism'.[25]

Ethically ambiguous conduct by lawyers and the negative public perception it can create have led to calls for accountability. There is growing public scrutiny over the conduct of corporate lawyers, for instance, who follow the instructions of their clients when such actions are contrary to the interests of shareholders. The Enron matter is one example that illustrates concerns by the public and by lawyers about privilege and loyalty to corporate clients.[26] It is not at all clear that corporate lawyers can simply do what their executive clients want. Some critics consider the privilege and confidentiality that attached to communications between the Enron executives and the company's lawyers a convenient means for lawyers to escape responsibility – especially criminal responsibility – for their actions.[27] The 'We're just lawyers, what do we know?' defence, coupled with the plea that 'Whatever we did know, we are duty bound to keep secret', is increasingly becoming ethically ambiguous. This is perhaps more so since the 2008 global financial crisis. Some members of the profession are also calling for new forms of restraints and constraints to curb and control commercial lawyers as well as the big law firms that have a diminishing connection with justice or its administration.[28]

There are also extraordinary examples of conduct that have significantly tarnished the public perception of the ethical leadership role of lawyers. According to international lawyer Philippe Sands, the quasi-legal justification given by the lawyers advising the US Bush Administration for the torture of Guantanamo Bay detainees is one example.[29] The conduct of the relevant politicians and their lawyers exemplifies some of the worst effects of a lack of reflexive capacity and ethical literacy. Sands describes the offensive conduct as including the writing of memos that gave legal justification for the abuse of prisoners in Abu Ghraib from 2002 when the cruelty started.[30] One memo, Sands states, reveals how:

> the lawyers go through all the different permutations of putting someone in a small box or a large box and then including in the box some sort of insect. And the lawyers go on at length about whether or not the insect bites . . . whether it can inflict a fatal sting or not and then whether or not to tell the person that there's an insect in there and what sort of insect it is.[31]

The intention is to submit the prisoners to their worst fears. Another memo, written in 2005, sets out techniques, including waterballing, waterboarding and walling, approved for use against suspected Al Qaeda operatives. The memos reveal that the use of waterboarding, for instance – which until recently was thought to have been limited to three men for one minute each – was in fact specifically used against two men a staggering 266 times. According to Sands, 'people are coming to the realization that, but for the lawyers', the outrageously cruel, inhumane and degrading treatment of the detainees 'would not have happened'.[32] These lawyers' special knowledge of the law was essentially used to assist government officials to evade the obligations of international conventions against torture.[33]

8.2.1 Loss of tradition as a diagnosis

Loss of tradition, some might say, is one explanation for the pressures often experienced in the legal profession that lead to ethically ambiguous and unprofessional conduct. The legal culture has changed markedly from a lengthy past in which the profession maintained an astonishing degree of homogeneity and conformity.[34] Today's profession, with the development of multidisciplinary practices, mega-firms, traditional and specialist firms, and incorporated legal practices, is far more heterogeneous than in previous times.[35] Market forces have impelled much of this change. There are now new contradictions flowing from incompatible beliefs and values about life and professional goals of legal practice. It is change that has also 'played out' on the identity of lawyers.[36]

Theories of modernity help to explain the effects of a decline in tradition on societies and on human beings.[37] For Beck, 'detraditionalization' leaves a vacuum where shared core values and ethics associated with past traditional social order once stood.[38] This void has been filled partly by market competition and economics. A consequence of change is that action must be validated and legitimated in light of incoming knowledge that has not been justified by trad-ition.[39] This can upset the ontological and normative order of those who routinely struggle to manage conflicts and tensions associated with incoming knowledge about how they should act. The struggle is to reinvent the 'self' as a good market citizen able to turn a decent profit from consumers of legal services while simultaneously striving to remain a 'virtuous professional' in today's 'risk society'.[40]

For practitioners, this involves a 'never-to-be-relaxed' monitoring of behaviour and its moral context. Giddens calls this process the 'reflexive monitoring of action', which can be applied to the self.[41] Giddens' theories are also applicable to law students. Symptoms of an ailing profession can be traced back to law schools, where evidence of bullying and harassment, emotional distress and mental impairment has also been found. In 2008, for instance, while a survey of 2,413 lawyers that included 738 law students from 13 law schools nationally found a high level of distress in all participants, it was particularly pronounced in students.[42] Indeed, the study found that 40 per cent of students reported psycho-logical distress severe enough to warrant clinical or medical assessment.[43]

The traditional law school curriculum, especially prior to the 1990s when ethics teaching in Australia rarely went beyond legal rules, has done little to develop the reflexive capacity, ethical literacy and emotional intelligence of students in prep-aration for practice.[44] This deficit could be a contributing factor.

8.3 Ethical illiteracy and emotional unintelligence: the link to traditional law school curricula

Research on the legal profession and legal education is probably most sophisti-cated and extensively documented in the United States. Trends evident in the United States, however, arguably parallel those in most law schools in Australia. Law school curriculum in Australia, as in the United States, follows a formalistic 'scientific' model.[45] Under this model, the law is broken down, as a subject of study, into separate doctrinal areas such as torts, contracts, property and criminal law. These are known as 'black letter law' subjects. Such subjects are typically taught early in the law degree. Students are therefore rarely explicitly exposed to any subjects directly addressing ethics or issues relevant to the social, cultural, political or ecological context of their future practice as lawyers until their studies are near completion.

In 2007, a review of best practice in legal education was conducted by Stuckley and his colleagues. Their review is critical of US law schools which teach students that to think intellectually like a lawyer requires careful consideration of both sides of disputes, yet also that to resolve legal problems requires adopting a 'critical, pessimistic and depersonalized' approach.[16] Stuckley describes this as 'a damaging paradigm' that trains students 'to see the worst in things' and to objectively 'define human beings primarily according to their legal rights'.[17] It is also an approach that is conveyed as the 'superior way of thinking' rather than as an important yet 'strictly limited legal tool'.[18]

Social justice practitioners in the United States are also critical of legal education. Boghosian, for instance, is critical of curricula which teach students that the nature of the lawyer–client relationship must be neutral and apolitical, even though 'the law school experience is anything but'.[19] She associates this definition of the lawyer's role as a passive representative of the clients' wishes with an erosion of altruistic values. Law students are taught that lawyers have 'no influence over legal doctrine, relevant social policies, or the principles guiding legal reasoning'.[50] Rather, this is the role of judges as 'lawmakers to determine what doctrine is', and the courts to determine when and which social policy arguments are relevant.[51] Students therefore learn early in their legal education that legal reasoning must be based on doctrinal neutrality, uninfluenced by emotions, imagination or moral considerations. Hence 'it is not lawyerly to stand up for what one believes.'[52] This homogenising process renders students especially vulnerable to internal conflict as they become 'less driven by their convictions' or alienated from their values.[53] Such observations about pedagogy and curriculum can also be made with equal strength in Australian law schools.

There are, of course, many justifications for organising the teaching of law around the review, dissection and assimilation of judicial opinion. If they are to persuade judges to rule in their favour, law students must learn to frame their legal arguments in a mode consistent with that adopted by lawmakers. The massive exposure to case law in legal education is not designed to open up thought processes directly addressing ethics, or to stimulate the imagination of students about the impact of their work on society as a whole. On the contrary, as Schlag points out: 'The *sine qua non* of the judicial opinion . . . is that it is supposed to shut down thought' to ensure the judge's order is actually heeded by the parties.[54]

Legal ethics subjects are also vulnerable to criticism for failing to teach law students the ethical dimension of law, how doctrines implicate moral questions, and the wider implications of their choices as lawyers.[55] This is perhaps most troubling when legal educators teach students to treat questions of professional responsibility as problems to solve in the course of representing clients by asking, in the words of Boghosian, 'What can I get away with without getting into trouble with the disciplinary board?' instead of 'What can a lawyer do for the good of society?'[56]

In Australia, there is some conjecture that there is a connection between the inadequacies in legal education and a high level of job dissatisfaction among young lawyers. The capacity to make ethical choices in busy law firms involves reflexive, ethically and emotionally intelligent human beings. According to Briton, this requires law schools 'to find ways to equip their students' with the skills and resilience needed 'to survive as lawyers'.[57] But this is only one part of the problem. The freedom to make ethical choices in the workplace also depends on the culture within law firms and the profession. For those students who 'remain vulnerable', the Legal Commissioner suggests 'some good old fashioned vocational guidance directing them to areas of practice where they'll be least at risk or perhaps to another career path altogether'.[58] Mental health experts like Hickie suggest that, as well as looking critically at the circumstances of employment – especially in the early years within the profession – there is an urgent need for law schools to develop strategies to support students while they are still in law school.[59]

These suggestions, and the criticisms of pedagogy and curricula highlighted in the US research, informed the development of my subject and my teaching approach.

8.3.1 Complexities of transitions from pedagogy to andragogy

My approach in the development and delivery of legal ethics as a subject is based on my intention to assist students to shift from a predominantly pedagogical approach to learning to an andragogical reflexive approach. That said, if pedagogy and andragogy sit at opposite ends of a spectrum, my approach typically falls somewhere in the middle. Much depends on the students in a given class. It is, however, a mistake to dichotomize too sharply the differences between pedagogy and andragogy. Whatever we do as legal educators tends to involve some element of both approaches.

This may be because law students in Australia are a complex blend of human beings. Some are undergraduate young adults who have only ever worked casually or part time. Others are more mature working adults, some of whom have been in the workforce for years. Some are postgraduate students. Most have never experienced work life in a busy law firm. The work experience of those who have worked in law firms tends to be limited to secretarial or administrative work.

This blend of adult students means that law students have varying levels of knowledge and work/life experience, a fact which contributes to the challenge faced by legal ethics teachers endeavouring to adopt the 'best' approach for teaching their subject. At James Cook University Law School, as at most law schools in Australia, teachers have very limited knowledge about the work, health or family commitments of the students enrolled in their subjects. This is especially so if it is the first time the teacher has taught the students.

The blend of students taking legal ethics means that empowering them to learn andragogically and reflexively from the limits of pedagogy can be challenging. A comparison of some key features of the two approaches may help explain why the transition from pedagogy to andragogy for students indoctrinated with a pedagogically orientated educational, cultural and normative scheme is a complex endeavour.

Prior to considering some of the benefits and shortcomings of pedagogy and andragogy in legal education, Table 8.1 offers a brief summary of early assumptions associated with both approaches. I will draw on some of these assumptions in the ensuing discussion.

Table 8.1 Pedagogy v andragogy

Assumptions about:	Pedagogical	Andragogical
The learner	Highly dependent on teacher for all learning	Increasingly self-directed, responsible for autonomous decisions
Learner's life experience	Limited – to be built on as a resource for learning	Broad – provides a rich resource for learning by self and others
Readiness to learn	Uniform by age-level and curriculum	Developed from a realisation of the worth/value of learning in enhancing their ability to address life issues and problems
Orientation to learning	Subject-centred	Task- or problem-centred
Motivation	By external rewards (competition for grades) and consequences of failure	By internal incentives, curiosity and extrinsically through life responsibilities and change
The teacher	Viewed as having superior knowledge and experience, very influential	Viewed as having a reciprocal relationship with learners, can have limited influence
Role	Assumes full responsibility for what is taught and how it is learned	Adopts facilitator posture and learning is negotiated with learners around life/work situations rather than subject matter units
Climate	Tense, low trust, formal, transactional, competitive, judgmental	Relaxed, trusting, mutually respectful, collaborative, supportive
Evaluation of learning	By teacher with grades, norm-referenced	By learner-collected evidence validated by peers and facilitator, criterion-referenced

Source: Adapted from Malcolm Knowles' work about assumptions associated with pedagogical and andragogical approaches to learning.[60]

8.3.2 *Legal pedagogy for transactional teaching*

The pedagogical approach to teaching, with its rigid vertical structure, may be of benefit to teachers and students. Teachers may find pedagogy a 'safer' approach to meeting published learning objectives. Students – even those with limited life experience and little motivation to learn – may be taught to attain objectives. However, notable tensions and contradiction about learning outcomes arise when the pedagogical approach is used to teach law students.

A criticism of a rigid application of legal pedagogy is that it tends to offer a transactional 'anti-dialogue' and anti-reflexive model of education. An anti-dialogue approach, as Freire puts it, is based on passive recipient, teacher-led 'communication'.[61] It is characterized by one-way transmissions from the techno-crat teacher as the 'sage' (one who knows, of authority) down to the students receiving knowledge (the silenced listeners, those whose thinking is done for them). This model is typically complemented by the use of complex problem-based questions to assess student retention of transmitted messages. Teaching problem-solving skills to law students, while necessary and important, can further hinder dialogue and reflexivity when such skills are taught through teacher-led examples and solutions. In essence, the technocrat's problem-solving stance is that objectives are achieved through a form of manipulation.[62]

Such manipulation, while serving to produce uniformity and conformity, also acts as the antithesis of what Freire refers to as 'problematizing'.[63] Problematizing requires certain 'realities' to be considered, such as social, cultural, historical and environmental realities in which the problem is immersed. Black letter law sub-jects are well suited to teacher-led transactional style teaching, as they do not require consideration of such realities, and consequently no dialogue about them is needed. Transactional law teachers are therefore free to proceed without worry about how the information is received. Power relations, hidden agendas or sub-texts conveyed in the language used are of no or little concern as long as the information imparted to students can be processed in an elaborate sequence to attain the 'correct answer' in examinations. The transaction is complete when students who rank highly in the final grades praise the 'sage', and the simple teaching style that offers a level of certainty through its rigidity, in the university student feedback system.

A notable deficit in a mode of teaching that keeps law students as docile listeners is that their consciousness develops with little experience of dialogue or opportunity for significant participation. In other words, to borrow Oscar Wilde's *bon mot*, students are left 'knowing the price of everything but the value of noth-ing'.[64] They know much about the law but very little about being an autonomous reflexive human being or acting with beneficence while maintaining dignity and respect for the fictitious autonomous 'client'.

Further, students who have been denied their say in law school through their duty to listen and obey may become unsure of themselves. They may develop a preference for engaging in dialogue. However, distrust takes hold and is almost always maintained towards those who attempt a dialogue with them. Distrust is also directed at the self by those students who doubt their ability, influenced by the myth of their ignorance. Students especially vulnerable to self-doubt have been found to be those who enter law school on a lower entrance score or who come from a low socio-economic background.[65] James Cook is a regional, open-access university that accepts lower entrance scores. The risk that ontological and normative insecurities will arise in those who fear academic shortfalls increases when students are relentlessly bombarded with rhetoric about the importance of grades for job placements, of winning legal arguments, of dispassion and objectivity, of corporate dominance and the competitive edge. A side-effect of such rhetoric is that students can lose their sense of altruism, of purpose as champions of a system of justice by righting social injustices.[66] As their perception of what it means to be a lawyer shifts, insecurities about how to manage the contradictions and tensions created by this change invade the self. A strong desire to conform takes over. Students at the end of their degree in predominantly pedagogically orientated programmes will likely need to be actively assisted to make the transition from passive to active and reflexive learners.

8.3.3 Transition to andragogy

The andragogical assumption is that adult students are not passive receptors of information but instead partners in the education process. A related assumption is that they possess, at some level, the capacity and will to be self-directed because of their life/work experiences. Such experiences should provide a powerful learning tool with which to contextualize content and allow the teacher to break out of the role of knowledge conveyor and assume a guide and mentor posture. This approach assumes an orientation to learning based on the students' experience of what is needed in the 'real world' of legal practice. However, some writers warn that, while the assumptions about adult learners are widely acknowledged through various successful adaptations of Knowles' work in different fields of study,[67] 'it is not certain whether adults actually behave or think in the way that Knowles assumes'.[68]

Law teachers intending to engage in a transition to a more andragogical reflexive style of teaching should note that such an approach is not readily accepted by students whose learning has largely been passive and silent. Although these students may well be culturally and legally recognized as adults, they may never have been enabled to participate in realising more meaningful learning outcomes for themselves. The lack of any equivalent of clinical placement for students in the early part of the law degree in most law schools is problematic.[69] Law subjects, including black letter law subjects, are often saturated with scenario-based learning through problem-solving. However, what is often lacking is any 'real-life' professional experience with which to benchmark such learning.

When teaching legal ethics to adult students who have not experienced the pressures of work in a busy law firm, the legal andragogical approach begins to falter. The information (a set of ambiguous conduct rules with accompanying statutory practice regulations) has to be transformed into knowledge that is considered by those receiving the information as relevant to their 'lived reality'. Words alone will not suffice. To optimise the transformation of words into knowledge, words must have contextual meaning – must be 'humanized', as Freire puts it.[70] This involves an extension of words beyond their 'basic meaning' so that the human relationships at their core are highlighted.

This process of education depends on 'basic factors' such as *how* and *what* 'human knowledge' is transmitted. It also depends on *who* transmits and the transmitter's chosen content, the delivery, the transmitter's superiority, culture, gender and other 'invasions' brought through the transmitter's version of the world.[71] The transmitter's experience of legal practice, for instance, can be a significant 'invasion' in terms of what information is transmitted. The transmission is likely to be different if the transmitter has never experienced practice. The attributes and life experiences of recipients of information are further considerations. According to Freire, these basic factors of human knowledge are the relationships that human beings have with the world; their human conditioning that governs their way of acting, of confronting the world and others. Only when these factors are taken into consideration can both the teacher and students become Freire's 'extension agents'.[72]

Teachers as extension agents try to establish relationships with their students in an attempt to alter or enhance existing knowledge with other knowledge. This can be achieved despite a teacher's penchant towards either a pedagogic or andragogic approach – or even a blend of these approaches.

To summarize, therefore, as with pedagogy there are some unresolved issues about andragogy.

8.4 Transforming pedagogically oriented students to a reflexive andragogic orientation

Taking into consideration Freire's basic relationship-building factors and the blended characteristics of the student groups, my approach to teaching and learning legal ethics involves two main components: (1) engaging with the subject-matter; and (2) enhancing reflexivity. My approach involves a two-way 'relational learning loop' between the teacher/facilitator and the students. The concept, adapted from Freire's work,[73] can be illustrated by a simple diagram (see Figure 8.1).

I explain my adaptation of the two components of my approach – engagement and reflexivity – separately as follows.

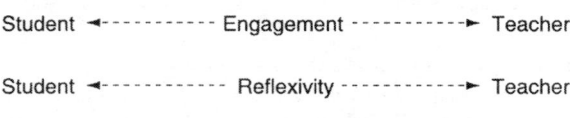

Figure 8.1 Relational learning loop (RLL).

8.4.1 Engaging with the subject-matter

Legal education, in the Freirian mode, has great appeal in the teaching of legal ethics. It provides a literacy method that allows 'the practice of liberty' in the sense that both the teacher and the students are freed 'from the twin thralldom of silence and monologue'.[74] This gives it a more andragogic bearing. Dialogue about the students' and teacher's personal values, morals and actions, past and present, is encouraged. Once dialogue opens up, there is an opportunity for relationships to be formed between those engaged in the joint search for knowledge. However, the development of my approach is flexible and contains variables that resonate to varying degrees within both andragogic and pedagogic approaches.

Freire's literacy method has five basic components, which I have adapted as follows:[75]

1   *Pro-dialogue.* My legal ethics subject focuses on good communication as a core value and skill for legal practice. It is a means of breaking down distrust. By way of example, the first session begins with an adult 'meet and greet' activity designed to engage students. I introduce myself by shaking hands with a random number of students. I then introduce myself to the class and ask the students to roam the room and introduce themselves in a professional manner to the students they have not formally met previously. This activity, as with all the activities in the subject, is reflected upon and discussed with the class. The different handshakes, postures and greetings are evaluated openly in terms of which might constitute best practice in a professional environment, and why. This presents an opportunity to begin quizzing the students about how they felt about being chosen for the initial handshake with the teacher. Typically and unremarkably, some students disclose suspicion and even 'fear' of this unfamiliar way of starting a subject. Others state that it made them 'feel special'. When those who are not chosen are asked the same question, some disclose relief at not being chosen, but there are consistently others who express a sense of 'having missed out'. This sense of 'exclusion' is then discussed in preparation for the next activity.

Once everyone has met, students are shown a slide show of simple images of different individuals. The images include individuals of various ethnicity, gender, socio-economic background and aesthetic beauty. Students are again asked to comment freely on their initial impressions of each person in the images. I have found this to be a useful activity for students to discover their sometimes subconscious biases and prejudices. Typically, the students begin by using emotionally neutral terms to describe the images. However, when given time, they tend to become more relaxed with what they say and use derogatory and emotive terms like 'crazy', psycho, 'ugly', 'dumb' and 'creepy' to describe some of the images.

The activity allows stereotyping and biases to begin to surface. The impressions, and the words used to convey these, are then unpacked in open discussion. I then link the importance of first impressions to good communication and language. I discuss human communication as a 'package' that goes beyond the spoken and written word. I stress the significance of first impressions on the development of trust relationships. Human senses that can affect how we perceive others include what we see (body language, facial expressions), what we hear (tone, pitch), what we feel (the grip of the handshake), what we smell (body odours, cigarette smoke, alcohol, perfume or aftershave), and so on.

Good communication is emphasized in my subject as a fundamental skill required by legal practitioners in their practice. This is supported by set readings from legal ethics texts and various annual reports by Legal Services Commissions that identify poor communication as a consistently significant complaint by clients.

Good communication is a linear thread running through the entire subject. It is a topic that everyone knows something about, allowing rich dialogue. However, this requires the educator to 'tune in' to the vocabulary universe of the students. Hence dialogue, I have found, requires an appropriate allocation of time to develop. Engagement is encouraged by providing students with a reflexive vocabulary, an 'active dialogue', and both critical and stimulating criticism so that the silence can disappear.

2   *Use of generative words with syllabic richness and a high charge of experiential involvement.* Legal ethics is enriched by the use of highly emotive words. Words explicitly or implicitly contained in professional rules of conduct, like 'trust', 'respect', 'power', 'dignity', 'veracity', 'candour', and so on, are used to form the themes of each session. As a new topic is introduced, the students are tasked, in groups, with defining the relevant thematic word. These meanings are shared with the class and then, as a class, we come to a shared agreed meaning of the terms in the context of legal ethics.

3   *A first codification of these words into visual images.* A shared definition of thematic words is intended to stimulate students submerged in a culture of silence to emerge as conscious makers of their own culture. Students' understanding of complex thematic words like 'dignity' and 'respect' can sometimes be limited and challenging to define individually or as a group. This challenge helps me illustrate the diversity of meanings across the ages and life stages of students, despite the common use of such words in the course of their law degrees. It also illustrates the diversity of meanings that may be applied to words by clients and the need for acknowledgement of audience.

4   *Decodification by a 'culture circle'.* Decodification occurs under the unassuming stimulus of a facilitator rather than a teacher in the conventional sense, but one who has become an 'educator-educatee'. Once a common meaning for words is agreed to by the class, those meanings are continually reassessed as we travel through the subject's curriculum and case examples.

5   *A creative new codification.* Defined words are given an 'extended' or 'contextual meaning'. First this occurs through a connection and application with the students' current conduct as human beings, and then in the context of the

conduct of an ethically literate member of the profession. This step is explicitly critical because it is aimed at self-assessment of action. Those who were formerly critically illiterate and non-reflexive now begin to reject their role as mere passive recipients of knowledge – mere 'objects' in nature and social history – and undertake to become 'subjects' of their own destiny.

Dialogue is therefore pivotal to the engagement process. Learning can begin once dialogue is active. Active dialogue allows subject content to be contextualized and teachable moments identified. Important feedback received during the semester can be incorporated into the remainder of the subject. Students develop a sense of 'ownership' of the content of the subject and the direction and extent of its flow.

8.4.2 *Enhancing reflexivity*

The second notable component of my approach to teaching and learning legal ethics is 'reflexivity'. As with engagement, reflexivity also offers a two-way relational learning loop whereby both students and 'teacher' engage in the process. Put simply, reflexive capacity means the capacity of human beings to *alter* their behaviour in future actions. This *altered state* must come as a consequence of the person having reflected upon her or his own former actions. Reflexive ethical literacy, therefore, involves the readjustment of actions and attitudes in response to new knowledge about the self's actions on others, ultimately to achieve and maintain a higher degree of ethical practice.

The reflexive process, as I use it, involves two main steps: (1) the acquisition, and (2) the integration of knowledge that results in change in the actor's action. Each of these steps involves distinct acts, as is illustrated in Figure 8.2.[76]

This reflexive process begins with monitoring information in the form of 'raw' data about the person's own actions. Such information is yet to be processed or reflected upon. Reflection requires a consideration of the objectives, means and efficacy of actions. In other words, reflection is a thought-reaction to incoming information about action. What is accepted assumes a new standing as knowledge – a fundamental first step in the reflexive process. The second step involves further action by the actor who uses the accepted knowledge to make sense of the world. Once knowledge is integrated with the actor's context, resulting in change – a 'transformation', some might say– there are indications that the reflexive process is active.

My approach to teaching legal ethics allows for careful consideration of the student's self as part of the context of change. The reflexive project of the self, as applicable to law students intending to enter the profession, allows for discussion

Step 1. Information* + Reflection** = Knowledge.

Step 2. Knowledge + Integration*** = *Reflexivity*

Figure 8.2 The two steps in the reflexive process.

about uncertainties and insecurities about their core values, what makes them happy, why they want to become lawyers, and so on. The challenge faced by law students – which is arguably faced by everyone – is to know how to manage the tensions between the quest for happiness, ontological security and increasing pressures of everyday working life. As stated earlier, ontological insecurity pertains to the present self and asks 'How do I reinvent myself so as to better function as a successful law student in order to avoid the perils associated with being an "unsuccessful" legal professional in the future?' For those wanting to make a good living out of being legal practitioners (the ends), the ethical dilemma intensifies when the way that this goal is reached (the means) is taken into consideration.

Reflexive capacity offers a means by which to better manage the insecurities generated from uncertainty and change, both as students and later as professionals. Only human beings who possess what Freire calls a 'thought-language', who act and are capable of reflection on themselves and their actions, are 'beings of relations in a world of relations'.[77] This is based on the idea that human actions condition and are conditioned by their own results or outcomes in the world. In a sense, it is a familiar concept that relates back to Sir Isaac Newton's 'displacement' theory.[78] Displacement is a useful concept in teaching legal ethics and professional conduct because it also represents the way power is exerted by the more powerful[79] (physically, economically, politically or socially, individuals or institutions) on the least powerful,[80] typically with negative effects.[81]

Early in my subject, I guide a discussion on why lawyers tend to be reported as unhappy professionals. The concept of 'harm' is given a broad meaning to include harm to the self, clients and opponents, the profession, broader society and the environment. The term is unpacked to illustrate the negative impact of normative, personal and ontological insecurity on lawyers as human beings and as professionals. The idea that the workplace can be an environment that socializes individuals into doing harm is also discussed. Through the use of readings on the topic of 'structurization',[82] I guide an open discussion on recent examples of corporate crimes and question whether law firms, as multinational organizations or as smaller local firms, can enlist their members to do harm. My goal is to inform students of possible encounters they may have with unethical cultures that challenge their professional ethics. Being informed may assist students to sustain their ethical and moral courage in the face of institutional, collegial and hierarchal pressures found ubiquitously in the workplace.

The idea that the modern legal profession lacks love for fellow human beings is discussed in a session on 'professionalism'. I use social science literature to highlight the 'traits' of the 'classic' professions, including 'altruism'. To engage students with this subject-matter, one activity involves each student circling 10 words out of a possible 30 provided to them. Students are to choose the words that best identify what they consider are the attributes of a virtuous legal professional. In small groups, the students are then asked to agree on 10 words out of those that were circled by individuals within the group. A spokesperson for each group shares with the class their agreed words. These are displayed on a whiteboard. Together, the class then selects the best five based on the number of times a word has been chosen by the groups. The teacher then draws the link between the words the students selected and those that appear in the profession's conduct rules. The intention is to give students a sense of connection with the conduct rules beyond simply reading words on a page. I have found that the students will recollect the five words the class chose and use these during the course of the subject.

Student feedback from the subject reaffirms that adult students enjoy learning in an environment that is rich with engaging activities. For example, some students said:

> This was the most informative class I have had in my law studies . . . I have thoroughly enjoyed myself. The experience gained from this session is invaluable. Thank you very much for providing this learning opportunity.

I now turn to the application of legal ethics. Law students, like clinicians in other highly ethically charged fields of practice, require a tool, a moral compass to help them navigate through life events that challenge their value system. Such a compass assists them on their quest to act as ethically literate 'virtuous' professionals. Hence, in the curriculum design of my subject, I adopted a 'principlist approach' for the application of legal ethics.

8.4.3 Philosophical underpinnings for the practical application of legal ethics

The scaffolding for my reflexive andragogical approach to teaching and learning legal ethics is built around a principlist approach. Such an approach to ethics provides universalist and abstract theories of principles. One version of this approach is based on four distinct but connected principles, rules and virtues, shown in Table 8.2.

This 'four-principle' approach was popularized by two bioethicists, Beauchamp and Childress, in the last quarter of the twentieth century.[83] This approach provides one of the most widely used frameworks for the application of ethics by professionals in the clinical setting. My adaptation of these four principles involves the legal practitioner balancing autonomy (respecting the capacity of autonomous clients to make decisions) with beneficence (acting in a way that benefits the client), non-maleficence (avoiding the causation of harm to the client) and justice

Table 8.2 A version of the principlist approach

Principles	Rules	Virtues
Respect for autonomy	Veracity	Compassion
Beneficence	Privacy	Dispassionate discernment
Non-maleficence	Confidentiality	Trustworthiness
Justice	Fidelity	Integrity

(distributing benefits, risks and costs fairly by treating all clients equitably) whenever these principles are in conflict.

Beauchamp and Childress supplement these principles with four 'rules' – veracity, privacy, confidentiality and fidelity – and four 'virtues' – compassion, dispassionate discernment, trustworthiness and integrity. They state explicitly that there are, of course, many other virtues that are important to the virtuous professional, like good character and moral emotions. The four that they have selected as of central importance to ethical practice in clinical health care, however, are equally significant in the legal practice setting.

Principle-based ethics is an approach with which this author is highly sympathetic, not least because it seems to cut across national, cultural, religious, political and philosophical divides. It is an approach that, in the words of one proponent, provides 'a common set of prima facie moral commitments, a common moral language' and analytical scaffolding for the application of ethics.[84] It is a useful approach to rekindle a spark for the belief in the sacredness of individual human beings by providing a foundation for self-control, and respect for all others.

My adaptation of this principlist approach involves unpacking these abstract concepts to provide the navigational coordinates for ethical conduct. The principles are not prioritized. Ethical problems are considered in context and through the prism of all four principles. The principle of autonomy, for instance, allows an opening for dialogue about power imbalances in the lawyer–client relationship that loom covertly over the duty to respect the autonomous client's decision-making capacities. The principles of beneficence and non-maleficence are well suited to discussions about the lawyer as fiduciary or agent of the client, especially in the context of using a system of 'billable hours'. This raises ethical contradictions with the profession's requirements of good communication and detailed cost agreements. Justice is a principle that allows for wider considerations of social justice, universal human rights and the environment when making judgments about the proper *balance* to be struck between competing ethical commitments when they are in conflict. Beauchamp and Childress have insisted on the necessity of making such judgments by emphasizing that:[85]

> Principles guide us to actions, but we still need to assess a situation and formulate an appropriate response, and this assessment and response flow as much from character and training as from principles.

Gillon, a proponent for the principlist approach, insightfully sums up the rationale for its use when he asks:[86]

> How are people to decide or be taught what constitutes virtue and what constitutes vice, what constitutes good character and what constitutes poor character, if they do not have some guiding moral principles against which to assess people's character dispositions?

Principle-based ethics is not, however, an approach that is without its opponents, and their criticism can be followed elsewhere.[87] For my purposes, it suffices to say that through the application of a simple rubric of four principles, particular ethical problems can be discussed. It is a tool that has served me well in developing the subject for final-year law students.

8.5 Teaching legal ethics in a reflexive andragogic learning environment

8.5.1 *The syllabus*

The syllabus for my legal ethics subject has been developing since 2006, after a review of the curriculum revealed that the subject – previously conducted as a two-day intensive workshop – was inadequate. Having taught predominantly commercial law subjects, I found developing a new legal ethics subject using a reflexive andragogic approach challenging yet personally fulfilling. The subject's objectives provide a necessary boundary around the theoretical content of the class. The syllabus states that 'the primary objective of the subject is to make you an effective, ethically literate legal professional'. It goes on to explain that this entails being a good communicator who is able to set aside personal biases in order to broadly and properly understand the underlying ethical principles discussed in various social and legal contexts.

Flexibility is also fundamentally important in my approach. If a pro-dialogue approach is taken, then teachers may need to 'let go' of content that is not crucial to meeting the requirements for admission.[88] In the early years of teaching the subject, I was not prepared for the encroaching effect that opening up dialogue with the students would have on the subject's content. The topics that trigger animated engagement by students are not always predictable. I have found that each cohort of students is different.[89] Consequently, instead of the two-hour lectures and one-hour tutorials that typically characterise how law subjects are taught at James Cook University, I ran legal ethics in four-hour face-to-face sessions that allowed for various class activities, group work and, most notably, time for discussions. Ethical dilemmas in the workplace can be highly emotive for students. The four-hour blocks provide time for greater participation by more students. This lessens the risk of silencing students and stymying their involvement in steering their learning.

8.5.2 *Readings*

Readings for each session are based on the session themes. Apart from the relevant provisions in the legislation and case law, I have included readings from other disciplines such as the social sciences. These provide a rich source of materials that have meaningful application. Take 'power' as a theme, for example. Law texts tend to focus on power imbalances that may arise in lawyer–client relationships and possibly in terms of potential conflicts of interest. Few, if any, drill deeper into more subtle issues like how power dynamics manifest themselves in law firms (with clients and among lawyers themselves) and their effects. Thompson, in his book *Promoting Equality*, identifies the use of jargon, stereotyping, stigma, exclusion and depersonalization as contributing factors to professionals' unintentional maintenance of inequality, discrimination and oppression.[90] Throughout my legal ethics subject, I link Thompson's factors to the practice of law as a way of illustrating how language connects with power in the communication process. For instance, I associate jargon with the technical language often used by lawyers when communicating with their clients.

Speaking 'legalese', while necessary at times, can create unnecessary barriers by reinforcing power differences between the parties. It can also alienate clients. The task is to reach an appropriate balance of technical and everyday language. This further involves a conscious avoidance by the lawyer of temptation to 'dumb down' communications, use inappropriate slang, or engage in private or personal denigration of the opponent in emotive cases. Such communication styles can bring into question the meaning of what is said or the professionalism of the lawyer. In my experience, the enviable skill of 'saying what we mean' with eloquence, courtesy and respect, mindful of our audience and others, is a quality enjoyed by too few.

Stereotyping and stigmatizing are often closely associated with exclusion through the use of derogatory and emotive language that overlooks or marginalizes certain groups.[91] Thompson also highlights the dehumanizing effect of the use of depersonalizing terms such as the 'elderly' and the 'disabled', or reference to a child as 'it'. Open discussions about the use of some of these words in everyday parlance allows for closer analysis of Thompson's factors and their application to the self. Awareness of the potential harms that can be caused to others by poor choices of words and how these are communicated better equips students to avoid harmful language and postures. Through this reflexive process, they become ethically literate communicators.

8.5.3 The classroom

I use this subject as an opportunity to help prepare students for the transition to a professional workplace. A horizontally level classroom instead of a tiered lecture theatre creates an atmosphere that more closely resembles a law office. Students can arrange the desks to form small groups. This allows the teacher/facilitator to move around the room freely and to join the groups by sitting down with them and engaging in the discussions. To reinforce the perception of a professional work environment, students are asked to come to classes in comfortable office wear. The subject outline also provides a brief explanation of classroom etiquette, which is fashioned from the profession's conduct rules.

8.5.4 Work simulated learning

To further develop students' interest I use stories, realistic scenarios and role-plays.

8.5.4.1 Stories

Teacher-directed storytelling is a powerful means of transmitting information in most cultures. Following a discussion in the first session about why students want to become lawyers – during which some characteristically state 'to help people' – I use a children's story to open up the concept of love for fellow human beings. The story, 'Where the Wild Things Are',[92] is an influential book for very young children on the cusp of literacy and the verge of learning about rules. The story's main character, a small boy symbolically dressed in a wolf suit, rejects his mother's rules and is punished by being sent to his room without dinner. After a journey into an imaginary world (a form of denial), he subsequently develops reflexive understanding of responsibility for his choices and actions. I draw parallels between the boy's journey and the law students' journey towards ethical literacy. My slide show is adapted from Des Manderson's engaging presentation at the 2004 Law and Literature Conference, for which he received a standing ovation.[93] Manderson's work provides a means of thinking about normative ethical theory, and is replete with interpretations of myths and symbols. For example, Manderson draws on Emmanuel Levinas' ethical theory to make sense of the controlling metaphor in the story, food. Levinas' distinction between hunger and love is explained as the fundamental distinction between egotism and altruism. I use the story as an entertaining way to explain the civilizing process, or 'awakening', that occurs when one reflects on the purposes and meaning of rules and law, and not just their forces.

I continue telling stories throughout the subject. The 'stories', however, are more serious as they are drawn from my own personal experiences while in practice.

8.5.4.2 Realistic scenarios

Having practised law is not a requirement for teaching law in Australia. It can, however, be useful in assisting students to analyse and critique 'near-life'[94] and 'real-life'[95] ethically challenging scenarios. Interesting scenarios can also be drawn from the experiences of practitioners or past students who are now in legal practice and who keep in touch with the teacher.

Students have consistently made favourable comments about this sharing of 'stories' of real life experience in my teaching. The following are just a sample:

> I appreciate your anecdotes on your experiences in the Mental Health Tribunal. They helped to illustrate the practical difficulties . . .
>
> Some real life stories . . . rather than regurgitated information from books helped me not only understand how tribunals operate but the difficulties that they face.
>
> The anecdotes gave me a better understanding of life as a young lawyer and how I should conduct myself.
>
> There is nothing in any subject that teach [*sic*] us the 'dos and don'ts' so to speak . . . it was good to learn from actual events or personal experiences.

> I always enjoy your insights into the legal profession . . . I think what a law
> degree lacks is this element of mentorship.

I am also finding that sharing authentic stories of experience fosters a connection
between the teacher and students that can persist well after the end of the subject.
I receive regular emails from past students who like to discuss with me ethical
problems they encounter in their workplaces.

8.5.4.3 Role-plays

In my subject, I develop skills-based activities as authentically as possible within
the budgetary constraints of a regional law school. Client interviewing skills, for
example, while not actively taught as part of the law degree at James Cook
University, are important for law students and well suited for incorporation into
my legal ethics subject. Development of interactive listening skills, how to meet
and how to take instructions from clients all form part of my subject's curriculum.
These skills are taught progressively in preparation for role-plays conducted at the
end of the subject. To add a heightened sense of realism, I use volunteers from
various organizations to act as 'difficult clients'.[96] These guests have special knowledge that places them in a good position to 'brief' students on their interviewing
performance and to answer questions generally.

In 2009, the role-plays received a 100 per cent response rate from students in
their feedback about what they considered the most significant thing that they had
learnt in the session. It was also the most passionate response overall. I include a
sample as follows:

> The role-plays were a wonderful exercise . . . it really brought home the
> potential situations we might find ourselves in with clients.
>
> I found it very interesting and useful to just watch . . . It gave me much to
> think about.
>
> This workshop was the most beneficial in identifying appropriate ways of
> dealing with clients not only in a legal way but also to analyze the situation
> and to remember our position and why the client has come to see us.
>
> Working in a law firm, I have been asked by the principal and solicitors
> to do preliminary interviews with clients or just to see them and find out
> what they want. So this lesson today was significant to me in the practical
> sense . . .

This feedback indicates that law students in general benefit from this type of
activity, whether they already engage in the process of meeting clients or not.

The next comment, especially, reaffirms the importance of my approach in
terms of enhancing the students' reflexive capacity and ontological security:

> As someone who suffers from a mental illness, I found the role-plays very
> personally confronting. I thought this was a very valuable role-play for myself

even though difficult and for other students as a way of exposing students to what it is like to 'manage' mental illness and its reality. I would HIGHLY recommend that this role-play is repeated for future students (especially your comments about treating people with mental illness with humanity and as 'real people who do remember and know right and wrong'. For me personally, I found these role-plays [were] a way for me to own my illness. Thank you.

8.5.5 Assessment

I have set different assessment types since 2005, ranging from an ethics CV to an ethics portfolio, formal examinations, assignments and oral presentations. I have found that, regardless of students' final grades, any form of assessment other than tests, assignments or examinations is not well received by students.[97] In 2009, I limited the assessment to an assignment in response to a fictitious law reform call for submission and four brief quizzes during the semester. This decision was met with support from the students, who appreciated one less examination at the end of semester. Student feedback was more favourable in 2009 than in previous years:

> I found the entire discussion helpful and . . . by doing the assignment helped to bring everything I learned together . . .

There was also a significant response to the lack of a formal examination:

> No exam! Thank you, thank you, thank you!

8.5.6 Feedback about the subject

At the end of each session, students are asked to fill in a brief self-assessment form about their performance in and out of class. The form asks students to identify their contribution to the discussions; what preparation they have done for the session (readings, voluntary problem questions, internet searches on the topic, etc); whether they assisted a peer by explaining a difficult concept or sharing information; and the most significant thing that they learnt from that day's session. I find these comments far more useful than end-of-semester formal student feedback. They are more tailored to gauging the student learning experience and engagement with the subject-matter.

Positive comments were also made by students on their day-to-day application of what they learnt in class, signalling a growth in professionalism through reflexive capacity. The following represent a sample:

> The most significant thing that I have learnt from today's session is the value of what I have undertaken . . . I can now look at what I have learnt since I started my degree and be proud of how far I have come. This subject gives me the confidence I need to enter the profession.

In terms of the whole course, I didn't know how much I could take from the subject initially because I thought I held a good ethic, however, I've definitely learned something new every week and enjoyed the style, etc. . . . an essential component to a law degree.

8.6 Conclusion

Recent reports indicating high levels of job dissatisfaction and the impaired emotional and mental state of law students, graduates and young lawyers are strong imperatives to question the adequacy of current approaches to legal education. There is no one theoretical approach for teachers who have a high degree of agency in improving ethical literacy outcomes for their students. This chapter outlines the scaffolding for shifting from a rigid pedagogic approach to a hybrid approach to teaching and learning legal ethics. Theories of modernity and reflexivity, andragogy and pedagogy, and universalist principles inform and explain my practice. They help me to evaluate and refine it. They make me more knowledgeable so that I can become a more effective teacher/facilitator who strives to make a difference for her students. The context in which I teach legal ethics aims to assist students to develop their vocabulary, knowledge and skills on their journey to ethical literacy and reflexive professionalism.

Notes

1 According to Schratz and Walker, teachers base their decisions on some kind of theory that is either implicit in everyday life or the kind that comes out of the academy. See M. Schratz and R. Walker, *Research of Social Change*, cited in J. Sachs (ed.), *The Activist Teaching Profession*, Buckingham: Open University Press, 2003, p. 82.
2 My use of the term 'reflexive capacity' is adapted from Giddens' meaning of reflexivity, which refers to the constant work required by individuals on their personal identity and sense of self to deal with the shifting and rapidly changing nature of modern life and the flexibility of our social roles. The concept that each person has a 'self', an identity that is individual and personal and therefore separate from 'others', can be connected to the notion of reflexivity, at least insofar as human beings can reflect on morally challenging questions and then alter both what they do and what they are. See A. Giddens, *Modernity and Self-Identity: Self and Society in the Late Modern Age*, Cambridge: Polity Press, 1991, p. 9.
3 ibid.
4 Indeed, in 2008 the Council of Australian Law Deans released its *Standards for Australian Law Schools*, which expresses an expectation that law school curricula will seek to develop in law students understanding and knowledge of the principles of ethical conduct as well as the role of lawyers including the 'internalization of the values that underpin the principles of ethical conduct and professional responsibility'. See Standard 2.3.3, www.cald.asn.au/docs/Standards_0308.pdf (accessed 27 November 2009).
5 M. Knowles, *The Modern Practice of Adult Education: Andragogy versus Pedagogy*, Englewood Cliffs: Prentice Hall/Cambridge, 1977.
6 See especially, P. Freire, *Education for Critical Consciousness*, New York: Seabury Press, 1973.
7 The term 'adult' is typically used in Australia to mean a person over the age of 18 years. Different writings in the area of adult learning can use different terms. For instance, 'legal pedagogy' as used by US educators often refers to postgraduate

students, and therefore adults. This is because, in the United States, the law degree is taught as a postgraduate degree. In the business sector, however, the term 'andragogy' generally refers to adults who have been in the workforce.

8 M. Kirby, 'Legal professional ethics in times of change', paper presented at the St James Ethics Centre Forum on Ethical Issues, Sydney, 23 July 1996.

9 Walker, 'Lawyers and money', paper presented at the St James Ethics Centre Lawyers Lecture, 18 October 2005. See www.ethics.org.au/about-ethics/ethics-centre-articles/ethics-subjects/law-and-justice/article-0465.html (accessed 11 June 2009).

10 J. Briton, 'Lawyers, emotional distress and regulation', speech delivered at the Bar Association of Queensland 2009 Annual Conference, Brisbane, March 2009, p. 6.

11 Giddens, *Modernity and Self-Identity*, p. 181.

12 Giddens defines 'ontological security' as 'a sense of continuity and order in events, including those not directly within the perceptual environment of the individual'. When the sense of familiarity and control that is generated from traditional norms and values is disrupted, ontological insecurity emerges. Hence fundamental social change requires the 'self' to engage in a process of reflexivity and reinvention. ibid., p. 243.

13 The 'self' is a specifically Western concept that attributes an identity that is individual and personal to each human being. See R. Billington, J. Hockey and S. Strawbridge, *Exploring Self and Society*, London: Macmillan, 1998, p. 255.

14 See, for instance, Bauman's concept of 'liquid modernity' characterized by people destined to live their lives against a backdrop of relentless upheaval and change. Those who have less capacity to engage in processes of reflexivity and reinvention experience greater levels of ontological insecurity. Z. Bauman, *Liquid Modernity*, Cambridge: Blackwell, 2000.

15 T. Blackshaw, *Zygmunt Bauman*, London: Routledge, 2005, p. 88.

16 ibid.

17 BeyondBlue and Beaton Consulting Annual Professions Survey, April 2007; Sydney University's Brain and Mind Research Institute survey of 2,400 lawyers found one in three solicitors and one in five barristers reported levels of depression associated with disability. One study reportedly found that 11 per cent of lawyers contemplated suicide every month and 15 per cent met the criteria for alcoholism. See the Tristan Jepson Memorial Lecture, 18 September 2008, cited in University of New South Wales, 'Depression a disabling problem in the legal profession'. See www.unsw.edu.au/news/pad/articles/2008/sep/Jepson_release.html (accessed 9 June 2009).

18 ibid.

19 The *Financial Review*, 15 July 2005, cited in Briton, 'Lawyers, emotional distress and regulation', 1.

20 BeyondBlue, 2007; the Tristan Jepson Memorial Lecture, 'Lawyers are human too', 19 September 2008; University of New South Wales, 'Depression a disabling problem'.

21 Various North American studies show that lawyers experience depression, anxiety, substance abuse, stress and suicide ideation at higher rates than the general population. See, for instance, D. Cassens Weiss, 'Lawyer personalities may contribute to increased suicide risk', *ABA Journal Law News Now*, 2009. See http://abajournal.com/news/lawyer_personalities_may_contribute_to_increased_suicide_risk (accessed 1 June 2009).

22 Briton, 'Lawyers, emotional distress and regulation', 1.

23 Tristan Jepson Memorial Lecture, 'Lawyers are human too'.

24 Briton, 'Lawyers, emotional distress and regulation'.

25 Walker, 'Lawyers and money', 7.

26 For a discussion of possible wrongdoing by Enron's lawyers, Vison and Elkins, see D. Ackman, 'Enron's lawyers: Eyes wide shut?', *Forbes Magazine*, 28 January 2002. See www.forbes.com/2002/01/28/0128veenron_print.html (accessed 24 November 2009).

27 See, D. Ackman, 'It's the lawyers' turn to answer for Enron', *Forbes Magazine*, 14 March 2002. See www.forbes.com/2002/03/14/0314topnews_print.html (accessed 7 May 2009).

28 Walker, 'Lawyers and money'.

29 P. Sands, *Torture Team*, London: Penguin, 2009.

30 Such memos flowed from the Office of Legal Counsel in the Department of Justice. The Office gives highly influential opinions to the US government. One of the memos is said to have been signed by the man who ran the Office, Jay Bibby. His deputy, John Yu, a Professor of Law at Berkeley Law School, largely wrote the memo. See the interview with Sands in T. Jones, 'Lawyer discusses US torture allegations', ABC *Lateline* transcript, 5 May 2009. See abc.net.au/lateline/content/2008/s2561815.html (accessed 6 May 2009).

31 ibid., pp. 1–2.

32 ibid., p. 3.

33 The UN *Convention Against Torture and Other Cruel, Inhuman or Degrading Treatment or Punishment* (CAT), UN Doc. A/39/51 (1984) was signed by Australia on 10 December 1985 and ratified in August 1989. The United States signed the Convention on 18 April 1988 and ratified it in October 1994.

34 M. Thornton, 'The legal profession, diversity in the profession: Gender, legality and authority', paper presented at the Australian Lawyer and Social Change Conference, ANU and National Institute of Social Sciences & Law, 22–24 September 2004, p. 2.

35 Variables such as the socio-economic status, sexual preference and ethnic background of Australian lawyers are not maintained by the Australian Bureau of Statistics or law associations. However, as Lamb and Littrich suggest, some general conclusions can be extrapolated from fundamental changes in Australia. These changes include a shift from a mainly British society in origin to a multicultural society, and the expansion of tertiary education opportunities in the 1960s and 1970s designed to encourage wider access to young Australians, women, Indigenous and non-English speaking people, and working-class people. See A. Lamb and J. Littrich, *Lawyers in Australia*, Melbourne: Federation Press, 2007, p. 63.

36 Thornton, 'The legal profession'.

37 A. Giddens, *The Consequences of Modernity*, Cambridge: Polity Press, 1995; Bauman, *Liquid Modernity*; J. Young, 'Cannibalism and bulimia: Patterns of social control in late modernity'. See www.malcomred.co.uk/JockYoung/cannibal.htm (accessed 15 January 2005).

38 U. Beck, *Risk Society: Towards a New Modernity*, London: Sage, 1991.

39 Tradition is a mode of integrating the 'reflexive monitoring of action' and the handling of time and space within the continuity of the past, present and future of the community. Giddens, *The Consequences of Modernity*, p. 37.

40 The term 'risk society' is used by Giddens to describe modern society at a time when traditional certainties and securities can no longer be assumed and science rather than nature dominates. Human manufactured risk generated by modernization processes carry new consequences that cannot be judged against the historical parameters of the past. These new sources of risk are derived from the progression of human action and development. They have not been experienced in earlier times and carry uncertainty based on conflicting and unreliable answers from Science, making them difficult to control. See A. Giddens, 'Frequently asked questions', London School of Economics and Politics website. See www.intellectualfootprint.com/abu/documentos/giddens-faq.pdf (accessed 8 June 2009).

41 Giddens' 'project of the self' is a process 'routinely' engaged in by human beings who monitor and reflect upon their conduct to 'keep in touch' with the grounds and reasons for what they do 'as an integral element of doing it'. Giddens, *Modernity and Self-Identity*, pp. 36–7.

42 The results of the research conducted by Professor Ian Hickie from the Brain and

Mind Research Institute were presented at the Tristan Jepson Memorial Foundation Lecture, 'Lawyers are human too'; N. Berkovic, 'Research finds depression very high in legal profession', *The Australian*, 19 September 2008. See www.theaustralian. news.com.au/story/0,25197,24367557-17044,00.html (accessed 7 June 2009).

43 Such findings about law students are well above those of the general population, estimated at 13 per cent. Berkovic, 'Research finds depression very high in the legal profession'.

44 The Pearce Report showed that there was little attention to legal ethics, legal theory or generic skills and there was a need for theoretical and critical perspectives. See D. Pearce, E. Campbell and D. Harding, *Australian Law Schools: A Disciplinary Assessment for the Commonwealth Tertiary Education Commission*, Canberra: AGPS, 1987. As reported by the Council of Law Deans, however, some law schools have since introduced ethics integrated across various law topics: S. Owen and G. Davis, *Some Innovations in Assessment in Legal Education*, Canberra: Australian Learning and Teaching Council, 2009, p. 69. See www.cald.asn.au/docs/altc_Davis_Owen_report_comb.pdf (accessed 15 January 2010).

45 The use of the scientific model introduced to law school pedagogy by Christopher Columbus Langdell in the late nineteenth century remains present, at some level, in almost all law schools in the United States today. See C. Langdell, 'Teaching law as a science', *American Law Review* 21, 1887, 123.

46 R. Stuckley et al., 'Best practices for legal education: A vision and road map', *Clinical Legal Education Association* 29, 2007, 34.

47 ibid.

48 L. Krieger, 'Institutional denial about the dark side of law school, and fresh empirical guidance for constructively breaking the silence', *Journal of Legal Education* 52, 2002, 117, cited in Stuckley et al., 'Best practices for legal education'.

49 H. Boghosian, 'The amorality of legal andragogy', *Stanford Agora* 3, 2003, 1. See http://agora.stanford.edu/agora/volume2/boghosian.shtml (accessed 9 September 2009).

50 ibid., 2.

51 ibid.

52 ibid.

53 ibid., 1.

54 P. Schlag, 'Ten thousand cases, maybe more: An essay on centrism in legal education', *Stanford Agora* 3, 2003, 2. See http://agora.stanford.edu/agoravolume2/schlag.shtml (accessed 12 June 2009).

55 Such choices include, for example, 'where to work, who to represent and what reasoning to employ when providing advice'. See Boghosian, 'The amorality of legal andragogy', 2.

56 ibid.

57 Briton, 'Lawyers, emotional distress and regulation', 8.

58 ibid.

59 Tristan Jepson Memorial Lecture, 'Lawyers are human too'.

60 M. Knowles, *The Modern Practice of Adult Education: From Pedagogy to Andragogy* 2nd edn, Englewood Cliffs, NJ: Prentice Hall, 1980.

61 Freire, *Education for Critical Consciousness*, p. 113.

62 Spender makes the point that 'language helps form the limits of our reality. It is our means of ordering, classifying and manipulating the world. It is through language that we become members of a human community; that the world becomes comprehensible and meaningful, that we bring into existence the world in which we live.' D. Spender, *Man Made Language*, 2nd edn, New York: Routledge, 1990, p. 3.

63 Freire, *Education for Critical Consciousness*, p. ix.

64 O. Wilde, *Lady Windermere's Fan*, Cambridge: Chadwyck-Healey, 1893.

65 A 1990 study of Harvard Law School students from working-class backgrounds said they felt inferior in the first year and reported higher levels of stress than their

classmates, in part due to fears of academic shortfalls. They sought to rebuild their esteem by changing their behaviour and adopting the values of the elite environment. See R. Granfield and T. Koenig, 'From activism to pro bono: The redirection of working class altruism at Harvard Law School', *Critical Sociology* 17, 1990, 57.

66 Boghosian, 'The amorality of legal andragogy'.

67 See, for instance, R. Jones, 'Teaching leadership and ethics to adults', The Citadel College of Graduate and Professional Studies, May 2007. See http://faculty.citadel. edu/jonesr/index_files/Teaching%20ethics%20to%20adults.doc (accessed 20 June 2009); S. Forrest III and T. Peterson, 'It's called andragogy', *Academy of Management Learning and Education* 5, 2006, 113; R. Solomon, 'Aristotelian virtues: Warrior, moral, business', in R.C. Solomon (ed.), *Ethics and Excellence: Cooperation and Integrity in Business*, Oxford: Oxford University Press, 1993, p. 199.

68 For instance, some research shows a gap between what young adult learners say they prefer and what they actually do when engaged in learning. See, for instance, a study by Choy and Delahaye, which found that young adult learners prefer only the 'feel good' aspects and are not ready to assume the learner responsibilities associated with andragogy. S. Choy and B. Delahaye, 'Andragogy in vocational education and training: Learners' perspective', *Proceedings 5th Annual Conference of the Australian VET Research Association* (AVETRA). Melbourne AVETRA, pp. 1–2. See http://eprints.qut.edu.au/archive/00006868/02/6868.pdf (accessed 17 July 2009).

69 This is an observation based on my experience of teaching adult students in the nursing, medicine and occupational therapy fields where clinical placements occur much earlier in their respective degrees.

70 Freire, *Education for Critical Consciousness*, p. 94.

71 ibid., p. 95.

72 ibid., p. 98.

73 ibid., p. 45.

74 ibid., p. viii.

75 ibid.

76 *Information can be in the form of direct or indirect 'feedback' to the person about how others have reacted to the person's actions; ** The process of 'filtering' information (through assimilation, categorisation, classification) will lead the recipient to either accept or reject the information as new knowledge or 'park it' for further possible reflection in the future; *** Freire uses the term 'integration' to mean a distinctively human activity that results from the capacity to make choices and to transform existing reality. See Freire, *Education for Critical Consciousness*, p. 4.

77 ibid., pp. 111–12.

78 Displacement theory stems from Newton's third law of motion, 'every action has an equal and opposite reaction'. See I. Newton, *Philosophiae Naturalis Principia Mathematica*, 1727, translated into English *The Mathematical Principles of Natural Philosophy* by A. Motte, London: Printed for Benjamin Motte, at the Middle-Temple Gate, in Fleet Street, 1729.

79 In this case, the teacher is the power holder, but when applied to the lawyer–client relationship, the lawyer tends to hold the power based on special knowledge and skills in connection with the law and legal system.

80 In this case, the student is the less powerful, but when applied to the lawyer–client relationship, typically this would be the client.

81 For examples of more contemporary applications of the displacement theory, see M. Fullivlove, 'Psychiatric implications of displacement: Contributions from the psychology of place', *American Journal of Psychiatry* 153, 1996, 1516; L. Vandermak, 'Promoting the sense of self, place and belonging in displaced persons: The example of homelessness', *Archives of Psychiatric Nursing* 21, 2007, 241; S. Stephenson, *Crossing the Line: Vagrancy, Homelessness and Social Displacement in Russia*, Aldershot: Ashgate, 2006. Also, more recently, the New South Wales government has used displacement theory to

argue that the removing of opportunity for crime or seeking to prevent crime by changing the situation in which it occurs does not actually prevent crime but simply moves it around: New South Wales Attorney General's Department, 'Displacement theory and crime prevention'. See www.crimeprevention.nsw.gov.au/Lawlink/cpd/ II_cpdiv.nsf/vwFiles/DisplacementTheoryFactsheet_2008.pdf/$file/Displacement TheoryFactsheet_2008.pdf (accessed 18 January 2010).

82 I use the term 'structurization' to mean the interplay between individuals and the structures and institutions in which they work. See, for instance, J. Darley, 'How organizations socialize individuals into evildoing', in J. Lancaster and D. Meltz (eds), *Business Law and Ethics*, Sydney: Pearson Education, 2006, p. 211.

83 The first edition of *Principles of Biomedical Ethics* by Beauchamp and Childress was published in 1979. The fifth edition was released in 2001.

84 R. Gillon, 'Defending "the four principles" approach to biomedical ethics', *Journal of Medical Ethics* 21, 1995, 323.

85 T. Beauchamp and J. Childress, *Principles of Biomedical Ethics*, 4th edn, Oxford: Oxford University Press, 1994, p. 67.

86 Gillon, 'Defending "the four principles" approach', 323.

87 Opponents of 'principlism', or at least leading proponents of more concrete, practice-based approaches to ethical decision-making, include those who claim that its principles do not represent a theoretical approach and those who claim that its principles are too far removed from the particularities of everyday human existence. See, for instance, the anti-principlism approaches of 'virtue ethics', which emphasizes attempts to identify and define ideals; 'care ethics', which focuses more on the needs of others and one's responsibility to meet those needs than on guiding rules; and 'consensus-based ethics', which emphasizes a blend of different ethical factors and methods including principles, circumstances, character, interpersonal needs and personal meaning. See generally the views of J. Kekes, *The Morality of Pluralism*, Princeton, NJ: Princeton University Press, 1993; S. Holm, 'Not just autonomy – the principles of American biomedical ethics', *Journal of Medical Ethics* 21, 1995, 332; T. Tomlinson, 'Balancing principles in Beauchamp and Childress', *Bioethics and Medical Ethics*. See www.bu.edu/ wcp/Papers/Bio/BiorToml.htm (accessed 29 May 2009).

88 Often content can be condensed, relocated to subsequent sessions, or covered in the readings or in assessment tasks such as assignments.

89 In 2007, for example, when the main statute regulating the profession, the *Legal Profession Act* 2004 (Qld), was significantly amended along with the Barrister and Solicitor Rules, students had much to say about the breadth of the legislation and conduct rule package. In 2008–09, Federal Court Judge Marcus Einfeld's very public disclosure of unethical and unlawful conduct while sitting on the Bench was highly topical and engaging for students.

90 N. Thompson, *Promoting Equality: Challenging Discrimination and Oppression in the Human Services*, Basingstoke: Palgrave Macmillan, 1998, p. 67.

91 For a sample of the breadth of literature on stigma, stereotyping and their effects on victims, their families and the wider community see SANE Australia, 'Stigma and mental illness', *Research Bulletin* 4, January 2007. See www.sane.org (accessed 20 May 2007); M.C. Angermeyer and S. Dietrich, 'Public beliefs about and attitudes towards people with mental illness: A review of population studies', *Acta Psychiatrica Scandinavica*, 113, 2006, 163; Michael Gelder, Susannah Rix, Howard Meltzer and Olwen Rowlands, 'Stigmatisation of People with Mental Illness' (2000) 177 *The British Journal of Psychiatry* 4, L. Crowley-Cyr and J. Cokley, 'Media, madness and ethical journalism', *Australian Journalism Review* 27, 2005, 53; A. Crisp et al., 'Stigmatisation of people with mental illness', *The British Journal of Psychiatry* 117, 2000, 4; National Coalition for the Homeless, *Hate, Violence, and Death on Main Street USA: A Report on Hate Crimes and Violence Against People Experiencing Homelessness in 2006*, Washington, DC: National Coalition for the Homeless, 2006; S. Hartwell, 'Triple stigma: Persons with mental

illness and substance abuse problems in the Criminal justice system', *Criminal Justice Policy Review* 15, 2004, 84.

92 The story was written by Maurice Sendak and published in 1963. It was released as a film in Australia in late 2009.

93 Professor Manderson is an Australian lawyer working at McGill University in Canada. The conference was held in Brisbane and the theme was 'Traumas of Law'.

94 'Near life' scenarios are fictitious scenarios used in the subject, such as role-plays and seminar questions.

95 'Real-life' scenarios are those derived from case law or personal experience.

96 By 'difficult clients', I mean those who present a challenge for unprepared lawyers in terms of getting clear instructions. Examples include incapacitated clients, those with no or little English, culturally different clients, and so on. In 2009 I invited the CEO of the Mental Illness Fellowship of NQ, who is also a clinician, to play the role of clients in various states of mental 'unwellness'. The faculty's Indigenous Representative and student mentor played the role of an Aboriginal woman seeking advice on a discrimination matter. A colleague from the Faculty of Medicine played the role of an elderly man with memory loss.

97 Students who completed the ethics portfolios and ethics CV completed the subject with better overall grades than students who sat formal examinations in this subject. Paradoxically, the three years in which I set an examination, I found the answers in exams were poorly developed and inadequate. This could be a result of any combination of factors, which will be the subject of further research. For some preliminary reflections, however, see L. Crowley-Cyr, 'Reflexive professionals or disempowered technicians? A case study of the risks of "McLearning" in a regional law school', *Journal of The Australasian Law Teachers Association* 1, 2008, 299.

9 Learning in justice: ethical education in an extra-curricular law clinic

Donald Nicolson

9.1 Introduction

This chapter has both a modest and an ambitious aim. The modest aim is to describe a method of teaching legal ethics in the context of a live client law clinic that focuses on providing access to justice rather than education, and where student involvement is largely extra-curricular. In 2003, I established the University of Strathclyde Law Clinic (USLC) with the primary goal of providing legal advice and assistance to those who could not afford legal services and did not qualify for legal aid, and the secondary goal of fostering a new generation of lawyers committed to using their legal skills to help those in need. The clinic now has an annual membership of around 200 student volunteers, who work in pairs providing advice and representation under the guidance of six student 'case managers' and the supervision of two part-time solicitors. In 2007, the Clinical Legal Practice (CLP) course was developed to reward students who had conducted at least two cases with advanced skills training and some academic credit for their clinic work. Subsequently, the course has run twice a year and is available to students at both Ordinary and Honours degree level.

However, given my interest in and views on legal ethics, it seemed natural to also teach ethics and to attempt to build on the clinic's aims to inculcate in students a sense of what I have previously described as ethical professionalism.[1] By this I mean that students will see ethics as central to their future professional status – that they will not be satisfied simply with applying professional rules or roles, but will independently evaluate their appropriateness in specific contexts; and that they will not see legal practice as simply involving the provision of competent services to those who can pay, but as involving some commitment to ensuring access to justice to those in need – either through their choice of career or via pro bono representation.

The more ambitious aim of this chapter is to draw on this experience of teaching ethics in a clinical context in order to contribute to the debate over whether and how teaching is best able to influence student moral development. Currently, there are strong competing theoretical views on whether ethical education[2] and law clinics[3] can have a positive impact on ethical development, but very little supporting empirical evidence. Drawing on the reflective diaries that CLP students submit as part of their assessment for the course, I will offer empirical evidence that, while based only on a limited sample, is unique in a number of ways. First, in contrast to the tentative conclusions of other studies,[1] the diaries provide clear evidence that a clinical experience may encourage the development of an attitude of ethical professionalism. Second, in contrast to other studies that have showed only that ethical teaching influences law students' moral reasoning[5] – which is only weakly related to actual moral behaviour[6] – this study provides evidence that teaching ethics, at least in the context of experience in a live client clinic that emphasizes social justice rather than educational aims, may begin to influence actual moral behaviour. In fact, contrary to those who question whether law schools can influence moral character,[7] there is even some evidence to support my previously expressed view[8] that combining ethical teaching with experience in live-client clinics, particularly extra-curricular clinics with a social justice orienta-tion, may enable law schools to positively influence the development of students' moral character, which I argue offers the best hope for influencing the future behaviour of lawyers.

9.2 Law clinics and ethical education

Given that moral behaviour requires the exercise of psychological functions, this argument begins with an understanding of what psychological components need to be affected by legal education in order to ensure moral development. Accord-ing to psychologists, moral behaviour requires four psychological components.[9] First, moral *sensitivity* enables moral actors to recognize moral problems in the first place. Second, moral *judgment* equips them to work out the correct response. Third, moral *commitment* ensures that they regard morality as important enough to prioritize over competing considerations like self-interest. Finally, moral *courage* helps moral actors to sustain this commitment in the face of competing pressures such as the demands of senior colleagues in law firms.

Currently, ethical education in most law schools is largely confined to teaching the formal professional codes of conduct, often only in the professional stage of training. At best, this might sensitize students and provide them with solutions to the type of ethical problems recognized by the codes. But, leaving aside the fact that many codes are limited to providing only vague principles of an aspirational nature, even codes that attempt to provide detailed solutions to all conceivable problems will inevitably contain gaps and ambiguities requiring the exercise of moral judgment. Teaching rules, even if it is accompanied by practice in applica-tion to hypotheticals, does not provide students with the requisite tools for dealing with situations where the rules do not provide answers or with the contextual complexities of real-life dilemmas.

Students also need exposure to competing approaches to the various problems arising in legal practice found in the legal ethics literature, along with the various general ethical theories upon which these approaches draw and information on the various pressures within the practice setting that will test the moral courage of practitioners committed to doing the right thing. More fundamentally, however, teaching rules does little to develop such commitment and courage – and, even if it did, ethics teaching is usually too limited and comes too late to reverse what is regarded by many as the implicit message of most legal teaching. Arguably, legal education contains a 'hidden curriculum'[10] to the effect that issues of ethics and justice are of little relevance to the real business of law, that rules are either there to be formalistically followed or manipulated in the interests of clients, and that a legal career is a means to success and financial rewards. As a result, according to research (albeit largely in the United States), legal education tends to undermine student idealism about using law to promote justice, and to engender moral and political cynicism, as well as a propensity towards ethically dubious behaviour.[11]

In such an environment, those who teach ethics in law schools should have four goals. First, given the implicit message that ethics is not important or at best simply involves keeping one's nose clean, law schools need to *inspire* an interest in ethics in students. Second, given that the current rules can never resolve all possible ethical dilemmas that might arise in practice, and given that these rules and over arching professional roles are highly contested, ethical education needs to *illuminate* the tools that ethical theory and applied ethical discourse provide for the resolution of ethical dilemmas. Third, given that these tools and ethical codes themselves always require the exercise of choice and judgment, ethical education needs to *illustrate* the ethical dimension of legal practice by giving students practice in resolving dilemmas. Finally, because recognizing ethical dilemmas and working out how to resolve them is insufficient by itself to ensure moral behaviour, ethical education needs to begin to *inculcate* in students the habit of identifying, evaluating and caring about ethical issues so that this becomes a more or less spontaneous response once in practice – especially when faced with the many countervailing pressures to compromise ethical values. According to contemporary moral psychology and virtue ethics, it is the development of relevant moral character traits that offers the best chance for prospective lawyers to display not only the necessary sensitivity and judgment to recognize and resolve moral problems, but also the commitment and courage to implement their decisions.

While I accept that law clinics cannot radically alter students' moral character, they can ensure that those with a strong ethical compass in their personal lives begin to adapt their values and character traits to the demands of professional life, hence developing what I call professional moral character,[12] and even start those with less developed character traits on a journey towards ethical professionalism. In other words, they may involve students in the sort of 'moral apprenticeship' that virtue ethics stresses as so important for character development.[13] Less ambitiously, law clinics may inspire an interest in, illuminate and illustrate issues of legal ethics and hence help students develop moral sensitivity, judgment and commitment.

Much of the benefit of live client clinics is thought to stem from the fact that handling real-life dilemmas and flesh and blood clients imparts an immediacy and provokes an engagement with ethics that are lacking in didactic and even interactive forms of teaching like tutorials and seminars. Where learning experiences are realistic, and relate to the fulfilment of future social roles, learning is said to be more profound and likely to lead to greater self-knowledge.[14] The 'disorienting moments'[15] or 'moral crises' that occur when prior assumptions and settled values jar with experienced reality may stimulate an 'engaged moral faculty',[16] whereas engaging with actual clients, particularly on an emotional level, may evoke feelings of empathy which are so important to the development of moral judgment and commitment.[17] Moreover, according to virtue ethicists and moral psychologists, any feelings of satisfaction or regret at their actions in representing actual clients and real dilemmas may affect character development,[18] whereas involvement in community work contributes to moral development.[19] Law clinics have other advantages. Because of their perceived expertise, clinic supervisors may function as influential moral exemplars, modelling good client relations, concern for how their actions affect others and an altruistic commitment to the community. In addition, clinics reveal the extent of unmet legal need, and social and legal injustice; students learn that legal practice can involve helping others, and this can be rewarding as well as intellectually challenging. Anecdotal reports suggest that this may inspire, or at least reinforce, altruistic aspirations in students.[20]

If clinic involvement can indeed foster a sense of ethical professionalism, then it seems plausible to suggest that, compared with most clinics which focus on students' educational needs and in which participation is usually relatively brief, the positive impact on moral development is likely to be greater in the USLC, where student involvement can last for up to five years,[21] where students are also exposed to ethical issues in mentoring fellow students and in sitting on ethics committees, and where attention to issues of ethics and justice need not be squeezed by other educational aims. More controversially, it can be argued that in putting social needs before education, extra-curricular clinics avoid the implicit message conveyed by educationally oriented clinics that it is the students' interests – now educational, but later financial – that take precedence over the interests of clients and the community.

Admittedly, the potential for fostering ethical professionalism will be seriously under utilized unless students are exposed to a theoretical basis to help them make sense of their experiences. Thus, without being alerted to the sort of ethical dilemmas that arise in practice, students might overlook those staring them in the face, whereas without exposure to a wide variety of ethical theories or positions on issues of legal ethics, they will not have the opportunity to explore alternative approaches to resolving dilemmas and to develop their own sense of professional values, which are arguably necessary to supplement and sometimes even supplant existing professional roles and rules.[22] Moreover: 'Learning occurs not in the doing but in the reflection and conceptualization that takes place during and after the event.'[23] Such reflection, aided by the critical evaluation of others, may help students develop the lifelong learning skills of the reflective practitioner.[24] Thus, according to Kolb's well-known learning circle,[25] reflection may lead to the adoption of new, or the adaptation of existing, theories about how to handle issues that can then be put into practice when similar situations arise. This new experience provides the material for further reflection, theory adaptation and theory testing, and so on.

9.3 The clinical legal practice course

Whereas many believe that more traditional forms of ethics teaching should precede clinical experience,[26] most CLP students – as the diaries reveal – are exposed to theoretical knowledge about legal ethics *after* they have encountered ethical dilemmas, either directly in the cases conducted prior to the course (an average of 4.75 for the students in this study)[27] or indirectly through overseeing other students[28] and/or sitting on the USLC committee which resolves ethical problems.[29] This is because the LLB curriculum covers issues of access to justice, and more briefly the regulation and constitution of the legal profession and basic ethical theory, but not legal ethics itself. On the five occasions on which the CLP course has run, ethics has been taught in anything from three to six two-hour seminars. Where there were only three, the first dealt with differing conceptions of professionalism and the current practice environment, the second with issues of client autonomy and lawyer paternalism, and the third with neutral partisanship,[30] with discussion focused on actual clinic cases. On three occasions, the first seminar was followed by one on ethical education and professional codes, while the final seminar was split into one on the problems of and justification for neutral partisanship and a second involving confidentiality and a more specific look at past cases in the light of alternatives to neutral partisanship. In addition, in order to help students make better sense of legal ethics, they were required to read up on moral theory and, given the emphasis on personal development, to discuss their five most important moral values.

Given the original aim of offering CLP to reward voluntary clinic activity, the remaining seminars were initially devoted to advanced skills development, but having quickly realized its value in fostering ethical professionalism, where staffing constraints permitted, I replaced this with up to five seminars on access to justice. Teaching was shared between me and two practitioners, though some sessions were also taken by experts in particular skills. The practitioners also took the majority[31] of hour-long weekly 'surgeries', which were devoted to discussing how to handle current cases and a court visit. Interestingly, while neither skills sessions nor the surgeries were meant to focus on ethics – indeed, one practitioner delights in semi-seriously modelling the amoral lawyer – growing ethical awareness led students to raise in class and/or their diaries ethical issues they saw as implicated in more practical concerns.[32]

Students were assessed on the basis of a class report comprising a reflective diary and two case files, and an essay evaluating relevant justice, ethical, legal and/or procedural aspects of one of their cases,[33] though Honours students were also orally examined. For the diary, students were required to submit weekly entries of a maximum of 500 words reflecting on their performance, what they were learning from the class and from their clinical experience, and how they might improve their performance. Entries could be submitted twice during the semester for my comments, to which students could then respond (maximum of 200 words), leading to a limited dialogue in which I was able to provoke deeper reflection and suggest further reading. Students were also invited to provide a short introductory overview of their diary, highlighting any note-worthy aspects.

9.4 Method

The findings reported below are based on 23 reflective diaries – though, because two took the course twice, only 21 students. No issues about sampling arose since I analysed all available diaries, with the only possible resulting bias caused by the fact that two students ignored requests for permission and nine diaries were destroyed due to university policy on retention of assessment work. Lacking experience in empirical research, I instinctively used a form of grounded theory in analysing the diaries.[34] Having already read them without any attempt at analysis when they were submitted for responses and assessment, I first conducted a closer reading with the aim of ascertaining what ethical issues were discussed. I then reread the diaries looking for evidence of moral development and its influences. As is common with this methodology, new themes emerged and earlier ones were modified during the writing up of the analysis and even the checking of footnotes. In presenting the findings, students have been anonymized through pseudonyms, case details changed and entries reproduced without correction to spelling and grammar. In order to provide an idea of the quantity of evidence for various phenomena, I have cited in the footnotes relevant diary entries by referring to the student's pseudonym and the semester week in which the entry was made.[35]

There are obvious limitations to relying on these diaries as evidence of the impact of clinical experience and ethics teaching on students' moral development. One is that they largely reflect merely what students say they think and feel, rather than how they actually behaved – though psychological research reveals a weak connection between moral views and behaviour,[36] and significantly there were notable occasions when students clearly had acted on their professed views. Obviously, also, the diaries cannot reveal how the students are likely to behave once they enter the more ethically challenging context of legal practice. Second, in a variation on the problem of the 'reactive effect' encountered in much qualitative research,[37] students might have consciously or unconsciously adapted their views to garner higher marks, though clearly some of the highest achieving students did not.[38] Finally, CLP students cannot be said to be representative of all USLC, let alone all law, students. While many say that they take CLP in order to gain additional skills, a few expressly refer to an interest in ethics and hence might be predisposed to ethics teaching in the same way that all USLC students are ostensibly predisposed towards altruistic service to the community. There are equally serious problems with the reported findings. My personal and intellectual investment in the Law Clinic and CLP as a means of influencing ethical orientation arguably render me even more than usually prone to subconscious bias in the interpretation of the data and the resulting narrative constructed, though to some extent the problem was mitigated by giving the students the opportunity to correct misrepresentations of their views.

9.5 Findings

Student reflection itself was highly subjective. Differences between students went well beyond changes in course content and the uniqueness of case experiences,[39] both in terms of register – from the purely intellectual discussion of the academic literature to the highly personal and even 'therapeutic'[40] discussion of emotions and values – and content – from learning about skills to reflecting not just on the set topics of ethics and access to justice, but also on the justice of substantive law and the legal process. Students also saw fit to comment on their legal education in terms of its silence on issues of legal ethics and justice, and the consequent negative impact of its message on students; its encouragement of student competitiveness and the domination of recruitment by the big firms; and the need for compulsory clinical legal education and pervasive ethics teaching. While these views were not unexpected in echoing the seminar reading, some went further to suggest reforms to the clinic and even to the course itself.

Nor was the subject-matter of reflection always predictable from the catalysing experience. Each semester began with an introduction to learning theory. For Lindsay, a questionnaire on learning styles provoked reflection on how he had treated his past clients,[41] whereas exposure to Kolb's learning cycle led Rebecca to a 'euphoric' revelation about how an earlier traumatic incident had caused her 'to revisit and incur the characteristics and emotions' experienced at the time and to develop a distrust of others which led to distancing herself from her classmates.[42] As a result of the 'personal journey' involved in writing the diary, she claimed to have gained greater self-knowledge and to have become more involved in the clinic.[43]

9.5.1 Learning from the course

Not all responses to class reading and discussion were as dramatic, but students were frequently stimulated to reflect on their personal values and ethical orientation, and how these might play out in practice,[44] with many admitting to not previously having considered their motivating moral values,[45] various issues of legal ethics[46] and professionalism,[47] and (notwithstanding their other courses) even the justice of the legal system.[48] Such reflection was enhanced by exposure to socio-legal research on the difficulties of maintaining one's values in the face of competing workplace pressures and academic discussion of the sorts of ethical problems that arise in practice. In this way, students can be said to have begun the process of developing their own sense of professional ethics[49] – even if, as some acknowledged, many issues remained to be resolved.[50] One seminar made Patrick realize that:

> my ideals to altruism will be tested when I start practising as a solicitor . . . I suppose I have been naïve to think that I could uphold my ideals and still become a successful lawyer. The seminar set me thinking seriously about the kind of lawyer I wanted to be and what my values really are.[51]

Similar insights led Vikram[52] and Becky[53] to question their decisions to pursue – and reinforced Jeremy's decision not to pursue[54] – a career in commercial law. More positively, Fiona was able to resolve previous doubts about how she could justify defending those accused of 'vile crimes',[55] and confirmed Elizabeth's choice of a career in civil rather than criminal defence advocacy.[56] Given that career choice will tend to be lawyers' most significant ethical decision, determining both the likely types of moral dilemmas they will face and the constraints on their ability to display moral integrity and altruism,[57] the CLP course can be said to have indirectly affected likely future behaviour.

To the limited extent that thinking is linked to behaviour, seminar reading and discussion may have a similar impact.[58] Thus students were provided with detailed reading on, not just the problems of legal ethics, but also the tools available for their resolution to be found both in competing professional legal ethics approaches to issues like lawyer paternalism, neutral partisanship and confidentiality, and especially the author's own contextual approach to ethics with its detailed decision-making schema,[59] and in the underlying ethical theories on which such approaches draw. Their diaries revealed students drawing as a matter of course both on ethical theory,[60] and on the concepts and arguments they had encountered in legal ethics literature – most notably views on moral development and ethical professionalism,[61] and particularly the contextual approach to ethics.[62] Moreover, many changed their views in response to the reading, class discussion and comments on their diary entries.[63] This occurred most frequently in relation to neutral partisanship, where many acknowledged reversing or limiting their initial support, with the catalyst often being one of the (but not necessarily the same) actual clinic cases discussed.[64]

Here, as in relation to arguments regarding a mandatory pro bono duty on lawyers or the altruistic dimension to professionalism,[65] students might have adapted their views to curry favour, though the fact that some expressly challenged my views indicated that not all students are so instrumental.[66] However, even if students retained their initial views, it can be argued that doing so after consideration of alternatives and being persuaded as to the justifications for neutral partisanship is an improvement on the current position whereby, in the absence of exposure to debates within legal ethics, students are likely to simply assume such justification – or, even worse, not consider the morality of the lawyer's 'hired gun' role at all. In fact, even if the students persuaded of the arguments supporting neutral partisanship go on to zealously 'over-represent' clients despite moral qualms, they are less likely to fall foul of the other alleged drawback to neutral partisanship, namely that its anaesthetization of moral conscience leads to the 'under-representation' of those most in need.[67]

Moreover, many students themselves were convinced that the course had affected their ethical orientation. To take one example, in introducing her diary Isla stated:

> I believe that my entries show a change in my attitude towards clients and their cases. For example in Week 3 I was adamant that it was above and

beyond the call of duty to show concern or compassion for my clients; how-ever in week 8 I found that my new case partner shared the same view which I used to possess . . . My partner's view was very pragmatic, 'if the client doesn't tell us all the information then that's their fault' . . . When I explained to him that it wouldn't be fair to judge the client by our personal standards I realized that I no longer agreed with my old perception of clients . . . [A]fter working with different clinic members and the CLP class I can appreciate that there are circumstances out with the client's control and I should not judge them by my own standards.[68]

9.5.2 Learning from cases

As Isla's reflection illustrate, clinic cases – both past and current, both students' own and those of others discussed in class – were a rich source of material for reflection and learning on issues of ethics and justice. Thus students came away from cases questioning the justice of law,[69] the effectiveness of legal remedies, and the fairness and transparency of legal proceedings.[70] For example, after success-fully helping a client who had been turned down by eight law firms, Isla com-mented that 'it appears . . . that the legal system is no longer fit for poor or "average" people it appears more geared towards businesses and the rich'.[71]

A wide variety of ethical dilemmas that arose in cases were discussed in class and in the diaries. One involved a conflict between the interests of a student in terms of career progression and those of his client,[72] and others issues of whether lawyer or police malpractice should be reported to the relevant authorities.[73] A fair number involved dubious tactics adopted on behalf of clients, such as seeking information in a way that came close to deception,[74] threatening collateral pro-ceedings as a means of pressurizing an opponent,[75] and taking advantage of an opponent's ignorance or lack of representation.[76] However, illustrating that virtu-ally every instance of client representation has an ethical dimension,[77] by far the most common issues arose in day-to-day dealings with clients. Thus every student reported grappling with and learning from dilemmas involving how to treat clients in a professional[78] and empathetic manner,[79] while not unduly raising their hopes[80] or impinging on their autonomy,[81] whereas some students' commitment to zealous representation was tested by clients who were unreliable or seen as untrustworthy, manipulative or lacking in gratitude.[82]

The way in which these issues were resolved demonstrates the value of teaching ethics alongside or after student immersion in real-life cases. Most directly, teachers and supervisors intervened to challenge student attitudes, as I did by encouraging students faced with their clients' non-attendance at meetings to try to put themselves in their shoes and to discuss matters with them,[83] and by alerting oblivious students to issues of dubious tactics.[84] Less directly, students clearly – and frequently explicitly – used their reading and class insights to question their actions in past cases and to handle current dilemmas, while some expressly acknowledged lessons learnt for the future.[85]

For example, the value of an ethics class was dramatically experienced by

Patrick, whose assertion of the value of tolerance in class a mere hour before interviewing a client inspired him to do all he could to help, notwithstanding that he considered the client to be untruthful and manipulative.[86] Two months later, after standing up to an aggressive opponent trying to pressure him into acting without instructions, he specifically acknowledged that compared with his partner who had not taken CLP, he had found it 'easier to make decisions on how to act in this situation mainly due to the knowledge I have gained through the CLP course'.[87] Similarly, faced with the option of the 'dirty trick' of using a former colleague who had to resign due to racial bullying in support of her client's claim of racial discrimination against a law firm, Rebecca cited chapter and verse of a seminar reading to justify using her morality to 'filter what I find to be immoral instructions' and finding out through 'moral dialogue' that her client also wanted to 'do the right thing'.[88] Five weeks later, however, after discovering that the defendant had lied, she methodically applied the contextual approach to ethics encountered in her reading and reversed her earlier rejection of the 'dirty trick'.[89] She also noted that her partner, who had been taught ethics in the diploma, 'did not view the matter as involving morality', commenting that this was 'a blatant example of the benefits of the CLP/Law Clinic education'.

While in most cases the application of ethical theory to practice was facilitated by the relatively unpressured clinical context, Rebecca was worried that her case would jeopardize her career prospects in the same area of practice as that of the defending law firm. Nevertheless, although realizing that she could be replaced by another adviser, she decided to test her 'drive and principles against that of personal and selfish gain' and continue with the case. Her further comment that in this 'test of character . . . without the clinic I would not have known that when it comes to it I am able to put aside personal gain for the sake of the right thing' perceptively echoes the view of ethicists that strong moral character is more likely to develop where individuals are subjected to difficult challenges.[90]

The diaries revealed the presence of other factors that enhance character development, such as student feelings of satisfaction or regret at their conduct of cases. For example, having successfully completed an 18-month case against all the odds, Lindsay commented:

> To say the least it was extremely satisfying . . . I now really understand why people get so much from the clinic on a personal level. In this case I got to help out someone . . . who would otherwise have been utterly vulnerable to people far stronger than herself.[91]

Later in the semester, Lindsay's experience in struggling to obtain better treatment for his disabled client illustrates how exposure to social injustice might conscientize students.[92] However, his diaries also show that clinics have an uphill struggle to overcome the pull of the better paid jobs on career choice.[93] Thus, while his experiences caused Lindsay to reconsider his career plans, he still admitted to being attracted academically and to 'the lifestyle and the rewards' of a corporate law career.[94] Similarly, Becky reported switching career plans from criminal to commercial law because of 'experiences in my personal life coupled with career opportunities presented to me'.[95] By contrast, Nicola stated that the 'possibility of making a positive difference to someone . . . reminds you of why you wanted to become a lawyer in the first place',[96] while Isla's satisfaction in successfully representing the client turned down by eight firms reinforced her desire to pursue a career which made a difference to the community.[97] Thus, at the very least, it can be said that law clinics may, as Harjinder argued, enthuse 'the many students [who] enter the profession with a genuine desire to tackle society's access to justice problems'.[98] Indeed, Isla revealed that by exposing her 'to the wide variety of options other than commercial law', the USLC had helped her to discover a 'social conscience':

> I didn't start my law degree to 'make a difference', my goal was simply to earn enough money so I can afford some of life's luxuries and have no financial troubles. However, having seen the positive effect my time and effort has had on clients of the clinic has changed my perspective and now, my ultimate goal is to find a job that provides both financial security and a chance to help communities or less fortunate individuals.[99]

Similarly, Calum admitted that before his clinic experience he had imagined a career in a large law firm and 'hadn't really considered the larger ideal of social justice . . . Now I find it impossible not to.'[100] For Mark, however, the impact of the clinic was more general in having a 'profound positive effect on my perception of ethics'.[101]

9.5.3 Learning from the clinic

No doubt, educationally oriented live client clinics might similarly affect moral development. However, some of the advantages of extra-curricular clinics suggested above[102] were highlighted by the diaries. One is that the students' greater caseload – an average of almost 10 for the CLP students who have now graduated and likely to be much higher for those who remain in the USLC[103] – as well as their role as case managers and in making decisions on ethics committees means that exposure to ethical dilemmas is likely to be much greater than in educationally oriented clinics. Thus, having acknowledged that being a clinic member for most of his university career and 'particularly taking the CLP course' has encouraged him to think about ethics, Vikram referred to sitting in on 'a number of interviews in which I found myself looking at the issues in a more ethical manner than I imagine I would otherwise . . . In a way, I have found myself having a part of a "moral apprenticeship".'[104] Indeed, his involvement in this case – like the experiences of Isla, Patrick and Rebecca discussed above[105] – shows that students with heightened moral awareness and understanding may engage those they supervise or partner in moral dialogue and a similar moral apprenticeship.

Also important to the sort of moral apprenticeship that fosters character development is the impact of role models. Thus one of the practitioners teaching CLP was twice mentioned. Her work as a legal aid lawyer and founder of an environmental law centre showed Isla that she could 'work in private practice and still achieve her ultimate aim of helping others',[106] whereas Seamus declared that by 'putting something back into the community' through her pro bono assistance of his client, she had acted as 'a positive role model to students' and been 'inspirational to me for my own career'.[107] A more immediate (and personally flattering) example was given by Patrick, who commented that one factor which helped overcome his distaste for his client in the first of his two cases discussed above[108] 'was Donald's "good nature" and commitment to social justice . . . this motivated us to carry out research late into the night!'

The other factor he mentioned was the clinic's ethos 'to help those with legal difficulties'. As already noted, all applicants for membership must sign up to putting client needs ahead of their own, and this ethos is reinforced in USLC literature, induction training and committee meetings, along with what I call a holistic approach which sees clients not simply as legal problems requiring technical, legal solutions, but as flesh and blood people with emotional and other personal needs who can be helped in many different ways. The diaries revealed that both the social justice and holistic aspects of this ethos influenced student thinking and behaviour. Thus Rebecca stated that the 'clinic ethos and environment' helped her through her dilemma over whether to continue her discrimination cases despite the risk to her career prospects:

> The altruistic ethos helped to reinforce my beliefs and allowed me to feel comfortable making a selfless decision in a profession surrounded by greed and self-importance. Without the clinic to strengthen and normalize my beliefs I do not know if I would have had the courage and conviction to act outside the norm. In the future, I will try to use the clinic as an example to justify acting altruistically rather than succumbing to peer pressure.[109]

Less dramatic, but equally passionate, was Orla's criticism of students from other universities attending a pro bono conference, who 'seemed to focus exclusively on the educational benefit which clinics provide to students', and her view that it is 'wrong to run a clinic entirely on this basis'.[110] Similarly, Seamus expressed the hope that 'within my own legal career I do not avoid the responsibility, mandatory or not, of pro bono',[111] while Grace vehemently opposed a proposal for a code of conduct imposing reciprocal obligations on clients, arguing that it would:

> distort the way we act pro bono – we do not do it to make ourselves feel good and to be thanked. Rather we act pro bono in order to make a difference to someone's life and to help them gain access to justice, whether we are to be thanked or not.[112]

Adoption of the holistic approach to client relations was equally evident. For example, in discussions over whether to help those without apparent legal solutions or how much time to allow for interviews, students accepted that they should help clients in whatever way possible, and that sometimes even listening to their problems, providing them with their day in court and encouraging them to move on with their lives may be valuable.[113] As Jeremy put it: '[T]he law clinic encourages us to appreciate people's problems as their reality.'[114] Similarly, Elizabeth insisted that clients must not be seen simply as legal problems but as 'people first and sometimes there are emotional needs and issues that we must first address before we can tackle the legal issues'.[115]

9.6 Conclusion

To the extent that the findings presented here represent a plausible reading of genuine views, they illuminate the hitherto largely theoretical debate about ethical education. Thus, contrary to sceptics, the diaries show that teaching can raise ethical awareness, equip students to deal with ethical issues and even affect (at least professed) ethical views and (at least in the context of the university environment) behaviour. They also show that live client clinics expose students to a wide range of ethical issues, particularly in relation to the appropriate relationship with clients, which may provide new, or deepen existing, insights into legal ethics – particularly if accompanied or followed by teaching and reflection. Clearly, their clinical experience reinforced the ethical orientation and career plans of some students, but it also seemed to alter that of others, and in some cases even affected their behaviour. Conversely, there is little evidence to support the view[116] that clinics engender cynicism.[117] On the contrary, many students cited their clinic experience as fostering a desire to help others either through their chosen career or pro bono work. To this extent, this chapter's more ambitious aim of showing that ethical teaching and clinical experience can foster ethical professionalism seems to have been achieved. In fact, the diaries also provide support for the impact of clinical experience on character development, at least in evidencing factors conducive to character development, such as the influence of role models, the experiencing of moral crises, and feelings of satisfaction and regret accompanying clinic experiences.

Of course, these diaries do not establish that all CLP, let alone all USLC, students will display a greater commitment to ethical professionalism once in practice. Nevertheless, the diaries of some CLP students[118] make it plausible to suggest that, compared with students whose ethical education is confined to learning professional rules, CLP students are likely to be more sensitive to, and better equipped to handle, ethical issues when professional rules run out or seem inappropriate. Indeed, like all USLC students, they may even have embarked on a process of professional moral character development – though whether this is the case and how robust such character is likely to be in withstanding the pressures of legal practice must await the results of a planned longitudinal study.

For similar reasons, these diaries do not demonstrate that long-standing student involvement in extra-curricular clinics with a social justice orientation are more likely to foster ethical professionalism than educationally oriented clinics with more short-lived student involvement. However, they do suggest that the USLC's social justice and client-centred ethos at least reinforced existing student attitudes, and even changed those of some students.[119] Moreover, the sheer level of case experience – both directly and indirectly – means that USLC students will have far more exposure to ethical issues than in most clinics, whereas the fact that CLP students were frequently able to relate their theoretical knowledge to previous case experiences is likely to ensure greater insights into their theoretical learning and a deeper imprint on their thinking. Indeed, the students were likely to further their ethical education after the course by repeating Kolb's learning cycle in the average of 4.15 cases subsequently conducted.[120] Although they will only benefit from guided reflection if – as five students have already done – they take CLP at both Ordinary and Honours levels, nevertheless the ethical tools they will have gained, especially those deriving from general ethical theory and a contextual approach to ethical decision-making, should equip them to engage in continuous self-reflection and to develop the habits of a reflective ethical practitioner.

Unfortunately, however – possibly because most USLC members do not want to jeopardize their career prospects by devoting one of their few options to a course focusing on ethics and justice – the very small proportion who have taken CLP means that this opportunity for experiential learning is currently being under utilized. While I have previously argued that ethical education can probably only have a long-lasting effect on a relatively small number of students, and it is probably better to provide a few with an intensive experience rather than many with a superficial experience,[121] the 40 or so students who have taken CLP thus far is too few. Partly for this reason, but also because of the general advantages of teaching law clinically, starting in 2010, students who are admitted into the USLC in terms of its current criteria will be able to graduate with a Clinical LLB, which will involve them using their clinic cases as an alternative form of assessment in relevant courses. In addition, two first-year courses will be partly given over to skills training and an introduction to legal ethics, ensuring an earlier start to the ethical development of USLC students, and hence meaning that clients and others are more likely to be protected from the sort of unethical behaviour which was occasionally revealed by the diaries. Then, in the third year, the CLP course will seek to further develop ethical awareness and commitment in the light of the students' intervening clinical experience. In addition, throughout the degree, students will discuss ethical as well as practical aspects of their current cases in regular surgeries, and reflect on issues of ethics and justice in a weekly diary. Given that such a practically oriented degree is likely to appeal to both students and prospective employers, hopefully many more USLC students will become exposed to the intensive and effective ethical education evidenced in the diaries analysed in this chapter.

Acknowledgements

I would like to thank the students whose stimulating diaries inspired this chapter for their patience in responding to frequent requests for information and providing helpful comments on an early draft. I would also like to thank Emma Boffey for her research assistance, Jo Winters for her careful reading of a draft, and Simon Halliday and Laura Piacentini for advice on research methods. Any errors or inadequacies are my sole responsibility.

Notes

1 D. Nicolson, 'Education, education, education: legal, moral and clinical', *The Law Teacher* 42, 2008, 145.

2 For an overview, see J.E. Moliterno, 'An analysis of ethics teaching in law schools: Replacing lost benefits of the apprentice system in the academic atmosphere', *University of Cincinnati Law Review* 60, 1991–92, 83–134 and more recently D. Webb, 'Ethics as a compulsory element of qualifying degrees: some modest expectations', *Legal Ethics* 4, 2001, 109–26.

3 Compare, for example, R. Condlin, 'The moral failure of clinical legal education', in D. Luban (ed.), *The Good Lawyer: Lawyer's Roles and Lawyer's Ethics*, Totowa, NJ: Rowman & Allanheld, 1983, pp. 320–4; N. Duncan, 'Responsibility and ethics in professional legal education', in R. Burridge and K. Hinett (eds), *Effective Learning and Teaching in Law*, London: Kegan Page, 2002; M. Jewell, 'Teaching law ethically: Is it possible?', *Dalhousie Law Journal* 8, 1984, 474, 507–10; T. Glennon, 'Building an ethic of responsibility', *Hastings Law Journal* 93, 1991–92, 1175; A. Boon and J. Levin, *The Ethics and Conduct of Lawyers in England and Wales*, Oxford: Hart, 2008, p. 60; D.L. Rhode, 'Into the valley of ethics: Professional responsibility and educational reform', *Law and Contemporary Problems* 58, 1995, 139, with e.g. R. J. Simon, 'An evaluation of the effectiveness of some curriculum innovations in law schools', *International Journal of Applied Behavioural Science* 2, 1966, 219; H. Sacks, 'Student fieldwork as a technique in educating students in professional responsibility', *Journal of Legal Education* 20, 1967–68, 291; J. MacFarlane, 'Look before you leap: Knowledge and learning in legal skills education', *Journal of Law and Society* 19, 1992, 306.

4 J. Palermo and A. Evans, 'Almost there: Empirical insights into clinical method and ethical courses in climbing the hill towards lawyers' professionalism', *Griffith Law Review* 17, 2008, 252 and, even more tentatively, A. Evans, 'Lawyers' perceptions of their values: An empirical assessment of Monash University graduates in law', *Legal Education Review* 12, 2001, 209.

5 E.M. Abramson, 'Legal education, punching the myth of the moral intractability of law students: The suggestiveness of the work of psychologist Lawrence Kohlberg for ethical training', *Notre Dame Journal of Law, Ethics & Public Policy* 7, 1993, 223; S. Hartwell, 'Promoting moral development through experimental teaching', *Clinical Law Review* 1, 1994–95, 505 and, more tentatively, S. Hartwell, 'Moral development, ethical conduct and clinical education', *New York Law School Law Review* 35, 1990, 131.

6 See, for example, J. Rest, 'The major components of morality', in W. Kurtines and J. Gewirtz (eds), *Morality, Moral Behaviour and Moral Development*, New York: Wiley, 1984, pp. 21–2; J. Rest, 'Can ethics be taught in professional schools? The psychological research', *Ethics Easier Said than Done* 1, 1988, 22; J. Rest et al., *Post Conventional Moral Thinking: A Neo-Kohlbergian Approach*, Mahwah, NJ: Lawrence Erlbaum, 1999, pp. 80ff.; S. Thoma, 'Moral judgments and moral action: Establishing the link between judgment and action', in J. Rest and D. Narvaez (eds), *Moral Development in the Professions: Psychology and Applied Ethics*, Hillsdale, NJ: Lawrence Erlbaum, 1994; A. Blasi, 'Bridging moral cognition and moral action: A critical review of the literature', *Psychological Bulletin* 88, 1980, 1.

7 R.M. Pipkin, 'Law school instruction in professional responsibility: A curricular paradox', *American Bar Foundation Research Journal* 1979, 247, 265ff; J. Carlin, 'What law

schools can do about professional responsibility', *Connecticut Law Review*, 4, 1971, 459; M. Robertson, 'Challenges in the design of legal ethics learning systems: An educational perspective', *Legal Ethics* 8, 2005, 222, 234.

8   Nicolson, 'Education, education, education'.

9   On what is required psychologically to ensure moral behaviour see, for example, Rest, 'The major components of morality'; Rest et al., *Post Conventional Moral Thinking*; Rest and Narvaez, *Moral Development in the Professions*, esp. Ch. 1; and on the advantages of moral character in this regard see, for example, D.K. Lapsley and F. Clark Power (eds), *Character Psychology and Character Education*, Notre Dame, IN: University of Notre Dame Press, 2005.

10 R.C. Cramton, 'The ordinary religion of the law school classroom', *Journal of Legal Education* 29, 1977–78, 247. See also Pipkin, 'Law school instruction in professional responsibility'; H. Lesnick, 'The integration of responsibility and values: legal education in an alternative consciousness of lawyering and law' *Nova Law Journal* 10, 1986, 633; K. Economides, 'Legal ethics: Three challenges for the next millennium', in K. Economides (ed.), *Ethical Challenges to Legal Education and Conduct*, Oxford: Hart, 1998, pp. xvii–xxxiii, who discuss, respectively, the latent, implicit or informal curriculum.

11 Usefully summarized in J. Chapman, 'Why teach legal ethics to undergraduates?', *Legal Ethics* 5, 2002, 68, 73–9.

12 Nicolson, 'Education, education, education', 160; D. Nicolson, 'Making lawyers moral: Ethical codes and moral character', *Legal Studies*, 25, 2005, 616.

13 D. Carr, *Educating the Virtues: An Essay on the Philosophical Psychology of Moral Development and Education*, London: Routledge, 1991, pp. 43, 242; R.S. Peters, *Moral Development and Moral Education*, London: George Allen & Unwin, 1981, p. 37.

14 See F. Block, 'The andragogical basis of clinical legal education', *Vanderbilt Law Review* 35, 1982, 321.

15 F. Quigley, 'Seizing the disorienting moment: Adult learning and the teaching of social justice in law school clinics', *Clinical Law Review* 2, 1995–96, 37.

16 J. Webb, 'Conduct, ethics and experience in vocational legal education: opportunities missed', in K. Economides (ed.), *Ethical Challenges to Legal Education and Conduct*, Oxford: Hart, 1998, p. 290.

17 See, for example, J. McDowell, 'Virtue and reason', *The Monist* 62, 1979, 331; D. Luban and M. Millemann, 'Good judgment: Teaching ethics in dark times', *Georgetown Journal of Legal Ethics* 9, 1995–96, 31; H.L. Feldman, 'Codes and virtues: Can good lawyers be good ethical deliberators?', *Southern California Law Review*, 69, 1995–96, 885, esp. at 904–8.

18 Cf. Carr, *Educating the Virtues*; Aristotle, *The Nicomachean Ethics*, Amherst, NY: Prometheus, 1978, especially Book II, Ch. I and Book VI, Ch. XIII; D. Luban, 'Epistemology and moral education', *Journal of Legal Education* 33, 1983, 636.

19 Rest and Narvaez, *Moral Development in the Professions*; Abramson, 'Legal education, punching the myth of the moral intractability of law students'; A.G. Lind, 'Educational environments which promote self-sustaining moral development', Paper presented at E Division, American Educational Research Association, April 1996.

20 Q. Johnstone, 'Law school legal aid clinics', *Journal of Legal Education* 3, 1950–51, 537; M. Rees, 'Clinical legal education: An analysis of the University of Kent model', *Law Teacher* 12, 1975, 136; M. Guggenheim, 'Fee-generating clinics: Can we bear the costs?', *Clinical Law Review* 1, 1994–95, 683; M.J. Kotkin, 'The law school clinic: A training ground for public interest lawyers' and S. Maresh, 'The impact of clinical legal education on decisions of law students to practice public interest law', both in J. Cooper and L.G. Trubek (eds), *Educating for Justice: Social Values and Legal Education*, Aldershot: Ashgate, 1997; I. Styles and A. Zariska, 'Law clinics and the promotion of public interest lawyering', *Law in Context* 19, 2001, 65; K. Tranter, 'Pro-bono ethos: Teaching legal ethics', *Brief* 29, 2002, 13.

21 Four-year Honours LLB, followed by a one-year Diploma in Legal Practice, though students might only take a three-year Ordinary LLB or a two-year accelerated LLB.

22 See Nicolson, 'Making lawyers moral'; D. Nicolson and J. Webb, *Professional Legal Ethics: Critical Interrogations*, Oxford: Oxford University Press, 1999.

23 H. Brayne, N. Duncan and R. Grimes (eds), *Clinical Legal Education: Active Learning in Your Law School*, London: Blackstone, 1998, p. 47.

24 See Webb, 'Conduct, ethics and experience in vocational legal education', 289–90; P.J. Spiegelman, 'Integrating doctrine, theory and practice in the law school curriculum: The logic of Jake's ladder in the context of Amy's web', *Journal of Legal Education* 38, 1988, 243; H. Lesnick, 'Infinity in a grain of sand: The world of law and lawyering as portrayed in the clinical teaching implicit in the law school curriculum', *UCLA Law Review* 38, 1990, 1157, 1184–5; J.H. Aiken, 'Striving to teach "justice, fairness, and morality" ', *Clinical Law Review* 4, 1997–98, 1.

25 See, for example, D.A. Kolb, *Experiential Learning: Experience as the Source of Learning and Development*, Englewood Cliffs, NJ: Prentice Hall, 1984.

26 For example, Luban and Milleman, 'Good judgment'; Nicolson, 'Education, education, education', 229; Webb, 'Conduct, ethics and experience in vocational legal education', 296; D. Webb, 'Inventing the good: A prospectus for clinical education and the teaching of legal ethics in England', *Law Teacher* 30, 1996, 294; D.R.F. O'Dair, *Legal Ethics: Text and Materials*, London: Butterworths, 2001, p. 128.

27 Though, admittedly, this was boosted by four students who had an average of 12.

28 Eight had acted as case managers, overseeing between 30 and 40 students.

29 This applied to all but four of the subjects of this study, and of these only one reported not discussing an ethical dilemma.

30 That is, the idea that lawyers should zealously represent their client's interests without consideration of the morality of their ends or the most effective means to those ends: see, for example, Nicolson and Webb, *Professional Legal Ethics*, Chs 6–8; the articles in 'Special Issue: Lawyers' duties, adversarialism and partisanship', *Legal Ethics* 7, 2004, 133–40, 167–275.

31 The others were used for discussing personal values or helping students to choose their essay topic.

32 Examples include the ethics of lying in a negotiation session, problems of respecting client autonomy following a letter-writing session and the impact of role morality following an advocacy class.

33 The essays were not analysed because they emphasized learning from reading rather than from case experience, and hence were unlikely to reveal ethical learning particular to clinical courses.

34 See A. Bryman, *Social Research Methods*, Oxford: Oxford University Press, 2008, pp. 56ff.

35 In relation to Ann and Seamus, Roman numerals denote whether the diary relates to the first or second time they took CLP.

36 See above at note 6.

37 See Bryman, *Social Research Methods*, p. 266.

38 See note 66 below.

39 For example, while all students discussed their values in class and visited the courts, not all reflected on these experiences, whereas there were notable differences between the reflection of those working together on cases.

40 Isla, 'Introduction'. In addition to Rebecca, discussed below, other examples include Mark's concern about class prejudice (Week 3) and Ann's exploration of vegetarianism and honesty in personal relations (II, Weeks 1 and 7).

41 Week 1; also Jeremy, Week 1.

42 Week 1.

43 Week 8.

44 For example, Elizabeth, Weeks 3 and 4; Fiona, Week 3; Grace, Week 8; Jeremy, Week 2; Nicola, Weeks 2 and 3; Patrick, Week 3.

45 Calum, Week 1.
46 Ann I, Week 4; Ann II, Week 3; Calum, Week 2; David, Week 11; Fiona, Week 3; Lindsay, Week 3; Nicola, Week 9; Tina, Week 7; William, Week 5.
47 Ann I, Week 3; Becky, Week 3; Calum, Week 2; Elizabeth, Week 5; William, Week 2.
48 Becky, Week 8; Mark, 'Introduction'.
49 See Isla, Week 8; also Becky, Week 6; David, Week 4; Lindsay, Week 10; Mark, Week 3; Patrick, Week 3; Rebecca, Week 2; Seamus I, Week 5.
50 Becky, Week 5; Isla, Week 3 and 6; Mark, Week 3; Patrick, Week 4.
51 Week 3; see also Karl, Week 9.
52 Week 6.
53 Weeks 3 and 6 (though she – like others (see note 111 below) – purported to resolve the contradiction between having 'dedicated 4 university years in the pursuit of social justice' and her desire for financial security and stability by committing herself to organizing pro bono within her future firm).
54 Jeremy, Week 4.
55 Weeks 5 and 7.
56 Week 7.
57 See Nicolson, 'Making lawyers moral', 623–4
58 Cf. Ann I, Week 4: 'The class could make me more ethical in the way I practice (if I become a lawyer), or it may just influence or encourage me to enter a particular area of law.'
59 See Nicolson and Webb, *Professional Legal Ethics*, Chs 8–10; Nicolson, 'Making lawyers moral'.
60 Becky, Week 2; Elizabeth, Weeks 3, 6 and 8; Isla, Week 10; Jeremy, Week 2; Karl *passim*; Patrick, Week 3; Vikram, Weeks 3 and 4.
61 Elizabeth, Week 5; Mark, Week 4; Rebecca, Week 2; Vikram, Week 4 echoing Nicolson, 'Education, education, education'.
62 See, for example, Becky, Week 2; Grace, Week 2; Harjinder, Week 2; Rebecca, Weeks 10 and 11; Seamus I, *passim*; Seamus II, Weeks 6 and 8; Vikram, Weeks 3 and 4–6.
63 In addition to many of the views (above), see, for example, Becky, Week 7; David, Week 2; Elizabeth, Week 6; Vikram, Weeks 5 and 6.
64 Mark, Weeks 4 and 6; Tina, Week 7; Vikram, Week 6. Calum, David, Grace and William, all Week 3. Becky, Week 6; Harjinder, Week 11; Patrick, Week 3; and Rebecca, Weeks 5 and 10 also rejected neutral partisanship, but without any apparent change of view.
65 Becky, Week 2; Elizabeth, Weeks 2 and 5; Jeremy, Week 3; Tina, Week 6; William, Week 7; Vikram, Week 2.
66 Grace, Week 3; Orla, Week 5; Seamus I, Week 5; Seamus II, Week 5.
67 See Nicolson and Webb, *Professional Legal Ethics*, Ch. 6; D. Rhode, 'Institutionalizing ethics', *Case Western Law Review* 44, 1993–95, 665.
68 Introduction and Week 8. See also the quotations from Patrick and Vikram below, and the general comments of David, Week 3; Fiona, Week 12; and Karl, Weeks 4 and 9.
69 Though for Calum, Week 11, his faith in law was restored by a notable case success.
70 Calum, Week 10; Grace, Weeks 2 and 7; Karl, Week 2; Mark, Weeks 2, 6, 8 and 10; Nicola, Week 6; Orla, Week 2; Patrick, Week 6.
71 Week 4.
72 Rebecca, Week 4.
73 David, Weeks 1 and 8; Fiona, Week 1; and Seamus I, Week 9 (same case).
74 Seamus I, Week 4; Grace, Week 1, also referred to her (more acceptable) controlling of information from a witness.
75 Elizabeth, Week 8 and Tina, Weeks 7 and 9 (same case). See also the similar dilemma discussed at note 88, below.
76 Lindsay, week 6; Grace, week 2 and William, week 5 (same case).
77 Cf. Nicolson, 'Education, education, education', 169.

78 Ann II, Week 8; Fiona, Week 5; Patrick, Week 3; Vikram, Week 3.

79 Calum, Week 2; David, Weeks 3, 6 and 7; Elizabeth, Week 3; Isla, Weeks 2 and 8; Jeremy, Week 11; Lindsay, Week 1; Mark, Week 5; Orla, Week 8; Rebecca, Weeks 5, 6 and 10; William, Week 9.

80 Harjinder, Weeks 1 and 8; Lindsay, Week 1; Orla, week 11; Rebecca, Week 2.

81 Ann I, Week 5; Becky, Weeks 5 and 9; David, Weeks 1 and 3; Fiona, Week 6; Grace, Week 5; Harjinder, Week 9; Jeremy, Week 7; Karl, Week 2; Lindsay, Week 7; Orla, Week 4; Patrick, Weeks 4 and 10; Rebecca, Week 4; Seamus II, Weeks 6 and 11; Tina, Week 6; Vikram, Week 4.

82 Elizabeth, Week 4; Isla, Week 3; Patrick, Weeks 2 and 4; Grace, Week 7; and William, Weeks 1 and 9 (same case).

83 Isla, Week 3: 'on reflection, I appreciate I can't judge a client by my own standards or how I am feeling . . .'; Elizabeth, Week 4; William, Week 1.

84 Seamus, Tina and Lindsay in the cases listed respectively above at notes 74 and 75.

85 In addition to examples in the text below, Becky, Week 9; David, Week 11; Elizabeth, Week 9; Harjinder, Weeks 1 and 8; Orla, Weeks 4 and 8; Seamus I, Week 4 and Seamus II, Week 6; Grace, Weeks 4 and 5; William, Week 9 (same case).

86 Week 2.

87 Week 10.

88 Week 5.

89 Week 10

90 J. Kupperman, *Character*, New York: Oxford University Press, 1991, p. 214.

91 Week 6. Similar sentiments were articulated by Calum, Week 11 and Isla, Weeks 4 and 5. Conversely Elizabeth, Week 9, expressed regret at her lack of tact and respect in dealing with a client's reluctance to divulge sensitive and private information; Becky, Week 8, doubted whether she had done enough for a client, 'spark[ing] a determination not to admit defeat so easily in the future'.

92 Week 10.

93 Many of the longest serving and most committed clinic students who took CLP have traineeships in commercial firms. The fact that Orla and Seamus came first and second in their LLB class suggests that students might associate high achievement with the better paid jobs – though Orla, like Isla (Week 4), saw her traineeship as a necessary stepping stone to environmental law, while Seamus (II, Week 5), like Becky (Week 3), stressed his commitment to doing pro bono work.

94 Lindsay, Week 10; also Week 7.

95 Week 2.

96 'Introduction'.

97 Week 4.

98 Week 7.

99 Week 5; also Elizabeth, Week 2.

100 Week 1.

101 Week 4; also Grace, Week 2.

102 See above at p. 174.

103 See below, note 120.

104 Week 3; also Harjinder, Week 7, referring to lessons learnt from reviewing cases as a case manager.

105 At notes 68, 87 and 89.

106 Week 4.

107 Seamus I, Week 3.

108 At note 87.

109 Week 4.

110 Week 7; see also Elizabeth's initial opposition to giving academic credit for clinic work: Week 1.

111 Week 5; also Becky above at note 53.

112 Week 10.
113 Becky, Weeks 2 and 5; Calum, Week 4; David, Weeks 3, 6 and 7; Elizabeth, Week 3; Harjinder, Week 1; Lindsay, Weeks 5 and 10; Rebecca, Week 7; William, Week 4; Vikram, Week 4.
114 Week 5.
115 Week 9
116 MacFarlane, 'Look before you leap'.
117 As expressed by Seamus II, Week 4, provoked not by his cases, but by seminars on access to justice, and negated by his professed determination to engage in pro bono work once qualified and continued commitment to his clients and clinic management. Similar commitment also qualifies William's comment (Week 9) that his experiences with an ungrateful and an untrustworthy client left him feeling 'a little cynical of clients'.
118 See above notes 68, 87 and 89.
119 For example, Isla above note 99; David, Weeks 2 and 8.
120 Although this was boosted by an average of 10 for four students, the last nine students to take CLP may continue to conduct cases for at least two more years.
121 Nicolson, 'Education, education, education', 162, 167.

10 Reading reported cases through a legal ethics lens

Linda Haller

10.1 Introduction

Courses on legal ethics and professional responsibility are notoriously difficult to teach,[1] and there remains a need to explore ways in which teaching can be enhanced. In this chapter I suggest a learning tool that I hope will prompt students to reflect on and critique the role of lawyers and the regulatory environment in which they practise. I suggest law lecturers use a resource that students respect and with which they are already familiar, but that is sometimes maligned in the legal ethics literature – the published law report. However, rather than advocate for a return to a doctrinal reading of the case as occurs in most other law subjects, I suggest that teachers encourage students to read the report through a legal ethics lens.

10.2 Reported or fictionalized?

Questions regarding the most effective resources for teaching legal ethics and professional responsibility have been the focus of debate in the pedagogical literature for quite some time. For instance, Carrie Menkel-Meadow and Bruce Green both note the limitations of using reported appellate decisions. Menkel-Meadow bemoans their 'eviscerated'[2] and closed nature; Green expresses concern that, even when incomplete official reporting is augmented by press reports, these can be unreliable and tell us very little about why the case developed as it did.[3]

To redress these shortcomings, Menkel-Meadow, among others, proposes that legal narrative and storytelling be used more often to form the basis of legal ethics teaching.[4] Narrative and storytelling can take many forms in legal ethics education. They include legal clinics where students come to know a real client and their story,[5] as well as class discussion of fictionalized versions of real cases, literature[6] and popular culture.[7] Green notes the advantages of fictionalized accounts as a means whereby students can explore the pressures, motivations, decision-making processes and relationships that lawyers encounter in much more detail than offered by a real, but abbreviated, reported decision.[8] However, as Green says, these fictionalized accounts suffer from one important drawback – they are not real, so it is too easy for students to dismiss them with the comment 'No real lawyer would act that way'.[9]

While some have suggested ways to respond to student resistance to fictionalized accounts,[10] it is argued here that law students might approach a legal ethics and professional responsibility course more seriously if reported decisions were used more often.[11] Perhaps the ideal is a 'fully fleshed out account'[12] of a real, reported case. However, the few examples of this that we do see[13] are likely to remain exceptional, given that participants may be unwilling to speak candidly about their experience or be constrained against doing so by duties of confidentiality. Even then, the personal accounts will reflect each participant's subjective reality.[14] These differing perceptions can be worthy of study in their own right. However, their existence reminds us that a search for any one, true, 'fully fleshed out' account may prove futile. The reported decision championed here reflects the reality as perceived by the judges who heard the case. This needs to be understood by students, but itself forms an important basis for ethical critique, as explained more fully below.

This chapter is not seeking to enter the debate over whether real or fictionalized stories are better. Each form has its strengths and weaknesses. Instead, the chapter simply notes that teachers of legal ethics and professional responsibility will sometimes lack the resources to create a fully fleshed out 'real' account or lack the novelist's ability to bring fictional characters to life,[15] and so may only have reported appellate decisions to work with. But, far from seeing these decisions as inferior teaching resources, I seek to demonstrate their power when read through a legal ethics lens, using the case of *Walmsley v Cosentino*[16] as an example.

When reading the case of *Walmsley v Cosentino* in the traditional, doctrinal way, it appears quite mundane. It is just a common law professional negligence case where the court ordered a solicitor to pay damages because he missed a statutory limitation period. However, when encouraged by the legal ethics teacher to read the case through a legal ethics lens focusing on questions of the role of lawyers and regulation, the case can take on a very different hue for the reader. This experience can be a powerful learning tool.

Others have noted the danger of lawyers, law teachers and students losing the ability to empathize with clients, or engage in critical self-examination.[17] It is suggested that students be asked to read the reported decision of a case like the one described in this chapter. At this stage, the teacher gives no prompts to students as to what they should be looking for in the case. Students have been trained throughout most of their time at law school to read cases in a particular, doctrinal way with the aim of gleaning legal principles from them. When students are asked to report on the case after their first, unguided reading, they are likely to report its *ratio* regarding the law of professional negligence. With guidance from the teacher, students are asked to reread the case – this time trying to be alert to broader, ethical issues. On this second reading, students can be shocked by their own failure in overlooking some of the ethical stories within the case. Would a layperson or student first entering the law school read the case differently? Is a layperson more likely than law students to have noticed the number of different lawyers who became involved in the case and the time it took to be resolved? Classroom discussion can explore possible reasons for the students' earlier over-sights. It may be at least partly because they have begun the process of socializa-tion into the legal profession and are accepting inferences from what is not mentioned by the judges in the court's decision that certain details are unimport-ant. That so much might 'slip beneath the radar' of the student's consciousness unless they read the case through a legal ethics lens adds to its power as a teaching resource. It leads them to consider whether they have become less reflective since they began training to be lawyers, and in particular less willing to critique the role of lawyers and self-regulation.

10.3 The case to be studied

This chapter redescribes *Walmsley v Cosentino*.[18] Briefly, the case involves a solicitor sued for professional negligence for not issuing court proceedings in relation to a personal injury claim arising out of a motor vehicle accident before a limitation period expired, and then failing to tell the client to seek independent advice by a certain date in relation to a possible claim against the lawyer. When read simply as a case adding to the common law of professional negligence, the case adds very little. Most lawyers, teachers and students are likely to overlook it in their research or dismiss it as insignificant. The case is legal authority for the proposition that, where a solicitor has failed to file proceedings in time, the solicitor will be in breach of his or her tortious duty of care to the client if the solicitor fails to tell the client not only that the client may have a cause of action against the solicitor and should seek independent advice, but also the date before which the client must seek that independent advice if they are to preserve their legal rights. This is all that a student in their final years of a law degree is likely to take from the case on their first reading.

I would now like to say a little more about the rich details that can be gleaned from the same case when read through a legal ethics lens. More detail about the 'legal ethics' facts of the case can be found in the appendix to this chapter; essentially, though, when the client Cosentino was first injured, he was a young man of 25, but by the time he finally obtained compensation he was a middle-aged man of 46, despite the fact that this was a simple 'crash and bash' car accident where the liability of the defendant was never at issue. The role played by the barristers in the case is particularly interesting. The instructing solicitor Walmsley briefed up to six barristers to ask the same question – 'Would the court grant an extension of time to sue the driver of the other car?' The extension was necessary because the solicitor had failed to issue proceedings within the statutory limitation period, a clear case of negligence.[19] The barristers briefed by the solicitor appeared to be aware of his negligence, and hence his position of conflict with the client,[20] but appeared to do nothing to protect or warn the client. By the time the client did become aware that he could sue the solicitor for missing the limitation period and did so,[21] ironically the solicitor's defence was that the limitation period to sue *him* had expired. This case had much to attract the interest of law students sceptical of fictional stories: what began as an apparently simple case turned into a saga that dragged on for 21 years with some of the features of a modern-day – though *real-life* – version of a Dickensian *Jarndyce v Jarndyce*.[22]

After we had spent class time contrasting the doctrinal and 'legal ethics' reading of the case, I set an assignment question that asked students to discuss the following statement about the case:

> It is surprising how little comment is made by the court in *Walmsley v Cosentino* [2001] NSWCA 403 as to the role the various lawyers – both barristers and solicitors – played. Perhaps in a case deciding questions of compensation this was understandable. However, the position would not have been much different if Cosentino had complained to a Legal Services Commissioner about Walmsley or any of the other solicitors or barristers involved in the case. Experience suggests that the current general law professional conduct rules and regulatory regime remain inadequate to ensure such a saga does not occur again in the future. At the end of the day, all we really have is our faith in the 'moral compass' of individual lawyers.

The two most important themes that can be drawn from the case are the role of lawyers and their regulation, but the case also provides interesting stories around a number of other issues relevant to legal ethics and professional responsibility courses, including conflicts of interest and legal culture. The discussion that follows will focus primarily on issues of role and regulation, and includes extracts from students' assignments to demonstrate the degree to which their reading of the case moved successfully from a doctrinal one about the law of negligence to one viewed through a legal ethics lens that was much more reflective on the role of lawyers and their regulation.[23] Despite some of the concerns in the literature noted earlier about the 'eviscerated' nature of appellate reported decisions and how this might limit their teaching potential in a legal ethics class, I would argue that it is in fact the brevity of the judgments in this case and the apparent decision of the appellate judges that it was not necessary to provide detail about or comment on the conduct of the barristers that is part of the power of this case as a teaching tool. This is the essence of the story according to judges as leaders of the profession, a theme to which we will return later.

The next section demonstrates the power of this case in exploring the role of lawyers. The chapter then goes on to describe the many stories the case holds in relation to the regulation of the legal profession.

10.4 The role of lawyers

Most teachers of legal ethics agree that justice is usually best served when various players in the legal system differentiate their functions and develop specialist expertise: when judges take responsibility for finally determining where justice lies in a particular dispute; when it is police and prosecutors who are responsible for proving a case against an accused; and when lawyers focus on the need to strongly assert the rights of clients. In other words, role is vitally important to achieving justice, and a lawyer[24] who commits to discharging that role – and that role only – thereby makes a strong moral commitment.[25] There were so many lawyers involved in *Walmsley v Cosentino* that it provides a good vehicle through which the teacher can compare and contrast roles – not only the roles assigned in a divided profession to the solicitors and many barristers acting for Cosentino, which are the main focus here, but also the roles of the lawyers acting for the driver and insurer of the driver of the other motor vehicle, who needed to decide whether to continue to negotiate after the Statute of Limitations had expired,[26] and whether to raise the statute in defence once proceedings were issued; and the roles of the lawyers acting for Walmsley and his professional indemnity insurers, who needed to decide whether Walmsley in turn should rely on the Statute of Limitations when sued by Cosentino.[27] Much classroom discussion can revolve around how each of the lawyers appeared to perceive their role and whether, in contexts such as *Walmsley v Cosentino*, it might be appropriate to broaden or reconceive that role.

Most students of legal ethics will learn that the traditional, standard conception of a lawyer's role places paramount emphasis on zealous representation of the client. This approach to lawyering draws its moral legitimacy from facilitating the moral autonomy of clients[28] and the adversarial system of justice.[29] Generally, however, it also accords with the economic incentive to please clients with the most ability to pay. A number of recent textbooks aim to highlight for students the unfairness of the traditional conception where there is unequal access to law.[30] These texts draw from the work of David Luban,[31] Deborah Rhode[32] and William Simon,[33] among others, who suggest lawyers take greater moral responsibility for redressing the balance in some contexts, including by providing *less* zealous and partisan representation to wealthy clients seeking to abuse the rights of others.

The reading of *Walmsley v Cosentino* through a legal ethics lens serves as a reminder to students that sometimes the danger is not excessive zeal, but rather a lack of zeal, whether through laziness, incompetence or excessive concern about paving a smooth career path or maintaining cordial relationships with superiors, colleagues and judges. As Ted Schneyer notes: '[A]gainst these forces, [the] norms of neutrality and partisanship [that underlie the zealous advocate approach] can play a crucial offsetting role.'[34] The crux of Walmsley is that Cosentino's lawyers were not zealous *enough*. This is not a case about zealous advocacy and its dangers, but the apparent *abandonment* of a client by his solicitor and many barristers. The role played by the barristers can be missed by students on their first (doctrinal) reading of the case. Students did become sensitive to the issue on their second reading of the case:

> Compounded against the backdrop of a natural instinct to delimit responsibilities and liabilities, ethicality is most easily achieved by embracing a myopic 'role' ethic . . . This can leave the lawyer oblivious as to the consequences of [their] conduct . . . This is the theoretical story behind *Walmsley*. All that was needed to prevent such injustice was for the barristers and other lawyers to take the extra step to ensure Cosentino acted upon their advice and to see

that justice was served. But . . . whether through weak values or a myopic focus on fulfilling their roles, reinforced by the inadequacy of the legal institution, the lawyers, both barristers and solicitors, played their crucial role in directing the saga.[35]

It is useful for students to see how Simon's theory of contextual judgment might apply in the circumstances of a real case such as this. While Simon acknowledges the importance and moral legitimacy of role, he thinks this largely depends on how well positioned a judge, rather than a lawyer, is to determine the merits of a case in a particular context,[36] and argues that a lawyer should take more personal responsibility for the law achieving a just outcome where there are failings in procedures or institutions.[37] What potential failings might students be able to identify in *Walmsley v Cosentino* sufficient to enliven Simon's entreaty? Would they be Walmsley's apparent intransigence in dealing appropriately with his earlier incompetence;[38] the lengthy delays before a formal decision-maker – whether judge or insurance company official – could determine a just outcome for Cosentino;[39] the lack of adequate and independent representation of Cosentino after his interests began to conflict with those of Walmsley; or Cosentino's apparent vulnerability and ignorance in relation to his possible claim against Walmsley? Would it be reasonable to expect any of the barristers to step out of their normal roles and take greater responsibility for obtaining a just outcome?

We will now explore and critique the differing roles of barristers and solicitors in more detail and in the context of *Walmsley v Cosentino*. Not all readers of this book will teach in a jurisdiction where the legal profession is divided into barristers and solicitors. However, the discussion that follows still has relevance to them. It provides an example of how a real, reported case can be used to demonstrate the inability or disinclination to see ethical issues, exercise ethical judgment or 'rock the boat' when tasks and information are divided among a number of individuals in a work team who also rely on each other for future patronage and financial reward.[40] On this particular occasion, the work team comprised barristers and solicitors. It is hoped that the discussion that follows will inspire teaching colleagues in other jurisdictions to consider using cases involving other organizational settings with the potential for similar ethical shortcomings, such as may occur within a large law firm or between in-house and external counsel.

10.4.1 Contrasting the role of barristers and solicitors

As more jurisdictions fuse their professions, thus allowing the public direct access to barristers, it is easy to gloss over the distinctive role that barristers have played in countries such as the United Kingdom and Australia. *Walmsley v Cosentino* provides a stark reminder that the Bar continues to portray itself as distinctively different from the solicitors' branch.

The case provides a valuable vehicle through which to explore the history and traditions of a divided legal profession and question why no barrister seemed to take responsibility for the client Cosentino's welfare. This is not necessarily an isolated aberration. Teachers can direct students to judicial comment[11] and Bar rules[12] that encourage barristers to remain quite distant from clients: an instructing solicitor should intervene between client and barrister; the barrister's primary relationship is with the instructing solicitor; it is the instructing solicitor who in turn liaises with the client. Courts continue to emphasize that a barrister is only expected to advise 'as instructed';[13] the instructing solicitor is the primary arbiter as to whether the barrister has discharged his or her obligations, and it is usually the responsibility of the instructing solicitor not the barrister to ensure the client understands their rights and obligations.[14] With this degree of distance, it is therefore perhaps not surprising that the barristers involved felt little or no responsibility for the client Cosentino.

Students recognized that the barristers in this case may have failed to broaden the frame of their advice from that given by colleagues previously because of concern about overstepping their role or second-guessing colleagues:[15]

> [A]ny moral obligation the barristers felt was not enough for any barrister involved to warn Cosentino. By the time the final had a cause of action against Walmsley. The failure to warn may have been the result of how the barrister was instructed, it is likely he appreciated Cosentino was blind to the fact of that barrister believing that he would be overstepping his role, considering none of the other barristers had commented. The systemic failure is evident, as the barristers appeared to take the view that they had performed their advisory role and did not have an obligation to intervene and comment on the failings of the solicitors.[16]

Traditionally, the legal profession – both barristers and solicitors – fiercely championed the need for independence from the state and from clients.[17] In jurisdictions where the profession is divided, barristers claim independence is more important to them than it is to solicitors,[18] and they support this through conduct rules that insist that barristers operate only as sole practitioners (thereby avoiding the influence from partners to which solicitors are subject) and that discourage direct access by clients.[19] But in *Walmsley v Cosentino* what was lacking was not independence from the state or from the client but from the *instructing solicitor*. Case law, professional conduct rules and commentary have been relatively quiet on this issue.

It is understandable that, just like members of other work teams, barristers would prefer to not question the work of the solicitor instructing them. Not only is this normally an inefficient duplication of role, but the barrister also relies on the instructing solicitor for future work. It is also valuable for students to discover that from time to time this professional relationship can experience tension; the Bar has sometimes had to revisit its own understanding of its role and relationship with instructing solicitors. At about the same time as the last of many briefed barristers was appearing on repeated, futile applications for an extension of time for Cosentino to sue the driver of the other vehicle, the New South Wales Bar was substantially rewriting its professional conduct rules. These included a new Rule

111, whereby the professional body indicated to its members that, if similar circumstances arose again in the future, their professional obligation was to take action:

> 111.   A barrister who believes on reasonable grounds that the interests of the client may conflict with the interests of the instructing solicitor, or that the client may have a claim against the instructing solicitor, must:
>
> (a)   advise the instructing solicitor of the barrister's belief; and
> (b)   if the instructing solicitor does not agree to advise the client of the barrister's belief, seek to advise the client in the presence of the instructing solicitor of the barrister's belief.[50]

A similar rule exists in the Code of Conduct for barristers in the United Kingdom.[51]

Students of legal ethics and professional responsibility need to become sensitive to the many purposes served by codes of conduct. These include legitimating the conduct of lawyers.[52] While the barristers in *Walmsley* did not appear to face criticism from the court for their failure to do more to protect Cosentino in the face of Walmsley's conflict of interest, it is possible that barristers in general have suffered embarrassment or feared a loss of future work from solicitors when placed in similar circumstances. The cab rank rule assists barristers to respond when asked 'How can you represent someone you know is guilty?'[53] Students can be asked to consider whether Rule 111 is similarly helpful to barristers trying to explain their action to irate instructing solicitors – 'The code demanded that I do it.'[54]

Students can also learn from studying this case that there is no clear and consistent guidance available to lawyers as to how to conduct themselves well: professional conduct rules and case law can be in tension.[55] Hence, in the context of *Walmsley v Cosentino*, professional codes of conduct do not affect the civil liability of lawyers,[56] and barristers who complied with Rule 111 could thereby find themselves in breach of duties of care under the general law.[57]

Students can be asked to consider why courts in the United Kingdom and Australia have only rarely considered what common law duties a barrister might owe the instructing solicitor, and why the position remains unclear and inconclusive. It may tell us much about the culture within the legal profession. In *Moy v Pettman Smith (a Firm)*,[58] a barrister gave evidence that she did not tell the lay client about his option of suing the instructing solicitor partly because of her perceived duty to the solicitor; however, in the UK Court of Appeal, Latham LJ was adamant that the barrister 'owed no duty to the appellants. Her duty was to Mr Moy and to Mr Moy alone.'[59]

The question of a possible duty at law was also considered in the Australian case of *Wilson v Carter*,[60] a case decided in New South Wales after *Walmsley v Cosentino*. In that case, Rothman J referred to professional conduct rules,[61] listing situations in which a barrister's potential conflict of interest would require the barrister to decline a brief. He extrapolated from these to suggest[62] that the law *prohibited* a barrister from advising the client of the solicitor's negligence.[63] His Honour went on to note that to advise the client of the solicitor's negligence would require the barrister:

> to breach the duty to the solicitor in order to comply with the duty to the client in circumstances where the barrister cannot be required to deal directly with the client and is not briefed (nor could be briefed) to advise on such a cause of action.[64]

However, if the position is as Rothman J says, this demonstrates to students the conflicted position at law of the barrister, in addition to conflicted position of the instructing solicitor. It also provides a powerful demonstration of the complex relationships between, and possible motivations behind, professional codes of conduct and the general law.

We could say that the facts in *Walmsley* were more extreme than those in *Moy v Pettman Smith (a Firm)* and in *Wilson v Carter*, given the number of barristers in *Walmsley* who allowed Cosentino to remain ignorant of his rights for many years. Students can be asked to then reflect on the question of whether at any point a *moral* duty to take action might arise for any of the many barristers involved, regardless of what professional conduct rules and the general law might have to say on the matter.

We can't be sure of the degree to which later barristers were ignorant of the advice given by those who came before them or the terms of Walmsley's brief to the barristers. However, as time passed, many of the ethical theories referred to earlier would suggest an increasing urgency to impose a broader frame on the advice than that sought by the instructing solicitor Walmsley. This broader frame would involve advising on *all* possible options for the client, even if the brief only asked for advice about an application for an extension of time. Some students were sensitive to this, and were more critical of the barristers who came later in time:

> [Barrister #2] had a conflict between giving Walmsley advice on how to manage liability in tort to Cosentino as well as providing frank advice for Cosentino. Other barristers briefed later by Walmsley were in a similar ethical position. Each later barrister had better notice of Walmsley's conflict and Cosentino's failure to pursue the action against Walmsley. Hence, each subsequent barrister had a stronger ethical obligation under a 'responsible lawyering' role ethic to expedite the administration of justice and inform Cosentino[65]
> . . . it is perhaps now easier to explain (although not necessarily condone) the conduct of Cosentino's barristers . . . They saw their job as only conveying 'independent judgment' on matters contained in the brief [and so] did not see Cosentino as a complete human being.[66]

The preceding discussion has sought to demonstrate how reported appellate decisions such as *Walmsley v Cosentino* have much to offer when read through a legal ethics lens. Our preceding discussion touched on the question of regulation within the legal profession. We will now look at that issue in more detail, again in the context of *Walmsley*.

10.5 Regulation of the legal profession

There is a danger in teaching the students of legal ethics and professional responsibility courses that regulation of the legal profession should only be considered in terms of admission and professional discipline.[67] Both teachers and students need to be drawn into considerations of the broader regulatory framework.[68] It is suggested that this is not difficult, as the students' earlier studies have prepared them well for this, and their imminent move into legal practice emphasizes the need to draw the threads of their law degree together. *Walmsley v Cosentino* provides a valuable vehicle through which to demonstrate how various forms of regulation play out in practice. In the following sections, we look at some of these forms of regulation and their potential efficacy in the context of *Walmsley v Cosentino*, looking first at civil liability for negligence and professional discipline before examining more indirect and informal influences on conduct, such as that exercised by colleagues. We are particularly interested in the likelihood of particular players – clients, courts, regulators and colleagues – taking action in contexts such as this.

10.5.1 Civil liability

10.5.1.1 The client

The case on its face is one about civil liability for professional negligence. Eventually the client Cosentino did become aware of his solicitor's negligence and did take action to sue, and in a sense this did 'regulate' the solicitor and in turn the legal profession. But a reading of the case through a legal ethics lens can demonstrate to students the limitations of civil liability as a form of regulation: it can be many years after the event and requires an individual to have suffered loss and be willing to initiate court proceedings. Here, the client Cosentino appeared happy to settle his motor accident claim for about $30,000,[69] but was a vulnerable and unsophisticated client reluctant to sue a solicitor he perceived to be a friend,[70] and it was 21 years before civil proceedings 'regulated' the conduct of the solicitor by ordering him to pay damages of $474,478. Students should be also asked to reflect on why the client chose not to sue any of the many barristers briefed to advise him.

10.5.1.2 The court

Even though 21 years had passed, could and should the members of the Court of Appeal who heard the negligence case have done more to 'regulate' the conduct of the solicitors or barristers in *Walmsley*? This raises a key question for all law students. as it draws on issues including the adversarial system of justice, the role of judges, responsible use of court privilege and natural justice for non-litigants (i.e. the barristers in this case). Judges, as leaders of the profession, sometimes choose to comment on the conduct of lawyers, even if the case before them is ostensibly about a narrower legal issue. Comments by judges have the advantage of being immediate, contextual and sometimes more effective than separate expensive and drawn-out disciplinary proceedings which may or may not occur. It could be argued that it is even more necessary for judges to comment if no one else is likely to complain about or investigate a lawyer's conduct, as appeared to be the situation in *Walmsley*. For instance, Goldberg J decided to take the opportunity to comment on the conduct of barristers involved in *White Industries v Flower & Hart*.[71] That case was a wasted costs application against solicitors for bringing a case for the ulterior purpose of delay and making baseless allegations of fraud. As in *Walmsley v Cosentino*, no barrister was made a party to the proceedings, although it is unclear why. Nevertheless, Goldberg J chose to comment on the conduct of the barristers but was later rebuked on appeal by the Full Federal Court. Despite the interest *outside* the court in the role played by the barristers in the case,[72] one of whom had since been appointed to the High Court of Australia, the Full Federal Court felt that, as the application for wasted costs in that case had been brought only against the firm of solicitors and not any of the barristers briefed, the barristers had not had an adequate opportunity to explain themselves, their conduct was largely irrelevant to the court's role and it would be unfair to draw adverse inferences against them.[73]

The judges in *Walmsley v Cosentino* also chose to limit themselves to what they saw as their own particular role and the immediate task before them. In the course of hearing the claim of professional negligence brought against the solicitor Walmsley, none of the three members of the Court of Appeal thought it appropriate to chastise Walmsley, let alone the barristers, for their failings. The strongest comment – though still muted – is during Powell JA's confirmation of the District Court judge's award of damages for vexation when he notes that 'Cosentino's distress at the delays incurred in the loss of his right to sue [the driver of the other car] was ... reasonably foreseeable'.[74] More surprisingly, while Powell JA notes that the motor accident claim proceeded in a 'dilatory way', he seems to blame the client and everyone *but* the solicitor Walmsley and the barristers for the delays.[75] Here, the members of the Court of Appeal have chosen to limit themselves to their immediate task – to decide whether the defendant Walmsley had breached his duty of care to the plaintiff Cosentino, and whether this had caused loss and the quantum of that loss. All of this provides fertile ground for classroom discussion regarding the regulatory role of judges.

Before leaving the issue of civil proceedings as a form of regulation, even if a client knows of their right to sue and does so, Australian students should be reminded that such proceedings have less regulatory potential in Australia where lawyers, both barristers and solicitors, are still able to claim the defence of advocates' immunity for work in court and for work out of court that is 'intimately connected' to their work in court.[76]

Students were alive to the issue of whether it would be appropriate in the course of the hearing of a claim for damages for negligence against the instructing solicitor for the Court of Appeal to comment on the willingness of barrister after barrister in the case to accept a brief to advise Cosentino,[77] but to then advise Walmsley *against* the interests of Cosentino. Some of these students queried whether questions of 'character and conduct' were perhaps more appropriately undertaken in disciplinary proceedings.[78] However, it is questionable how effective professional discipline would be in the context of this case.

10.5.2 Professional discipline

The facts of the case portray Cosentino as an unsophisticated and trusting client – not one to exercise his rights to complain to a Legal Services Commissioner. With guidance from their teacher, students can explore how this may be of concern in a regulatory system that is largely reactive to client complaints. Even if Cosentino or some other person or entity had complained about the solicitor Walmsley's incompetence, professional discipline has traditionally limited itself to questions of dishonesty and character.[79] The case can be used as a prompt for students to consider whether Walmsley's incompetence should have disciplinary consequences in addition to civil liability for negligence. Some students preferred a clear regulatory divide between discipline and civil liability:

> The combination of inadequate independent oversight and excessive trust leaves consumers vulnerable where lawyers fail to recognize major conflicts of interest [but] . . . it appears harsh to impose disciplinary measures on incompetent but innocent lawyers.[80]

Students should also be able to justify the position they take. As I have tried to emphasize in this chapter, throughout their reading of *Walmsley* through a legal ethics lens, they should be encouraged to reflect on the degree to whether any of their responses may be coloured by their own imminent entry into the legal profession.

Also of interest is whether the conduct of the barristers in this case could and should have had disciplinary consequences. If Cosentino appeared unlikely to complain about his solicitor, it seemed even less likely that he would complain about the more distant barristers. This is confirmed by empirical evidence that barristers are subject to far fewer complaints than solicitors[81] (just as they are less likely to be sued). It is useful to explore the reasons for this with students, as well as critique the conduct of the barristers in this case: given that a commissioner can initiate an investigation of conduct even in the absence of a complaint by a client,[82] and given that the barristers' conduct was not subject to review in civil proceedings as was the conduct of the solicitor Walmsley, *should* the Legal Services

Commissioner have filled this regulatory gap by taking more interest in their conduct?

The preceding discussion has focused on formal regulation. We will now demonstrate how *Walmsley v Cosentino* can be used to critique the informal regulation that can occur through professional colleagues.

10.5.3 Informal 'self'-regulation by colleagues

A common theme in legal ethics and professional responsibility courses that include some sociology[83] or history of the profession is the profession's ongoing quest for self-regulation. While at the level of formal law this debate has been lost, and the profession is now largely regulated by external bodies,[84] empirical studies demonstrate the important influence that colleagues can have.[85] This is a form of informal self-regulation. Much has been written about more proactive, aspirational and supportive ways in which high ethical standards are encouraged, such as through healthy 'ethical infrastructures'[86] within large law firms. *Walmsley v Cosentino* can be used to highlight the dangers for solicitors operating in sole practice or in small firms without a community of support.

Walmsley v Cosentino also provides a case study of informal self-regulation in action – or perhaps inaction. Three solicitors and up to six barristers were involved in pursuing an application for an extension of time which most of them knew was futile. While the barristers seemed very willing to encourage the solicitor Walmsley to take steps to ensure he was indemnified by his insurers if the client sued him,[87] no barrister appeared to have seen a responsibility *to their profession* to regulate colleagues by advising Walmsley strongly to cease acting for Cosentino or by giving the client Cosentino advice about his options in the face of Walmsley's negligence.

Class discussions can explore the many possible reasons for this. One student thought it was partly due to the way in which, by default, lawyers are presumed to be ethical:

> The presumption that the legal profession is inherently ethical discourages lawyers from critically assessing their own as well as their colleagues' behaviour. Therefore self-regulation inevitably leads lawyers to set their colleagues' conduct as their benchmark . . . This may also explain why barrister after barrister took no action regarding Cosentino's situation – their previous colleagues did nothing, therefore inaction may not have seemed so 'unethical'.[88]

Another argued that the duty to the profession should extend to the lawyers representing the insurer of the driver of the other vehicle, GIO, and Walmsley's insurer, LawCover:

> It is possible that the lawyers' responsibilities to the law and to the profession, as well as to the public interest in the professionalism of lawyers, may have

outweighed any duty they might have had to their client to adopt the dubious course of watching Walmsley destroy Mr Cosentino's rights without lifting a finger in protest . . . [Barrister #2] . . . might have more actively encouraged Walmsley to advise Mr Cosentino to get independent legal advice; the lawyers representing the GIO might have tried to obtain instructions from their client to ask Walmsley whether he would be issuing proceedings as the date approached on which the action would become statute-barred; and the lawyers representing LawCover did in fact take the commendable course of instructing Walmsley to advise Mr Cosentino to seek another solicitor.[89]

While classes on legal ethics and professional responsibility often focus on the relationship of loyalty between client and lawyer, *Walmsley* raises issues around the nature of loyalty between colleagues – in this case, between barrister and instructing solicitor and between successively briefed barristers. Professional conduct rules often prohibit lawyers from making adverse comments about other lawyers.[90] This is usually portrayed as necessary to uphold the public's respect for the courts and the administration of justice.[91] However, there may also be regulatory advantages in encouraging instructing solicitors to be extremely candid to barristers about misgivings they have about the client, the strength of the client's case and their own performance in preparing the client's case without being in fear of the barrister reporting them. The duty of confidence between client and lawyer is thought to achieve instrumental ends of placing the lawyer in a position to counsel the client to do the right thing – a form of informal regulation of client conduct;[92] others have thought there may be merit in an 'ethics guru' or ombudsman within a large law firm owing a duty of confidence to junior lawyers.[93] Similarly, a duty of confidence owed by a barrister to the instructing solicitor[94] could facilitate the barrister counselling the solicitor to take responsibility for their omissions. Some students who saw merit in a system in which it was the ethical norm for lawyers to report misconduct or poor service were also concerned about making this a mandatory form of regulation, as they thought this might undermine the trust necessary for informal regulation between colleagues.[95]

10.6 Conclusion

No resource in the teaching of legal ethics and professional responsibility is necessarily better than others: each has strengths and weaknesses. Fictionalized accounts might allow us to explore issues of motivations and relationships in much more detail than provided by abbreviated reported decisions. In contrast, reported decisions will sometimes earn greater respect from students because of their reality and familiarity to students. While we continue to seek out ways to improve the quality of *all* of the teaching resources we use, this chapter has sought to encourage teachers to consider more closely the teaching potential of reported cases than they may have done to date; the previous 'bad press' of the reported appellate decision in the pedagogical literature may have overlooked their potential power as a teaching tool when read through a legal ethics lens. Students may learn powerful lessons about themselves by what they didn't see on their first doctrinal reading of a case, as well as uncover compelling ethical stories, including those about role and regulation as described here.

APPENDIX 10.1: *WALMSLEY V COSENTINO* – A TIMELINE[96]

13 August 1980	Cosentino is injured in a car accident when another driver, Upton, turns right into his path. At the time he is a 25-year-old contract tiler.
February 1981	Cosentino asks the solicitor Walmsley to act for him to sue Upton to obtain compensation for his injuries and loss of income.
1981–84	Very little progress is made over the next three years, partly because Cosentino is sometimes slow to respond to correspondence from Walmsley.
August 1984	GIO (the insurer of the driver of the other vehicle, Upton) offers Cosentino $16,000 compensation.
August 1985	GIO threatens to withdraw its offer.
12 August 1986	*The Statute of Limitation period to sue Upton, the driver of the other car, expires. At any time from now Cosentino could have issued proceedings against the solicitor Walmsley for loss of the chance to sue Upton.*
8 October 1986	Barrister #1 joins the stage, to settle the Statement of Claim against Upton. Apparently the barrister does so without querying the prior expiry of the Statute of Limitation period.
April 1987	Barrister #2 gives advice.[97] The barrister advises that the client has *no chance*[98] of obtaining an extension of time to sue Upton. The remainder of the advice focuses heavily on the interests of the briefing solicitor, Walmsley, and no advice is given as to how to best protect the interests of the client, Cosentino. *Clearly, barrister #2 is in a position of conflict in attempting to simultaneously advise the instructing solicitor and the lay client.*[99] *Nevertheless, the barrister perseveres, suggesting all is not lost, as GIO still appears willing to negotiate.*
27 April 1987	Walmsley tells Cosentino barrister #2's advice about likely quantum of damages, but not the remainder of barrister #2's advice (i.e. that the application for extension of time had 'no chance').
November 1988	Barrister #3 is briefed to advise on an extension of time application and confirms barrister #2's advice – 'no chance'.
December 1988	Barrister #4 briefed. He replies in March 1989, giving Walmsley a glimmer of hope regarding an extension application but emphasizing the need for Walmsley to do nothing that might jeopardize Walmsley's professional indemnity insurance. Apparently no advice is given regarding client Cosentino's best interests.
September 1991	(Two and a half years later) Barrister #5 is briefed. Walmsley is still acting for client Cosentino but admits to barrister #5 he (Walmsley) is 'extremely negative' about continuing to negotiate with GIO on Cosentino's behalf.

(*Continued Overleaf*)

APPENDIX 10.1: (Continued)

January 1992	Walmsley and Cosentino have a heart-to-heart discussion. For the first time, Walmsley tells Cosentino: 'If I don't get an extension, you could sue me.' Cosentino asks Walmsley if Walmsley is insured. Walmsley replies that he is and Cosentino says: 'I want you to keep acting for me'.
	The Court of Appeal later holds that Walmsley breached a tortious duty of care owed on *this* occasion[100] by failing to tell Cosentino that if he was to sue Walmsley, he needed to issue court proceedings by mid-August of that year (1992).
December 1992	Barrister #5 (first briefed in September 1991) agrees with the advice of barristers #2 and #3 (application for an extension of time would be 'futile') and drafts a letter to GIO for Walmsley to send, still seeking settlement on behalf of Cosentino.
December 1992	Walmsley asks his professional indemnity insurer, LawCover, for permission to write to GIO (i.e. to continue to act for Cosentino). Finally, the client Cosentino instructs other solicitors, although there is no immediate improvement in his position. *It is possible that a court could have found that Cosentino's time to sue Walmsley had expired by this date.*
February 1993	Walmsley writes to Cosentino, thanking him for his loyalty but wrongly giving Cosentino the impression that the barristers had been more hopeful about the extension application's chance of success than they had been, and blaming the client's current predicament on recent High Court authority. Solicitor #2 is arranged by Walmsley. Arguably, that means solicitor #2 may have some sense of loyalty to Walmsley and may not provide the independent advice that the client desperately needs. As if to confirm our worst suspicions, solicitor #2 briefs barrister #6.[101] As with four of the barristers before him, the question still being asked in the brief to barrister #6 is whether there may be some hope of an extension of time. Still, no solicitor or barrister appears to turn their mind as to whether action against Walmsley might be in the client Cosentino's best interests, rather than the further pursuit of a futile extension application.
May 1994	Cosentino instructs solicitor #3. Still no lawyer ends the futile pursuit of extension applications. Solicitor #3 briefs barrister #7 to appear on an application for extension. It is dismissed by the court.
June 1994	*Bar Rule 111 comes into force.*[102]
23 December 1994	At last, on the eve of Christmas and perhaps bringing a touch of Dickens' *Christmas Carol* into the scene, the course of action most beneficial to the *client* Cosentino, which could have been pursued as early as 13 August 1985 (eight years earlier) and would probably have been settled by Walmsley's professional indemnity insurer, is pursued. Cosentino's solicitor #3 sues Walmsley. To add insult to injury, and in one of a number of ironies of the case, Walmsley relies on the same Statute of Limitations that has led to this debacle. The essence of his defence is: 'You can't sue me for missing a period of limitation because you in turn have missed the period of limitation for suing *me*.'

| 30 August 2000 | District Court delivers judgment in favour of Cosentino. Walmsley (perhaps under pressure from his insurers) appeals. |
| 21 November 2001 | New South Wales Court of Appeal delivers judgment in favour of Cosentino, now 46 years old. The quantum has ballooned from a figure that Cosentino may have accepted 21 years ago of less than $30,000 to a judgment of $474,478 plus costs. |

Notes

1 D. Rhode, 'Teaching legal ethics', *Saint Louis University Law Journal* 51, 2007, 1047; L.A. Weeman, M.C. Regan Jr and S. Gillers, 'Twenty years of legal ethics: Past present and future' (symposium transcript), *Georgetown Journal of Legal Ethics* 20, 2007, 328; E. Chambliss, 'Professional responsibility: Lawyers, a case study', *Fordham Law Review* 69, 2000, 821; M. Robertson, 'Challenges in the design of legal ethics learning systems: An educational perspective', *Legal Ethics* 8, 2005, 239; D. Rhode, 'Legal ethics in legal education', *Clinical Law Review* 16, 2009, 43; cf. R. Cramton and S. Koniak, 'Rule, story and commitment in the teaching of legal ethics', *William and Mary Law Review* 38, 1996–97, 154.

2 C. Menkel-Meadow, 'Telling stories in school: Using case studies and stories to teach legal ethics', *Fordham Law Review* 69, 2000, 788, 793.

3 B. Green, 'There but for fortune: Real-life vs fictional "case studies" in legal ethics', *Fordham Law Review* 69, 2000, 987.

4 K. Economides and M. O'Leary, 'The moral of the story: Toward an understanding of ethics in organisations and legal practice', *Legal Ethics* 10, 2007, 5.

5 C. Menkel-Meadow, 'Two contradictory criticisms of clinical legal education: Dilemmas and directions in lawyering education', *Antioch Law Journal* 4, 1984, 297.

6 For instance, 'Being Atticus Finch: The professional role of empathy in *To Kill a Mockingbird*', *Harvard Law Review* 117, 2004, 1682.

7 For instance, A. Scherr and H. Farber, 'Popular culture as a lens on legal professionalism', *South Carolina Law Review* 55, 2003, 351.

8 Green, 'There but for fortune', 987.

9 ibid., 994.

10 Scherr and Farber, 'Popular culture', 379.

11 Cramton and Koniak, 'Rule, story and commitment', 177.

12 Green, 'There but for fortune', 995.

13 Recent examples include T. Floyd and J. Gallagher 'Legal ethics, narrative, and professional identity: The story of David Spaulding', *Mercer Law Review* 59, 2008, 941 (John Gallagher was the first to interview David Spaulding, 38 years after the celebrated case of *Spaulding v Zimmerman* 116 NW 2d 704 (Minn Supreme Ct, 1962)); R. Abel, *Lawyers in the Dock: Learning from Attorney Disciplinary Proceedings*, New York: Oxford University Press, 2008 (three of the seven lawyers studied by Abel agreed to be interviewed).

14 Economides and O'Leary, 'Moral of the story', 7.

15 Green, 'There but for fortune', 994.

16 *Walmsley v Cosentino* [2001] NSWCA 403.

17 M. Nussbaum, 'Cultivating humanity in legal education', *University of Chicago Law Review* 70, 2003, 272.

18 *Walmsley v Cosentino* [2001] NSWCA 403.

19 *Kitchen Royal Air Force Association* [1958] 1 WLR 563.

20 A lawyer owes fiduciary duties to the client and so must avoid conflicts between their personal interest (in this case, defending a negligence action) and the duty owed to the

client (to pursue a successful negligence action): *Spector v Ageda* [1973] Ch 30. In most cases, this fiduciary duty will require the lawyer to cease acting for the client; an ongoing duty of care requires the lawyer to also advise the client to get independent legal advice about the possibility of suing the lawyer.

21 Refer to Appendix, 23 December 1994.
22 Charles Dickens, *Bleak House* (first published 1854). Bleak House includes the story of *Jarndyce v Jarndyce*, a case dragging through the English courts from one generation to the next.
23 It would also be valuable to formally survey students as to whether they find this use of case law as a source of narrative to be useful. At the moment, the only feedback has been informal, but all of that has been positive.
24 The term 'lawyers' is used generically and includes both barristers and solicitors where the legal profession is divided.
25 W. Simon, *The Practice of Justice: A Theory of Lawyers' Ethics*, Cambridge, MA: Harvard University Press, 1998, p. 139; D. Luban, *Lawyers and Justice: an Ethical Study*, Princeton, NJ: Princeton University Press, 1988, pp. 146, 147.
26 Refer to Appendix, 12 August 1986. Reliance on the Statute of Limitations is another favourite topic in legal ethics debates: G.C. Hazard and A. Dondi, *Legal Ethics: A Comparative Study*, Stanford, CN: Stanford University Press, 2004, p. 175; Compare the approaches of Luban, *Lawyers and Justice*, pp. 9–10, 47; T. Dare, 'Merezeal, hyper-zeal and the ethical obligations of lawyers', *Legal Ethics* 7, 2004, 24; Simon, *The Practice of Justice*, p. 33.
27 Refer to Appendix, 23 December 1994.
28 S. Pepper, 'The lawyer's amoral ethical role: A defense, a problem and some possibilities', *American Bar Foundation Research Journal*, 1986, vol. 4, 613.
29 D. Luban, 'The adversary system excuse', in D. Luban (ed.), *The Good Lawyer: Lawyers' Roles and Lawyers' Ethics*, Totowa: Roman and Allanheld, 1983.
30 For instance, C. Parker and A. Evans, *Inside Lawyers' Ethics*, Melbourne: Cambridge University Press, 2007.
31 Luban, *Lawyers and Justice*.
32 D. Rhode, 'Rethinking the public in lawyers' public service: Pro bono, strategic philanthropy, and the bottom line', *Fordham Law Review*, 2009, vol. 77.
33 Simon, *The Practice of Justice*.
34 T. Schneyer, 'Some sympathy for the hired gun', *Journal of Legal Education* 41, 1991, 23.
35 Zoe Zi Wei Wong, law student, University of Melbourne, citing R. Gordon, 'A new role for lawyers? The corporate counselor after Enron', *Connecticut Law Review* 35, 2003, 1185; and D. Luban 'The ethics of wrongful obedience', in D. Rhode, *Ethics in Practice: Lawyers' Roles, Responsibilities and Regulation*, Oxford: Oxford University Press, 2000.
36 Simon, *The Practice of* Justice, p. 140.
37 ibid., p. 141.
38 By ceasing to act and advising the client to get independent advice.
39 As distinct from the negligence of the driver of the vehicle that injured Cosentino.
40 C. Parker, A. Evans, L. Haller, S. Le Mire and R. Mortensen, 'The ethical infrastructure of legal practice in larger law firms: Values, policy and behaviour', *University of New South Wales Law Journal* 31, 2008, 163.
41 *Doe d Bennett v Hale* (1850) 15 QB 171 at 182, 185; *New South Wales Bar Association v Livesey* [1982] 2 NSWLR 231 at 233; G. Dal Pont, *Lawyers' Professional Responsibility*, 4th edn, Sydney: Thomson Reuters, 2010, p. 47; A. Boon and J. Levin, *The Ethics and Conduct of Lawyers in England and Wales*, 2nd edn, Oxford: Hart, 2008, p. 30.
42 New South Wales Bar Association, *The New South Wales Barristers' Rules*, Rules 74–80.
43 '[T]he task of a barrister in giving opinions was . . . widely regarded as being to answer the specific questions on which he or she was briefed for advice. Counsel was

not expected to go beyond matters on which the opinion was sought, although he or she might, and generally would, do so on noticing something material that might have been *overlooked by those instructing.' Heydon v NRMA Ltd* (2000) 51 NSWLR 1 [365], McPherson AJA (emphasis added). His Honour went on to note that the extent of a barrister's duty had not altered; 'It is one thing for counsel to notice some incidental point outside the scope of his brief and draw attention to it. It is quite another thing to impose upon counsel a duty of care to advise on some matter which is beyond the scope of the brief or retainer.' *Heydon v NRMA Ltd* (2000) 51 NSWLR 1, [309], Malcolm AJA.

44 For instance, New South Wales Bar Association, *The New South Wales Barristers' Rules*, Rule 17.

45 We are told in the judgment that one of the first barristers briefed to advise was subsequently appointed to the District Court bench: *Walmsley v Cosentino* [2001] NSWCA 403, [12].

46 Olivia Draudins, law student, University of Melbourne.

47 R. Gordon, 'The independence of lawyers', *Boston University Law Review* 68, 1988, 1.

48 For instance, New South Wales Bar Association, *The New South Wales Barristers' Rules*, Rule 5: 'Barristers should exercise their forensic judgments and give their advice independently and for the proper administration of justice, notwithstanding any contrary desires of their clients' and NSW Bar Rule 18: 'A barrister must not act as the mere mouthpiece of the client or of the instructing solicitor and must exercise the forensic judgments called for during the case independently, after appropriate consideration of the client's and the instructing solicitor's desires where practicable'. See www.nswbar.asn.au/docs/professional/rules/Rules_july2008.pdf (accessed 24 February 2009).

49 Dal Pont, *Lawyers' Professional Responsibility*, p. 371; Boon and Levin, *The Ethics and Conduct of Lawyers in England and Wales*, p. 30. Robert Gordon notes that this 'British recipe for independence . . . did not survive the [American] Revolution': Gordon, 'The independence of Lawyers', 54, with no divided profession in the United States and all US attorneys having equal contact with clients.

50 It is not known whether the inclusion of this rule was prompted by this case and the apparent inaction of the barristers in relation to Walmsley's negligence, or whether the timing is simply a coincidence. The new New South Wales Barristers' Rules became Statutory Rule No. 207 and were published in *Government Gazette* 78 of 10 June 1994, p. 2779. They came into operation on 1 July 1994. The wording of Rule 111 has remained unchanged since 1994. The current rules can be viewed online. See www.nswbar.asn.au/docs/professional/rules/Rules_july2008.pdf (accessed 24 February 2009). Equivalent rules exist in all other Australian jurisdictions: Dal Pont, *Lawyers' Professional Responsibility*, p. 144.

51 Arguably, the UK rule exacerbates the difficulty for barristers struggling to clarify their loyalties: the rule refers to instructing solicitors as 'professional clients' to distinguish them from 'lay clients': *Code of Conduct of the Bar of England & Wales*, Rule 303. 'A barrister: (a) must promote and protect fearlessly . . . the lay client's best interests and do so without regard to . . . any consequences to. any other person (including any professional client or other intermediary or another barrister); (b) owes his primary duty as between the lay client and any professional client . . . to the lay client and must not permit the intermediary to limit his discretion as to how the interests of the lay client can best be served.' See www.barstandardsboard.org.uk/standardsandguidance/codeofconduct/section1cod eofconduct/partiii_fundmentalprinciples/#302 (accessed 25 January 2010). *Code of Conduct of the Bar of England & Wales*, Written Standard 3.3: 'A barrister should always be alert to the possibility of a conflict of interests. If the conflict is between the interests of his lay client and his professional client, the conflict must be resolved in favour of the lay client'. See www. barstandardsboard.org.uk/standardsandguidance/

codeofconduct/writtenstandardsfortheconductofprofessionalwork (accessed 25 January 2010).

52 Gino Dal Pont, 'What are rules of professional conduct for?' *New Zealand Law Review* 1996, 254.

53 Boon and Levin, *The Ethics and Conduct of Lawyers in England and Wales*, p. 72.

54 That Rule 111 is designed to assist barristers is also suggested by its mandatory wording: Cramton and Koniak, 'Rule, Story and Commitment', 175.

55 ibid., 174.

56 *Maguire & Tansey v Makaronis* [1997] HCA 23; (1997) 188 CLR 449.

57 F. Zacharias, 'The myth of self-regulation', *Minnesota Law Review* 93, 2008–09, 1184.

58 *Moy v Pettman Smith (a Firm)* [2002] EWCA Civ 875.

59 ibid. at [43] per Latham LJ. The other judges agreed. See also C. Hollander and S. Salzedo, *Conflicts of Interest*, 3rd edn, London: Sweet & Maxwell, 2008, p. 244, where the authors argue that a duty could be owed where there was no conflict, such as where a barrister's incompetence caused loss to both client and instructing solicitor. Hollander and Salzedo suggest that no common law duty could be owed to the instructing solicitors in *Moy* simply because that would have conflicted with their duty to the client; cf. *Hilton v Barker Booth* [2005] UKHL 8, [6].

60 *Wilson v Carter* [2005] NSWSC 1351.

61 Namely, where: 'The barrister is a potential witness, but not a party, in proceedings between client and solicitor; the barrister has information which may be confidential to either the solicitor or client and may not be known by the other party, or; the barrister may have reasonable grounds to believe that his or her own conduct may be attacked.' Citing New South Wales Bar Association, *The New South Wales Barristers' Rules*, Rule 87.

62 However, the question remains an open one as this was an application for summary judgment and the court thought the arguments deserved full argument at hearing.

63 *Wilson v Carter* [2005] NSWSC 1351, [80].

64 ibid. at [81].

65 Mark Jones, law student, University of Melbourne.

66 Melinda Han, law student, University of Melbourne.

67 Cramton and Koniak, 'Rule, story and commitment', 170.

68 D. Wilkins, 'Who should regulate lawyers?', *Harvard Law Review* 105, 1992, 801; Cramton and Koniak, 'Rule, story and commitment', 172.

69 *Walmsley v Cosentino* [2001] NSWCA 403, [24].

70 ibid. at [25], [31].

71 *White Industries (Qld) Pty Ltd v Flower & Hart (a firm)* (1998) 156 ALR 169 (Goldberg J).

72 Australian Broadcasting Corporation, *His Honour*, Television programme, broadcast 14 September 1998. See www.abc.net.au/4corners/stories/s18184.htm (accessed 25 January 2010); R. Ackland, 'Bench tips a bucket on the reckless and worthless', *Sydney Morning Herald*, 16 January 2004. See www.smh.com.au/articles/2004/01/15/1073877962996.html?from=storyrhs (accessed 26 January 2010).

73 *Flower & Hart (a firm) v White Industries (Qld) Pty Ltd* [1999] FCA 773, [47].

74 *Walmsley v Cosentino* [2001] NSWCA 403, 59.

75 ibid. at [9].

76 *D'Orta-Ekenaike v Victoria Legal Aid* [2005] HCA 12.

77 And presumably accept a brief fee paid by Cosentino to do so. We are not told the basis on which the barristers were paid. Even if they were advising on a 'no win, no fee' or pro bono basis or were paid by Legal Aid, this does not excuse them from the duties owed to avoid further harm to Cosentino.

78 Olivia Draudins, law student, University of Melbourne.

79 R. Abel, *The Making of the English Legal Profession 1800–1988*, Washington: Beard Books, 2005, p. 252.

80 Brad Smorgon, law student, University of Melbourne.

81 John Forbes suggests it is also at least partly due to the fact that barristers don't handle client money: J. Forbes, *The Divided Legal Profession in Australia: History, Rationalisation and Rationale*, Sydney: Law Book Company, 1979, p. 259; R. Abel, *English Lawyers Between Market and State: The Politics of Professionalism*, New York: Oxford University Press, 2003, p. 393.

82 For instance, *Legal Profession Act 2004* (NSW), s 504.

83 Chambliss, 'Professional responsibility'.

84 Zacharias, 'The myth of self-regulation'.

85 L. Mather, C. McEwen and R. Maiman, *Divorce Lawyers at Work: Varieties of Professionalism in Practice*, New York: Oxford University Press, 2001.

86 Parker et al., 'Ethical infrastructure', 158.

87 Refer to Appendix, April 1987 and December 1988.

88 Melinda Han, law student, University of Melbourne.

89 Jemima O'Callaghan, law student, Melbourne Law School, University of Melbourne.

90 Dal Pont, *Lawyers' Professional Responsibility*, p. 487.

91 ibid.

92 W. Simon, 'The confidentiality fetish', *The Atlantic*, 2004. See www.theatlantic.com/doc/200412/simon (accessed 26 January 2010).

93 Parker et al., 'Ethical infrastructure', 180.

94 The court in *Wilson v Carter* thought that a barrister may owe an instructing solicitor a duty of confidence: *Wilson v Carter* [2005] NSWSC 1351, [80].

95 Jemima O'Callaghan, law student, University of Melbourne.

96 Commentary is in italics.

97 The court mentions in passing that this barrister was subsequently appointed to the Bench: *Walmsley v Cosentino* [2001] NSWCA 403, [12].

98 Emphasis added.

99 See discussion in main text: Hollander and Salzedo, *Conflicts of Interest*, p. 244; *Wilson v Carter* [2005] NSWSC 1351; cf *Moy v Pettman Smith (a Firm)* [2002] EWCA Civ 875, [43] per Latham LJ, stating that no duty is owed to the instructing solicitor.

100 The separate duty owed on this date appears to have been found by the Court of Appeal so as to avoid Walmsley being able to rely on the Statute of Limitations in Cosentino's claim against him.

101 It is possible that this was the seventh barrister, as the reporting becomes unclear on this.

102 Discussed in more detail in text.

11 Coming to terms with legal ethics assessment

Justine Rogers

11.1 Introduction

There has been a noticeable burst of energy recently among the legal professions of England and Wales to develop legal ethics education. The leaders of the Bar Council and the Law Society, the representative bodies of both the Bar and the solicitors' profession respectively, have become actively interested in ethics education. They have, in many instances, framed it as essential to the survival of the profession, as a cure-all to the threats (internal and external) to public confidence and trust, to the profession's distinctive identity, and therefore to its special place in society.[1] In the current (post-Clementi, post-Legal Services Act 2007) climate, the professions' regulatory bodies, the Bar Standards Board (BSB) and the Solicitors Regulatory Authority (SRA), are subjecting the professions to more managerial activity than ever before. Part of this activity involves a keener interest in means by which to assess and certify the professional standards and ethical qualities of their members. They have struggled thus far to devise robust assessment strategies, and have sought the consultation of academics on how to proceed. There is, however, strikingly little guidance emerging from the legal academic context.

Assessment strategies document – usually in measurable terms – the knowledge, skills, attitudes and beliefs of learners. Assessment is a 'potent driver for learning',[2] shaping the learning experiences and learning behaviour of students and trainees. It therefore has the potential to cultivate deep understanding and reflection among learners and teachers alike. Assessment is a means for teachers and trainers to articulate, consolidate and certify learning objectives. For learners, it serves as formative or ongoing feedback – feedback that is otherwise gleaned through informal means and day-to-day cues. In fact, assessment conveys to learners crucial messages about the value of what is being taught relative to the wider learning objectives and environment in which they find themselves. Ethics assessment, in particular, can allow teachers and trainers to detect, discuss and address problematic issues and deviant behaviour. However, with a few exceptions, legal ethics assessment remains an unimaginative and tentative enterprise. Indeed, many academics perceive it as futile.

This chapter reviews the nature of the considerable challenges and limitations that currently beset legal ethics assessment – those that have generated doubt, even cynicism, about its value. The premise of this chapter is that legal ethics assessment is chiefly important and needs to be developed for reasons that are distinct from, but not wholly or always incompatible with, the aims of the professional bodies and that, in order to progress, it is necessary to better come to terms with its difficulties as well as appreciate its possibilities. Drawing on the legal education and wider assessment literature, the first and major part of this chapter consolidates and analyses three broad reasons why there is such profound distrust in ethics assessment and legal ethics assessment in particular. The second part of the chapter examines the case of medical ethics assessment and suggests that it provides a worthwhile framework that could be adapted by legal academics to assess legal ethics.

As a note, this chapter also relies on some of the qualitative interview material gathered by Professor Kim Economides and this author for a (2009) report for the Law Society of England and Wales, *Preparatory Ethics Training for Future Solicitors*.[3]

11.2 Reasons for cynicism about legal ethics assessment

11.2.1 Assessment favours narrow approaches to ethics

The most dominant criticism of ethics assessment among certain academics and practitioners is that it favours a narrow, and therefore inadequate, version of ethics. Assessment can indeed confine the ethics programme from the start. This is because assessment, in the strictest sense, concerns itself with objective measurement and is traditionally summative or a one-off test. The standards of validity and reliability, then, apply: the assessment instrument must in fact measure what it sets out to measure, and must procure results that are independent of the subjective views of the assessor. However, not every aspect of professionalism or version of ethics is equally amenable to these standards. Surdyk, in her study of medical ethics, neatly sums up the way in which assessment supports certain definitions of professionalism over others, those that test quantifiable knowledge and skills over, for instance, the habits and virtues of the person being assessed. She says:

> Some knowledge components of professionalism lend themselves more readily than others to use of objective assessment tools. For instance, various quantitative measures are frequently used to test cognitive grasp of components such as ethical principles, advance directives, informed consent, and business ethics. Likewise, efforts exist to assess skill acquisition in some components of professionalism, such as applied ethical reasoning. Other components, however, such as altruism, respect, and integrity, are seemingly less amenable to objective assessment because of their subjective nature.[4]

The examples of knowledge components of professionalism provided above can easily be substituted with legal equivalents, such as lawyers' duties to other participants in the legal sector and the lay client, as well as those laws and principles governing the practices of the organizations in which lawyers work. Creating an assessment regime carries a high risk that a range of possibilities for engaging with the ethics of law and lawyers are put aside or pared down (consciously or otherwise), while those dimensions that most easily satisfy the standards of objectivity are prioritized. The most straightforward alliance between content and assessment are those learning frameworks that test the aspiring or new lawyer's knowledge of the relevant professional Code of Conduct and his or her skills relating to its correct application.

Indeed, when handling legal ethics, the professional bodies and legal educators at each stage of education and training tend to work from a code-based version of ethics. Given that these codes represent what the professions stand for – their essential, public claims for legitimacy and trust – it is perhaps unsurprising that they serve as the focus for the ethics instruction. During their education and training, and especially at the post-academic stages, aspiring and new lawyers are systematically presented with and sometimes tested on their core professional duties as found in the codes. These codes convey a philosophical emphasis on independence and the rule of law, and a practical focus on lawyers' duties to the court, other lawyers and the lay client. More recently, these duties have been supplemented by accounting and financial regulations, and by anti-discrimination legislation.

There are a handful of academic programmes that employ wider and more imaginative approaches to ethics than this, such as the use of clinics, simulations and e-learning.[5] In other universities where ethics instruction exists, nearly all of these courses involve some exploration of the social context and philosophical meaning of the professional rules (and other issues about the legal profession and the role of law in society).[6] Nevertheless, the code continues to govern both the academic and vocational stages. There is, in this way, a strong, pre-existing bias towards a narrow construction of ethics, and it should be stressed that decisions about how to assess legal ethics arise within a context in which its meaning has already been heavily influenced. In other words, while assessment is more clearly compatible with a codes-based approach because of its traditional concern for objectivity, it is not the 'fault' of assessment that this formulation of ethics dominates.

In any case, given the narrowness of content and the strength of quantitative principles in ideas about assessment, the ethics assessment of lawyers is often relatively simple. At the academic and vocational phases for both legal professions, knowledge of the code and other legal obligations tend to be taught through methods that test the recall and application of these rules, such as multiple-choice or short-answer questions. These tasks, in effect, ask students for the repetition of declarative or factual knowledge, and sometimes evidence of procedural knowledge or skills of application (evidence of knowledge of when to use the particular rule). This type of assessment is known by its critics as a 'replicative' approach to ethics assessment,[7] since it tests the learner's skills in recollection and repetition, and asks them to reproduce or replicate the routines and values embedded in the codes.

Many scholars and some practitioners have rejected the code-based or 'replicative' models. In 1998, Goldsmith and Powles, two Australian scholars, condemned these 'technical and strategic' models as 'outmoded and objection-able' on the grounds that they are 'uncritically based upon traditional notions of education and skills [which] in all probability no longer fits contemporary circum-stances' and operate 'in the interests of a dominant professional group or ortho-doxy'.[8] Barnaby, an Australian solicitor citing other scholars and practitioners, outlined the myriad limitations of a code-based approach to ethics instruction:[9]

> Firstly, codes assume that ethical behaviour can be achieved through a mech-anism of external control[10] . . . [whereas] codes cannot address the notion that 'being ethical' is fundamentally an internal process[11] . . . codes do not motivate people to be ethical. Secondly, codes generally regulate only vertical relation-ships, that is, practitioner-client relationships and this ignores the importance of a broader grid of relationships including those between peer colleagues, relationships in work places, and hierarchical relationships between more experienced practitioners and newer practitioners.[12] Thirdly, positing a response to ethics in a code tends to then take attention away from any broader ethical issues which are not amenable to codification.[13] These broader issues might include: access to justice; human rights; the impact of law on vulnerable groups in the community and issues of character and professional identity.[14]

A senior solicitor at a large UK firm pointed out that a code-based approach is not always practically useful for practitioners facing day-to-day ethical dilemmas. She stated that when ethics is reduced solely to client *care*, important issues like client *choice* do not get raised: 'How do we deal, for instance, with the client who wants to clear land in another country?' She believed that solicitors, from trainees to senior partners, need a formal context within which to reflect on the complex role of solicitors and precisely to what point their duties extend. '[A solicitor is] an officer of the court with professional duties to colleagues, clients, and regulators and [arguably with duties] to other communities and countries?' This solicitor was just one of several lawyers we consulted who identified the code-based approach to ethics as outmoded, as too self-contained in practice. Barnaby's summary pre-figures some of the additional problems with ethics assessment that have been identified in the scholarship, discussed in the following sections.

11.2.2 Ethics are simply not assessable

Another reason for widespread cynicism among scholars is the perception that ethics – or what would amount to them as satisfactory versions of ethics – are simply not assessable. Incidentally, the professional regulators and associations are currently advancing broader conceptions of legal ethics, moving from technical, knowledge-based or merely 'replicative' ideas about ethics to those that emphasize the virtues and behaviour of the practitioner. These bodies are seeking to develop robust assessment regimes, consistent with their outcomes and entity-based approaches.[15] The latter refer to aspects of regulatory models whereby educators and workplaces are made responsible for devising training programmes – in this case, the substance of ethics training and assessment – and simply must prove to the regulators that certain pre-specified outcomes are met. These approaches valorize assessment since for the regulators assessment serves as a mechanism of feedback, quality assurance and accreditation.

From 2010, for instance, the new outcomes-based Legal Practice Course, the vocational training course for solicitors, will involve a compulsory written assessment for 'professional conduct and regulation'. As for the training contract, the workplace-based and final phase of training for solicitors, the SRA (the Solicitors' Regulatory Authority) has accentuated virtues linked with skill and character, such as integrity, effective communication, working with others, self-awareness and development. Of course, these standards accompany others, many of which advance different and perhaps competing priorities, such as client handling, business awareness and workload management. Nevertheless, the SRA has recognized the potential of work-based learning to promote reflection on handling of ethical and practical issues in a supported environment, and has enlisted organizations to develop and approve new learning and assessment methods for trainee solicitors in the workplace as part of a workplace-based learning pilot. Meanwhile, the Bar's new Bar Professional Training Course encompasses revitalized 'professional ethics' requirements. Mere knowledge or recall of the code is no longer enough. The formal rationale of the course is to:

> instill and build up in students the essential qualities of ethical behaviour at the Bar by nurturing and developing to a high level these existing attributes in students. Encompassing more than the knowledge and formalities outlined in the Professional Code of Conduct, this will furnish far reaching and fundamental knowledge of ethics that underlies practice at the Bar.[16]

The workplace phase of training or apprenticeship for barristers, pupillage, continues to be subject to the teaching style and philosophy of the individual pupil supervisors, and whether and to what extent they recognize and then share the ethical dimensions and implications of their work. However, pupils must attend a session on ethics as part of their compulsory training through the Inns of Court. Moreover, more and more chambers are providing their pupils with separate ethics sessions, such as formal code-based hypotheticals or informal roundtable discussions of the sorts of ethical problems more senior practitioners have encountered. The assessment is by way of immediate oral feedback, usually informal.

Nonetheless, there is a conspicuous lack of experimentation coming from the legal academic community when it comes to ethics assessment – activity that could help prepare law students for their working lives after university, as well as support, and ideally extend, these professional initiatives. Based on the appraisals of the regulators, it is evident that the vocational course providers are struggling with ethics assessment. It is unclear as yet how the law firms will proceed.

The lack of options and general inertia emerge, to some extent, from a general feeling among many scholars that ethics are not assessable. For these commentators, ethics concerns a wide set of habits, dispositions, beliefs and reflections that simply cannot be broken down or measured. According to this perspective, assessment indicators are likely to have very little connection to these processes, processes that are mostly internal. The potential gap between the assessment outcomes and the true beliefs of the person being assessed is a sticking point. An influential Canadian scholar, Arthurs, identifies this as one of the reasons why few law schools accept that students could or should be tested for ethical 'competence', since 'a course in legal ethics – like a course in, say, real estate or labour law – requires only that students study the syllabus, not that they believe in it'.[17] Certainly, satisfying an assessment programme by displaying certain awareness and values does not guarantee their internalization. Osborn, in a study of medical education, demonstrated how professional values espoused in institutional and programme policies were seemingly disregarded and subsequently challenged by medical students with decidedly different life experiences and expectations than those who formulated them.[18] Indeed, when it comes to ethical qualities, it has long been accepted that the evaluation of people's beliefs and attitudes is notoriously difficult, if not impossible.[19]

Furthermore, various scholars have emphasized that being ethical is also a social process – something that occurs in contexts that are governed by role expectations, hierarchies, discourses and specific work environments.[20] These scholars point out that being ethical may not be reducible to a set of measurable or valid competencies. Indeed, one of the major hurdles when it comes to ethics assessment is its rigid attachment to objectivity and repeatability. In practice, moral decision-making is subject to more fluid, complex and ongoing factors, like role models, organizational cultures, and work communities and specialties. Barnaby argues that even approaches to ethics assessment that look at whether forms of philosophical reasoning are applied correctly to specific case scenarios can erroneously confine the 'content and parameters of moral discourse':[21] 'Reason, on this construction, equates with equality, autonomy, uniformity and impartiality. Yet it discounts responsibilities, vulnerabilities, particularity, care and relationships.'[22] Goldsmith and Powles assert that 'conceptions of professional responsibility need to be developed in ways that exceed, even disrupt, mainstream approaches to ethical instruction'.[23]

Other commentators argue that ethics instruction should be an open and openly social process that leads participants in time to become practitioners who are 'thoughtful, wise and contemplative'.[24] Some scholars argue that legal educationalists need to take more seriously the impact of business and business ethics on lawyers' practice and ethics, and that much could be learnt about professional ethics through storytelling.[25] Ethics instruction may even mean cultivating a sense in the learner or trainee of legal practice as morally defensible, and therefore personally engaging.[26]

The criticisms reveal high expectations of ethics education and assessment. However, it is also simply the case that, as Surdyk argues: 'Part of the problem is a lack of familiarity with qualitative assessments as credible and valid evaluation tools that can be used to gain insight into professional behaviours or the lack thereof.'[27]

11.2.3 Ethics assessment is not feasible

A third form of malaise about ethics assessment emerges not so much from doubts about its validity (or lack thereof) as its feasibility given the wider learning environment in which ethics instruction occurs. The first section of the chapter identified and analysed an essential background feature in legal ethics assessment, which was the pre-existing authority of the professional codes, and outlined some of the reasons why its primacy was rejected by many commentators. There are several other contextual factors that contribute to a sense of wariness about ethics assessment. These are conditions that, critics argue, are inhospitable to the sorts of reflection required for worthwhile learning, feedback and reflection to take place.

One of these factors is the way in which ethics instruction is typically regarded and handled. Ethics is widely perceived by academic and vocational educators as simply another component in an already crammed curriculum. Furthermore, the relative infancy of ethics as a discipline, and the paucity of innovative models and content upon which to draw, mean that even within so-called pervasive courses, ethics is widely treated as a bolt-on. On top of this, at the academic stage, universities are already geared towards the traditional modes of assessment, exams and coursework. This means that traditional modes of ethics assessment based on hypothetical problems remain dominant. Castles, an Australian scholar, warns that if legal ethics is taught with an emphasis on practical problem-solving, law students are unlikely to see that legal ethics is anything more than a gloss on the substantive law.[28] As for the vocational courses, Boon argues that these are environments potentially inhospitable to deep thought and reflection regarding professional roles and responsibilities because the courses are already long, intensive and relatively expensive to deliver.[29]

A compounding issue is student attitude and motivation. A professor in medical ethics we consulted noted that students vary in their interest in ethics, which in turn presents further challenges for assessment. Indeed, often it is the students themselves who resist unorthodox or qualitative approaches to teaching and assessment:

> Assessment is more challenging than the instruction. Students vary considerably in their interest in medical ethics and one challenge is to bring on board those who have low initial interest. Some students like the opportunity to think about the complex issues in ethics and tolerate the lack of definitive answers to many of the issues. Other students like to come away from a seminar with particular clear facts. Keeping the interest of both types of student is a challenge.

In addition, the internal hierarchies and cultures of the workplace govern, to a large extent, the learning attitudes of new lawyers, including towards formal ethics instruction. In order to be effective, the routine behaviour of practitioners needs to be consistent with the objectives of any ethics instruction and assessment. This author's forthcoming DPhil thesis describes in detail the ways in which pupils (or trainee barristers) tend to value the advice and experiences of practitioners, particularly their pupil supervisors, over their earlier formal legal training. Typically, when faced with conflicting messages, pupils readily revise, replace or suppress their own beliefs and what they have learned during their academic and professional courses with the views, practices and conduct of their supervisors and seniors. As Duff put it in the medical context, 'In truth, trainees learn what they see.'[30]

A final source of concern is the likely meaning of the outcomes and entity-based regulatory models that govern, in particular, the vocational training phases (the professional courses and subsequent workplace training). While the new regulations concerning ethics and professional conduct are formally designed to give course providers and workplaces permission to experiment with assessment, this may not represent the substantive guidance required for those actually responsible for ethics assessment to develop non-orthodox programmes. An outcomes approach, combined with the other environmental factors, may lead to uncertainty and conservatism since, for reasons that have already been made clear, it is far easier to satisfy outcomes by assessing knowledge (recall, identification and application) of professional rules and even their aspirational underpinnings than complex processes of ethical behaviour. The general uncertainty about how to proceed may explain in part why the regulators have been so flexible or non-instructive when it has come to ethics assessment, beyond suggesting the use of the traditional approaches – namely multiple-choice and short-answer questions.

This chapter has so far drawn together three broad reasons for the widespread cynicism and uncertainty about legal ethics assessment in order to more fully understand its difficulties: that it favours a narrow version of ethics, is invalid and is not feasible. These reasons coalesce into a dominant concern about the presence and meaning of a technical approach to ethics, a concern that is, for the most part, legitimate. The current ethics assessment practices do not in fact typically depart from objective, summative and narrow modes of evaluation. The consequences are, moreover, that many of the lessons about the ethical qualities of law students and lawyers are transmitted in the informal curricula of universities, law schools and legal organizations. It is now the professional bodies and the law firms themselves that are addressing these gaps.

Having mapped the challenges and limitations of legal ethics assessment, we will now investigate some of the practical lessons that have emerged from the experience of medical ethics education.

11.3 Lessons from medicine

A professor of medical ethics at the University of Oxford whom we consulted as part of our report[31] made the following remarks:

> I think ethics in legal education is like medicine 20 years ago. At that stage most doctors and medical schools said, 'What is the point? You pick up ethics on the job and besides there isn't much.' They look ridiculously old-fashioned now.

It would be difficult to state with any certainty how far behind the medical profession the legal profession is in terms of the ethics education of its members. Moreover, it would be misguided to view the medical profession as free of the sorts of challenges that hem in legal ethics education. Indeed, an associate professor at one of Australia's most prestigious medical schools identified several obstacles to a robust ethics framework, many of which were strikingly similar to those described above. These included the difficulties in changing the institutional cultures of medical schools and hospitals (where, she said, ethical situations are often ignored until they become imperative), low levels of student interest and motivation, and the sheer variety of ethics issues according to fields of practice. In short, ethics education remains a challenge for the medical profession.

Nevertheless, on the basis of the volume and quality of the literature, there is more widespread acceptance of the significance of ethics training and assessment, and more numerous attempts to advance and develop them in medicine than in law. Wong and Cheung, academics at the Department of Psychiatry at the University of Hong Kong, have affirmed that: 'Since assessment is a strong motivator for learning and the mode of assessment influences learning behaviour, assessment in ethics is essential in any medical curriculum with an ethics course.'[32] Duff, at the University of Florida, has outlined the steps his department and medical school have taken to 'bring professionalism to center stage in the minds of students and residents', including assessment. He states:

> Professionalism is the first competency listed on the student and resident evaluation form. Presentations on professionalism are an integral part of orientation for first-year students and the White Coat Ceremony for the third-year students. Similar presentations occur during the orientation program for new residents and are part of faculty development workshops. In addition, our department recently adopted an extensive new annual evaluation form devoted solely to an assessment of professional behavior.[33]

In his book, *Measuring Medical Professionalism*, Associate Professor Stern, at the University of Michigan Medical School, distinguished some of the myriad benefits of measuring professionalism, including detecting deviant behaviour, providing formative feedback and rewarding those physicians who are especially altruistic, humanistic and compassionate.[34] Building on these rationales and approaches, one highly valuable tool from the medical ethics literature that legal educators could adapt is the 'Know-Can-Do' learning pyramid.

11.3.1 The 'know-can-do' learning pyramid

Professor Alastair V. Campbell and his colleagues at the Centre for Biomedical Ethics at the National University of Singapore produced the following version of the 'Know-Can-Do' learning pyramid (see Figure 11.1).[35]

Wong and Cheung explain how the pyramid represents the different levels of learning and assessment:

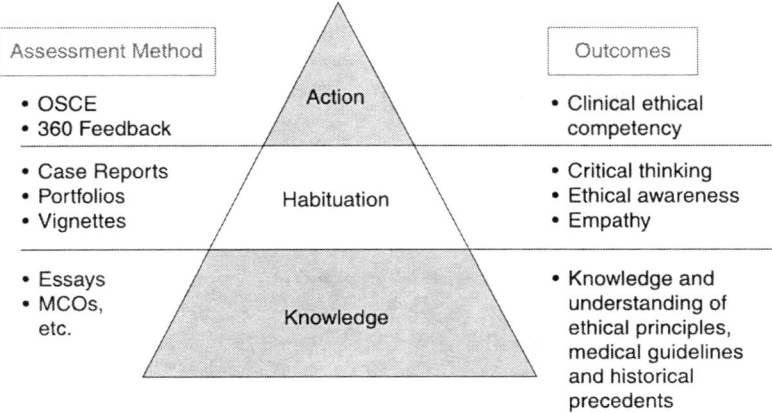

Figure 11.1 Learning outcomes and matching methods of assessment in key areas of medical ethics education.

The bottom of the pyramid, the 'know' level, refers to the knowledge of theories, concepts and principles in medical ethics. This is essentially the cognitive component of medical ethics education. The 'can' or habituation level in the middle refers to the students' ability to select and apply what they have learned from the 'know' level . . . This level pertains to the possession of application skills. At the top, the 'do' or action level refers to one's behaviour in a clinical setting when not under scrutiny, and refers to attitudes and performance in actual practice, which arguably is the most relevant outcome of ethics education.[36]

The pyramid shape also represents the increasing complexity of the teaching and assessment outcomes as one ascends the levels in the hierarchy. Campbell et al. add:

All three of these levels are what we need to be aiming for. At times, we can see the impact of the irresponsible behaviour of medical students on their careers later on. From that point of view, clearly, knowledge is not enough. Knowledge is needed for habituation, to shape the mould within which a student behaves so that there emerges action of a kind that is clinically appropriate and effective.[37]

11.3.2 Assessment at the 'know' level

The diagram also includes common methods of assessment for each level. Assessment at the 'know' level may include essays and multiple-choice questions. Wong and Cheung use different examples for each level and have positioned case reports, for instance, as part of the knowledge level, instead of the 'can' level as do

Campbell and colleagues. In any case, case reports are a good illustration of how an assessment task should be regarded primarily as a learning experience, an opportunity for the student or trainee to exercise qualities such as responsibility, judgment and sensitivity. Wong and Cheung note that, in case reports:

> Students are then expected to perform some or all of these tasks: identify ethical issues, consider courses of action and select what they consider an appropriate action and then justify this decision. In this process, students can demonstrate their ethical sensitivity, their knowledge of the ethical analytical framework, their skills of analysis, reasoning and reflection.[38]

Myser and colleagues propose that the report be based on a case identified by the student. Since the student is responsible for identifying an ethically problematic case, this has the advantage of being student-centred, and may both encourage reflection and enhance ethical sensitivity.[39]

11.3.3 Assessment at the 'can' level

Assessment at the 'can' level will be different. According to Wong and Cheung, the 'do' level refers to how medical students or doctors actually behave in practice when interacting with patients. As such, 'to assess medical students' competence in selecting and applying knowledge in clinical practice requires a performance-based assessment'.[40] They describe the Objective Structured Clinical Examination (OSCE) as the most widely adopted method at this level. Campbell and colleagues have included it at the higher 'do' level. An OSCE typically involves a student interacting with a standardized (or a real) patient, depicting a clinical scenario within a fixed period of time.[41] The student's performance is marked according to whether or not the student exhibits certain behaviours listed on a checklist.[42] Other appropriate assessment methods may involve face-to-face, formal evaluation sessions – these have significantly improved the detection of unprofessional behaviour in clerkship settings[43] – or role-play with subsequent review of simulated clinical cases.[44]

Newble, in the context of trainee nurses, devised a groundbreaking assessment method, based on the critical incident technique. The procedure involves evaluators describing or writing down the most critical incident they perceived when observing the individuals at work, either because it was conspicuously good and effective, or unsatisfactory.[45]

Wong and Cheung argue that portfolios are the most promising tool for evaluating how students perform in the 'real world' over a period of time:

> A strength of this approach is that the evidence about the students' attitudes comes from a wide range of sources and is documented in the portfolios. This may include the ratings and views of clinicians, members of the multidiscipli-nary team (for example nurses) and patients. It also includes the students' own commentaries on the patients they have seen and their reflection on them.[46]

The UK Postgraduate Medical Education and Training Board (PMETB) supports all evidence for assessment being incorporated into a portfolio with room for reflection, and a final summative review so long as 'the synthesis of the evidence and the process of judging is made explicit'.[17] The Australian associate professor in medicine we consulted said she favoured portfolios and case reports, finding them less 'fraught' than OSCEs.

Moreover, the Law Society's own consultants proposed the use of a portfolio for the training contract stage.[18] They suggested that it should be incorporated into a final assessment interview by external assessors. This interview should include a number of hypothetical questions and be accompanied by a critical incident assessment, which would be a tape-recorded simulation with ethical issues embedded in it. The interview could overcome the pitfalls with portfolios – specifically, like any self-reported assessment, 'if an ethical issue has been missed or not recorded then it is gone and cannot be assessed'.

11.3.4 Assessment at the 'do' level

Methods that have been used in medicine to assess the 'do' level include 360-degree evaluations that are used to solicit feedback from patients, co-workers, peers and instructors, which may be effective in identifying deficiencies in professionalism.[49] Peer- and self-assessments are other favoured methods because the qualities of moral decision-making and character do not present themselves as stable characteristics and are often exhibited in contexts other than those directly observed or supervised by faculty.[50]

A more progressive proposal found in the medical literature is to employ humanism 'connoisseurs' to qualitatively evaluate medical trainees' professionalism.[51] Such connoisseurs would possess expert knowledge, training and experience in the interpersonal aspects of the art of medicine, allowing them to deconstruct concepts such as empathy, compassion, integrity and respect into their respective key elements while evaluating physicians' behaviours as an integrated, cohesive whole. Through the use of a rich descriptive vocabulary, humanism connoisseurs would provide valid formative and summative feedback regarding competency in medical professionalism and humanism. In the process, they would serve to counteract the relative marginalization of professionalism and humanism in the informal and lived curricula of medical trainees.

Stern's book[52] outlines in great detail many of these methods, such as critical incident reports, peer assessment and the portfolio. He also describes several others, including standardized clinical encounters, assessment of moral reasoning evaluations, surveys to assess individuals and institutions, and measurements of specific elements (empathy, teamwork and lifelong learning). Moreover, the rationale of the book is wholly consistent with a complex and versatile assessment programme as conveyed in the pyramid.

The PMETB has recently singled out workplace-based assessment as an under-utilized area. Workplace-based assessment, it argues, has high validity because of its authenticity of assessing actual performance. In terms of assessment methods, the PMETB approves a 'basket' of methods for different contexts, including direct observation, multi-source feedback, trainer's reports, research, critical incident (significant event) review, video assessment and case-based discussion. It provides a suggested work-based assessment checklist,[53] as well as a Personal Development Plan (for trainees before meeting with an educational supervisor).[54] Again consistent with the pyramid approach, it affirms the necessity for a multifaceted assessment strategy: 'Because of the complexity of assessing medical proficiency in areas such as "probity" and "professionalism", the assessment strategy must also be flexible enough to capture and assess opportunistic evidence as it arises.'[55]

In addition, Stern has identified the characteristics of effective assessment, including: triangulation (multiple settings and multiple observers) to address the challenge in determining whether those observations and measurements are representative of how the person (and the institution) will behave in all situations; a realistic context; a situation that involves conflict – that is, choices between equally worthy values – and transparency and symmetry, whereby all levels are evaluated using the same methods.[56] He provides a useful set of criteria, including these, for designing assessment of professionalism.[57]

The PMETB report also provides a useful assessment framework, including integration, evidence-based, positive standards (not just 'lack of negative evidence'), transparency, relevant feedback, recruitment of assessors and lay input.[58] It highlights areas for improvement, including the need to develop and validate assessment tools, to define roles and responsibilities of people involved in the training, to train assessors and to support the system with adequate funding.[59] Indeed, one important lesson to emerge from the experience of postgraduate medical education is that having a list of outcomes without clear and credible guidance for organizations may mean that the trainees are left without the support they need to really achieve these standards. As Grant puts it: 'Competences alone do not describe professional performance, but deconstruct it.'[60] Further, the challenge to assess well includes developing curriculum content as well as instructional methods. Tools such as the electronic clearinghouse initiated by the American Society for Bioethics and Medical Humanities have been highlighted by Surdyk as providing 'an excellent source for locating and building on ethics curricula currently used in teaching hospitals across the country. In addition to its role as a resource for content and activities, the clearinghouse will provide a framework from which consensus principles of ethics education can be drawn.'[61]

Medical educators appear to be taking ethics assessment more seriously than legal educators. They are less fixated on objectivity and repeatability, and more concerned with creating the motivation and opportunities for their students and trainees to practise certain ethical behaviour, and to engage with and reflect on a range of ethical issues, over time and from multiple perspectives. The case of medical ethics assessment provides much in the ways of guidance and resources from which legal educators might draw. It demonstrates that ethics assessment is not only feasible but, when formulated carefully, immensely worthwhile. Ethics assessment represents a means of fostering deep understanding about the moral implications of law and lawyering, and better communication and reflection among students and their teachers, and trainees and their seniors.

11.4 Conclusion

This chapter has examined some of the reasons for the distrust in and uncertainty about legal ethics assessment. This has revealed more sharply the reasons why it remains an under developed aspect of legal education and training, principally because of a widespread wariness about its easy alliance with technical, codes-based approaches to ethics. Nevertheless, assessment represents a crucial driver of the learning experiences and behaviour of students and lawyers. It is certainly not the only driver, and other instructional methods that have been identified as worthwhile in ethics education – like storytelling and formal dialogue – should also be developed. However, assessment is a crucial component of ethics education. Moreover, ethics instruction and feedback occur anyway, whether as formal provision or through the routine conversations and tacit cues of learning and working contexts. Legal educators need to use tools like assessment to become more aware of these processes, and to influence the ways in which these messages are understood by learners and trainees.

In addition, as the professional bodies become more heavily committed to assessment, and turn to law firms and other organizations for robust solutions, it is the responsibility of legal academics in particular to provide more substantial guidance on what should be propelling the assessment experiences of aspiring and new lawyers and workers. Training the assessors, and the ongoing knowledge and financial input needed for the development of this training, will continue be significant considerations – particularly in a context where when the regulators appear to want to push most of the costs for devising assessment strategies to the vocational institutions and workplaces. Legal academics need to start helping to shape these activities, rather than continuing to see them as bothersome, undesirable or irrelevant.

The experience of the medical profession provides several possibilities for progress at each phase of legal education and training. The 'Know-Can-Do' pyramid embodies many of these. Most importantly, it stresses that all three levels of the pyramid contribute to the overall objective of ethics education. In this way, the model serves as an organizing tool for educators and as a useful way of overcoming the conceptual trap by which the limits of knowledge-based approaches are used as evidence for the futility of the endeavour as a whole. As this chapter has demonstrated, the cynicism about knowledge-based approaches encumbers legal ethics assessment. The knowledge level, as this diagram shows, is only one aspect of ethics assessment. Further, it is a decisive one. In addition, the diagram symbolizes the importance of explicitly matching the method of assessment to the learning outcomes in devising assessment schemes, since the former invariably shapes the latter. Legal academics should be encouraged to see assessment as a larger enterprise and to make these connections.

For some commentators, assessment is simply too technical and not designed to capture the ethical intricacies of the attitudes, reflections and social encounters that lawyers (and other workers) experience in the course of their daily practice. However, the case of medical ethics assessment demonstrates that this view is outdated and perhaps careless. Most of the concerns outlined in the first part of this chapter, while legitimate, are not in themselves adequate reasons for not moving forward and attempting to devise appropriate methods that actually facilitate deeper, more reflective ethics education and more open social interactions when it comes to ethical issues encountered in practice. In fact, the reasons for concern represent compelling motives for movement, not indifference. As Hamdorf and Hall put it, 'it is generally agreed that it is better to measure uncertainly the significant than to measure reliably and validly the trivial'.[62] Moreover, a wide range of assessment methods exist to get at even the most subtle forms of professional behaviour, with the emphasis on cultivating responsibility, judgment and sensitivity rather than the 'right' answer. Legal educators and trainers need to be encouraged to experiment with and develop these methods, to evaluate them and to find formal ways of sharing their experiences and resources with others.[63]

Finally, I note the observation of Campbell and colleagues that emphasizes the underlying linkages between the liberal professions and disciplines, and the importance of a holistic approach to ethics teaching and assessment:

> Firstly, there is now a wide acceptance that medical ethics has to be multi-disciplinary and multi-professional. It cannot be the business of one particular academic discipline or the concern of any single profession. Secondly, it should be academically rigorous, and taught in a manner that is clearly related to research, as the other academic subjects in the medical curriculum must be. Thirdly, it ought to be fully integrated into the medical curriculum both horizontally and vertically so that there is a seamless transition between whatever is being taught at that time and the ethical issues. Ethics should not be regarded as an add-on or after-thought to the main business of medical education.[64]

When it comes to legal ethics assessment, the law schools and professional bodies appear to be lagging behind some of the other professions. Nevertheless, this also means that there are already some fairly well-trodden paths forward.

Notes

1 See, for example, the foreword of Paul Marsh, then President of the Law Society, in K. Economides and J. Rogers, *Preparatory Ethics Training for Future Solicitors*, Law Society, 2009. See http://eric.exeter.ac.uk/exeter/handle/10036/64973 (accessed 18 December 2009).

2 UK Postgraduate Medical Education and Training Board (PMETB) Workplace Based Assessment Subcommittee, *Workplace Based Assessment*, London: PMETB, 2005, p. 6. See www.pmetb.org.uk/media/pdf/3/b/PMETB_workplace_based_assessment_paper_(2005).pdf (accessed 11 February 2008).

3 Economides and Rogers, *Preparatory Ethics Training*.
4 P. Surdyk, 'Educating for professionalism: What counts? Who's counting?', *Cambridge Quarterly of Healthcare Ethics* 12, 2003, 157.
5 For example, University of Strathclyde, the University of Northumbria and City University.
6 S. Chandler and N. Duncan, *Survey of Ethics Teaching* (forthcoming); Summary at Annex A of Economides and Rogers, *Preparatory Ethics Training*.
7 A. Goldsmith and G. Powles, 'Where now in legal education for acting responsibly in Australia?', in K. Economides (ed.), *Ethical Challenges to Legal Education and Conduct*, Oxford: Hart, 1998.
8 ibid., p. 145.
9 S. Barnaby, 'Legal ethics for the real world: A model for engaging first year law students', *QUT Law and Justice Journal* 4, 2004, 6. See www.law.qut.edu.au/ljj/editions/v4n2/pdf/Barnaby.pdf (accessed 18 December 2009).
10 M. Castles, 'Challenges to the academy: Reflections on the teaching of legal ethics in Australia', *Legal Education Review* 12, 2001, 81, 89.
11 C. Taylor, 'Two theories of modernity', *Hastings Centre Report* 25, 1995, 24, 32.
12 P. Isaacs, 'Social practices, medicine and the nature of medical ethics', paper presented at the Society for Health and Human Values Spring Regional Meeting, Youngston State University, Youngston, Ohio, 17–19 April 1998, 13–14.
13 Castles, 'Challenges to the academy', 90; N. Preston, *Understanding Ethics*, Sydney: Federation Press, 1996, pp. 198–9.
14 B. Hamilton, 'Getting them early: Teaching a critical perspective on legal ethics and adversarialism in an introductory LLB unit at the Queensland University of Technology', *Legal Education Review* 12, 2001, 105, 117–18; Lord Woolf, 'The education the justice system requires today', speech delivered at the 29th Lord Upjohn Lecture, Inns of Court School of Law, 14 June 2000.
15 E. Chambliss, 'MDPs: Toward an institutional strategy for entity regulation', *Legal Ethics* 4, 2001, 45–65.
16 Bar Standards Board, *BPTC Handbook*, final version 1 July 2009, para. 2.2.4. See www.barstandardsboard.org.uk/assets/documents/BPTC.pdf (accessed 18 December 2009).
17 H. Arthurs, 'Why Canadian law schools do not teach legal ethics', in Economides, *Ethical Challenges to Legal Education and Conduct*.
18 E. Osborn, 'Punishment: A story for medical educators', *Academic Medicine* 75, 2000, cited in Surdyk, 'Educating for professionalism', 158.
19 Surdyk, 'Educating for professionalism'; S. Illingworth, *Approaches to Ethics in Higher Education: Learning and Teaching in Ethics across the Curriculum*, Leeds: Philosophical and Religious Studies Subject Centre, Learning and Teaching Support Network, 2004.
20 There is a wide literature that suggests the workplace is an important site, rich in learning opportunities: see J. Webb, M. Maughan and W. Purcell, *Project to Support Implementation of a New Training Framework for Solicitors Qualifying in England and Wales*, London: The Law Society, 2004. See www.lawsociety.org.uk/documents/downloads/becomingtfrwebb.pdf (accessed 1 February 2008). The workplace is also viewed as the central context for adult socialization and ethical development: see Winfree et al., 'On becoming a prosecutor: Observations on the organizational socialization of law interns', *Work and Occupations* 11, 1984, 207; Anderson-Gough et al., *Making Up Accountants: The Organizational and Professional Socialization of Trainee Chartered Accountants*, Aldershot: Ashgate, 1999.
21 Barnaby, 'Legal ethics for the real world', 5.
22 M.U. Walker, 'Feminism, ethics, and the question of theory', *Hypatia* 7, 1992, 23, 24–25; C. Gilligan, *In a Different Voice: Psychological Theory and Women's Development*, 2nd edn, Cambridge, MA: Harvard University Press, 1993, pp. 31–2, cited in Barnaby, 'Legal ethics for the real world', 5.

23 Goldsmith and Powles, 'Where now in legal education for acting responsibly in Australia?', 140.

24 D. Schön, *The Reflective Practitioner: How Professionals Think in Action*, New York: Basic Books, 1983, cited in Barnaby, 'Legal ethics for the real world', 19.

25 K. Economides and M. O'Leary, 'The moral of the story: Toward an understanding of ethics in organisations and legal practice', *Legal Ethics* 10, 2007, 5–25; B.R. Mescher, 'The business of commercial legal advice and the ethical implications for lawyers and their clients', *Journal of Business Ethics*, 2007. See www.springerlink.com/content/k177j56n04p76475 (accessed 19 February 2008).

26 R. O'Dair, *Legal Ethics: Text and Materials*, London: Butterworths, 2001, p. 5.

27 Surdyk, 'Educating for professionalism', 157

28 M. Castles, 'Challenges to the academy: Reflections on the teaching of legal ethics in Australia', *Legal Education Review* 12, 2001, 82.

29 A. Boon, 'Ethics in legal education and training: Four reports, three jurisdictions and a prospectus', *Legal Ethics* 5, 2002, 34–67.

30 P. Duff, 'Teaching and assessing professionalism in medicine', *Obstet Gynecol* 4, 2004, 1363.

31 Economides and Rogers, *Preparatory Ethics Training*.

32 J.G.W.S. Wong and E.P.T. Cheung, 'Ethics assessment in medical students', *Medical Teacher* 25, 2003, 5.

33 Duff, 'Teaching and assessing professionalism', 1363.

34 D.T. Stern (ed.), *Measuring Professionalism*, Oxford: Oxford University Press, 2006.

35 Permission was kindly granted by Professor Campbell and his colleagues to reproduce their diagram as found in A.V. Campbell, J. Chin and T. Voo, 'How can we know that ethics education produces ethical doctors?', *Medical Teacher* 29, 2007, 431–6. The diagram was adapted from G.E. Miller, 'The assessment of clinical skills/competence/performance', *Academic Medicine* 65, 1990, 563–67.

36 Wong and Cheung, 'Ethics assessment in medical students', 5.

37 Campbell et. al., 'How can we know that ethics education produces ethical doctors?', 432.

38 Wong and Cheung, 'Ethics assessment in medical students', 6.

39 C. Myser, I.H. Kerridge, and K.R. Mitchell, 'Teaching clinical ethics as a professional skill: Bridging the gap between knowledge about ethics and its use in clinical practice', *Journal of Medical Ethics*, 21, 1995, cited in Wong and Cheung, 'Ethics assessment in medical students', 6.

40 Wong and Cheung, 'Ethics assessment in medical students', 6.

41 J.P. Collins and R.M. Harden, 'AMEE Medical Education Guide No. 13: Real patients, simulated patients and simulators in clinical examinations', *Medical Teacher* 20, 1998, 1–6.

42 Wong and Cheung, 'Ethics assessment in medical students', 6.

43 P.A. Hemmer et al., 'Assessing how well three evaluation methods detect deficiencies in medical students' professionalism in two settings of an internal medicine clerkship', *Academic Medicine* 75, 2000, 167–73.

44 Duff, 'Teaching and assessing professionalism'.

45 D.I. Newble, 'The critical incident technique: A new approach to the assessment of clinical performance', *Medical Education* 17, 1983, 401–3, cited in Wong and Cheung, 'Ethics assessment in medical students', 7; see also K. Economides and J. Smallcombe, *Preparatory Skills Training for Trainee Solicitors*, London: Law Society Research Study No. 7, The Law Society, 1991, Annex 3.

46 Wong and Cheung, 'Ethics assessment in medical students', 6.

47 PMETB, *Workplace Based Assessment*, 8.

48 Webb, Maughan and Purcell, *Project to Support Implementation of a New Training Framework for Solicitors*.

49 Duff, 'Teaching and assessing professionalism'.

50 S. Ginsburg, G. Regehr, R. Hatala, N. McNaughton, A. Frohna, B. Hodges et al., 'Context, conflict and resolution: A new conceptual framework for evaluating professionalism', *Academic Medicine* 75, 2000, cited in Surdyk, 'Educating for professionalism', 157.

51 D.A. Misch, 'Evaluating physicians' professionalism and humanism: The case for humanism "connoisseurs" ', *Academic Medicine* 77, 2002, 489–95.

52 Stern, *Measuring Professionalism*.

53 PMETB, *Workplace Based Assessment*, Appendix 1.

54 ibid., Appendix 4.

55 ibid., p. 8.

56 Stern, *Measuring Professionalism*, pp. 8–9.

57 ibid., p. 11.

58 PMETB, *Workplace Based Assessment*, pp. 10–12.

59 ibid., pp. 14–15.

60 J.A. Grant, 'Changing postgraduate medical education: A commentary from the United Kingdom', *Medical Journal of Australia* 86, 2007, S12.

61 Surdyk, 'Educating for professionalism', 158.

62 J.M. Hamdorf and J.C. Hall, 'The development of undergraduate curricula in surgery, III: Assessment', *Australian and New Zealand Journal of Surgery* 71, 2001, cited in Wong and Cheung, 'Ethics assessment in medical students', 7.

63 See Barnaby, 'Legal ethics for the real world' for an excellent illustration of sharing resources, in this case a fascinating online ethics programme for first-year students.

64 Campbell et al., 'How can we know that ethics education produces ethical doctors?',

Index